To Hell with Honor

To Hell with Honor

Custer and the Little Bighorn

Larry Sklenar

UNIVERSITY OF OKLAHOMA PRESS : NORMAN

Library of Congress Cataloging-in-Publication Data

Sklenar, Larry, 1937–
    To hell with honor: Custer and the Little Bighorn / Larry
Sklenar.
        p.   cm.
    Includes bibliographical references and index.
    ISBN 0-8061-3156-X (alk. paper)
    1. Little Bighorn, Battle of the, Mont., 1876.   2. Custer, George
Armstrong, 1839–1876.   I. Title.
    E83.876.S54   2000
    973.8'2—dc21   99-38632
                                                              CIP

Text design by Gail Carter.

1 2 3 4 5 6 7 8 9 10

To Claire and the boys (Scott, Duane, and Steve)

CONTENTS

ILLUSTRATIONS

PHOTOGRAPHS

MAPS

PREFACE

When George Armstrong Custer died at the Battle of the Little Bighorn, he was thirty-six years old. Nearly all of the soldiers who rode with him were younger than that, as were the Sioux and Cheyenne warriors who defeated him and his command on 25 June 1876.

Of course, the burdens of waging war have always fallen predominantly on the young. I continue to be amazed that the men who flew U.S. bombers in World War II were so terribly young, most of them barely twenty years old. Their responsibilities were so great. The pilot, besides trying to achieve his objectives in the most perilous of circumstances while looking out for himself, had in his care the lives of nine or so crew members. That has always seemed to me such a lonely way to die, even when that crew went down together. The thought of those boys falling dead or dying through sky to earth is haunting in the extreme.

And so it is with Custer and his band of men. The great Hunkpapa spiritual leader Sitting Bull, in one of his visions, saw the soldiers falling headlong into the Indian village days before the Seventh U.S. Cavalry was routed on the banks of the Little Bighorn—falling, falling, iron feathers into fire, sans heads, sans arms, without weight except in memory. For Americans especially, but for the world at large as well, the image of the famous "last stand" has persisted in every imaginable form of expression until this little fight (no more than twenty bombers flaming out of the blue) has metamorphosed into myth—the solitary Custer standing upright to the end, his troopers formed into clots of wounded and dying men, with no one to watch the going down but foes. Whether or not one believes in the myth, the event still captivates, as it has for better than a hundred years.

But beyond the mythic proportions of Custer's defeat, there is a reality, and the aim of this book is to get at the facts as they can be gleaned from the gargantuan body of material available to the researcher, the analyst, and the student of the battle. At the center of the great controversy is Custer himself. Other commanders have also died with their men, captains with their crews, but Custer is different, maybe because he so closely resembles the classic tragic figure, the great man with a fatal flaw that leads to his undoing.

Certainly Custer was a popular figure. To the Union side in the Civil War, he must have seemed a great man. He was the "boy general" to the Northern press, made famous by the many articles extolling his bravery under fire. His golden hair flowed. His uniforms, for a short season, bordered on the garish. The truth is that he was brave, he did lead his units to many victories, he was highly regarded by the officers under whom he served, and in his manner of dress and command he was not unlike Jeb Stuart, the cocky and flamboyant head of General Robert E. Lee's Confederate cavalry. Although generally popular with his men, even during the Civil War Custer had his detractors—not many, but a few, mostly those who resented his rapid rise in rank.

After the war, Custer remained a horse-soldier, as lieutenant colonel of the newly formed Seventh Cavalry. On duty in the West, rarely fighting Indians, he established a spotty record. Without question, some of the luster adhering to his Civil War reputation dulled, but to many he remained the darling of those glory days. Thus when he and a significant portion of his Seventh Cavalry were crushed by an overwhelming force of Sioux and Cheyennes, some were shocked and some were not surprised (they said). The latter said that he had always been too reckless—not the youthful recklessness that gathered battle flags and cannon when it mattered to the Union cause, but an adolescent selfishness set free on the open plains, without regard for authority, without proper respect for the people he was bound by order to subdue. He got what he deserved, his detractors said.

This is the story of Custer's last fight. Although I had been fascinated by the subject for many years, I chose to delve more deeply into the mystery after my retirement from government service, chiefly because of three books: Paul Andrew Hutton's *The Custer Reader*, W. A. Graham's *The Custer Myth*, and Robert M. Utley's *Cavalier in Buckskin*. I had read other Custer books (mostly negative), yet the volumes cited above not only whetted my appetite with respect to the man and his final ordeal but also described the scope of the controversy and indicated sources one might investigate to acquire a more complete understanding of the riddle that had so engaged people. An analyst by inclination and experience, I could not resist the puzzle, so that casual reading turned into pursuit of primary sources, a visit to the battlefield, and a piecing together of the fragments that now constitute the story I believe to be nearly the whole truth of what happened at the Little Bighorn.

The trend in recent years has been to discover some new source of information to explain the outcome of Custer's defeat, with emphasis on the final phase of the battle. In the mid-1980s, archaeological excavations at the battlefield produced an impressive array of bones, bullets, and buttons. Out of this hodgepodge of artifacts, some investigators attempted to write the definitive account of Custer's defeat, even though parts of the field had been corrupted by millions of souvenir-hunters. Time-motion studies, psychological profiling (with group and individual traumas and psychoses), and acoustical experiments have sought to bring "science" (with appropriate charts and graphs) to bear on the outcome of the fight.

During the same period, students of the battle have tried to pierce the mystery by more closely examining Sioux and Cheyenne testimony— certainly a valid path of inquiry, since these Indians were the last to see Custer and his command alive. None of this information was new (like the soldiers, the last Indian participants died many years ago), but such eyewitness accounts deserved more careful study than accorded them when they were dismissed as the tales of cowards, liars, or incompetents. When all is said and done, the Indians were at least as honest as the whites, although their testimony is clouded by the necessary intervention of interpreters (some using sign language) and by the inexactness of Indian allusions to time, army formations, and geographic locations.

All of these approaches have value, and I make use of them when appropriate. But just as this book is not a biography of Custer, so neither is it a treatise on the injustices done the American Indians nor a close study of their culture. This is the historiography of one relatively small battle initiated by the Seventh U.S. Cavalry at the behest of the government it served, on behalf of a confused policy driven by many special interests. By pure happenstance, Custer found himself at the center of one of the largest military operations ever conducted against one of the largest concentrations of Indians on the North American continent. This book means to show how and why he failed to enforce government edicts at that moment, though enforcement was bound to happen eventually.

Since the book concentrates primarily on the military campaign, I have necessarily focused on army sources. None of this information has been newly discovered. In one form or another, the interviews, correspondence, and other papers reflecting participant accounts have been around for many years. My sole contribution is the analysis, and in that I have been as objective as my reading of the facts and my intelligence will permit, recognizing that subjectivity even in science is an ever-present and inescapable condition.

One last word on sources: at the core of the controversy is the question of whether Custer made mistakes or whether several subordinates (Major Marcus Reno and Captain Frederick Benteen) were derelict in the performance of their duties. Key to the official position of these two latter officers is the transcript of the Reno Court of Inquiry, a U.S. army tribunal assembled in 1879 to look into Major Reno's (and, by extension, Captain Benteen's) performance during critical phases of the battle. I have read and reread the record of those proceedings in an effort to get at the truth of what happened and, more particularly, to determine how it was that there could be such divergent views regarding specific events. My conclusion is that some officers committed perjury in direct contravention of their duty and obligations, which is more despicable than their original failings resulting from personal weakness or deliberate avoidance of the obvious. Some readers will have difficulty accepting that the lying occurred, but during the course of this book, the case will be proved.

With that as a basis for believing certain witnesses while disbelieving others, I will demonstrate that Custer did have a battle plan different from any advanced by scholars thus far; that he had sufficient reason to conclude that his scheme might be successful, with minimum bloodshed; that he made decisions in accordance with army regulation and his best instincts as an experienced commander; that his logistical tail (mule train) was a major impediment; that certain subordinates could not surmount the limits of their personalities in a desperate situation and so contributed to the failure of the mission; and that Custer made a totally unselfish commitment to save the bulk of his regiment by taking his wing into a diversionary posture in full expectation that the surviving elements of the Seventh would rally to his aid. Along the way, I will discuss the causes of the schism between Custer and Benteen, the nature of the officer corps within the regiment, the manner of men who served in the Seventh, and the plans and circumstances leading up to the Battle of the Little Bighorn.

In an undertaking of this sort, several people deserve thanks for their generous contributions. My deepest appreciation goes to Robert M. Utley, who read this book in its various stages and who encouraged me to keep going. He was instrumental in getting the thing done, and he knows how much I have valued his counsel and assistance. Words escape me.

I am also indebted to Brian W. Dippie, who gave the manuscript a fair reading. His essay on the place that this work occupies in the body of Custer literature is a small masterpiece.

In his review of the manuscript, Jerome A. Greene provided additional confidence that my analysis is plausible and that my conclusions are consistent with the evidence presented.

Of course, a book needs a publisher, and I would not have met the University of Oklahoma Press without the initiative of Acquisitions Editor Randolph Lewis, who saw merit in my writing and who pushed the project.

Beyond that, within the body of institutional helpers, no one was more important than the late Dennis Rowley, a curator at the Harold B. Lee Library, Brigham Young University. Bless him and his assistant, Ellen Copley. The staff at the Little Bighorn Battlefield National Monument and the U.S. Army Military Institute also furnished important information.

James Court provided valuable comments and photographs on the terrain east of the Little Bighorn River.

Closer to home, I thank Mickey Rankine for her assistance in providing the computer support necessary to the final form of the book.

And more than anyone else, my wife, Claire, is the heroine of this piece. She read every page of this work repeatedly. It helps to have a good friend close at hand.

For any errors (there must be some), I alone am the culprit.

To Hell with Honor

CHAPTER ONE

A DIRTY LITTLE WAR

The death of George Armstrong Custer and nearly half his command at the Battle of the Little Bighorn captured the attention of America in a way that no other engagement in the Indian Wars had done. The business of absorbing the aborigines into the outskirts of white civilization gained a momentum it might have lacked but for Custer's fatal decision on 25 June 1876 to attack a Sioux and Northern Cheyenne village ostensibly too large for his Seventh U.S. Cavalry to handle, in a manner perceived as foolishly proud, uncommonly stupid, or incredibly brave. The name of Custer has dominated the event from the first, even though hundreds of soldiers and warriors died in that clash of arms on a most desolate piece of earth. The Plains Indian way of life was already doomed, but Custer's last fight mobilized a recently reunified nation to accelerate the movement toward a final resolution.

This is not to say that the Battle of the Little Bighorn defined the "Indian problem" or led directly to a universal and totally satisfactory accord. After all, European settlers in North America had been pushing Indians westward out of their natural habitats for more than two hundred years, and a century after Custer's death, fundamental legal and ethical questions regarding the treatment of the native inhabitants are still being debated. But if the Custer defeat marked the zenith of the Plains Indians' expression of power, that humiliation also galvanized the people and the institutions of the reunited United States to settle all Indian issues by force, if necessary, forgoing the niceties of peaceful negotiation and treaty-making, however flawed and even corrupt those earlier efforts at peaceful accommodation may have been.[1]

After the Seventh Cavalry had been crushed by Sioux and Cheyenne warriors, America reacted with dismay and outrage. Newspaper headlines throughout the country resounded with calls for action. In accordance with legal authorization for an "expansible" army, the U.S. president was able to increase the size of companies from seventy to one hundred soldiers. Young men joined the Seventh as "avengers" to complement the residue of "bloodhounds" who had survived the worst humiliation of the post–Civil War cavalry, all no doubt possessed by the idea of getting even with the "red heathen." The war of "Civilization" against "Barbarity," with the army as the "advance guard," as General William Tecumseh Sherman called it, was about to reach a denouement in the American West, in partial fulfillment of Custer's own unintended prophecy that it would take "another Phil Kearny massacre to bring Congress up to a generous support of the army." For the military establishment, such an awakening was indeed limited, sufficient only to finish the pesky Indian problem, which had its own long, sad chronicle of broken promises and greedy exploitation.[2]

Within a year after the Little Bighorn fight, the remnants of the great Sioux confederacy—led in the West by the Lakota (Teton) tribe—were essentially under U.S. government control on reservations. With the surrender and killing of Crazy Horse of the Oglalas in 1877, the war on the plains was effectively over, and with the return of the Hunkpapa Sitting Bull and his small band from Canada in 1881, any real hope of restoring the nomadic life central to the Lakota culture vanished forever. For generations to come many Indians would blame Custer personally for the outcome, even though he died in a battle that for the Sioux was their single greatest military triumph, an exquisite piece of work by arguably the most skilled individual horsemen on the continent.[3]

The U.S. Army was the instrument for enforcing federal policy on the western frontier, and the cavalry, because of its greater mobility, was the primary action arm. In truth, the military establishment had limited ability to influence the nuances of change manufactured by civilian leadership in the nation's capital. Even with the election of General Ulysses S. Grant to the presidency in 1869, the army found itself chasing after overall plans and specific programs devised by the executive and legislative branches of the government to deal with the Indian problem. Army officers argued mightily for a greater voice in the management of Indian affairs, but the country and its elected representatives were in no mood to entrust the recent saviors of the nation with too much power.

In 1866 Congress had authorized army strength at several times the level existing before the Civil War—primarily to deal with Reconstruction, coastal defense, and frontier protection—but the people retained a healthy suspicion of a peacetime military, which might be tempted to assume dictatorial powers in order to solve problems. In real terms, the size of the army had been approximately 18,000 at the start of the Civil War. During the conflict, the Union forces numbered several millions of volunteers from the states, but when the fighting machine was demobilized in 1865–66, these citizen-soldiers were mustered out of the army, and in their place was a vastly shrunken thing made up of enlisted men more often than not indifferent—even hostile—to the duties they were expected to perform. The authorized strength of the regular army as set by Congress in 1866 was roughly 54,000, decreasing to 37,000 in 1870 and to 25,000 in 1874. Even these numbers are misleading because actual manpower was never up to authorized levels. With so much yet to be done, the army in post–Civil War America was a pitiful shadow of the formidable Union hulk that had brought the South to its knees.[4]

The primary function of the army immediately after the war was the implementation of Reconstruction policies. The army walked a thin line between the views of Radical Republicans, who were bent on a dramatic remaking of Dixie, and those of a resistant Democratic president, Andrew Johnson (1865–69), who, being from Tennessee himself, was inclined to be more lenient toward the former Confederate states. Although armed with the best of intentions, Johnson's Republican successor, Grant (1869–77), fared no better. Reconstruction was virtually dead by the mid-1870s, but still one-fifth of the army was kept busy quelling riots in the South, pursuing a growing Ku Klux Klan, and chasing moonshiners. From 1866 to 1876, the army performed its constabulary duties with varying degrees of success but never so well as to endear itself to the American public. The soldiers were simply national policemen, not the hometown heroes of the Civil War. They were despised in the South and shunned in the North, separate from and barely connected to the ocean of people they were meant to serve.[5]

Out in the West, beyond the Mississippi and Missouri Rivers, fractions of this truncated military apparatus were manning isolated outposts, conducting tiresome patrols, and escorting private and commercial parties across the vast expanse of land seemingly bereft of redeeming qualities— land so unattractive, in fact, that General Sherman would find the trans-Mississippi area nearly useless to the civilization he would later trumpet as essential to its taming.[6] The evolution of official attitudes toward the western plains was directly proportional to the enterprises that saw value in the area's exploitation. As railroads, mining interests, ranchers, and homesteading farmers drifted toward the setting sun in increasing numbers, an irresistible national urge was unofficially promulgated and promoted. For a country that had recently whipped the states'-rights Southerners into submission, the hesitancy of American Indians to show respect for the idea of an inviolable United States could not be countenanced. The expression of Manifest Destiny predated the Civil War by more than a decade, but with the bitter taste of that expensive victory still in their mouths, the people of the rejuvenated union adhered to the idea even if they could not call it by its name or recite the language of its definition.[7] The nation of states was growing, and regardless of the reservoir of ordinary decency residing in its collective soul, a small army of mostly unspecific men was expected to pound heads if necessary to force any outsiders into line.

Rounding up hard-to-catch Indians was work that appealed to few soldiers. Pride in country and duty were attributes common to nineteenth-century Americans imbued with the Victorian virtues inherited through the strained but uncut umbilical to mother England. However, many of the common soldiers who served in the postbellum army were recent immigrants from parts of Europe other than England, and in the eyes of the general population, they and their comrades in arms were "bummers, loafers, and foreign paupers," a rabble of ne'er-do-wells who could not find proper employment in the civilian sector. For these men, Victorian ideals were no more than that, and for many of them, the obligation to serve their country was about an escape from personal difficulties, about a yearning for adventure, about a free ride to the gold and silver fields, or maybe just about a way to be fed and clothed for a year, for a season. But regardless of the cultures from which they had come, they were finally creatures of the white,

Protestant, and middle-class society that set the standards of conduct and judged them accordingly.[8]

Custer was a product of these times. Born into a middle-class and very Methodist family in New Rumley, Ohio, on 5 December 1839, he was by the age of fourteen spending most of every year in Monroe, Michigan, with his half sister, Lydia Reed, and her family. Over the years, although frequently separated from his family, Custer retained strong bonds with his parents, his brothers (Nevin, Thomas, and Boston), and his sister (Margaret, or "Maggie"). In the company of his family, close friends, or other relatives, Custer took pleasure in games and practical jokes for his entire life, and he possessed a self-deprecating humor too seldom mentioned as a feature of his personality. To these people, he was "Autie" (a childhood mispronunciation of Armstrong), who seemed always willing to share his sense of adventure and even the little money he possessed. On the other hand, to some men during the Civil War but especially afterward, Custer was an arrogant and egocentric showboat who boasted too much and who inflated reports about the accomplishments of his commands—as well as being a swindler and a womanizer.[9]

Certainly, as a young man, Custer chased the girls and may have had his way with one or two. At the U.S. Military Academy at West Point, he apparently was treated for a case of gonorrhea, probably contracted during a visit to the brothels in New York City. He also consumed alcohol to excess before and in the early years of the Civil War, and his capacity for cursing a blue streak was enhanced during that conflict under the informal tutorship of his senior officers. By the time the war ended, however, he had managed to bring all of his "vices" under control except for gambling, which seemed to suit his innate propensity for risk-taking. All in all, he was a bit of a wild boy, thoroughly convinced that in following his instincts, he would find his destiny as dictated by the God of Battles. In this sense alone, he was a fatalist, as men in combat must always be.

As terrible as the Civil War would prove to be for the nation as a whole, it was a serendipitous event for Custer, as fortuitous as had been his entrance into West Point and his eventual graduation, the genesis of the often cited and highly ironic "Custer's luck." Like most of his academy classmates, who served on both sides of the conflict, Custer was an eager warrior. But whatever his daydreams and whatever his enthusiasm, he could not have foreseen the sequence of events that would carry him to success under a variety of commanding officers, his rapid promotion to brevet (honorary commission) brigadier general, and the fame that would result from coverage of his exploits by the popular press. Of course, he was not the only "boy general" in the Union and Confederate Armies, and he was not the only one who rode fearlessly as officer-fodder at the head of his troops into the jaws of hell, but he was special. History has adjudged him to have been perhaps second only to General Philip Sheridan in his courage and skill as a Union cavalry leader, displaying exceptional abilities to command in the field from Gettysburg, down the Shenandoah Valley, and to Appomattox Courthouse, where Custer received the first indication of the South's willingness to surrender the Army of Northern Virginia. To mark the surrender, Sheridan presented Custer's wife with a small table used in preparing the surrender documents; he included a note saying that no one had done more than her husband to bring the conflict to a successful conclusion.

Custer never won a more important prize during those Civil War years than Elizabeth Bacon. Known as "Libbie" to family and friends, she was a beautiful and intelligent young woman, who succumbed to Custer's persistent courting only after a long period of clandestine communication and in spite of her father's initial resistance to the match. Eventually, her stern father (Judge Daniel Bacon) was won over, partly by the new brevet brigadier general's entreaties and partly perhaps by the inevitability of the engagement. On 9 February 1864, Libbie and Autie were married in the First Presbyterian Church in Monroe. This was Libbie's church; Custer chose to worship a personal and nondenominational God.[10]

For the last year of the war, Libbie spent as much time as possible in the company of her husband, often in the field under the most trying of circumstances. When apart, they exchanged titillating correspondence, including references to pet names for parts of their bodies. Obviously Libbie was no prude, and as rigorous as their life was at that juncture, she was amenable to fighting through the difficulties as he fought his way to fame, if not prosperity. One only has to read the last letters exchanged between them to realize that regardless of the strains in their marriage, the mood swings, the jealousies, the arguments over finances, and the absence of children, Libbie never wavered in her support and her care for that fallible piece of flesh she had labored with such dedication to protect. From the moment of his death until her own death at age ninety, she remained the steadfast partner she had been during their happier times of adventure and exploration together. Not able to imagine any head but Autie's on her pillow, she steeled her fragility after his death and guarded his reputation against the plethora of after-action what-ifs that would haunt her widowhood.

The post–Civil War army in which Custer continued to serve was in some disarray. The military was expected to enforce Reconstruction policies that were at best unclear. In dealing with the Indian problem, the army was a confused tool of schizophrenic schemes concocted within the federal government in response to pressure from myriad competing special-interest groups. Commercial concerns in the West wanted the army to drive the Indians out of the way while religious and humanitarian organizations in the East hoped to educate the "savages" to the path of industry and civilization. The Interior Department and its Bureau of Indian Affairs looked after their charges, providing arms and ammunition for the hunt, while the army suffered the consequences of superior weapons in the hands of already able warriors. Congress slashed appropriations in programs designed to honor treaty obligations, alienating the various tribes and hindering the government agents operating on the reservations and the soldiers trying to minimize depredations in the field, even while unscrupulous traders cheated the Indians and the government. Held in low esteem by a general population as perplexed by the Indian question—and by Reconstruction—as was their government, the army entered a "dark age" that would last for twenty years after the Civil War. Civilian versus military, line versus staff, West Point graduate versus volunteer, cavalry versus infantry: the army was rife with its own tensions, all of which were exacerbated by congressionally mandated reductions in total force strength, which in turn stimulated increased appeal to political patronage among officers striving for the few plum positions and rare promotions.

When Custer was mustered out with the volunteers in 1866, he did not have many career choices. His name recognition and status as a bona fide hero might have opened the door to a term or two in Congress, but Libbie was opposed to that course, and Custer himself must have recognized that his poor oratory skills, restlessness, and action-oriented personality were not suited to political campaigning and service. Also, he had no commercial or financial savvy, as he would demonstrate in his lifelong effort to amass a small fortune without the business acumen to achieve that goal. In fact, his ventures into money-making schemes were generally disastrous and in several cases involved some unsavory characters, the episodes tending to taint Custer with guilt by association. He had always been able to write well enough, and with Libbie's help in refining this talent, he would turn out many articles for *Galaxy* and *Turf, Field, and Farm,* but such work was occasional, not a livelihood. Similarly, he might have felt some real yearning to become an actor, like his good friend Lawrence Barrett, but that was not a realistic option, even though Custer would have brought to the stage extraordinary energy, strong sentiments, and a comic side deriving from the frivolity that had defined his youth before war had fixed his visage with a public mask severe enough to command authority.

Custer's only viable career choice was to remain in the army, specifically the cavalry. Following his last Civil War assignment in Texas (where errors in judgment magnified existing tensions), Custer was offered and accepted an appointment as lieutenant colonel in the regular army, although General Sheridan had attempted without success to obtain a full colonelcy for his protégé. General Sherman said that Custer "gracefully subsided" to the lieutenant colonelcy from his brevet rank of major general (two stars conferred in 1865), but in real terms his commission represented a two-grade promotion. By the end of 1866 Lieutenant Colonel Custer was off to become second-in-command of the Seventh, then being formed in Fort Riley, Kansas, as part of the congressionally mandated increase in army strength from pre–Civil War levels. The Seventh was nominally commanded by a full colonel, but more often than not Custer headed the regiment in and out of garrison.[11]

In December 1866, just about as Custer was joining his new unit, Captain William J. Fetterman and eighty soldiers were killed in a decoy-and-ambush ploy implemented by Sioux warriors, including the young Crazy Horse. This was the Fort Phil Kearny (northern Wyoming) debacle to which Custer later alluded. Nearly coincident with Fetterman's reckless and vainglorious foray, which stunned the army and the general populace, the government in Washington, D.C., was making plans to conclude another in a long list of nearly meaningless treaties with the Indians. In 1867, while Custer and the Seventh were engaged in fruitless chases after Cheyenne villages at the behest of settlers on the central plains, a government commission was charged with persuading the Cheyennes especially to remove themselves to reservations in Indian Territory. The result was the Medicine Lodge Treaty, which may have pleased reformers back East but which simply confused the issues and did not stop Cheyenne warriors from committing depredations in white settlements.[12]

The Seventh Cavalry did not meet with much success during its first year on the job as it grappled with the strange business of subduing Indians on the central plains, roughly between the North Platte River and the Texas Panhandle. The whole army was having difficulty coping with problems in the area, but for Custer particularly the tasks were daunting and the results embarrassing. Usually charged with pursuing bands of uncooperative Indians, he found that trails petered out and whole villages disappeared almost under his nose. In addition, many of the enlisted men in the regiment—as in virtually all military components then serving on the frontier—found the duty hard, the work irksome, and the pay too low for the aggravation. They deserted by the scores.

Frustrated and impatient with the general state of affairs during his first experience as an Indian-fighter, Custer made a series of mistakes— including leaving his post without clear orders in an effort to determine Libbie's whereabouts and safety—leading to his court-martial and suspension from service. He was reinstated in less than a year and was available to command the regiment at the Battle of the Washita, the most famous of his encounters with Indians until the Little Bighorn. The winter campaign against mostly Southern Cheyennes located on the Washita River in Indian Territory (present-day western Oklahoma) was a significant victory for Custer, especially within the army chain of command, but influential humanitarians in the East regarded the attack and loss of life as pointless and unjust. The victory at the Washita may have done much to assuage Custer's feelings of inadequacy as a field commander, but the results did not materially affect his career.[13]

Also during 1868, another peace commission, including General Sherman, was persuading a limited number of Lakota chiefs to sign the Fort Laramie Treaty, which specified that the Sioux would reside on a reservation encompassing much of present-day South Dakota in exchange for certain government concessions, including the abandonment of forts along the Bozeman Trail. The treaty was a highly technical document not fully understood by the chiefs, who were not in a position to speak for all of the members of their communities. Two features of the Fort Laramie Treaty would have a direct bearing on Custer's misfortune at the Little Bighorn. One was that the Black Hills—which were as symbolically central to the Sioux culture as they had been to some of the Indian peoples displaced by the westward push of the Lakota—were part of the land set aside for the original reservation. The other was that a huge tract of land in the Yellowstone country of present-day Montana and Wyoming was designated "unceded Indian territory," which whites were not to enter without permission from the tribes. Unhappily, other legalistic provisions of the treaty permitted such trespasses. Besides being an exercise in noncommunication between very different cultures, the agreement was a sham in many respects, and "nontreaty" stalwarts such as Sitting Bull and Crazy Horse— now designated "hostiles"—were as determined to ignore its strictures as white men were to find loopholes in its maze of expedients.[14]

By 1869, Grant was in the White House, fully committed to a peace policy that would effectively turn the management of the Indian problem over to religious groups enthused by the prospect of proselytizing the Indians to their civilized Christian point of view. The Quakers were apparently the first of the denominations to press the matter with Grant, but others soon followed, some going so far as to institute full-fledged lobbying efforts to acquire control over one Indian agency or another. The idea was that the groups would choose members to serve as agents at the various reservations, ensuring not only that the wards of the government got fair treatment but also that they would be educated in Christian doctrine while they were trained to perform useful work such as farming.[15]

The peace policy reflected the quintessential Victorian proclivity to balance moral salvation with practical relief for the downtrodden. The intervention by men of God was expected to produce clean and respectable Indians who would, by the assumption of daily tasks, be beggars no more. No longer would they be unregenerate paupers dependent on the largesse of the government, nor nomadic savages living in filth as they trailed aimlessly and endlessly after herds of buffalo and elk; with proper attention, they might henceforth become productive members and possibly citizens of a progressive Eurocentric society. The concept appealed to Grant, who "had settled in his own mind that the great result of the Civil War was that America was one nation, with a national norm, a single idiom."[16]

Some Indians benefited from the plan, but most did not, in large part because they resisted the constraints imposed on their freedom to roam. They did not take to growing potatoes or corn or any other crop on the hardscrabble or dusty ground available to them, when by nature and tradition they were bound to hunt and fight, without compass or clock. Only in the frigid months did they come into the agencies to take advantage of government annuities, though at other times they visited long enough to trade animal pelts or other native products for manufactured goods, including weapons. Like the government they served, the mostly well-intentioned clerics and their lay agents lacked the key to persuade the native inhabitants of the West to accept the white man's ways.

The government's shift in emphasis away from reliance on the military may have convinced Custer that it was time for a different kind of assignment. He applied in 1869 for the position of Commandant of Cadets at West Point. Although Colonel Samuel Sturgis, recently appointed commander of the Seventh, endorsed his application, Lieutenant Colonel Emory Upton instead received the assignment, effective in July 1870. Upton was clearly the better choice. The commandant was responsible for ensuring that the cadets were taught tactics for the three arms of the service, as well as for overseeing the general curriculum, discipline, and administration. Custer may have felt that he needed a tour outside purely line/field duty, but he must have realized that the only way he could fulfill the requirements of the job was to turn upside down his own record of undisciplined behavior and lax study habits at the academy, instilling in the cadets a determination to do the opposite of what he had done. In all probability Custer lacked the intellectual focus and rigidity of temperament for the assignment, but the corps of cadets as a whole might have adored him.

Many commentators have made much of the fact that when Custer graduated from West Point in 1861, he ranked last in a class of thirty-four. The truth is that nearly twice that many cadets had entered with Custer four years earlier, and besides those who had departed to join the Confederate armed forces at the start of the Civil War, a number of others had dropped out because of the rigors of the curriculum and the severity of the discipline. So even though Custer was probably a mediocre student more inclined to have fun than to apply himself, he did survive the ordeal, presumably by applying his quick wit and by cramming (or purloining an exam) when faced with failure and possible expulsion. His amassment of demerits for mostly minor infractions of West Point's code of conduct was extraordinary and at the end came close to keeping him from graduating at all. In sum, one has to admire his determination and resiliency, even as his deficiencies as a serious scholar make it obvious why the more cerebral Upton (a contemporary of Custer's and also a "boy general" during the Civil War) was chosen to fill the commandant position.[17]

Thwarted in his attempt to get the West Point job, Custer spent the period of 1870–72 in Kentucky performing Reconstruction duties and purchasing horses for the cavalry. For part of that time, he was on leave, enjoying New York society and gambling at faro or at the Saratoga race-track. Also, at about the middle of this pleasant interlude, he returned to the West in order to accompany Russia's Grand Duke Alexis on a hunting trip, which proved to be a great success. By the spring of 1873, Custer and Libbie were back on the frontier, stationed at Fort Rice while the new quarters for the Seventh Cavalry were being built at Fort Abraham Lincoln in Dakota Territory. During the summer of that year, the Yellowstone Expedition occupied Custer and nearly all of the Seventh in support of a Northern Pacific Railroad survey; Libbie returned to her and Autie's home in Monroe. The expedition included several sharp fights between the Seventh and Sioux warriors, and in these confrontations, Custer displayed the tactical skills usually associated with his name.

The Black Hills Expedition of 1874 was more placid. One purpose was to explore the possibility of establishing an army fort on territory considered important to the Sioux and other Indians and by treaty part of the Great Sioux Reservation, but the trip ended up being a virtual picnic. As a by-product of this sojourn, it was confirmed that gold existed in the Black Hills in sufficient amounts to warrant further examination and possible exploita-tion. Again it was Custer who would be blamed for opening up the "Thieve's Road," but Custer's first reports were restrained regarding the prospects of finding precious metals in paying quantities. Besides, an irreversible momentum had already been established by white men determined to pursue all avenues leading to the dream of easy wealth.

The following year was mostly uneventful except for the U.S. government's failed efforts to buy the Black Hills from the Sioux, leading to a growing feeling that the army would have to apply force in order to settle the issue. By the fall of 1875, President Grant and his military and civilian advisers were agreed on a policy that would drive the Sioux onto reservations, in the absence of their peaceful compliance with government ultimatums. For Custer, the winter of 1875–76 would have been an interval of quiet waiting had it not been for his good-intentioned but fundamentally flawed entrance into an executive-congressional brouhaha related to a kickback scheme involving senior officials and Grant's brother. By being dragged into a political quagmire, which resulted in Secretary of War William W. Belknap's resignation, Custer was denied the opportunity to command the military expedition of 1876 and was nearly prevented from leading his beloved Seventh Cavalry into what would eventually become its entrance into historical and mythical lore.

For a year or two after the Little Bighorn disaster, the nation had a clear policy and a military establishment equipped with the wherewithal to implement it. Granted, this was a stern policy, aimed at driving the Indians off the open plains and onto reservations, but at least it was free of that perpetual flux that had characterized Washington thinking for the first decade after the Civil War. On the other hand, with the various tribes significantly weakened by protracted confrontations during all seasons against an army of seemingly infinite proportions in endless pursuit, the outcome was never really in doubt, whether Custer and his command had fallen or not.

During the eight years of Grant's administration, some two hundred engagements were fought between the army and the Indians even while the peace policy remained in force. By the end of Grant's second term in 1877, General George Crook had conducted a vigorous campaign in Arizona, the army had won the Red River War, Custer had intruded as directed into the Black Hills, and the Little Bighorn battle had ended. The missionary zeal of the religious groups was flagging, while the railroads and wagon trains carried hordes of eager settlers, ambitious entrepreneurs, and assorted adventurers westward. At the same time, the buffalo were disappearing as white hunters conspired unintentionally with desperate Indians (forgetful of their own spiritual and dependent relationship with the beast), disease, and other factors to significantly reduce the size of the herds.

Diverse pressures were still at work on the frontier, and if Grant's idea of peace through Indian reformation was not dead by the time he left office, it was suffering from a terminal illness, made moribund to a degree by his own inconsistent decisions.[18]

The army had never really developed a coherent strategy for confronting the Indians. Few in the service gave thought to the subject, and for even these few, the hardly innovative ideas during the 1868–76 period pertained chiefly to conducting winter campaigns (to suppress warrior mobility), converging columns (to catch stationary villages in a vice), and using mule trains versus wagons as the support-supply component (logistical tail). In keeping with their Civil War experiences, Sherman and Sheridan from time to time referred to "total war," which envisaged eliminating the Indians' ability to subsist. But in truth, it was easier for these officers and the army as a whole to give vent to their impatience with the Indian problem and to contemplate plans for future foreign wars than to face the vagaries of actual involvement on the frontier.

As a consequence, there was no army policy regarding the suppression or conquest of the Indians. Every officer had to do the best he could, guided by his own experience in the field. These conditions made Custer an invaluable asset to the army leadership, which was obliged to depend on instinct and invention to defeat the Plains Indians. Expressing the views of many other officers, General Sherman said that fighting the Indians was "at best . . . an inglorious war, not apt to add much to our fame or personal comfort." He added, "To accuse us of inaugurating or wishing such a war, is to accuse us of a want of common sense." Throughout the chain of command, the army wanted the problem to go away, and if any of the senior officers injudiciously used the word "exterminate," they referred to the intractable nature of the dilemma, not to the Indians as a people.[19]

In May 1875 Colonel Sturgis wrote a letter to his son James, who was about to graduate from West Point. As the nominal commander of the Seventh Cavalry, Colonel Sturgis might have been expected to recommend the mounted arm of the military to his boy. Such was not the case. .

In Artillery, you always have refined stations and access to books and refined society, while the Cavalry are thrown out to the frontiers, away from all books, society and other refining influences—and it is hardly necessary to tell you, after what you have seen, that temptations increase a thousand fold, for drinking, gambling and all kinds of dissipation which destroys so many young officers. . . . The more boyish notion which cadets so often entertain of being mounted and dashing about on their horses, I hope will find no place in your mind in making up your choice. An Indian, for that matter, is mounted also and does a great deal of dashing around, but for all that, he is an Indian still. You I hope will take a higher view of your future than all that.[20]

Assuming that young James (nicknamed "Jack") had an opportunity to join the artillery, he declined his father's advice: he selected the Seventh and died with Custer at the Little Bighorn. That Colonel Sturgis would make such a recommendation is not so surprising in light of the fact that until Custer's death, he spent virtually no time with the regiment he was supposed to command. His recitation of reasons for avoiding service in the cavalry pretty well captures the essence of the perception of the army in the West. To Sturgis, the cavalryman was little more than an Indian in uniform, with more vices and less pleasure in what he did.

Colonel Sturgis and other officers had a clear distaste, if not contempt, for army life and duty on the plains. Their attitude was typical. Approximately 20 percent of the officers assigned to the Seventh Cavalry were absent when the regiment took the field in the spring of 1876. Some were undoubtedly "coffee-coolers" (a military characterization for those who avoided action in the field), some not. There is no evidence that any of them were chomping at the bit to partake of that long, hard ride with Custer and their fellows after an apparition called glory. It took a special kind of man to engage enthusiastically in that gritty and almost always unproductive business—a restless man, a tireless man, a man who thrived in the outdoors, who found respite in retreat from the refinements of civilized society, who actually wanted to cavort with Indians in the wild. In face and experience, Custer had grown suddenly older during that spring, and if it was the boy in him that wept unabashedly for one more chance to court death, it was a battle-hardened but psychologically wounded soldier who recognized that time to roam free was running out.

In 1874 some of Custer's *Galaxy* magazine articles had been compiled and published in a book entitled *My Life on the Plains*. Early in that volume, he expressed a sympathetic view of the Indians' plight: "If I were an Indian, I often think I would greatly prefer to cast my lot among those of my people adhered to the free open plains rather than submit to the confined limits of a reservation, there to be the recipient of the blessed benefits of civilization, with its vices thrown in without stint or measure." A part of him must have always felt that way, although at other times he betrayed a less agreeable attitude toward the Indians, including an avowed intention to ride down and kill those involved in depredations against white women and children.[21]

In the course of his short life, Custer had as many faults and made as many mistakes as most other men. He may have had too much confidence in his ability as a field commander, but timid men rarely got the job done. He obviously liked showy displays of force and esprit de corps in the face of the enemy, but that was his style, and it had worked on many occasions during the Civil War. He may have appeared too considerate of some men and not considerate enough of others, but once on the battlefield, he showed little favoritism, even when that might have served his interests.

What would have saddened and angered Custer was how badly he was used by the men of the Seventh Cavalry who lived after him. When honesty was covered over by a veneer of respectability at a public charade two and a half years after his death, much that had meaning in the Victorian values and the military code of conduct smelled to high heaven in that place, for that time and henceforth, with regard to a brother soldier who deserved at least a frank review of the facts surrounding his death.

In January 1879, an army court of inquiry convened in Chicago to examine Major Marcus Reno's performance at the Little Bighorn. Much like a civilian grand jury, the court of inquiry was charged with hearing the evidence and with determining whether Reno had behaved in such a way as to warrant further action by the army or the government, including taking administrative measures or even conducting a court-martial, if the latter was still possible in Reno's case. Although Reno was the focus of the court's attention, the actions of Captain Frederick Benteen were bound to be discussed, and as a by-product of the testimony, Custer's military decisions during the battle would be scrutinized and judged.[22]

The officers forming the tribunal were Colonel John H. King (Ninth Infantry), Lieutenant Colonel W. B. Royall (Third Cavalry), and Colonel Wesley Merritt (Fifth Cavalry), the last another of the "boy generals" who had served with Custer under Sheridan during the Civil War. Lieutenant Jesse M. Lee served as the recorder of the court, a kind of quasi-prosecutor authorized to summon and interrogate witnesses. To serve at his defense counsel, Reno retained Lyman Gilbert, an acquaintance and an assistant attorney general in Pennsylvania.

The moving force behind the Reno Court of Inquiry was a former Union Army officer, magazine editor, and dime novelist named Frederick Whittaker. Within six months of the Battle of the Little Bighorn, Whittaker had produced a highly controversial biography of Custer. Obviously using material provided by Libbie and one or more unidentified Seventh Cavalry officers, Whittaker's book—an extraordinary accomplishment in so short a time—treated Custer as entirely heroic. The biography took Reno and Benteen to task for failing to carry out their orders and for remaining fixed in place when it was clear that Custer's component was under attack.[23]

In June 1878 Whittaker had formally petitioned Representative W. W. Corlett of Wyoming Territory to have the U.S. House of Representatives' Committee on Military Affairs look into Reno's conduct. However, the House adjourned before any action could be taken on the matter, and instead Reno himself requested the army court of inquiry in order to clear his name. In Whittaker's mind, this was a clever ploy on Reno's part, since a court-martial, for whatever cause, had to be instituted within two years of the events in question, making it uncertain what the army could do under such a statute of limitations even if it determined that Reno was culpable in some respect.[24]

Adding to the bizarre nature of the proceedings, Reno was under two years' suspension from duty when the court of inquiry convened. He had been court-martialed in May 1877 for making improper advances to Mrs. Emiline Bell, who was the wife of Captain James M. Bell, Seventh Cavalry, and who, apparently, had enjoyed the advances of numerous other men. A graduate of West Point, Reno had served with some distinction in mostly staff assignments during the Civil War, but his tours on the frontier were more often than not characterized by heavy drinking and by brooding, quarrelsome behavior. By 1880, he would be court-martialed again—for getting involved in a drunken brawl in a post trader's store and for being a "Peeping Tom." In this case, the object of his voyeurism was the daughter of Colonel Sturgis; Reno was found guilty and was finally dismissed from the service. Even at this late date, some have argued that Reno was unjustly cashiered, but beyond question he exhibited over many years a pattern of behavior that suggested a social misfit.[25]

But when the court of inquiry met in 1879, the forty-four-year-old Reno apparently hoped to save his questionable reputation by proving that he was completely guiltless in the Little Bighorn affair. Described by the *Chicago Times* as "a rather short, thick-set man, with a large head and heavy German-looking face," Reno needed to fight off Whittaker's accusations of incompetence and cowardice. As the court officer charged with the prosecution of the case, Recorder Lee had an obligation to gather testimony supporting an opposite argument.[26]

In Chicago's Palmer House, headquarters of General Sheridan's Division of the Missouri, the atmosphere was electric with public interest. The *Times* had said of Custer's defeat that "no occurrence of modern times carried such a shock to the American populace," comparing the event to the assassination of President Abraham Lincoln. That hyperbole aside, the people of the nation did expect that what happened in Chicago would contribute significantly to a greater understanding of how the best-known of the army units then engaged in the cause of Manifest Destiny could have come to such an unhappy end. The army as a whole was under siege, and no amount of professional allegiance or congenial reunion could deflect the reality that the whole civilian world was watching. A public perception of an unfair hearing and wrong conclusions could send the U.S. military establishment reeling.[27]

What Major Reno needed was for some member of the Seventh Cavalry's officer corps to substantiate his version of the events. Within the army grapevine, soldiers familiar with the aftermath of the battle contended that references to Reno's cowardice were rampant throughout the regiment, but these men were not called to testify. Even if they had been willing to share their stories, they were outsiders and their evidence was no more than hearsay. Within the Seventh, however, there might have been officers willing and able to recount the extent of Reno's failings unless a person of indisputable integrity could be found to attest to the veracity of Reno's version.[28]

The Reno side found that person in Lieutenant George D. ("Nick") Wallace, a gangly six-foot-plus Seventh Cavalry officer who had been the regiment's engineering-topographical officer, responsible for keeping the itinerary during the Little Bighorn campaign. How Wallace came to be the savior of Reno's reputation is not known. Shortly after the battle, Reno appointed Wallace the regimental adjutant, but that hardly seems adequate reason for the young subaltern and graduate of West Point to commit outright perjury. There can be no doubt that Wallace agreed to corroborate Reno's fabrications, but whether Wallace simply felt sympathy for Reno's plight or whether he succumbed to the idea of unit and overall army solidarity will always remain a mystery.

There were reports that officers met in Reno's room in the Palmer House, partook of the host's whiskey and cigars, and agreed on how they would testify. Some of the surviving officers surely did visit Reno's quarters, but a number indignantly denied that they had ever done so, which was probably true. Once Reno had co-opted Wallace, the rest of the officers were hamstrung unless they were willing to contradict a promising and popular young man like Wallace in order to tell the truth about a person like Reno, whom few in the regiment respected.[29]

The court called twenty-three witnesses over a period of twenty-six days. Included on the witness list were officers, enlisted men, and white scouts who had survived the Little Bighorn fight, as well as nonparticipants such as Lieutenant Edward Maguire, an engineering officer whose rather imperfect map of the battlefield was used to identify points of interest as the testimony unfolded. In the presentation of his case, Recorder Lee followed a logic that is hard to fault. After questioning Lieutenant Maguire on his map based on an examination of the battlefield, Lee called Wallace to the stand, doubtless meaning to obtain from him the broad outlines of Custer's advance up Rosebud Creek to the valley of the Little Bighorn River. It had been Wallace's responsibility as topographical officer to record the route and significant events, which were encapsulated in an official report ending just as Custer and Reno separated to begin the assault on the main Sioux and Cheyenne village—or, as we shall see, just as Wallace left Custer's side, with Custer's permission, to join Reno in the opening attack on the Indian encampment.

Wallace told a number of little lies, but when he told the court that he was always in close proximity to Reno (and was therefore able to corroborate Reno's version of events), he told a whopper. Whatever Recorder Lee thought he had learned in the pre-inquiry questioning of Wallace, he must have been shocked by what he heard now. Reflecting their obvious glee, Reno and Gilbert immediately requested that the court lift its ban on the taking of notes by reporters. Their request was granted. The *Chicago Times* (whose reporters were adept at taking notes, whether sanctioned or not) observed: "It is evident from the testimony of Lieut. Wallace that there is going to be some difficulty in locating the blame in the case under examination." In the battle of public relations, the Reno side—"if we can claim to have sides here," Gilbert proclaimed magnanimously—had clearly won the opening skirmish.[30]

For the next two weeks, Recorder Lee questioned a broad assortment of witnesses, including a contract surgeon, an enlisted man, a white scout, and an interpreter, all of whom provided evidence different from that furnished by Reno and Wallace. In his cross-examination of these four individuals, Gilbert undercut their testimony by getting them to admit that they could not recall whether Lieutenant Wallace was near Major Reno. Gilbert also played on the court's prejudices in favor of officers and against the private soldiers and civilians, who lived "in the suburbs of the army." For example, Gilbert noted, the white interpreter belonged to "a class familiar to the army," and by having lived with an Indian woman, he had in effect fornicated with the enemy. Testifying against the word of two officers, both graduates of West Point, the four witnesses came off as confused and inconsistent.

As conclusive evidence of his importance to the Reno side, Wallace was the only surviving Seventh Cavalry officer recalled to the stand when it came time for Gilbert to present his case. In effect, Wallace simply repeated what he had said during his first appearance, but Recorder Lee—obviously frustrated by the young subaltern's insistence and likely knowing the truth—pressed the lieutenant on the question of whether he had always been near Reno. Judging by the rapid-fire persistence of Lee's queries, we can surmise that Lee believed Wallace was lying to protect Reno.

The proof of Wallace's deliberate perjury did not appear for many years. In 1909 Lieutenant Charles Varnum, chief of scouts with the Seventh during the Little Bighorn expedition, wrote to the researcher Walter Mason Camp and said that Wallace had been with Custer when Reno left to begin his attack on the Indian village. This account was given to Camp while Varnum was still on active duty, assigned as professor of military science at the University of Maine. In nearly the same language that he used in his letter to Camp, Varnum later reiterated his recollections in two separate memoirs found after his death. Nowhere does he make an overt statement aimed at discrediting Wallace, but the incident that places Wallace with Custer—not with Reno—is so detailed that it stands out in the three Varnum narratives, suggesting that he may have meant to leave posterity a kind of Rosetta stone to assist in unraveling the mystery of the court's conflicting testimony.[31]

The full magnitude of Wallace's lies told in support of Reno's falsehoods will be explored in the course of this book, as the incidents occur in the chronological examination of the battle. But just using common sense, it is odd that no one on the army side at the court of inquiry—with all its amassed knowledge of command structures—wondered aloud why Wallace would be with Reno when, as Custer's engineering officer charged with keeping the itinerary of the march, he should properly have been with the head-quarters staff.

But the evidence is persuasive that Wallace did lie and that other officers shaded the truth or did not volunteer information that would have explained Custer's intentions and the reasonableness of his decisions on the verge of battle. One source of unknown reliability suggested that years later Wallace ("with tears in his eyes") told another story, one different from that expressed to the court. Although Wallace went on with his army career, he was killed at Wounded Knee in 1890, dying with full knowledge that he had helped bury the whole truth by slow, insidious increments, skewing history for generations to come, presumably in the name of honor.[32]

The one officer who took perverse pride in having impeded the search for truth was Captain Benteen. Later he stated: "As to queries before the Court of Inquiry, these I would answer now as I did then, and shield Reno quite as much as I then did; and this simply from the fact that there were a lot of harpies after him." Benteen also noted: "The Court of Inquiry knew there was something kept back by me, but they didn't know how to dig it out by questioning, as I gave them no chance to do so; and Reno's attorney was 'Posted' thereon." Certainly, the latter statement indicates some measure of collusion, but Benteen had a jaundiced view of the military justice system, as reflected in the following quotation from one of his letters: "Now, if people think there is no chicanery—or whipping the devil around the stump, in military law, why, they are not in it, so to speak. I know it, for I've seen it. You can write it on your tablet that Capt. Wallace would have done nothing of the kind!" For one who had so few qualms about manipulating the truth while under oath, Benteen does seem to protest a bit too much in defense of Lieutenant (later Captain) Wallace, raising the likelihood that someone had sniffed out the young subaltern's role in the Reno whitewash.[33]

Reno did get off this hook. The officers of the tribunal concluded that they could find in Reno's performance of duty nothing that required "animadversion" from the court. The army as an institution must have been greatly relieved that the court of inquiry could find no cause to bring Reno up on charges, which would probably have necessitated some kind of administrative action, since a court-martial was apparently out of the question. Although senior officers may have felt that even the spectacle of a public hearing had "hurt the army badly," it would have been far worse if a West Point graduate and career man like Reno had been found guilty of cowardice in the face of the enemy. Under scrutiny from a penny-pinching and military-phobic Congress, the army had larger concerns about future appropriations dependent on public support, even as the temporarily enlarged forces were finishing up that dirty little war in the West.[34]

It is impossible to prove beyond the shadow of a doubt that the army dictated the outcome of the Reno Court of Inquiry, but there are intriguing suggestions that at least some of the Seventh's officers felt pressured by the army command to close ranks regarding Reno's behavior. One commissioned officer supposedly said, "They have got the whip over us." He added that there was information set aside that could make the witnesses "uncomfortable" and that there "was no use trying to stand [alone] against the whole gang."[35]

In his correspondence, Benteen partially exposed the cynical set of players who took pleasure in having thwarted the search for the truth:

> I heard not a criticism on the nature of my evidence in the Reno case, tho' Gilbert has written me since that it was wholly satisfactory to army people.[36]

Benteen seems so proud of his accomplishments that one can almost see his barrel chest puff with the thanks of a grateful nation. However, from the public's point of view, the whole court of inquiry exercise must have appeared hardly worth the effort. It did not settle anything about the Battle of the Little Bighorn except that the army and the government had washed their hands of the affair. If Whittaker's biography had tended to myth-ologize Custer, Reno's day in court cut the Civil War hero down to size—and diminished him as a military leader in ways that apparently could not be repaired by appeal to the sworn testimony of fellow officers.

But if Custer was simply dead to the army, and if Benteen delighted at having consigned Custer to a historical hell, both the army and Benteen were much in error. As the long-suffering, fiercely loyal Libbie always believed, and as Lieutenant Varnum may have secretly hoped, the ghost of the real Custer at the Battle of the Little Bighorn can be found in a close reading of the primary sources, even in that record of deliberate mendacity that temporarily saved Reno and that distorted Custer's intentions and actions.

CHAPTER TWO

NATURAL ENEMIES

Blunt and sarcastic, Captain Frederick Benteen gave perhaps his finest public performance at the court of inquiry. Whether or not he meant to be entertaining, the *St. Paul Pioneer Press* at least thought that Benteen was "the humorist of the Reno inquiry and his caustic comments on the march" enlivened "an otherwise dull report." The article noted that Benteen "took the stand with military precision, and an air of considerable dash, which awakened the admiration of the ladies and the envy of the gentlemen."[1]

It was good courtroom theater, but Benteen's testimony was—by his own admission—designed to impede the investigation into the truth of what had happened at the Little Bighorn, and if his testimony also undercut the reputation of Custer, that suited Benteen as well. An intensely proud man, he had been hurt by the Custer family, and that personal pain seethed over the years into bitterness, even into a hatred for everything associated with the inner circle from which he had been excluded—not that he cared about being ostracized. Or so he claimed.

As Benteen liked to tell the story of their first meeting at Fort Riley, Kansas, during the winter of 1866–67, Custer trundled out his order book reflecting the success of his units during the Civil War, making an impression that Benteen thought not favorable. In Benteen's words, he "had been on intimate relations with many great generals, and had heard of no such bragging as was stuffed into me on that night." At this introductory meeting, Custer also produced his valedictory order to his division, which Benteen said "abounded with bluster, brag, and gush." Benteen, countering

26

Custer with a kind of one-upmanship that was to characterize his relations with almost everyone else as well, let Custer read a copy of General James Wilson's brief and concise farewell address to his troops. When Libbie remarked on how beautifully written Wilson's composition was, Benteen took satisfaction in having put Custer—who disliked Wilson—in his place.[2] Even allowing for Benteen's exaggeration and probable telescoping of several encounters into one (unless he had had Wilson's address in his pocket), their initial tête-à-tête must have been fraught with many of the fundamental differences that would divide the two men for the full course of their relationship.

Some five years younger than Benteen at the time of their meeting, Custer had blue eyes, a florid complexion, a golden mustache, and golden hair that curled down to touch the shoulders of his slender, nearly six-foot frame. His exceptional strength was reflected not so much in his lean, high-cheekboned, almost feminine face as in his hands, toughened by wind and sun and by outdoors, athletic endeavors. And out of his small, weak mouth—partially concealed and made more manly by the mustache—spilled words, first rapidly, then haltingly, his voice increasing in pitch as he strived to keep pace with his hyperactive mind. If he wanted to convey authority, Custer had to slow down, bring the torrent of feelings under control, and mentally—even physically—grab the whirlwind and hold it in check. In the process, he risked boring his audience. One of his boyhood friends recalled: "Custer had not the gift of oratory of a public speaker at all, neither was he a great conversationalist."[3] It was said that on at least one occasion when Custer joined other officers around a campfire, his companions one by one invented excuses to leave the place and their commander's tiresome dissertations.[4] If necessary Custer, feeling himself to be dull and unengaging in everyday chitchat with people outside his family circle, held the attention of his interlocutors by force of will, by the authority of rank, by blurted orders, by the example he set, and by reference to his considerable reputation for bravery under fire.

In addition to having no skill as an oral storyteller, Custer had a limited subject matter on which to draw, especially when dealing with strangers. He read little beyond military history, and even at that he was a deliberate reader, possibly because his thoughts ran in many directions at once, limiting his ability to concentrate. He would rather watch a play than pore

27

over a book, would rather fall down laughing at the antics of a comedian than pass the time in small talk. If he was a success in New York and Washington society, his acceptance stemmed from what he had done in the Civil War, from his celebrity status. He was a doer. His life was defined by action, by war, by hunting, by dogs and horses, by the feel of the world around him. In his quiet moments, when he was ensconced securely in his study or in his tent, Custer's thoughts must still have come in random bursts until they could be assembled and captured in written form, perhaps a letter or perhaps an article for *Galaxy* magazine.

With close associates or relatives, Custer might speak more freely, laugh, and play pranks. Then he was the man that his friend, the actor Lawrence Barrett, knew, a man whose "voice was earnest . . . soft . . . with a quickness of utterance which became at times choked by the rapid flow of ideas, and a nervous hesitancy of speech, betraying intensity of thought." Barrett remembered Custer as "peculiarly nervous" and "reticent among strangers, even to a fault." Barrett added: "This reticence often caused him to be misunderstood." But to Barrett, Custer was "sunny" and "affectionate," and though "utterly fearless of danger, he seemed in private to become as gentle as a woman." Obviously, this is a kindly portrait painted by an ardent admirer and as such could not be expected to reflect the whole of Custer's personality, but it does represent the man as remembered by many who knew him well.[5]

As Benteen and Custer sat opposite one another, all that Benteen could have known about Custer was by way of rumor and reputation. Benteen, prematurely gray at thirty-three, smooth-faced (like "an overgrown drummer boy," the *Chicago Times* would say three years later), and somewhat bug-eyed, must have been irked just a little that he was obliged to be interviewed by this young demigod of war—a man who, in Benteen's opinion, was the product of press and propaganda, no larger in stature or accomplishment than many of the men under whom he had served.[6]

And so Benteen—glib but deferential, perhaps sucking on his corncob pipe—stared down his new regimental commander. Within days, Benteen would be able to gauge the full measure of this Custer person and his cronies as they competed at poker. The fact that Benteen was even invited to play suggests something about the relationship in its early stages. Poker was always more than a game of chance with Benteen, who not only invariably won all the chips but also was able to compute in exact terms the nature of his adversaries. Benteen was wide awake to the bluff and the bluffer. Surely it added to his annoyance that this upstart Custer—faltering of speech, quite ordinary, with his wife hovering to mitigate failure—should be in a position to exercise command and control over his future. But in the beginning, none of this mattered because Benteen was quite willing to get along, whatever characterizations and attendant sarcasms may have flitted through his fertile mind as he calculated the cut and jib of this so-called *beau sabreur*.

Born into a strongly secessionist Virginia family that had moved to Missouri early in his life, when the Civil War started Benteen had defected to the Union cause in spite of his father's threats to disown him and in spite of his own apparent bias against blacks. Commissioned as a first lieutenant in 1861, he joined the Tenth Missouri Volunteer Cavalry the following year as a major and rose to the rank of colonel in charge of a "colored unit" by war's end. He was recognized repeatedly for effective leadership. During the war, Benteen served under James Wilson (corps commander) and Emory Upton (division commander) late in the conflict as the Union Army in the West pushed across Alabama and Georgia. For that duty he was recommended for the brevet rank of brigadier general, but he did not actually achieve that grade until after his retirement from the army nearly thirty years later.

When the volunteers were mustered out in 1865, Benteen was appointed a captain in the Seventh Cavalry. Ironically, he would conclude his career in the regular army as a major in command of the black Ninth Cavalry, one of the two "buffalo soldier" regiments that served with distinction during the Indian Wars. For Benteen, being in charge of a black unit at the end of such a long and illustrious career was clearly a cruel blow. As he put it, he preferred retirement in 1888 to remaining "with a race of troops" that he could "take no interest in—and this on account of their 'low-down' rascally character."[7] What he failed to mention was that he had been court-martialed for drunkenness and disrobing in public to fight with civilians, had been suspended from rank for one year at half pay, and had elected to take a disability retirement during the period of suspension.[8]

Although Benteen claimed that he had no regrets about his many years of military service, he complained frequently about the costs to him personally.

In a letter to Private Theodore W. Goldin, Benteen observed that such service had cost him ten thousand dollars out of pocket beyond his pay and that he had lost four children while his family endured life on the frontier.[9] Actually, he calculated the ten thousand dollars based on neglect of his property interests in Georgia (presumably a residence in Atlanta and 170 acres outside the city) rather than real expenditures; he supposedly always had money while in the service and paid his bills only in cash. As for the children, their loss was a true and terrible indicator of the cost of living far from civilized society. The four children had died of spinal meningitis, from which Benteen himself had suffered, and though he may possibly have transmitted the disease to them, no medical proof exists to support such a conclusion.[10]

Partly because he was a frugal man, Benteen moaned bitterly and repeatedly that in the fall of 1868 Custer had asked him to advance Libbie one hundred dollars for essentials and had not repaid the loan for a year, and then without interest. The intriguing features of this transaction are that Custer asked him to provide the money, perhaps knowing that Benteen was one of the few officers with money to lend, and that Benteen agreed to provide it, indicating that relations between the two men had not yet soured completely. In a historic instance of the pot pillorying the kettle, Benteen would call Libbie and Margaret Custer Calhoun (sister of Custer and wife of Lieutenant James Calhoun of the Seventh) the most "penurious" and "parsimonious" of people, a judgment reached after his years of dealing with these apparent witches of the Custer clan.[11]

Whatever else may have gone into shaping his personality, certainly there was something of the stereotypical southern gentleman in Benteen. When his enormous pride was wounded, honor had to be satisfied. For example, some years before the Little Bighorn, he and Major Marcus Reno had a disagreement over some unidentified matter in the officers' club at a post trader's establishment. They may have been under the influence of "bug juice," but in any event, according to Benteen, he tried to reason with the stubborn Reno, who in turn attempted to bully Benteen. Then, as Benteen later recounted, "I slapped his jaws for him till his ears must have rung; told him he was a dirty S.O.B., and if he wanted any other kind of satisfaction, I was only too ready to afford it." From that incident, Benteen concluded that Reno respected him, although it apparently created a gulf between them. Likewise, in the presence of about a dozen officers, Benteen called Captain Thomas Weir a "damned liar" on the subject of the Little Bighorn battle, and when Weir said that this meant "blood," Benteen invited him to select a pistol so that they could "spill the blood right here!" Later, on meeting Benteen, Weir extended his hand, which confused Benteen, who nonetheless "had his accurate measure."[12]

After the Battle of the Washita, Benteen had a similar confrontation with Custer and drew the same conclusions. The Washita was in fact the defining moment in the relationship between the two men, and for that reason there is merit in examining, in some detail, that battle and its repercussions. The year was 1868, and Custer was still in suspension from rank and pay as a consequence of a court-martial proceeding the previous year on a variety of charges. Without Custer to lead the Seventh, Lieutenant Colonel (brevet Brigadier General) Alfred H. Sully, commander of the Third Infantry as well as the District of the Upper Arkansas, reportedly agonized over who should be placed in charge of the regiment as it prepared for a winter campaign against the Cheyenne Indians. Sully felt that Major Joel Elliott lacked the experience to lead such an expedition, and he was apparently not satisfied that any other available officer could command the Seventh.[13]

Early in the fall of that year, according to Benteen, a representative of General Philip Sheridan's Department of Missouri headquarters offered him the command, which was to be accomplished by giving Elliott and another senior captain leaves of absence. Benteen asserted that he "politely but firmly declined the compliment," suggesting instead that the unexpired portion of Custer's one-year sentence (now almost over) be remitted so that Custer might rejoin the Seventh. Benteen's stated reason for declining command of the regiment was that perhaps Custer had learned his lesson and would now exhibit "more sense and judgment." In Benteen's mind, Custer was allowed to return because Benteen had "recommended" it, an act of generosity that Benteen later regretted, since Custer was, according to Benteen, "worse instead of better" when he came back from his forced vacation.[14]

Although it is entirely possible that Benteen spoke on Custer's behalf, thus forgoing a chance to lead the regiment instead of remaining in his company-level assignment, his opinion probably carried less weight than he imagined. General Sheridan was partial to Custer and would have needed no urging to summon one of his favorites back into action, especially as the army was about to begin its short-lived policy of "total war" against the Indians in the West. One feature of this policy was the winter campaign, which was designed to take advantage of the fact that in the winter the Indians would be less mobile than during the summer months and could therefore be more easily found and defeated. The purpose was to make all segments of Indian society experience the horrors of war as fully as the warriors. To achieve these objectives, Sheridan summoned Custer back from Monroe on 24 September 1868: "Generals Sherman, Sully, and myself, and nearly all the officers of your regiment, have asked for you, and I hope the application will be successful. Can you come at once?" Before final approval had been received from the War Department, Custer was on his way back to the field.[15]

One of Custer's first acts was to assign horses by color to the various companies. Each company commander was allowed to pick, by seniority, the shade of his choice. The purpose was to provide a modicum of unit identity and therefore esprit de corps. It was not a new idea (Napoleon had used it) and in the future would be incorporated into cavalry doctrine as the norm.[16] As Benteen described the "horse trade," he was absent when it occurred and, as a consequence, lost what Sheridan had supposedly called "the finest mount he ever saw a troop of cavalry have." Benteen claimed that he lost quality bays and browns, which were replaced by other bays, but he made no mention of favoritism in the exchange. He did protest that the colors had been assigned "in the field at the beginning of the severest campaign that ever cavalry underwent."[17]

Presaging the Little Bighorn expedition, Sheridan's plan in 1868 envisaged three converging columns, one of which was the Seventh Cavalry. Also, Sheridan's written orders to Custer were similar in tone and substance to those that General Alfred Terry would issue to Custer in 1876. Sheridan wrote: "These directions are only general and may be varied by circumstances or by your own judgment. The object of this movement is to operate against hostile Indians, should any be encountered they are to be attacked, their villages destroyed and stock killed."[18]

From Custer's point of view, the village on the Washita River discovered on 27 November stood at the terminus of a trail made by a large number of Indians who had earlier committed depredations. In keeping with his orders, Custer prepared to initiate an assault on the Cheyenne village, attacking from several directions in the early morning hours of a bitterly cold day, under circumstances that precluded the kind of reconnaissance an officer might make to prevent surprise from enemy forces in adjacent camps. Although allegedly secretive regarding his intentions, Custer met with his subordinates to formulate a plan of attack.[19]

As the units took their positions, a single shot from an unidentified source caused the assembled components of the Seventh Cavalry to sweep down on the sleeping village, including some fifty lodges. The fight was a total mismatch. The peaceful Cheyenne chief Black Kettle was killed, as were men, women, and children. In keeping with Sheridan's orders, the lodges were burned and the ponies were slaughtered.

Benteen had not been present when Custer had conferred with his officers before the attack on Black Kettle's camp. Benteen's company was back with the wagon train, serving as a guard and as a reserve force, but as the other units prepared to begin the attack, Custer ordered him to rejoin the command. The officer who carried Custer's instructions was Lieutenant Edward Godfrey, who said that when he returned with Benteen's troop, the various squadrons were taking their positions. Assigned to Major Elliott's battalion, Benteen's company was apparently late getting into position.[20]

In his narrative of the battle, Captain Albert Barnitz noted several times that Benteen did not appear as quickly as expected, though he did arrive "at length" as dawn was breaking. The regimental band was supposed to play the Seventh's battle song, "Garry Owen," as a signal to start the onslaught, but frozen spittle precluded more than a toot or two, thus contributing to the confusion and preventing a fully synchronized attack from several directions. Such glitches were of little import, since the Cheyenne village was taken completely by surprise and was soon overwhelmed, resulting in the deaths of some one hundred Indian "combatants" and about twenty soldiers. The regiment also captured fifty or so women and children and killed more than eight hundred ponies.[21]

The last into position, Benteen's company was one of the first onto the field. According to Benteen, he and his unit "broke up the village before a trooper of any of the other companies of the 7th got in, and we protected the fifty-five squaws and children we captured." Then he, a sergeant, two privates, and a scout "surrounded" the herd of more than eight hundred ponies—no mean feat in itself—and drove them to a place where they were all slaughtered by Custer.[22] Custer was not the lone executioner, of course. Several companies under the command of Lieutenant Godfrey first tried to cut the throats of the ponies, but since there were obviously too many horses for such a time-consuming operation, the Seventh Cavalry shot the animals, the most prized possessions of the Indians. Custer did take part in dispatching the large herd, but he also ensured that enough of the beasts were saved to accommodate the captured women and children.[23]

Benteen believed that he had almost single-handedly won the Battle of the Washita. He had broken up the village, captured the survivors, and rounded up all the ponies. If true, those extraordinary exploits ought to have earned him a high degree of praise in his commander's official report, but this did not occur, at least not to Benteen's satisfaction. This perceived oversight constituted one of the central causes of friction between Benteen and Custer.

Two other events of the battle would also have a lasting effect on this relationship. The first was Benteen's killing of an Indian youth, between twelve and twenty-one years of age, depending on the version of the story. To Benteen, it was a clear case of self-defense. When the young man raised a weapon and attempted to shoot Benteen, the captain killed him. Trained from an early age to use weapons of various kinds, Indian adolescent boys were often regarded as warriors in a fight; thus Benteen was probably justified in defending himself, particularly since a gun had been fired in his direction. However, amid all of the confusion and killing at the Washita, this occurrence persisted in the memory of the Seventh, suggesting that at least some of the regiment relived the moment to Benteen's disadvantage. It would come up again in discussions between Benteen and Custer.[24]

The second incident is writ larger in the history of the Washita and would become a kind of cause celebre in Benteen's later dealings with Custer. Although the Cheyenne village had been surprised while it slept, some of the inhabitants managed to escape the surrounding force. As one of these groups was running from the scene, Major Elliott led a contingent of eighteen men in pursuit, reportedly shouting as he left, "Here's to a brevet or a coffin!" Unknown to Elliott or anyone else in the command at that time, other, stronger Indian encampments were located in the vicinity. No one knows for sure what happened after Elliott's contingent departed the Washita site, but Indian accounts and subsequent investigation determined that within a distance of several miles, the relatively small body of volunteers was itself trapped and destroyed to the last man, having formed into the classic "last stand" defense as the Indian opponents circled in for the kill.

In Benteen's opinion, Custer should have done more at the time to determine the fate of Elliott's party. However, when Elliott left, the battle was still winding down, and Custer was not aware of the major's exit and no one else seemed to know exactly where he had gone. Afterward, Custer was preoccupied with burning the village, killing the ponies, and assembling the captives as an increasing number of Indians from the other camps were gathering on the distant hills. Additionally, the wagon train was somewhere in the rear, protected by only a small number of soldiers and therefore vulnerable to attack by Indians from the nearby encampments.

According to Lieutenant Godfrey, Captain Edward Myers went "down the valley about two miles but found no trace" of the major and his men.[25] Similarly, Sergeant John Ryan, who served in the same company as seven of the men in Elliott's detachment and who therefore had a personal interest in the fate of the group, later commented that Custer had indeed looked for Elliott but that the searchers had been driven back.[26] Even Benteen had to admit that Elliott, like himself, "'pirating' on his own hook, allowed himself to be surrounded and died like a man."[27]

Although Custer may have wondered and even worried about the nearly twenty men now missing in action, he was clearly concerned about the mass of warriors who had formed on the hills around him. They were threatening, not only to the column of soldiers but also to the wagon train, which was not yet in sight. Instead of retreating from danger, Custer did the unexpected by advancing his command in the direction of the adjacent camps, colors flying and the band playing "Ain't I Glad to Get Out of the Wilderness." The warriors withdrew to protect their homes, and after dark, Custer reversed his course back up the valley of the Washita and recovered the wagon train, with no losses. Custer probably could not have pulled off this tactical coup had he not had in his possession the fifty-some women and children captives. Although these noncombatants were not hostages in the narrowest meaning of that word, doubtlessly it occurred to Custer that family-oriented warriors would not attack the Seventh with the women and children marching in the middle of the makeshift parade.

Ostensibly distressed that Major Elliott and his followers had been left unrecovered on the field for several weeks, Benteen wrote a letter to a friend describing the loss of his comrade, with whom he had served during the Civil War. Writing about a month after the battle, Benteen imagined how the forsaken party might have "strained their yearning eyes in the direction whence help should come," while the bulk of the regiment remained in the village performing perfunctory tasks, including the slaughter of ponies. In sum, Benteen suggested that Custer left Elliott's party to its fate. When the letter was published, then picked up by prominent newspapers, Benteen may have regretted writing it, but he had sufficient ego and pride to stand by his utterances no matter how patently untrue they were.[28]

In a tale often told, when Custer got wind of the Washita exposé, he announced his indignation. Custer assembled his officers, switched his legs with his riding whip, and challenged the guilty individual to identify himself. Benteen boldly stepped forward, spinning the cylinder of his revolver to ensure that it was working properly, while the general paced and stammered. Yes, Benteen announced with customary bravado, he was the culprit, at which point Custer sputtered something about seeing Benteen again, then declined to pursue the matter further. Although there were apparently others present, this was always Benteen's story. In his eyes, Custer "wilted like a whipped cur." From that day forward, Benteen noted: "Custer had respect for me, for at the Washita in 1868, I taught him to have it."[29]

Perhaps Custer relented because he understood the real cause of Benteen's intemperate outburst. Benteen did deserve respect for his performance at the Washita. Maybe he had even earned some kind of special recognition, of the sort that accrued only to Custer as the commander of the expedition. Speaking just on his own behalf, not for the other officers and men who had fought and died at the Washita, Benteen eventually revealed the true reason for his bitter feelings.

> And I was head and front at the Battle of the Washita, though *I was most grandly ignored there* [emphasis added] on account of a letter I wrote to a friend who unwisely allowed a portion of it to be published. When it was seen, I admitted having written it, and Custer took mean advantage to punish me in a sly way for it.[30]

Now, late in his life, Benteen acknowledged for the only time the actual stimulus for his Washita account, though even here he distorted the sequence of events. As he would have it, he first wrote the account (and regretted that it was published, not that he had sent it), then he was ignored for his contributions, and then Custer got even.

In *My Life on the Plains*, Custer explained that when preparing his official report after the battle, he had not had the time to await written submissions from all his subordinates on their part in the fight and so had requested brief oral summaries of important points. The substance of Custer's report was repeated in Sheridan's General Field Orders No. 6 of 29 November 1868, just two days after the engagement with Black Kettle's Cheyenne village. The only officers mentioned by name were Custer and those killed—specifically, Major Elliott and Captain Louis M. Hamilton, for whom Custer had a special fondness.[31]

Custer's reaction to Sheridan's laudatory comments did reflect at least a small measure of insensitivity and possibly rationalization. To Custer, praise for the regiment's performance was more important than a "budget of brevets, worded in the regular stereotyped form and distributed in a promiscuous manner."[32] Maybe these thoughts, expressed after the fact in *My Life on the Plains* (Benteen called it *My Lie on the Plains*), were meant to explain his decision—to assuage the feelings of all the participants—but as Custer knew, he had benefited greatly from the brevet system, and his failure to appreciate the importance of such an acknowledgment for other men constituted at least a severe case of shortsightedness. On 2 December 1868, the War Department invited General Sheridan to "forward the names of officers and men deserving special mention," but Custer declined to do so on the grounds that it would be unfair to single out individuals for commendation.[33]

Brevets and medals did matter, though their issuance did not mean a dollar more for the men who received them. Right or wrong in his assessment of Benteen's particular contributions vis-à-vis those of all the other officers and men, Custer did bask in the glory—however tainted—that stemmed from the Washita battle. To an extent, he deserved that recognition, if only because of his insightful extrication of his regiment from the jaws of disaster—in many respects a disaster much like a later predicament from which he would not escape. But when Custer slighted Benteen, and accepted praise for himself, he made an enemy.

37

Contrary to Benteen's claim regarding the sequence of events, Custer first ignored him, and on 22 December—several weeks after Custer's report—Benteen, in a fit of pique, wrote his misbegotten letter to a friend. Whatever his personal remorse that Major Elliott had been lost and left, Benteen by his own admission believed that in chasing after the escaping Indians, his erstwhile comrade had done just the sort of thing that any aggressive and ambitious officer might have attempted. It is not quite fair to say that Benteen felt nothing about Elliott's death, but by the facts, it was the lack of mention of himself that mattered most to Benteen.

For the rest of his life, Benteen would insist that he had no interest in receiving special recognition for having done his duty. He told Private Goldin that he had garnered a "sufficiency of commendation" over the years. It supposedly embarrassed him that Major Reno had chosen to cite him for heroism at the Little Bighorn, although almost without exception the survivors praised him for taking control and possibly saving the remnants of the regiment. The cause of his alleged unease was that first of all, he had "little regard for his [Reno's] opinion," and second, the other officers objected that they had not been mentioned in Reno's official report. According to Benteen, he had not been consulted by Reno, but if he had been given the opportunity, he would have recommended several of the officers for brevets. In his mind, that these subalterns would hold him responsible seemed a great injustice.[34]

Benteen's first reference to this unwarranted carping by the other surviving officers appeared in a letter he wrote to the *Army and Navy Journal* in January 1877, soon after Whittaker's biography of Custer was published. Alluding again to the "Major Elliott affair" and denying that he had disobeyed Custer's orders at the Little Bighorn, Benteen concluded his missive by discussing at some length "the Society of Mutual Admiration" then existing in the Seventh Cavalry. None of the participants were identified, but based on Benteen's subsequent correspondence, the group was apparently made up of all the survivors except Lieutenant George D. Wallace. Thus, for Benteen, a new factionalism had been created out of the flotsam and jetsam of the Little Bighorn, even though the accused source of division within the Seventh had been laid to rest in a shallow grave along that river.[35]

Though it was true that easygoing "Old Man" Benteen had little difficulty making friends, he was less adept at sustaining relationships. By his own admission, he was his own worst enemy. In his declining years, he acknowledged that he had "been a loser in a way, all my life rubbing a bit against the angles—or hair—of folks, instead of going with their whims." He added, "But I couldn't go otherwise—'twould be against the grain of myself." He "had a happy facility of making enemies of any one I ever knew." He was a poor politician and could not let questions of supposed injustice go unchallenged. As he said, "In Russia I'd be a Nihilist sure!"[36]

One person he surely rubbed the wrong way was Libbie Custer. Although Custer himself had a well-documented inclination to let bygones be bygones, Libbie was less likely to give up her grudges, especially where her husband's reputation was involved. In the aftermath of Benteen's Washita letter, her rage must have been monumental. That particular event was never addressed explicitly in any of her written accounts of life with the Seventh, but many other small insults were, and in a recurring theme, she admitted that she could not help but wear her loyal and unforgiving heart on her sleeve. She said that her husband "could not endure to see me show dislike for anyone who did not like him." But she noted that she "felt myself dishonest if I even spoke to one whom I hated." She thought her husband too much attached to President Abraham Lincoln's generous idea of "with malice toward none, with charity for all." Such an attitude made no sense to her, particularly if the offender did not apologize in public, which would have been an utter impossibility for Benteen. "To ignore injury and praise what is praiseworthy is the highest form of nobility," she said. "I could not do it. My soul is too small to forgive." Unlike her husband, she could not set aside the "temptation to retaliate."[37]

The role of any garrison commander's wife was limited almost by definition to organizing and managing the social activities of the post to which her husband was assigned, but it would be absurd to suppose that a wife did not exercise some sway over the direction of her spouse's decisions insofar as personalities were concerned. Custer was aware of the dangers of such influence. In 1873, as they were about to move into the newly constructed Fort Abraham Lincoln in Dakota Territory, Custer wrote Libbie: "I presume you wish you were here, to give the Lt. Colonel a little advice about the designation of these companies. For this reason I am glad you are not here. I should not wish it thought that I had been influenced in the matter. . . . It is a difficult and undesirable task to make

these decisions."[38] Clearly Libbie had injected her opinion into past delibera-
tions on such matters, which determined which officers and their units
would be assigned to the better facilities. In Benteen's case after the Washita,
the depth of Libbie's outrage may have been decisive. Benteen had publicly
and irrevocably besmirched her husband's good name and his greatest
triumph against the Plains Indians.

The extent of Libbie's involvement was undoubtedly known to Benteen.
In correspondence some three decades later, he made repeated references
to a possible reconciliation with Custer's widow, a course of action apparently urged by friends of his. His attitude was that if she would say that it
would be "pleasant" to receive him, he would "gladly pay my respects." He
added: "I believe her principal objection to me is that it was told to her that
I said 'Custer never killed anything but horses anyway!' Now, I don't plead
guilty to the expression she has attributed to me—could not, when I had
so many choices . . . that would have better shown up my opinion of her
husband, but then you see, what's the good of saying anything?"[39] The
shadow of the Washita affair fell well into Benteen's twilight years, and he
could not yield any more than Libbie could.

Whatever Libbie's influence in the wake of the Washita battle in 1868,
Benteen rightly faulted Custer for his exile in 1869 to Fort Dodge, a remote
and relatively incommodious outpost. As Benteen put it, Custer paid him
off "in almost spot cash" for having written the infamous letter. According
to Benteen, the banishment was carried out even though Custer knew that
Benteen had recently lost a child, even though Benteen's wife was ill, and
even though Benteen did not want the assignment.[40]

The result of this sequence of events was that Benteen felt betrayed by
Custer and his minions after having performed heroically at the Washita.
No one involved was without blame, but to the self-righteous Benteen, as
he packed his wife and lone surviving child off to St. Louis so that they
might be spared the indignities and inconveniences of Fort Dodge, it was
a signal injustice. At the earliest opportunity, Benteen extricated himself
from the situation and rejoined the regiment at Fort Hays.[41]

For Benteen, the Washita affair was seminal in terms of his relationship
with Custer. Bizarrely, it was the subject of a conversation between the two
men on the very eve of the march to the Little Bighorn. At that time, many
of the officers drank, sang, and made out their wills in preparation for their

rendezvous with death, which must have appeared—especially to the fatalistic or superstitious—a palpable eventuality. In this atmosphere, Custer and Benteen engaged in a debate described by Lieutenant Richard E. Thompson, then assigned to the Sixth Infantry.

> On the night of 21 June, at the mouth of the Rosebud, a group of officers, including Custer and Benteen, sat discussing the possibilities of the campaign, and Benteen and Custer engaged in some personalities and recriminations. Benteen said that if they were to get into a fight he hoped he would be better supported than he was at the Battle of the Washita. Custer then twitted Benteen of shooting an Indian boy in battle, and Benteen went on to explain why he had to do so to defend his life. . . . The discussion of matters between Custer and Benteen waxed rather warm at this time, and it was plain to be seen that Benteen hated Custer.[42]

The reported incident illustrates the degree to which the Washita battle preyed on Benteen's mind.

Although not nearly as relevant to the Little Bighorn as the Washita, Benteen's recollections of the Canyon Creek engagement in 1877 shed additional light on his willingness to rationalize and distort events, as well as to denigrate those with whom he served. The particulars of this brief fight with the Nez Percés are less important than the fact that Benteen was unhappy in a reserve role, was willing to divide the regiment in order to hurry after Indians, and suggested that he personally could catch them by riding the men and horses fifty miles a day even though the regiment lacked complete knowledge of the size and disposition of the enemy. In a series of letters, writing as if he were wearing blinders regarding his own criticisms of Custer at the Little Bighorn, he described how he had urged such action. He described Colonel Samuel Sturgis (commander of the Seventh) as a "coward." Benteen ranked Sturgis with Reno and the rest of the senior officers in the regiment as "a crowd of chumps." He wondered whether "a finely-toothed comb, well dragged" could "have pulled out of the whole army a sorrier set." Benteen added: "Sturgis treated Reno like a dog. Reno was a far better soldier than Sturgis, and that isn't much praise." When nothing was occurring worthy of his attention, Benteen had the time to strip his "fine silk fishing line" so that he might engage in his favorite pastime. "My fishing pole of birch was my spear on that ride," he said.[43]

Slow in the rear, fast in the lead: that was Captain Frederick Benteen. With his fishing gear as ready as his rifle, he was as prepared for peaceful and watchful waiting as he was for active engagement. Perhaps his superiors should have realized that Benteen was the ideal cavalryman for bringing an enemy to battle. Or perhaps they all believed that he could not be trusted in the lead position, that he was too impetuous, too lustful after the official recognition he claimed to disdain, too much like the kind of ambitious glory-hunter that Custer was supposed to be.

The wedge that circumstances had driven between the two men was sharp and went deep. The two were very different in temperament. Benteen was complacent, even lackadaisical in garrison; Custer sought any means to avoid the tedium and inactivity of post life and could not sit still for the everyday business of living. Custer avoided gossip-mongering; Benteen rejoiced in it. Benteen was a binge drinker; Custer did not imbibe and disliked the habit in others. Custer still inclined to a personal reserve capable of misinterpretation by strangers in spite of his success and rank, still stammered when excited, still flushed crimson when challenged or embarrassed, and still snapped at signs of insubordination. This was the man Benteen called "quite ordinary" in every sense. This was the man Benteen hated not with nonchalance but with passion.[44]

Given the persistence of Benteen's negative feelings toward the Custers, one would hardly expect to find a high level of understanding or compassion in his commentaries, which more often than not were based on reports from "Dame Rumor." That he had to depend on camp gossip for the ugliest of his stories is not surprising, since between the Washita and the Little Bighorn, he was rarely in the company of those he could not stand. Thus Benteen was able to say, without proof or compunction, that Custer had slept with his black cook, with an Indian maiden, and with the wife of another officer. No doubt he derived much amused satisfaction from thoughts of Custer copulating with the cook.[45]

Later in life, Benteen said that he had "not learned to love [Custer] yet." He added: "And it comes . . . from bitter experience with him, from which no harm ever came to me, so I'm not vindictive." Continuing with his episodes of self-delusion, Benteen noted that he had never been afraid of

Custer. "Custer liked me for it, and I always surmised what I afterwards learned, de facto, that he wanted me badly for a friend; but I could not be, tho' I never fought him covertly." Benteen was indeed vindictive, and given a choice, he did prefer to speak beyond the glare of public scrutiny, spreading vicious rumors in the dark corners of correspondence. By his own admission, he was like "a goose doing his mess by moonlight."[46]

Benteen's correspondence reveals an imperfect man at war with the world and with himself. The enemy whose company he could not keep, could not keep his. Two truly brave soldiers reached out and scarcely touched one another, except to cause pain. Had the better angels in Benteen prevailed, he would not have written that fateful and fundamentally untruthful letter about the Battle of the Washita, and in the relative comfort of Fort Lincoln, he might have been embraced by the family he finally could not abide. Or perhaps the hurt and unbridgeable break would simply have been delayed.

CHAPTER THREE

AS FAMILIES GO

The anti-Custer faction—if there was such a faction—were the people in regiment which had all of the hard duty to perform, and who did it nobly, because they loved their country and the "Service."

No favors were ever asked for by them, and none would have been granted them by Custer had they been requested.

The fact of the matter is, the regiment was in terrible shape from the very beginning, and Custer was the grand marplot and cause of it all.[1]

So said Captain Frederick Benteen twenty years after the Battle of the Little Bighorn. He would not have led a rebellious group or belonged to one. He was too stubborn, independent, and cantankerous to organize or join a cabal of officers seeking to redress general grievances or simply trying to "pepper" Custer with small annoyances. In the first place, he had as little regard for most officers who served in the Seventh Cavalry as he had for Custer, and second, it would have required the expenditure of more time and energy than he was inclined to spare on behalf of anyone else's interests. In one of his letters, he remarked that he did not even want his only son to join the army because of cliques, which obviously in his mind included more than the Custer gang or the surviving officers who sniped at him and Major Marcus Reno and who failed to send congratulatory notes on the occasion of his promotion to brigadier general.[2]

The most serious schism within the Seventh had occurred in 1867–68, when Custer opened himself up to criticism by fellow officers who already had reasons to resent his youth and to envy his success. His court-martial in that year provided the perfect opportunity for them to vent their feelings and to punish him. He had flaunted army regulations by leaving his post without proper authority, had abandoned men in order to serve what were essentially selfish ends, and had ordered soldiers shot while they were attempting to desert. Naturally, Custer vigorously defended his actions, and in fact arguments can be made that some of what he did was not only human but also legal. But he did not appeal the judgment against him; instead he quietly (though restlessly) waited for the year's suspension to pass. Less important than his actions and the sentence of the court, however, is the fact that there seemed to be a clear delineation of regimental factions resulting from witnesses declaring for or against him.

Custer's actions before his 1867–68 suspension did not help his case. He again displayed some of the petty authoritarian attributes that had caused him trouble in Texas at the end of the Civil War. Accustomed to dealing with officers and men more fully committed to military service, and used to conflicts in which there was action daily, he stumbled badly on the frontier. Granted, he was trying to force a newborn regiment into full maturity, but he himself was still a young man trying to understand the requirements of peacetime garrison management. Much was expected of him, and he could not make the post–Civil War soldiers as good as he wanted. His impatience with the mission, with the resources at his disposal, and with his own ineptitude was apparent. He put on his imperious face, and it did not work.

Subordinates complained about high-handed behavior or petty orders or official rudeness or lack of recognition, the same litany of complaints and grievances that often drive men in competitive and difficult circumstances to blame the boss. Perhaps some of them gathered in quarters or tents or around campfires and shared their troubles about the tyrant at the top, but there is no evidence that they conspired to achieve some common objective. If there were factions in the Seventh after 1867–68, they were temporary alliances of professional soldiers driven by shared but individual desires not to be bored, not to be ignored, and to advance in rank even at the expense of their cohorts of the moment.

Although writing of the period just after the war, an entry in Libbie's diary probably captured the essence of the continuing problem:

> At a military banquet the drink-loosened tongue recounts some tale of past injustices—never too long past for the slightest detail to be forgotten. What injustices? Oh, having been thwarted when on the point of being assigned to a post where duty was light and pleasure perpetual. Or having had baseless charges preferred against one. Or having been overslaughed.
>
> At a military dinner there may be little to eat, but never a lack of grievances.[3]

In Custer's view, even though his subordinates might be upset with him or the army in general, they would come to their senses if simply left to themselves. At least, that is what he told Libbie, and an unwillingness to counsel officers on points of dissatisfaction is consistent with his personality. It is hard to imagine him having a heart-to-heart with any of his subalterns. Even with his brother Tom, he depended on Libbie's good influence to curb the younger sibling's unhealthy appetites.[4]

Of course, Tom was not the worst offender in the regiment. Drinking and drunkenness were common in the army among officers and enlisted men alike. For those posted to the western territories, winters were spent normally in garrison, and the summer months were occupied with expeditions or specific missions in the field. While in garrison, men drank to relieve loneliness or boredom or to satisfy a habit; while in the field, they drank to get through the "extra tired time" or to stiffen their spines for hard riding and fighting and bad food. The Seventh Cavalry had always had plenty of heavy drinkers, and in 1876 it was no different. Unfortunately for those who were fond of spirits, Custer was not.

Custer's attitude toward alcohol doubtless stemmed from his own experience earlier in life, when he had discovered that under the influence of demon rum, he tended to become a giddy fool. By all accounts, he was saved by confessing his sin to his half-sister, Lydia Reed, who exorcized the evil through moral suasion. In an era marked by Victorian middle-class morality and evangelical fervor, Custer's conversion under Lydia's influence is probably not so remarkable, but in exercising his newfound abstinence in the presence of men on the brink of extinction (the Civil War) or excruciating boredom (the frontier), he must surely have come off as somewhat self-righteous to some of them. However, he was in fact surprisingly tolerant of the practice among his officers as long as they were not inebriated on duty and did not let their drinking interfere with the execution of orders.[5]

Of the garrisons available in Dakota Territory in 1876, certainly Fort Abraham Lincoln was the most desirable, a fact recognized by Custer and probably every other officer in the regiment. The obvious reason was that Fort Lincoln was the headquarters of the Seventh, with access to a key part of the command structure, but its location also offered a connection to civilization through Bismarck on the Missouri River and the terminus of the Northern Pacific Railroad. Bismarck itself was a boomtown of unpaved and muddy streets with low, weather-stained houses mostly dedicated to the businesses of fodder, alcohol, laundry, and prostitution. Thus, even though Fort Lincoln was hardly Eden, it was better than the alternatives. Fort Rice was "one of the most God-forsaken spots on earth," and after a stay at Fort Rice, Fort Lincoln "seemed the quintessence of luxury and comfort." Fort Totten was smaller and even more remote than Fort Rice.[6]

The post at Fort Lincoln had been built in 1872 for the infantry, then enlarged over the next year to accommodate six companies of cavalry. Facilitated by faulty insulation called "warm paper," the post commander's home burned down in 1874, and Custer supervised its reconstruction during that year, ensuring that it was built to suit Libbie's tastes. The residence, located at the center of "officers' row," was flanked by homes of similar construction, designed as duplexes to accommodate two individual officers or families. Such houses seemed "hastily constructed, as the wind blew through unseen crevices and rattled the windows." Lighted by kerosene lamps and candles, the medium-sized living rooms sometimes included old canvas tenting to add warmth, retaining the heat generated by a stove in the middle of the room. The furniture often included campstools and unpainted chairs, with possibly a fur rug or two covering the floors. If the officer was enterprising, the furnishings might include a piano delivered from St. Paul, supplemented by a guitar, a banjo, or a violin. The dining room might consist of wooden planks stretched across two carpenter's horses.[7] There was little incentive to expend a great deal of energy on improving the appearance of these homes, however, because officers and their companies changed station so often. Additionally, under the custom of "ranking out"—in which more-senior officers bumped subordinates from quarters—it must have been nearly impossible to feel any sense of long-term security.

The Custer home was more spacious and elegant than the others, in part because it represented the center of social life for the officers, their families, and guests. As mistress of the post, Libbie did what she could to keep the social scene humming along. For small affairs, there was the rented piano; for large occasions, the regimental band performed at dances and hops, maybe featuring Virginia reels, square dances, waltzes. There were charades and amateur theatrical performances, practical jokes, and romps. Other activities included riding and shooting, horse racing, baseball, and picnics. Once a month or so, officers and their wives might attend a ball or drama given by the enlisted men. Books and newspapers were treasures, often reread many times during the course of weeks or longer.

Most of the indoor activities occurred in the Custer home, although all of the officers' residences were considered "social thoroughfares," depending entirely on individual popularity. Libbie cared about keeping her own restless husband occupied, if not entertained. And she worried over the junior subalterns who joined the regiment, fearing that they might be inclined to follow the lead of certain of the older men, particularly during "the tameness and dead calm" of winter. She fretted especially for "the young officers who came to the regiment from West Point, fearing that the sameness and inactivity of the garrison life would be a test to which their character would succumb."[8]

While Custer eschewed the perils of drink, he was known to bet a thousand dollars in a poker game on a bluff and lose, or to wager five hundred dollars on a horse race and win. He had triumphed over gin and had curtailed his cursing to a rare oath, but his fight against the roll of the dice was inconsistent, and the rush obtained from high risk was a demon he could not finally defeat. Gambling was a habit he indulged to the end, although he proclaimed from time to time that he was able to resist the temptation.

All in all, Libbie Custer was a faithful companion and friend as well as wife to her husband. Spiteful, vindictive, and unrelentingly cold to enemies of the general, she was equally loyal and giving to family and close associates. There is no doubt that she and Autie were always in love, and there is no evidence that he was ever involved with any other women. Had he been, the lightning speed of the army grapevine—facilitated and energized by the people who resented and envied Custer—would have informed his wife first of all and would have been reflected in the memoirs and private correspondence of men other than Benteen. Even Custer's supposed liaison with Monahsetah, an attractive young Cheyenne, is about as likely as the myth that Rain-in-the-Face ate Tom Custer's heart after the Battle of the Little Bighorn. Although Custer alluded to Monahsetah, who was at least seven months pregnant when she was captured at the Washita, several times in *My Life on the Plains* he specified that she provided valuable service as an interpreter during the early part of 1869.[9]

Again, the final letters written by Custer and Libbie before his death at the Little Bighorn contain no hint of strain in their marriage, no coolness in their romance of a dozen years, no curtness, no accusatory or unkind language. Doubtless seeking her approval, he expressed pride in the work he was doing, asked that she not be anxious about him, and indicated that he was obeying her "instructions" to remain near the column. In Libbie's last letter (never received by Custer), she praised his recent articles. She said that she felt "the greatest apprehension" for him on "this dangerous scout." She concluded the letter: "I shall go to bed and dream of my dear Bo." "Oh, Autie," she added, "if you return without bad news the worst of the summer will be over." Of course, the news of that summer was as bad as it could get for Libbie.[10]

In the spring of 1876, the Seventh was perhaps not as good as its reputation. The nominal commander of the unit, Colonel Samuel Sturgis, was not present, having been detached to engage in recruiting duties. He had shown no vigor in many years and was rarely with the regiment, and besides, General Philip Sheridan preferred Custer. Major Joseph Tilford was on leave, and Major Lewis Merrill was serving as chief of the military staff to President Ulysses Grant at the Centennial Exhibition in Philadelphia. Neither were Lieutenants William Craycroft and James Bell available for duty. Captain Charles Ilsley was aide-de-camp to General John Pope, and Lieutenant Henry Jackson was on detached service with the signal corps. Captain John Tourtellotte was aide-de-camp to General William Sherman, Captain Owen Hale was on detached service in St. Louis, and Captain

Michael Sheridan served his brother as aide-de-camp, a position he had held for many years. Lieutenant Charles Braden was on sick leave, and Lieutenant Edwin Eckerson, recently assigned to the Seventh, was on regular leave. Lieutenant Ernest Garlington was on detached service, and Lieutenant Andrew Nave was on sick leave. Lieutenant Charles Larned, probably the most pretentious and supercilious officer in the Seventh, was on duty as assistant professor of drawing at West Point, where he would remain for most of his career.[11]

In short, eleven of forty-one officers assigned to the Seventh were not on duty, and although some of the missing might fairly be called "malingerers" or "coffee coolers," the fact is that the presence of certain officers might have changed the equation at the Little Bighorn. Custer did request the return of Merrill (ostensibly an "enemy") to the regiment. This transfer was approved at lower levels, but President Grant himself vetoed the move, and the possibility cannot be ruled out that Merrill was disinclined to join his old nemesis and thus influenced the final decision. Whether Merrill would have made any difference is problematical. Benteen thought he was a poorer officer than Reno, but on the other hand, Merrill would have pushed Benteen one rung lower in the command structure.

In the beginning of 1876, there was a real question as to whether Custer would lead the expedition against the Sioux and Cheyennes in the unceded territory, since he had allowed himself to be sucked into a congressional inquiry on the subject of post traderships and possible malfeasance by Secretary of War William W. Belknap. Although he had no direct knowledge of the issues being discussed, Custer had strong feelings about the selling of such profitable enterprises, which involved kickbacks to politicians and resulted in detrimental consequences for military personnel. Many in the army considered Custer's stance both correct and courageous, but to President Grant, it was an affront and an aggravation. Not only was his secretary of war in jeopardy, but his own brother was implicated in the scandal. In the end, Belknap resigned before he could be impeached, and Grant denied Custer the opportunity to lead the expedition into the field, in fact indicating that Custer could not even accompany his own regiment. Only the intervention of Generals Alfred Terry, Sheridan, and Sherman allowed Custer to head up the Seventh, under the overall command of Terry. Custer was deeply wounded by Grant's position (as understandable as it might have been), especially since the president would not even allow Custer to present his side of the story.[12]

General Terry had a high regard, one might even say affection, for Custer. In a letter written on the eve of the congressional hearings, Terry informed Custer that he was sorry an appearance was required: "I fear it will delay our movements." He added, "Your services are indispensable." A lawyer by education, Terry was almost universally portrayed as a kind and gentle man, unversed in Indian warfare but willing to rely on men who were. In spite of stories that Custer bragged that he would "cut loose" from Terry, as he had from other superiors, Terry knew his firebrand subordinate and in fact planned a campaign that cast Custer in a leading role.[13]

The question is whether the Seventh Cavalry, as it formed at Fort Lincoln in the spring of 1876 to begin what would become the Little Bighorn expedition, contained true factions. Certainly the kind of clearly defined cliques that had existed in 1867 were not now present. On the other hand, the regiment did include a number of officers who were obviously closer to the inner circle than others, and in that sense alone, some were more "in" while the rest were "out." In terms of hard-core opponents of Custer, these included only Reno and Benteen, who apparently also hated one another and thus could not have created a faction in the narrowest meaning of the word. Had Merrill, Larned, and possibly certain other absent officers been present, there might have been a collection of men sufficiently cohesive in their dislike of Custer to constitute a faction of the sort that supposedly contributed to the disaster at the Little Bighorn.

Following are brief biographical sketches of the officers who rode with the Seventh. They are presented in an order that reflects their status relative to the Custer "inner circle" of the regimental family. No factions are apparent.

Captain Thomas Ward Custer was five years younger than his brother Armstrong. In 1861, at the age of sixteen, he enlisted as a private in the Twenty-first Ohio Infantry. During the Civil War he won two Medals of Honor. As a consequence of one battle, for which he received a medal, he had a scar on his left cheek where hair would not grow; he also had a split forefinger on his left hand, and his initials were tattooed on one arm. He was described as freckle-faced and restless. He shared Armstrong's predilection for practical jokes, but despite an "abiding fondness" between the two men, Libbie thought that her husband was "too severe with his brother, for in his anxiety not to show favoritism he noticed the smallest misdemeanor," transgressions he might well have overlooked in others. Custer did worry that Tom sometimes drank to excess, but the two men were extremely close until the end of their lives.[14]

First Lieutenant James ("Jimmy") Calhoun was several months older than Tom and was married to Margaret (Maggie) Custer, the general's sister. When he was finally assigned to the Seventh in 1871, he thanked Custer for the assistance given, adding: "If the time comes you will not find me wanting."[15] In his biography of Custer, Frederick Whittaker called the blonde, six-foot Calhoun Custer's dearest friend, which means that the description probably came from Libbie. He was also characterized as a gentleman's son, very quiet, reserved, and sensitive, with refined literary tastes yet full of life and fun.[16]

Captain George Wilhelmus Mancius Yates was appointed second lieutenant of the Second Cavalry following service in the Civil War, but within a year he was appointed captain in the Seventh. His wife, Annie, was a close friend of Libbie's, and he was one of Custer's favorites. At the Little Bighorn, Yates commanded F Troop, or the "Band-box Company," so named because of its fine "spit and polish" military appearance.[17]

First Lieutenant Algernon Emory ("Fresh") Smith joined the Seventh in 1867 as a second lieutenant. In 1870 he sought disability retirement for a Civil War wound that made it difficult for him to lift his left arm above shoulder level, but he withdrew the application after treatment. At the Little Bighorn, he commanded E Troop, the "Gray Horse Troop." He was called a modest individual, and he and his wife, Nettie, were intimates of the Custers.[18]

First Lieutenant William Winer Cooke, known as "Cookie" or the "Queen's Own," was Canadian-born, over six feet tall, with Dundreary whiskers. According to some, he was the finest horseman, the fastest runner, and the best shot in the Seventh. He was generally regarded as dependable and brave and was quite close to the Custer family for many years.[19] He joined the Twenty-fourth New York Cavalry in 1862 when he was eighteen years old, giving his age as twenty-two, and within two years was appointed second lieutenant. He finally achieved the rank of first lieutenant before being mustered out. In 1866 he obtained a commission as second lieutenant in the Seventh, and a year later Custer recommended him for promotion to captain, but the recommendation was rejected, and he advanced only one grade. The eldest of four sons of a wealthy Ontario physician, he was apparently a very able and persistent petitioner on his own behalf, which hardly made him unique in the army scheme of things during or after the Civil War.[20]

Captain Thomas Benton Weir, born in Ohio in 1838, attended the University of Michigan and enlisted in the Third Michigan Cavalry in 1861, soon after getting a commission as second lieutenant. After the war he served on Custer's staff in Texas, and he was appointed first lieutenant coincident with the formation of the Seventh in 1866. A year later he was promoted to captain.[21] Like other members of the Seventh, Weir drank to excess on occasion, but he was described as "very well read, and social in his disposition" by Captain Albert Barnitz, who was decidedly a teetotaler but who was glad to see Weir return to the regiment in 1867 because he was a source of intelligent conversation. Given this opinion of Weir and the fact that he was an educated and eligible bachelor, we can easily understand how Libbie might have found him an attractive companion and why Custer might have been worried enough to leave his post without permission and so get himself court-martialed. The scuttlebutt was that in the summer of 1867 Custer received an anonymous letter (allegedly written by Lieutenant Charles Brewster at the urging of Custer's cook) stating that the general had better hurry home to keep track of his wife. Several sources told essentially the same story: namely, that when Custer caught up with Weir, he forced his subordinate to kneel and beg for forgiveness. According to Captain Barnitz, Weir did "unaccountably" lose his hair that summer and was wearing a wig. Whether Weir's shedding was caused by a touch of cholera or by a nervous condition stimulated by Custer's actions is not certain.[22] In December 1876, while on recruiting duty in New York City, Weir died of "congestion of the brain," a mysterious surcease to say the least. Because of his untimely death at the age of thirty-eight, he was not available to testify at the Reno Court of Inquiry, where he may have had the courage, which he showed at the Little Bighorn, to speak the truth about Custer's plight.

Captain Myles Moylan enlisted in the regular army in 1857 at the age of nineteen, then worked his way up to first sergeant in a company of the Second Dragoons. In 1863 he won a commission as second lieutenant in the Fifth Cavalry, and during that year he was dismissed from the army for being absent without proper authority. He reenlisted under an assumed name, worked his way up to sergeant, within six months was commissioned first lieutenant, and was promoted to captain by 1864. Mustered out after the war, he enlisted again as a private in the regular army and was assigned to the Seventh; Custer promptly made him sergeant major of the regiment. Almost immediately Custer and other senior officers endorsed his application for a commission, which he received by December 1866. Within six years he was promoted to captain. Probably no one else on the roster of the Seventh's officers demonstrated greater ambition, persistence, and resiliency than did Moylan. Moylan was married to Charlotte Calhoun, the sister of Lieutenant James Calhoun.

Second Lieutenant Charles Albert Varnum, unmarried, turned twenty-seven on the eve of the regiment's departure for the Little Bighorn, at which time he was in charge of the scouts. He had graduated from West Point in 1872 and had participated in the 1873 and 1874 expeditions, where his connection with Custer, who appreciated courage, was cemented. "I must have been on fairly intimate terms with General Custer for he was the kind of man who kept officers at a distance as a rule. . . . I had been in two pretty sharp Indian fights in 1873 under him, and that therefore I had gotten into a relationship that made him lenient with what he would have regarded as impudence on the part of some officers who did not know him so well."[23] Eventually Varnum would reach the rank of colonel, and he was awarded the Medal of Honor for courageous action at Wounded Knee, where his friend George Wallace was killed at his side.

Captain Myles Walter Keogh was the archetypical soldier of fortune. Unmarried and thirty-six years old at the time of his death, he had been born in Ireland. He left home to join the Papal Guards while he was still a teenager, was eventually commissioned as an officer, and was awarded the Medaglia di Pro Petri Sede by Pope Pius IX. During the Civil War he attained the rank of brevet lieutenant colonel for meritorious service; although normally consigned to staff duties, he sought out action whenever he could. For the period of 1866–76, he was captain in command of I Troop, Seventh Cavalry. But Keogh missed the Battle of the Washita and the 1873 and 1874 expeditions because of other temporary assignments or authorized leave and thus had as little experience fighting Indians as Major Reno. In addition, he was characterized as unpopular in the regiment because he was a habitual drunkard who caned enlisted men and who turned the management of his everyday affairs (his attire and finances) over to his striker (soldier-servant) because he could not cope. However, Custer said in 1871 that he "would rather have [Keogh] stationed near us than many others," even though Keogh had treated Custer "unfairly," an apparent reference to Keogh's position during Custer's 1867 court-martial (another example that Custer did not hold a grudge).[24]

First Lieutenant Edward Gustave Mathey was the consummate "scrounger" in the Seventh, and whether by coincidence or through recognition of his innate sense of how to procure needed goods, he ended up with the logistical tail during both the Washita and the Little Bighorn fights. Because of snow blindness at the Battle of the Washita, Mathey remained with the wagon train and turned over his position with an attacking company to Captain Louis Hamilton, who died for his eagerness to join the assault. At the Little Bighorn, Mathey was assigned to look after the mule train carrying ammunition and other supplies. According to one story, if asked to do so, Mathey could find just about anything, from whiskey to a box of tacks. Not surprisingly, on the Little Bighorn expedition he stored his own saber, and several demijohns of liquor were carried in the packs to accommodate that "extra tired time" of the officers. It is impossible to hazard a guess as to what else Mathey might have stashed for possible emergencies or pleasure.[25] Within the regiment, he was known as "Bible Thumper" because of his propensity to use blasphemous language. Benteen thought that he was one of the men who did Custer's "dirty work."[26]

First Lieutenant Francis Marion ("Gibby") Gibson was twenty-eight years old at the time of the battle. He had joined the Seventh in 1867 and was promoted one grade in 1871. He participated in both the Yellowstone and the Black Hills expeditions. He was married to the younger sister of Lieutenant Donald McIntosh's wife. As the regiment was preparing to depart Fort Lincoln in the spring of 1876, Custer asked Gibson to join Company E as second-in-command to Lieutenant Smith. Gibson was apparently inclined to do so, but his wife dissuaded him on the basis of a premonition of disaster. So Gibson remained with H Troop and the "level-headed Benteen," and the position in Company E was taken by young Lieutenant Jack Sturgis.[27]

Captain Thomas H. French served in the regular Union infantry for the last year of the Civil War and by 1868 had been promoted to captain. Before joining the army, he had worked as a clerk in the diplomatic bureau of the State Department; he may have obtained his commission through letters written by his uncle. He was assigned to the Seventh in 1871.[28] His survival at the Little Bighorn may have been a circumstance he found difficult to bear. His most famous letter suggests that he may have sought death during Reno's retreat from the valley and that he may have contemplated shooting Reno, a man he apparently loathed. He did not participate in the Reno Court of Inquiry, however, because he was himself being court-martialed for getting drunk, losing his horse, and dallying with two laundresses. Whether he drank before the battle is not known, but he certainly imbibed afterward: an army surgeon declared in late 1878 that French had been drinking excessively for three months and was "incurable by ordinary methods of treatment." Following a seventeen-day trial in early 1879, he was found guilty and was sentenced to dismissal from service, but President Rutherford B. Hayes commuted the sentence to suspension from rank on half pay for one year. Before the year had elapsed, French sought reinstatement on the grounds that he had no interests or home outside the army, but the War Department chose to retire him involuntarily, and he died of apoplexy in 1882.[29]

First Lieutenant Edward Settle Godfrey was tall, with a large nose and bushy mustache. He was considered a good officer who did not get involved in regimental differences, but later in life he defended Custer, became a close friend and confidante of Libbie's, and continued to detest and blame Reno. Godfrey's career is somewhat unusual in that he enlisted in the Twenty-first Ohio Infantry in 1861 at the age of seventeen, was honorably discharged several months later, gained an appointment to West Point in 1863, and graduated in 1867, ranking fifty-third in a class of sixty-three. These are fairly modest beginnings for a man whom Captain Barnitz found to be snobbish about his West Point education (as well as lazy and undisciplined) during his early months in the Seventh after his graduation.[30] He eventually became a general in the army. Any close association with the Custers was more apparent after the Little Bighorn than before, although in 1874 Godfrey thanked Custer for the "unfailing kindness and consideration" he had shown during the Black Hills expedition.[31]

First Lieutenant Donald ("Tosh") McIntosh was born in Canada and was the offspring of Scotch and Indian parents. He may have suffered from some ostracism because of his mixed-blood parentage, although this is not obvious from the available evidence. Tall, with a kind face, dark eyes, and snow-white teeth, he was called "one of the most beloved officers of the regiment." This assessment came from his sister-in-law, who characterized him further as having a "keen sense of humor" and a brilliant mind, especially regarding military science.[32]

Second Lieutenant Winfield Scott Edgerly would later, like Godfrey, become a general in the army; also like Godfrey, he had an inauspicious start in terms of his class ranking when he graduated from West Point in 1870: fiftieth in a class of fifty-eight. Edgerly was another of the officers who simply tried to perform his assignments well, without any special connection with one group or another, although in his own correspondence he referred to having dined with Custer during the 1876 expedition and to having spent off-duty time with Lieutenant Cooke and Captain Tom Custer. Edgerly described one incident in a letter to Libbie after the battle, saying that Custer had come out of his tent and Edgerly had remarked about the excitement of catching up with the Indians. Custer had replied: "It all depends on you young officers. We can't get Indians without hard riding and plenty of it!" At the time, Edgerly was thirty, and Custer was thirty-six.[33]

Second Lieutenant Benjamin Hubert Hodgson graduated from West Point in the same year as Edgerly, with a slightly better class ranking, and immediately thereafter joined the Seventh. Short and good-looking, "Little Benny" was killed during Custer's last fight. In one of the many harsh ironies of the Little Bighorn, Hodgson had apparently planned to leave the army in the spring of that year but had withdrawn his resignation "for the fun of one last campaign."[34]

Second Lieutenant George Daniel Wallace attended West Point with Varnum and Henry Harrington and considered Hodgson to be one of his best friends. Regardless of what Wallace did on Reno's behalf after the battle, there is no evidence that he felt any ill-will toward Custer personally before the Little Bighorn. When Wallace was killed at Wounded Knee in 1890, he and Varnum were searching Indians for weapons.[35]

Second Lieutenant Henry Moore Harrington, like Wallace and Varnum, graduated from West Point in 1872, joining the Seventh at that time. Not much information exists to assist in placing Harrington within the regimental family, though he served under Tom Custer in C Company. He was on leave when the Seventh was ordered into the field in 1876, and he telegraphed to say that he was giving up his leave in order to join the expedition. He died in the fight, but his body was never identified.

Second Lieutenant William Van Wyck Reily was ill on the eve of the regiment's departure and could therefore have remained at Fort Lincoln, but he chose to go anyway. In 1875 he had been appointed a second lieutenant in the Tenth Cavalry but three months later had been transferred to the Seventh, so that he had just arrived when the regiment started for the Little Bighorn.[36] He also died in the battle.

First Lieutenant James Ezekiel Porter graduated from West Point in 1869 and was commissioned a second lieutenant in the Seventh immediately thereafter. Promoted in 1872, he transferred to Company I, where he served under Keogh. He was presumed killed at the Little Bighorn because his coat was found in the Indian village, but his body was never identified on the battlefield.

Second Lieutenant Luther Rector Hare spoke little about the Little Bighorn after the battle, but what he did say was generally critical of Custer's decisions, particularly the decision to divide the regiment. The *Chicago Times* in 1879 described Hare as "a black-haired fiery-eyed warrior, with tawny skin and a face so furrowed by exposure to the elements" that he may have been "either 20 or 40 years."[37] Graduating from West Point in 1874, he had been with the Seventh for less than two years when it left Fort Lincoln. For most of that time, Hare had been with his company in the South.

Second Lieutenant John Jordan Crittenden was another of the "boy officers" with the Seventh. Crittenden came from a prominent Kentucky family that had been divided by the Civil War. Only twenty-two at the time of his death, he had attended West Point for three years but had failed to graduate because of a "deficiency in philosophy." The real reasons were that he was apparently too young, immature, and intimidated by the rigorous academic environment. He then petitioned President Grant for a commission in the army and in the fall of 1875 was appointed to the Twentieth Infantry. Shortly after assignment, he was injured when a shotgun cartridge exploded in his face, causing him to lose his left eye. He should have been recuperating with his own unit, but knowing of the Seventh's imminent departure, he asked his father to persuade Custer to let him fill one of the vacancies in the officer ranks.[38] Colonel Thomas Crittenden, commander of the Seventeenth

Infantry, was successful in his petition to Custer, and his only son, John, was granted leave from the Twentieth and was assigned to L Company as second-in-command to Calhoun. The father's advice to the young man was to do his duty and never retreat, and the colonel is said to have remarked to someone else, "If he does not come back, I never again can look his mother in the face."[39] The son did not come back, and his mother and father were devastated. Colonel Crittenden did not return to his regiment. The colonel insisted that John be buried where he had fallen at the Little Bighorn, whereas the remains of all other identified officers were removed.

Second Lieutenant James ("Jack") Garland Sturgis graduated from West Point in June 1875 and requested assignment to the Seventh, in spite of his father's objections. Colonel Sturgis, nominal commander of the Seventh, was disdainful of the cavalry and of service in the West. Within a month of his son's assignment, he wrote to Custer, thanking Custer for showing kindness to Jack. The colonel added that although Fort Lincoln was "a more desirable place having a much larger garrison," he felt that his son ought to transfer to Fort Rice, indicating that he wanted Jack stationed away from regimental headquarters.[40] After the Battle of the Little Bighorn, Colonel Sturgis blamed Custer for his son's death, and he said so openly and bluntly.[41]

Captain Thomas Mower McDougall was the son of a brevet brigadier general. McDougall was appointed a second lieutenant in the Tenth Louisiana Volunteers of African Descent at the age of eighteen in 1864, and after being mustered out a year later, he accepted a commission in the infantry, where he remained until being assigned to the Seventh in 1870. He was promoted to captain in 1875. McDougall is another of those officers difficult to place in relation to the Custer inner circle.

Major Marcus Albert Reno, also a graduate of West Point, was some five years older than his commander. Of all the officers in the Seventh, he had more reason than most to resent Custer. Although he had established a respectable record in the Civil War, his service, like Keogh's, was limited largely to staff functions. During his time with the Seventh before the Little Bighorn, he never fought an Indian. Nevertheless, while Custer was in limbo because of the Belknap hearings in Washington, Reno immediately applied for command of the Seventh. The Seventh's contract surgeon, James DeWolf, had favorable first impressions of Custer, but he stated: "Reno who commands my wing I cannot like." Ironically, DeWolf was killed during Reno's retreat from the valley at the Little Bighorn.[42] Private Charles Windolph probably best summed up the general attitude toward Reno: "A lot of the troopers didn't care much for Custer, but it looked as if Major Reno would command the regiment if Custer didn't arrive. And most of us didn't know or care a great deal about Reno. . . . He'd never fought Indians, and he didn't seem to be very popular with either the men or the officers."[43] Even Benteen considered the heavy-drinking Reno stubborn and disagreeable and, as already noted, rated him extremely low on the scale of cavalry officers. Reno would die in 1889 following an operation for cancer of the tongue, with tertiary syphilis listed as a secondary cause of death. One historian has suggested that the syphilis, contracted while he attended West Point, may have contributed to some of his more peculiar behavior.[44]

Captain Frederick William Benteen was a bitter enemy of Custer. His background and his attitudes toward the Custers were discussed in the previous chapter.

First Lieutenant Charles Camilus DeRudio falls farthest outside the family. As Lieutenant Charles A. Woodruff commented: "If you saw DeRudio, you met the bitterest anti-Custer man I ever met unless he has changed; he was at the time simply venomous." However, DeRudio was a minor player within the regiment, more a character actor than a leading light.[45] Having emigrated to the United States from Italy, where he claimed to have been involved in militant revolutionary activities, DeRudio enlisted as a private in the New York Volunteers in 1864 and was later commissioned a second lieutenant in the Second U.S. Colored Infantry. DeRudio was assigned to the Seventh in 1869 and was promoted to first lieutenant in 1875. Shortly before the regiment departed Fort Lincoln in 1876, Custer appointed his good friend "Fresh" Smith to command E Troop in the absence of Captain Charles Ilsley, and although some people thought that Custer did so because he had little confidence in DeRudio, who was second-in-command of E, Smith was actually several years senior in grade—a fact of army protocol that did not prevent DeRudio from taking umbrage at the decision. Also, in later years DeRudio would complain that Custer had suggested that he return an honorary sword and that at the Little Bighorn, the general had borrowed binoculars that were never returned.[46] Benteen called DeRudio "a fearful liar" and indicated that when the "Count" did not have a friend in the regiment after the battle, Benteen took care of him even though he knew DeRudio was "an out and out shyster." He added: "I treated him as a gentleman—which he was not!"[47]

◆ ◆ ◆

This was the set of Seventh U.S. Cavalry officers who gathered under Custer at Fort Lincoln to begin the one-month trek in pursuit of recalcitrant Indians. Without specific reference to this group of officers, when Custer was tweaking Libbie in 1873 for her attempts to influence his personnel decisions, the general had remarked, "Personally I should like to have every one of them with me at Lincoln." Libbie had once called the regiment "a medley of incongruous elements," an astute characterization that certainly applied to these men: old friends, the general's brother, a Frenchman, an Italian, a Canadian, a half-blood, Irishmen, "rankers," an infantryman, and West Point graduates, some of whom were so young that they had scarcely experienced garrison drill, let alone combat. Except for Reno's envy and Benteen's hatred of Custer, the men were compatible enough that under normal circumstances, the regimental commander could expect full cooperation in the conduct of the government's most ambitious operation against the Plains Indians.[48]

Unable to purchase the Black Hills and unable to keep white men from exploiting the potential financial windfall (an Interior Department geology team had confirmed the existence of gold in 1875), the U.S. government had no choice but to accede to demands in the West for decisive action to obtain the Black Hills territory. Miners were spilling onto the land in increasing numbers while Lakota leaders like Sitting Bull and Crazy Horse were determined to stand firm against the white onslaught. The Indian chiefs were content to fight a defensive war to resist further incursions, but the young men of the tribes were still committing depredations that helped to justify the government's actions.[49]

President Grant met with Secretary of War Belknap, Interior Secretary Zachariah Chandler, Commissioner of Indian Affairs E. P. Smith, and Generals Sheridan and George Crook in November 1875 to devise a strategy for achieving their objectives. The resulting decision gave the Indians until 31 January 1876 to relocate from all of the unceded territory to the government agencies; after that date, all bands not reporting would be considered hostile, and the matter would be turned over to the army for resolution. Indian runners were sent out with the notification, but such hit-and-miss means were not likely to reach all of the Indians, many of whom would nevertheless have ignored the decree had they heard it.[50]

On 1 February, Secretary Chandler informed Belknap that the question of the unwilling Indians was in the hands of the War Department and the army. Although General Crook and his forces marched out of Fort Fetterman in March with the hope of hitting hostile Indians while winter weather prevailed, snow storms hampered his movements, and a subordinate officer botched the one opportunity to achieve even a partial victory. Not until May were the converging columns of General Crook (north from Wyoming), General Terry (west from Fort Lincoln, with Custer and the Seventh), and Colonel John Gibbon (east from Fort Ellis, Montana) ready to move out in rough concert—nearly four months after the arbitrary deadline for Indian compliance.

And so the Seventh assembled in the mist during the early morning hours of 17 May 1876. In addition to the six companies stationed at Fort Lincoln, companies from Fort Rice, from Fort Totten, and from duty in the South had also arrived. They had collected on the open land several miles south of Fort Lincoln and bivouacked there until the march began, the whole regiment together for the first time in ten years, camping in tents and awaiting orders. The expedition was supposed to have commenced on 15 May, but rain delayed the departure for two days. At 3 A.M. on the seventeenth, the regiment was aroused, and by 5 A.M. the "general" (the signal to break camp) was sounded; two hours later the Seventh was "marching in column of platoon around the parade ground of Fort Lincoln," with the band playing "Garry Owen," an Irish drinking song and the battle tune that had accompanied Custer and his men since the Washita.

> The affect of the bodies of troops emerging from the mist and fading into it once more was weird in the extreme. First in the procession rode General Terry accompanied by his staff. Next came the forty Ree [Arikara] scouts. After them the band of the Seventh Cavalry, playing an air which we did not know to be "Garryowen," though we had no difficulty in recognizing the quick-step which followed— an air never gay to army women's ears—"The Girl I Left Behind Me."

Next in order was the Seventh Cavalry. Riding at its head were General Custer and his beautiful wife, who accompanied him as far as the first camp. Next came a battery of Gatling guns, each drawn by six horses. . . . Three companies of the Seventeenth Infantry closed the procession.[51]

To Libbie, watching the gathering in the hazy sunrise, the column of cavalry seemed a mirage "equally plain to the sight on the earth and in the sky." Some in attendance may have thought this would be another pleasant summer outing, but Custer and many of his men doubtless hoped for more, although there was scant prospect of extracting glory or fame from a war that few seemed to want against an enemy unlikely to stand still for a fight. The tearful good-byes in front of the officers' quarters and along "Suds Row" (where the laundresses and the wives of enlisted men lived) suggested at least the pain of separation. And soldiers did die in such enterprises.[52]

CHAPTER FOUR

MEN AND BOYS

On the plateau west of Fort Abraham Lincoln, the infantry and 150 wagons
waited for the Seventh to complete its parade through the post and for the
married officers and enlisted men to say their good-byes. The rain had
stopped for the moment, but the ground was soft, and the heavily laden
wagons sank into the mud as the caravan re-formed, then inched toward its
first stop at the Heart River campsite, about thirteen miles distant. In the
wake of the train straggled a large group of cavalry recruits and others who
were obliged to march with the infantry because horses had not arrived in
time. The brief interlude of martial pageantry was too soon over, and the
hard work of a summer campaign had begun.

Ninety or so enlisted men did not depart with the regiment. A number
were left behind to tend company gardens or to look after company
property. A few were too sick or too old for the arduous adventure ahead.
One was a cook, and one was an orderly for Libbie Custer. Thirteen were
in confinement at various locations for desertion or some other serious
infraction of army regulations. Those left in garrison at Fort Lincoln were
probably content with their fate, particularly since rigid supervision and
discipline were bound to be relaxed in the absence of the post commander
and the other officers of the Seventh.

On the other hand, certainly many of the men of the Seventh eagerly
anticipated the expedition, as an opportunity to escape the confines of the
post where they had endured the daily rounds of closely monitored drill
and labor and where every day, from reveille to taps, had been filled with

the drudgery of necessary and makeshift duty. Although such work varied according to the station from which a company came, there was a sameness about the routine, from fatigue (manual labor) details to long boring hours in dirty and overcrowded barracks. At the Dakota forts, the men likely engaged in cutting wood, sawing ice for summer use, disposing of garbage, obtaining water, cleaning stables, shoveling snow, or performing any number of other such activities that served the needs of the post and kept the men busy. And of course they needed to feed and groom their horses, a task that was probably relatively pleasant, since any trooper worth his salt understood the importance of a healthy mount and had likely developed a genuine fondness for his animal. Every now and then the men might actually fire a weapon, although ammunition was scarce and target practice rare. In good weather, they might engage in mounted maneuvers, usually by company and sometimes by platoon, and infrequently they might turn out for inspections or formal ceremonies. For relaxation, they could play cards, drink whiskey, make music and sing, tell stories, give dances and plays, and if there was a "hog ranch" nearby, enjoy the company of a prostitute. But these pleasures required leisure time and sometimes money, and the enlisted man had severely limited amounts of either. The average trooper was usually in debt to someone, perhaps a friend, a sutler, or a sergeant.

If a soldier performed well and looked sharp, he might be selected to serve as orderly for the post commander, in which case he could rightly be called slave for a day. Also, until 1870 officers could legally hire enlisted men as "strikers" for five to ten dollars a month, and even after being out-lawed, the practice continued for many years. The term *striker* was still in use in 1876 at the Little Bighorn as a euphemism for "body servant." Officers needed enlisted personnel to cook their food, put up their tents, fetch their belongings, care for their horses, and perform other tasks. Depending on the personality of the officer, such duty was more often sought than avoided.[1]

Except in those circumstances in which a soldier worked directly for an officer, there was a vast gulf between those in command and those at the bottom of the enlisted ranks. The private spoke to the sergeant, the sergeant to the second lieutenant, and so on up the chain. Even under special circum-stances, there was rarely more than perfunctory communication between

65

officers and privates in the "Old Army." It is little wonder that a post and regimental commander like Custer would seem a remote and aloof figure.

The only enlisted man on intimate terms with Custer was Private John Burkman, an illiterate German immigrant whose chief function was to look after Custer's horses, dogs, and other pets. Burkman's long service and his total loyalty to the Custer household are well recorded in recollections of Custer, the martinet who supposedly treated his animals better than his men. According to Private Charles Windolph, "If anyone made the slightest remark against Custer, John would threaten to kill him." Although the relationship between Burkman and Custer was punctuated by occasional misunderstandings, which were caused largely by the general's quick temper and for which Custer invariably apologized, Burkman was indeed both a trusted servant and the epitome of the common soldier, and his fidelity extended to Libbie and the Custer memory long after his leader's death. In an army so rigidly stratified, such relationships were indeed rare. If enlisted men went to officers with stories, they would not be believed. These understood rules of nonfraternization would have unfortunate consequences at the Little Bighorn, where even a bit more inquiry into what enlisted men had seen and heard might have made a difference.[2]

A private's pay was thirteen dollars a month (reduced from sixteen dollars in 1871), but the low wage and hard duty did not deter the many men who enlisted in the army and were assigned to the Seventh. Neither did these factors inhibit the substantial number who reenlisted for a second or third tour. If a man signed up for more than a five-year stint, he had probably come to regard his company as a family that would feed, shelter, and clothe him. Because the company was the basic unit within the more amorphous Seventh U.S. Cavalry, men tended to identify with that component.

It was extraordinary for more than six companies (out of twelve) of the Seventh to be assembled in one place at any given time. Therefore, since companies were rotated among the various garrisons in the West and the South, for a trooper to even see the regimental commander, either nominal (Colonel Samuel Sturgis) or actual (Custer), was exceptional. For many men, however, service in the army had little to do with money, devotion to duty, or patriotism; they enlisted with the intention of satisfying more private and selfish needs. These men fulfilled the expectations of the general populace, which regarded the soldier as a shiftless and unskilled person who could not make a living at more respectable work.

On the whole, this was an unfair characterization, but fashioning a career in the civilian sector at that time was undeniably difficult. The country was still suffering from the repercussions of the 1873 financial crisis, and good jobs were scarce. For the many Irish, German, and other recent immigrants especially, service in the military offered an avenue of escape from a hard life in the city while at the same time it provided a measure of security until something better came along. Young men from small towns and farms also found temporary homes in the army. Some joined for the sheer adventure. Some—thieves or worse—were running from the law. Some had jilted a girl back home, and some had been jilted. If nothing else, the army furnished free transportation to the West, where men had reason to believe they might find gold or silver or at least a respite until they had the wherewithal to seek more promising occupations. It was not unusual for a man to enlist in the fall, serve through the winter, and desert in the spring, thus following the long line of "snowbirds" already drifting across the prairies in pursuit of some probably undefined dream.

Desertion was a continuing problem in the post–Civil War army. In 1875 the adjutant general reported that for the five previous fiscal years, there had been thirty thousand desertions. During 1875 there were only twenty-five hundred desertions, or roughly 10 percent of the entire army, somewhat reduced from previous years. The Seventh had its share of desertions, before and after the Little Bighorn. But except for the period of Custer's early frontier service, when as many as forty men deserted at one time, the regiment's record under him is probably no better or worse than that of other units of the same size. All commanders marched their men hard and had about the same regard for their welfare.[3]

In the final analysis, the army won the Indian Wars by wearing down the enemy, using a virtually limitless supply of manpower to pursue, through all seasons, a more mobile but increasingly constricted foe. Those soldiers who disdained the long and painful chases for so little recompense did desert, but some returned under assumed names or in response to presidential or other pardons. In addition, although desertion was punishable by death during the Civil War and by branding and tattooing thereafter, discipline had been sufficiently relaxed by 1874 that a soldier who had deserted but was later in good standing could get off with forfeiture of pay or perhaps hard labor.[4]

Of the approximately seven hundred enlisted men of the Seventh who left Fort Lincoln, only a small percentage were shirkers and ne'er-do-wells who had deserted or would again. The soldiers had indicated their previous occupations on their enlistment forms: plumbers, painters, teachers, engineers, cabinetmakers, weavers, candy makers, cooks, farmers, artificers, brakemen, machinists, musicians, shoemakers, brush makers, bakers, boatmen, and laborers. Private William A. Lossee, of Brewster Station, New York, enlisted in September 1875 at the age of twenty-six, listing his previous occupation as "showman." Assigned to Company F, he was killed at the Little Bighorn some nine months later, before he could realize his ambition of becoming perhaps the P. T. Barnum of San Francisco or Denver.[5]

The hundred or so cavalrymen without horses who followed the caravan out of Fort Lincoln were primarily recruits. According to Private Jacob Horner, he and seventy-seven other new men were among those who marched out of the post unmounted. When the fort did not have enough animals to accommodate the entire regiment and when additional animals did not arrive, an order was issued for the horseless troopers to remain behind; however, at the last moment, Custer reversed the order "so that every available man should go along," apparently with the understanding that horses would be provided somewhere on the Yellowstone. Horner further stated that the trailing troopers "wore cavalry boots and they were not built for walking. In no time at all our feet were blistered." Although Horner's testimony may be accurate regarding the size of the "recruit" force that followed the expedition, the total number of soldiers who dropped out of the regiment between Fort Lincoln and Rosebud Creek was much larger. For various reasons, but mostly because of the shortage of mounts, about 120 troopers would not march with the Seventh to the Little Bighorn.[6]

With its tail of walking men, the ponderous column slogged forward out of Fort Lincoln. The 150 wagons (114 government vehicles, each pulled by six mules, and 36 contract wagons, each towed by two horses and driven by civilian teamsters) were formed in columns of four and were flanked by pack animal and cattle herds, which in turn were flanked by companies of cavalry and outriders. Next came the artillery (two Rodman and two Gatling guns) and the infantry (three companies from the Sixth and the Seventh), then General Alfred Terry and his staff, including Lieutenant Edward Maguire and the four-mule ambulance carrying his engineering equipment. In advance of them, two troops of cavalry constituted the "pioneers," whose function was to clear the road and build the bridges and who had several wagons of their own to hold the tools essential to their work. In the lead, as always, was the irrepressible Custer and one of his companies to guide the way, select the campsites, and kill the game. During the trip, Terry had to put Custer under arrest several times for getting too far in front of the cavalcade, but it is unlikely that the general made his young friend "lead the pelican" (give up his sword and ride at the rear of the column). In fact, Terry valued Custer's pathfinding ability, although occasionally he may have had to forcefully remind Custer to slow down. However, the short trip to the first stop, at the Heart River camp, was leisurely and uneventful.[7]

Libbie Custer and Maggie Calhoun accompanied the expedition as far as the Heart River. The sutler and the paymaster were also along for the first leg of the journey. The men had not been paid for four months, and after the evening meal on 17 May, the paymaster did his job and "enlivened" the hearts of the boys, said Sergeant John Ryan. The "blood sucking sutler" was then able to do his work, selling the men "his vile whiskey, rotten tobacco, and high priced notions," added Private Peter Thompson. If the soldiers had been paid at Fort Lincoln, "some of the troopers would have undoubtedly deserted," Ryan concluded. Apparently Terry and Custer both also believed that if the men had been paid off before leaving garrison, they might have dissipated their energies in the fleshpots of Bismarck and its environs, then deserted or become too sick to participate in the campaign.[8]

On the morning of the eighteenth, Libbie, Maggie, the sutler, and the paymaster returned to Fort Lincoln with an escort. Private Burkman later described the parting of Custer and his wife: "Even now, after all these years, it brings a lump into my throat, remembering how she clung to Custer at the last, her arms tight around his neck, and how she cried. She wasn't one to take on usually, but seemed like she just couldn't go back and leave him that day. There were tears in his eyes too and he kept telling her she was a soldier's wife, she must be a brave little woman, soon he'd be back and then we'd all have good times at Fort Lincoln again." The soldiers prepared to move west. Custer would continue to lead the march under the watchful but mostly tolerant eye of General Terry.[9]

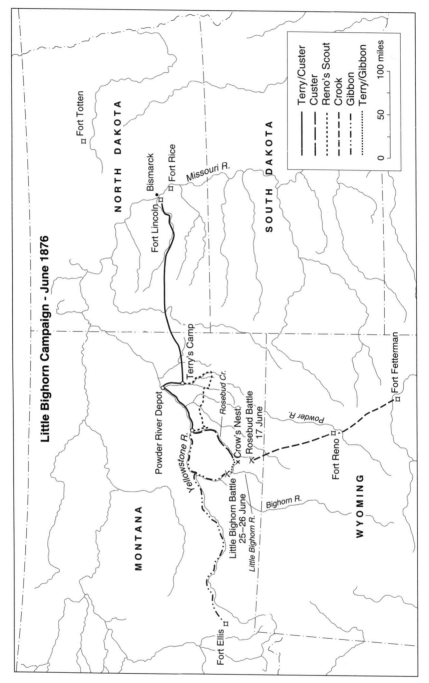

Little Bighorn Campaign - June 1876

Terry/Custer
Custer
Reno's Scout
Crook
Gibbon
Terry/Gibbon

0   50   100 miles

NORTH DAKOTA

SOUTH DAKOTA

MONTANA

WYOMING

Fort Totten

Bismarck
Fort Lincoln
Fort Rice

Missouri R.

Fort Fetterman

Fort Reno

Fort Ellis

Powder River Depot

Terry's Camp

Rosebud Cr.

Crow's Nest
Rosebud Battle
17 June

Powder R.

Yellowstone R.

Little Bighorn Battle
25–26 June

Little Bighorn R.

Bighorn R.

Military expedition of 1876

For the next week the column marched some ten to twenty miles a day. By 26 May it had entered the Bad Lands. The valleys were narrow, and the water was alkaline. Terry occasionally joined the advance, but it was Custer who found the way through the tortuous country. Some men became ill, and one man was bitten by a rattlesnake. Within four days the command was at the Little Missouri River, where Custer departed with four companies to scout for any signs of hostile Indians. After a trip of forty-five miles, he returned on the same day without detecting any evidence of the quarry.

On 31 May the expedition resumed the march up and down steep buttes, only to be stalled again for several days in a "disagreeable" snowstorm, causing Terry to become impatient with the delay. Conditions had improved by 3 June. The first dispatches were received from Colonel John Gibbon, who was on Rosebud Creek. Terry was tired and began to ride in an ambulance as the column moved over the rolling hills interspersed throughout the Bad Lands. Custer had no shortage of energy, riding fifty miles in one day. He was proud of the fact that he could keep going while others were exhausted. By 7 June the command was in sight of the Powder River.[10]

Since leaving Fort Lincoln, the chief impediments to the column's advance had been inclement weather and the hard country, which required hauling the wagons up and over land barely suited to a single man on horseback, land so high and narrow that the fall seemed forever. And yet the expedition had gone forward, covering as many as forty miles in a day. On 10 June Terry returned from meeting Gibbon on the Yellowstone, and he ordered Major Marcus Reno to take the right wing (six companies) on a scout up the Powder River.

From the time the regiment left Fort Lincoln, it had been divided into two wings, one commanded by Reno and the other by Captain Frederick Benteen. By definition, a *wing* in cavalry parlance was one-half of a regiment or, on certain occasions, of an army. Benteen was surely content with the command of one wing, since he believed that he had driven Custer to the decision. In his convenient hindsight, his political connections had forced Custer to give him a wing, when in fact Benteen was the senior captain and third in the pecking order behind Custer and Reno. As for Reno, he probably harbored some dim and disappointed hope that he might run the entire regiment, but in truth he must have been satisfied—

perhaps even relieved—at being in charge of the other wing and second in overall command of the Seventh while it was in the field.[11]

The six companies in the right wing under Reno were B (Captain Thomas McDougall), E (First Lieutenant Algernon Smith), F (Captain George Yates), I (Captain Myles Keogh), and L (First Lieutenant James Calhoun), and C (commanded by Second Lieutenant Henry Harrington rather than Captain Tom Custer, who had apparently already begun to serve as his brother's aide-de-camp rather than company commander). Even though Custer had managed to keep Tom by his side, the ache of seeing his brother-in-law and his close friends depart with Reno must have been severe. Five of the six companies sent on Reno's scout to locate the trail of the Indians would be annihilated with Custer at the Little Bighorn.[12]

Terry's instructions to Reno were to search up the Powder River and cross over to the Tongue, then travel down that stream to the Yellowstone. Besides the six companies, Reno's expedition included pack mules (eleven per company) and a Gatling gun battery. Using packs was a new experience for the soldiers, and the vast majority of the animals were not accustomed to carrying such heavy loads, since they had been selected from among those mules that until recently had been pulling wagons. A noncommissioned officer and four men from each company were assigned as packers, and they were taught how to tie the "diamond hitch" by civilian employees. The sawbuck and aparejo (Spanish) varieties of packsaddles were used; the latter type was more secure and successful, but because relatively few were available, this type was used primarily for the ammunition. The soldier-packers had difficulty during the whole scout with falling cargo and balky mules. Similarly, the Gatling guns proved to be an annoying burden on this sojourn: they either fell apart or had to be disassembled and carried in pieces over rough terrain. The half-blood Mitch Boyer (who was part Sioux) and a contingent of Arikara scouts (including Bloody Knife, Custer's favorite) accompanied Reno's wing.[13]

While Reno scouted up the Powder, the rest of the expedition followed the river north to its junction with the Yellowstone, where the soldiers established a supply point known as the Powder River base camp or the Yellowstone depot. The selection of this particular ground for a base camp was based on Terry's original intention of trying to trap the hostile Indians between the Tongue River and Rosebud Creek, where it was thought they might be located, but information known only to Colonel Gibbon—and confirmed by Reno's scout—soon made this plan obsolete. As it turned out, the depot would have little bearing on the expedition except as a holding area for most of the wagons, some of the infantry, cavalrymen without horses, and the regimental band.[14]

The steamboat *Far West* arrived during this period, and the sutler John Smith again had an opportunity to unload some of his goods, including liquor. For a dollar a pint, soldiers could fill their three-pint canteens, with the permission of their commanders. With four months' pay in their pockets, surely enlisted men as well as officers took advantage of the chance to celebrate a welcome break in the long, almost continuous march from Fort Lincoln to very near the end of their journey.[15]

While Terry moved to the mouth of the Tongue River aboard the *Far West*, Custer marched in the same direction from the Yellowstone depot early on 15 June with his headquarters and Benteen's wing of six companies. Instead of a wagon train to encumber his march, Custer was now burdened by the same impediment that would annoy Reno's scout and that would plague the Seventh throughout its later advance into battle: the hard-to-manage mules. Although the swing and leader mules had been carefully selected from the wagon teams as the best animals to transport essential supplies, some 150 animals had already been detached for the Reno scout, so that Custer must have been left with at least some of the less pliable wheeler mules. Therefore, although men in Benteen's wing had been hastily trained to pack the independent beasts, Custer's half of the regiment advanced with difficulty. As Private Theodore Goldin described the movement, the novelty of the ordeal for men and mules was largely responsible for the fact that it took several days to cover a mere forty miles. In any case, Custer was on his way with some three hundred men to a rendezvous with Terry and Gibbon, but by all accounts, the regimental band was not present. According to Goldin, the band assembled on a knoll near the mouth of the Powder River and played "Garry Owen" as Custer's column moved out of the depot.[16]

To Custer, continuing on the journey without his beloved band must have been somewhat akin to leaving Libbie behind. Both were talismans in his life. He was upset that the *Far West* did not include Libbie among its passengers when it arrived at the Yellowstone depot, and he was obviously put off by the decision to unhorse band members so as to disperse their mounts to other members of the regiment.[17] As Private James Wilber recalled, "Custer wanted to take the band beyond Powder River, but Terry would not consent to it."[18] That this was a matter of contention between Custer and Terry is borne out by the fact that a field order was issued on 14 June at the mouth of the Tongue River: "The regimental band and the dismounted men of the Cavalry will remain at the depot at this point."[19] It is unlikely that Terry would have felt compelled to put the instruction in writing unless Custer had argued on behalf of taking the band along.

The band members were soldiers first of all and musicians simply by dint of the regimental commander's discretion. In fact, regimental bands had been abolished by the army act of 1869, so that thereafter the Seventh and other units were obliged to support their ensembles out of a regimental fund or by individual subscription.[20] The Seventh had had a band since its organization, and even after the function was officially discarded, recruiters were aware of the need for musicians and made an extra effort to find and enlist them. Colonel Sturgis, in his 1875 letter regarding his son, had told Custer to be patient regarding musicians because they came in to the recruiter's station rarely. He added, "There is a whole army of them wanted."[21]

As an indication of the importance that Custer attached to the band as an integral part of his commands, a bandmaster who had served under him during the Civil War quoted Custer as saying that if his superiors offered him three brigades with a band or four brigades without, he would take the three. Though possibly an exaggeration meant to make the bandmaster feel needed, this expressed preference probably did reflect Custer's state of mind at a time when such alternatives were more theoretical than real. He had never been forced to make that kind of choice before.[22]

From the moment he assumed command of a brigade in the Civil War, Custer had had a band, and he had used it in combat situations as a psychological weapon. Bands had other uses as well. On more than one occasion Custer employed the band as his voice to tell friends and enemies that he was sorry or that past differences could be forgotten and forgiven. In addition, Private Horner remembered that Custer would often station the band on high ground to play "stirring tunes" while the men worked. "He knew we worked faster when there was music," Horner said, "and I have to admit that we could always march better when the band played."[23]

By using the white horses belonging to the seventeen band members, mounts were apparently available to six hundred or so soldiers in the Seventh. For reasons that are not entirely clear, but presumably caused by some snafu in the staff support system, the eighty or so horses that were supposed to appear at either Fort Lincoln or the Yellowstone depot did not materialize. On the other hand, the time required to train a horse was much greater than the time needed to educate the rider in drills and maneuvers, so that it is hard to understand how animals recently purchased could have been properly schooled in the field before being used. Besides the horses that failed to appear, another forty or fifty mounts must have been taken out of service along the way, being either in poor condition generally or fatigued from the long march already conducted. Otherwise, the Seventh would not have been reduced by 120 men, and the band would not have had their animals taken from them. As it was, at least a few troopers began the Little Bighorn expedition on horses that were somewhat less than prime.[24]

The Reno scout of the Powder-Tongue ended on 18 June. Instead of limiting himself to the course specified in Terry's orders, Reno picked up the trail of a large Indian band (some 350 lodges) and followed it all the way to Rosebud Creek. Thus Reno traveled almost 250 miles in eight days, or nearly 30 miles a day over some very rough terrain, rather than making the shorter trip, of possibly six days' duration, as projected by Terry. Whether the longer journey was instigated by Reno himself or whether he was encouraged in the decision by subordinate commanders like Yates and Keogh or by the scout Mitch Boyer is not known. Regardless, only two days behind the Indians, Reno declined to continue pursuit, ostensibly on the grounds that rations were running out but possibly influenced by his scouts' opinion that the wing would find more Indians than it could handle.

Terry was obviously annoyed that Reno had been gone several days longer than expected and that men and horses had been worn out by the extra distance covered. Reno's scout was meant to be a routine intelligence-gathering mission, which would only tangentially affect plans already made, but in confirming that the Indians were moving away in a south-western direction along the Rosebud, Reno now forced the commanding general to rethink his intentions and move with urgency. Besides disliking the fact that his orders had been disobeyed, Terry could not have been happy about hearing bad news—namely, that any pursuing force would have to ride farther and faster to catch up with the enemy and that any coordinated pincer action would be more difficult to achieve. Terry's opinion of Reno's ability as a military leader and as a man was now probably almost as low as it would be after the battle.

By the afternoon of 21 June, Custer had joined Terry and Gibbon on the *Far West* at the mouth of the Rosebud. Instead of continuing with his original plan of trying to corral the Indians between that stream and points east along the Tongue, Terry outlined a strategy that still envisaged dividing his forces but that shifted the objective to the land lying between the Rosebud and the Bighorn, possibly even on the Little Bighorn River. Like General Philip Sheridan's strategic plan for three widely separated, converging columns, which he could not have expected to end up at the same place at the same time, Terry's scheme would position his forces in such a way that their lines of march would so compress the space within which the Sioux were active that the tribes might be defeated or discouraged.

As Terry and the senior officers discussed the matter aboard the steamboat, they were unaware that General George Crook's substantial force in the Sheridan triad had been fought to a standstill a week earlier almost due south of where they stood and a scant forty miles from where Custer would be defeated at the hands of many of the same warriors. According to Terry's plan, Custer's Seventh would constitute the rapidly moving strike force aimed up the Rosebud while Gibbon's infantry and a battalion of the Second Cavalry (some 450 men all together) would travel westward along the Yellowstone until they turned up the Bighorn, parallel to but slower than Custer's advance. Terry would go with Gibbon.

Terry's instructions to Custer were detailed, but they gave his subordinate wide latitude in executing them.

> It is, of course, impossible to give you any definite instructions in regard to this movement, and were it not impossible to do so, the Department Commander places too much confidence in your zeal, energy, and ability to wish to impose upon you precise orders which might hamper your action when nearly in contact with the enemy.

Terry added that he expected Custer to conform to the instructions unless the officer saw "sufficient reason for departing from them." As already noted, these "orders" were similar in tone to those given by Sheridan to Custer before the Washita battle. They directed a trusted officer to use his best judgment in achieving an objective, which in accordance with federal policy was first of all to find the Indians, then move them if possible and fight them if necessary. The words "zeal, energy, and ability" were surely chosen by Terry himself, not some staff officer, and were exactly the qualities that Terry must have had in mind when he cautioned Custer against becoming entangled in political intrigues that might prevent Custer from rejoining the regiment that spring.[25]

In the blame-laying aftermath of the Little Bighorn fight, Captain Robert P. Hughes (Terry's brother-in-law and aide-de-camp) and Major James Brisbin (Second Cavalry) attempted to show that Custer had disobeyed explicit orders, but their efforts were exposed after the discovery that the copy of Terry's instructions they were using had been deliberately altered. In attempting to spare Terry any blame in the affair, they served the good general and his memory poorly. Similarly, they and others sought to discredit an affidavit made by one of Custer's servants, who claimed to have heard the following dialogue between Terry and Custer on the eve of the latter's departure:

> Terry: "Custer, I don't know what to say for the last."
> Custer: "Say whatever you want to say."
> Terry: "Use your own judgment and do what you think best if you strike the trail. And whatever you do, Custer, hold on to your wounded."[26]

In his instructions, Terry wanted Custer to go up the Rosebud to the point where Reno had left the trail of the Indians, then to proceed to the headwaters of the Little Bighorn, all the while feeling to his left (south) so that the Indians could not escape around that flank. Under the circumstances, this was a sensible enough plan considering the information available to Terry. The maps were inaccurate as to landmarks and exact distances, since few white men had explored the region. Although Custer agreed to the plan of operations, he knew—as did some of the scouts and possibly others—that the Indians would not sit still while one or two columns of soldiers marched around them, thus allowing themselves to be "so nearly inclosed . . . that their escape [would] be impossible," as Terry's orders proposed. Whether Terry counted on Crook operating to the south is not known, but the only junction mentioned is the one anticipated between the columns of Custer and Gibbon.

The instructions give no date for when such a meeting was expected, but the officers on the *Far West* probably did attempt to calculate distances and times on their imperfect maps. In a real exercise in futility, Brisbin—at Terry's request—went so far as to trace the routes of the two columns and to indicate their respective camping places with pins. Though they may have wanted to establish an approximate date on which the separate commands could meet and so catch those sitting-still Indians, the officers at the council of war could not have been so foolish as to view such a date as more than a weakly conceived supposition.[27]

In his first report after the battle, Terry indicated that Gibbon's column had been expected to reach, "in all probability," the *mouth* of the Little Bighorn on 26 June, but in a follow-up report, the commander of the expedition stated that the day of confluence at the mouth of the Little Bighorn had been set exactly on 26 June and that if Custer had simply taken the "wide sweep" that was proposed by Terry, all would have been well. The absurdity of this afterthought is demonstrated by Terry's reference to his plan as the most promising for bringing the infantry to bear on the outcome, when it was well-known that foot soldiers were of limited use in Indian fighting. As an infantry officer, perhaps Terry felt he needed to make that point. Besides, Gibbon, in his report on the expedition, noted that as he envisaged his line and time of march, it would take approximately six days for his column to reach the Little Bighorn, meaning that the earliest he could reach the point of the projected connection was 28 June.[28]

Apparently Terry offered Brisbin's battalion of the Second Cavalry and the Gatling gun battery to accompany the Seventh, but Custer refused these additions for several reasons. First of all, Custer and Brisbin did not get along, and Custer thus would not have wanted to place Brisbin in a senior command position. Custer was on the verge of abolishing the wings then led by Reno and Benteen, and the inclusion of Brisbin would have complicated the arrangement he had in mind. Also, Custer retained the conviction that the Seventh could handle any force of Indians it might encounter, and he may have reasoned that taking the Second Cavalry would leave Gibbon's column susceptible to attack and defeat. Later, even Brisbin would acknowledge that everyone in Gibbon's command understood the logic in Terry's determination to make the Seventh the primary strike force.[29]

As for the Gatling guns, even though they might have been effective against a static opponent, they would merely have been an encumbrance on the trail of a fast-moving enemy over severely broken ground. Each gun was accompanied by a two-wheeled ammunition carrier, both pieces pulled by four condemned cavalry horses. During the Reno scout, the two guns were actually abandoned (and retrieved later) because soldiers got tired of dragging them over rough spots. If Custer did not already have a fully formed negative opinion regarding the suitability of the Gatlings on such an expedition, the experience of the Reno scout surely convinced him. Apparently Lieutenant William Lowe was on the verge of tears when Custer refused to take Lowe's detachment of Gatling guns along.[30]

By the evening of 21 June, the pieces of the plan were in place. The sutler was again on hand to sell his liquor and other wares, including quarter-dollar or half-dollar straw hats for the officers and men who might prefer such comfort instead of the heavy, broad-brimmed, government-issue headgear. In the camp of the Seventh, "officers' call" was sounded, and Custer issued orders that the pack mules would carry fifteen days' ration of hardtack, coffee, and sugar (along with twelve days' ration of bacon), as well as fifty rounds of carbine ammunition per man. Another one hundred rounds of carbine ammunition and twenty-four rounds for pistols were to be carried by each trooper on his person or in his saddlebags. Each soldier would also take twelve quarts of oats for his horse.[31]

Whatever the regimental commander said, the company was the primary operating unit, and each commander was expected to manage the day-to-day operations of his organization, although most officers were more or less inclined to let the first sergeant do the actual work. The authorized size of companies (or troops) at this time was 70 enlisted men, including 54 privates, 1 first sergeant, 5 sergeants, 4 corporals, 2 trumpeters, 2 blacksmiths/ farriers, 1 saddler, and 1 wagoner. All companies had been understrength from the time they had departed Fort Lincoln. The regiment was authorized 845 enlisted men (the 70 for each company, plus 5 for staff and bandmaster functions), but the assigned or actual manpower available was 791, and out of that total, 16 soldiers had been taken out of the ranks to play in the band.

The companies had been in even worse shape until the Mounted Recruiting Service had supplied additional recruits during the months preceding the expedition. Whatever the individual merits of these new men, they at least represented an augmentation of the "skeleton" units on paper. For the purposes of the inquiry here, the recruits are divided into two groups: the "fresh" recruits, those who joined the army between January and April 1876; and the "recent" recruits, those who enlisted during the September-December 1875 period. The reason for this delineation is purely arbitrary and is used here merely to convey degrees of indoctrination and training. In no sense is it meant to suggest the quality of the soldier or individual skills in riding and shooting, since judgments or correlations in such areas are impossible. Those young men recruited during the previous autumn had simply spent more time in the service, had experienced at least some good weather in which to drill, and as a group were presumably more comfortable on a horse, with a gun, and in the interpersonal associations that might prove beneficial in battle. Except for the rare veteran who had reenlisted, none of these men—like many of the horses they rode —had ever heard the sounds of war, smelled the odor of gunpowder, or seen death and destruction while engaging a skillful and frenzied enemy.[32]

The effective fighting strength of the twelve companies is described generally below. Note that this broad delineation does not account for all of the troopers detailed elsewhere within the regiment.

Company A: Captain Myles Moylan commanded. His second-in-command, First Lieutenant "Fresh" Smith, had been detailed to E Troop, and Second Lieutenant Charles Varnum was in charge of the detachment of scouts. The second-in-command was First Lieutenant Charles DeRudio. Out of an assigned strength of fifty-five enlisted men, ten were elsewhere: three at the Yellowstone depot, two with the pack train, four on detached service, and one in confinement. Out of the effective fighting force of forty-five, only six were recent recruits, and none were fresh recruits. Overall, this was an experienced and only moderately depleted company.

Company B: With First Lieutenant William Craycroft on detached service and Second Lieutenant Benjamin Hodgson serving as adjutant to Reno, the commanding officer, Captain Thomas McDougall, had First Sergeant James Hill as second-in-command. The company was the largest, with an assigned strength of seventy-one, but twenty-two were fresh recruits, seventeen of whom had been left at the Yellowstone depot. Another four veterans were also at the base camp, including a trumpeter and a soldier who had shot himself in the foot, the quintessential excuse for remaining out of battle. Of the five men on detached service, two were serving as orderlies for Libbie Custer and Terry. Three were in confinement. Two were elsewhere in the regiment. Thus the largest company on paper had only forty men available to guard the pack train, the eventual mission of the troop.

Company C: The acting commander was Second Lieutenant Harrington, with Captain Tom Custer serving as aide-de-camp to his brother and with First Lieutenant Calhoun being in charge of Company L. The first sergeant was Edwin Bobo. There were no fresh recruits, but out of a total assigned strength of sixty-six, fifteen were recent recruits and ten of those would go into battle. With seven men left at the Yellowstone depot, eight with the pack train, two sick, three on detached service (a sergeant tending the company garden at Fort Lincoln), and two in confinement, only forty-four were available for the fight. Out of that total, one would be used as a messenger and at least five would drop out before the company was committed. In short, this was a relatively weak company of less than forty men, one-quarter of whom had served for less than a year, and was led by a junior officer, although Captain Tom Custer was never far from his unit.

Company D: The assigned strength of this company was sixty-four, but only forty-seven men were available because thirteen were left at the Yellowstone depot, including four recent recruits; also, one man was sick, and three were on detached service (two tending the company garden at Fort Lincoln). None accompanied the packs. Of those riding with the company, nine were recent recruits. Captain Thomas Weir commanded, assisted by Second Lieutenant Winfield Scott Edgerly and First Sergeant Michael Martin (First Lieutenant James Bell was on leave of absence). All things considered, this was one of the stronger companies, with excellent leaders.

Company E: By any measure, the Gray Horse Troop was the most dis-combobulated component of the regiment. With Captain Charles Ilsley on detached service, First Lieutenant Charles DeRudio detailed to Company A, and Second Lieutenant William Van Wyck Reily with Company F, command responsibilities fell to First Lieutenant Smith (acting regimental quartermaster and deputy of A Troop) and young Second Lieutenant Jack Sturgis. Frederick Hohmeyer was the first sergeant. The company had an assigned strength of sixty-one, but twenty-three of the men were somewhere else, leaving only thirty-eight to join the battle, under commanders they hardly knew. Of the twenty-three who were not present, four were at the Yellowstone depot (one sick with constipation), ten were with the pack train, one was ill in garrison, one was in confinement, and seven were on detached service (one with Terry and one serving as a hospital attendant on the *Far West*). Three of the five sergeants were absent—at the depot, with the packs, or on detached service. This was indeed a depleted unit (possibly under the eventual command of the inexperienced Sturgis), which would be asked to serve as the point during the final phase of Custer's attack on the Indian village.

Company F: Captain Yates seems always to have been near Custer, and his "Band Box" troop should have been one of the premier companies at the Little Bighorn. With First Lieutenant Henry Jackson and Second Lieutenant Charles Larned on detached service, Yates had Second Lieutenant Reily and First Sergeant Michael Kenney as backup to his command of sixty-seven enlisted men. Yet thirty-one would not accompany the troop into the last battle: ten were at the Yellowstone depot (including one cooking for the band, one attending to Custer's baggage, and one serving with the quartermaster department), six were with the pack train (including an orderly looking after Yates's extra horse), ten were on detached service (one gardening at Fort Lincoln and one guarding company property there), two were in confinement, and one was an orderly for Reno. Two were absent for unexplained reasons. The company had no fresh recruits and fourteen recent recruits, nine of whom would go in with Custer's advance. This unit, with twenty-nine soldiers who might be called "veterans," was of passable quality.

Company G: With Captain John Tourtellotte on detached service, First Lieutenant Donald McIntosh commanded the troop. Second Lieutenant George Wallace was serving as engineering officer for the regiment, and the first sergeant was on furlough, meaning that McIntosh was virtually alone in providing senior leadership, particularly since two of the five sergeants were also missing. The company had fourteen fresh recruits assigned to the unit, but eleven of them had been left at the Yellowstone depot and one was with the pack train. Five other soldiers were at the depot, including four veterans, two of whom were tending to the company and ordnance wagons. Six men were on detached service, one attending to company property at

Fort Lincoln and one, a trumpeter, remaining in Louisiana. Of sixty-six soldiers assigned to the company, only some thirty-eight were with the unit proper. Although heavy with recruits on the rolls and weak in numbers, the company was decidedly veteran in years of service as it went into battle.

Company H: This was Benteen's company. He was assisted by First Lieutenant Francis Gibson (Second Lieutenant Ernest Garlington was on leave of absence). The first sergeant was Joseph McCurry. Of the fifty-five men assigned to the unit, twelve can be placed elsewhere: two at the Yellowstone depot (another who shot himself in the foot and one who was watching company property), five on sick call at Fort Rice, one with the pack train, one with Custer, and three in confinement. The company had no fresh recruits and five recent recruits. With the first sergeant, five sergeants, and three corporals present, it was one of the strongest troops in terms of numbers and experience.

Company I: Captain Keogh commanded, and First Lieutenant James Porter was his second-in-command. Second Lieutenant Andrew Nave was on leave. The first sergeant was Frank Varden. Of the sixty-five men assigned, twenty-eight were not present: six at the Yellowstone depot, including two sergeants, one of whom was identified as a mechanic; eight with the packs, including a sergeant and five veterans; five sick; eight on detached service (including a sergeant-orderly for Terry and three at the Fort Lincoln post bakery, company garden, and quartermaster); and one in confinement. Thus only thirty-seven men entered the battle, including just one sergeant (James Bustard) besides Varden, two trumpeters, no fresh recruits, and two recent enlistees. At the Little Bighorn, this small but tested company would have difficulty with command and control in an impossible situation.

Company K: With Captain Owen Hale on detached service, leadership fell to First Lieutenant Edward Godfrey, supported by Second Lieutenant Luther Hare until the latter was detached to serve with Varnum's scouts. First Sergeant DeWitt Winney would eventually fill Hare's position as second-in-command. For reasons that are not clear, twenty-two members of this troop were left at the Yellowstone depot; eight fresh recruits were part of this number, but so were thirteen veterans, two of whom were sick. Five men were on detached service, including another who was serving as orderly for Terry; three were sick at Fort Lincoln; and three were elsewhere in Custer's column. Only two soldiers were detailed to the pack train. Why such a large number of troopers were dispersed out of this company is not known, but the group of thirty-four who remained out of an assigned strength of sixty-nine consisted of almost all veterans and a healthy complement of noncommissioned officers.

Company L: As with E Troop, command of this company fell by default to an officer outside the unit—in this case, to First Lieutenant Calhoun. Titular head Captain Michael Sheridan had been on detached service for many years, and First Lieutenant Charles Braden and Second Lieutenant Edwin Eckerson were also not available. Second-in-command fell to Second Lieutenant John Crittenden, a junior officer detailed from the Twentieth Infantry, and the first sergeant was James Butler. This company took forty-six of its sixty-seven assigned men into battle. Those left behind included only six at the Yellowstone depot, taking care of regimental records, looking after company property, guarding the cattle herd, or remaining behind because of sickness. Oddly, the three enlisted men—including a sergeant— on detached service are listed as tending the company garden at Fort Lincoln. Even more strangely, eleven soldiers were apparently with the packs, and of that number, one was a sergeant, seven were veterans (including Private Burkman), and three were recent recruits. Although the commanders were relatively junior, and although three of five sergeants were somewhere else, the unit could be considered veteran in essential makeup.

Company M: This troop was easily the least affected by the diversion of soldiers to other duties. It was led by Captain Thomas French, who was assisted by First Sergeant Ryan, since First Lieutenant Edward Mathey was managing the packs and Second Lieutenant Jack Sturgis had been detailed to Company E. Of the sixty-three men assigned, only six were absent: four at the Yellowstone depot (one looking after company property), one sick, and one farrier on detached service. However, the strength of fifty-seven men may have been somewhat diluted by the presence of seventeen recent recruits (none having been left at the depot). With its complement of noncommissioned officers virtually intact, and with French in command, M Troop was as formidable as any available to Custer.

◆ ◆ ◆

Any analysis of such an admixture of variables must be, finally, a best guess. Nonetheless, the available information indicates that out of an assigned strength of 791 enlisted men, more than 90 (in confinement, sick, or performing other duties) did not accompany the regiment out of Fort Lincoln. Another 120 or so cavalrymen were left at the Yellowstone depot (including roughly 30 fresh and 10 recent recruits), leaving 575 to 580 men with the Seventh as it moved to the mouth of the Rosebud. Why some 80 "veterans" were left at the base camp is a riddle not easily solved, and whether that number would even have made any difference to Custer is unknown.

Besides the quasi-official reasons given (tending company property, cattle herds, or wagons), some men were noted as having "played up sick" and others as simply surrendering their horses to men who wanted to go on the campaign. These explanations are difficult to accept at face value, but it is possible to imagine individual soldiers making a deal—with an understanding wink from the senior sergeants—to go or to stay. Regardless of legitimate reasons or shenanigans, no more men could go to battle than there were horses to carry them, and the subtraction of 120 troopers for the lack of mounts is the more telling number.[33]

Assuming that these calculations are valid approximations, the regiment had 575 to 580 men and 28 officers (plus 3 surgeons), for a total of 606 to 611, which is consistent with Varnum's estimate that there were 605 soldiers on the march and with Sergeant Ryan's belief that there were about 600 men in the command. Out of this aggregate, 50 or so of the enlisted men, only a very small percentage of whom were recruits, would eventually be assigned to attend to the packs. Eleven fresh and 70 recent enlistees, a bit less than 15 percent of the total, would accompany the combat units.[34]

Extrapolations of this kind are useful for projecting the mass of men available to the company commanders, but they are deficient in defining the manner of men who sallied forth to do battle with people they neither knew nor generally cared much about. For example, if the records are correct, Private Francis Milton of F Troop enlisted for a second tour at the age of eighteen in 1871, meaning that he was as young as thirteen when he initially signed up for service in the cavalry and was twenty-three when he died, a veteran, at the Little Bighorn. Company G's Corporal John Hammon enlisted in 1873 at the listed age of eighteen, but he was only fifteen at the time; thus he was really eighteen when the fight began and was made sergeant on the initial day of fighting after the acting first sergeant was killed. Private Theodore Goldin of G Troop joined the service in April 1876 at the announced age of twenty-one; in fact he was seventeen and barely beyond the reach of his parents in Wisconsin. Such stories are rife in the annals of the Seventh and no doubt of the army as a whole. In the assemblage that was this regiment, mere boys had signed on the dotted line, as had men in their late twenties and thirties, some already hardened by earlier service and some just beginning the search for their identity under fire.[35]

For both enlisted men and officers, a pall reportedly settled over the camp on the evening of 21 June. Lieutenant Godfrey described it as "a presentiment of their fate." Nearly all took the time to write letters home and to make arrangements for the disposition of personal effects and mementos. Around a fire on the banks of the Yellowstone, Custer and Benteen traded barbs about the Washita. Possibly Benteen thought that he had again won the contest of words, whereas Custer perhaps tried to put behind him another example of unjust criticism beyond his ability to refute to the satisfaction of old opponents. The other officers in attendance may have looked away in embarrassment, then slowly risen and quietly disappeared.[36]

The Arikara scouts sang their dirges, accompanied by tom-toms and encouraged by Custer, who "had the heart like an Indian." An Arikara noted, "If we ever left out one thing in our ceremonies, he always suggested it to us." While the scouts wailed to the deities dear to them, Custer's dog, Tuck, began to bellow a kind of death howl of his own—or at least so it seemed to the superstitious and totally loyal Private Burkman, who tried to quiet the hound.[37]

CHAPTER FIVE

HOW THEY LOOKED

Fluttering guidons marked the positions of the separate companies as the regiment assembled to depart the banks of the Yellowstone. On restless horses, men ragtag by military standards formed in column of fours as the Seventh Cavalry prepared to advance southward. Without benefit of the band's full-toned rendition of the regiment's battle song to spur them on, massed trumpets playing the march would have to do as the proud men of the Seventh paraded past the senior officers. The men moved forward to a future imagined differently by individual soldiers, with some laughing and talking, some swallowing doubt amid shouts of mutual encouragement, and some simply remaining afraid and without an avenue of escape from a duty until now only dimly understood. It was noon on 22 June 1876.

Private Charles Windolph thought that the men were pleased to be part of the Seventh, "an outfit that had a fighting reputation, and . . . were ready for a fight or a frolic." Long after he had survived the battle, he noted: "There wasn't a man in it who didn't believe it was the greatest cavalry outfit in the entire United States Army."[1] But for French-born Private Jean Baptiste Desire Gallenne, there was another way to view the start of this decisive campaign: "I am sick since three days, I feel so unhappy, so sad, that I wish God had called me away from this life," he wrote in his journal on 22 June and later communicated in a letter to a priest.[2]

Reviewing the troops were General Alfred Terry, Colonel John Gibbon, Custer, Major James Brisbin, and perhaps a coterie of staff members, who returned salutes and made a pleasant comment to each of the Seventh's other officers as they passed. Apparently these four officers exchanged remarks on the fine appearance of the regiment, especially the quality of the horses in the ranks. Gibbon's men were said to have cheered as the Seventh snaked off, company by company, into the distance. All in all, the mood was positive, if not jovial. Whatever forebodings each officer felt lay hidden beneath the blare of trumpets, the rattle and clank of equipment, the thunder of a thousand hoofs, and the promise of six hundred able soldiers riding to do battle with an enemy that would surely have to be run to ground.

As they were saying good-bye, Colonel Gibbon suggested that Custer not be greedy and that he leave some Indians for the other column, to which Custer is alleged to have replied enigmatically,, "No, I won't."³ Much has been made of this final exchange, particularly as an example of Custer's egotism, but as Lieutenant Charles Varnum explained this "bit of pleasantry," Gibbon meant only to convey that he knew Custer was always ready to fight and that Gibbon wanted to help if he could.⁴ Terry, Gibbon, and Brisbin were likely distressed that they were being left behind at that highly charged emotional moment, but none of them—Brisbin included—could have done otherwise than to wish Custer well as he left to catch up with the head of the column.

The soldiers of the Seventh probably did not look as fine as the reviewing officers thought or said. The regiment had been on the march for more than a month, through rain, hail, snow, and heat, with few opportunities for the men to wash themselves, let alone their uniforms. Blue jackets or blouses had faded to gray or had turned purple from the weather. Government-issue hats could not have retained their shapes or their colors, and at least some of the men had purchased the straw head-coverings offered by the sutler. Certainly a few had already shed their regular blouses to expose white or checked cotton shirts bought at their own expense. Like Custer, many of the men had cut their hair short before leaving Fort Abraham Lincoln, but with thirty days of growth on their heads and faces, they were surely a shaggy bunch, uncaring of their appearance and unconcerned with the niceties of regulation now that they were in the field and perhaps on the verge of battle.

Thus, by choice or by necessity, they were by and large a dirty and smelly congregation of men, indifferent to their daily grooming under circumstances that would not improve. For added protection while in the saddle, some of the men used white canvas to reinforce the seats and inside legs of their trousers. Underneath, they wore heavy underwear, which was standard regardless of the season. Many of their faces had been sunned leather-tough and brown.

Each trooper was armed with the Model 1873 Springfield (.45-caliber breech-loading or trapdoor single-shot) carbine, about seven pounds worth of weapon, as well as Model 1873 Colt (.45-caliber six-shot, called the "Peacemaker") revolvers. Nobody carried a saber. The McClellan saddle weighed some 20 pounds, and the other gear (ammunition, overcoats, blankets, tent flies, rations, mess kits, and pots and pans) added another 100 pounds or so to the load that a horse would have to carry. Assuming that the average cavalryman weighed about 140 to 150 pounds, the horses were toting close to 300 pounds at the outset. The evidence indicates that troopers lessened the burden on their precious steeds by dumping pieces of the cargo along the way—an overcoat here, a blanket there, a cooking utensil anywhere. On the eve of battle, at least a few of the soldiers would even discard what was left of the twelve quarts of oats they were required to carry for the horses, simply dumping the contents in front of the animals and using the empty sacks instead to hold spare clothing.[5]

Regardless of any cavalryman's individual decisions regarding the importance of nonessential accoutrements, all would have held tightly to their weapons, their ammunition, their canteens, their rations, and probably the extra shoes for their mounts. Regimental orders called for each soldier to carry one hundred rounds of carbine ammunition (fifty in their belts and fifty in their saddlebags) and twenty-four rounds of pistol ammunition. Again, the testimony of the troopers themselves suggests that some carried less than the amount specified either because they had a different under-standing of the "order" (for example, eighty instead of one hundred rounds) or because they chose to disregard the instructions; others, on the other hand, carried more than the amount specified because they wanted to lessen the burden on their pack mules, which transported approximately twenty-six thousand rounds of ammunition. The significance of these differences is not so much that all manner of men failed to comprehend or even deliberately disobeyed orders but rather that the men represent distinct variables in a contest of arms that has generally been analyzed as if instructions and consequent actions were one and the same. Thousands of separate and highly personal decisions were made, and many of these did not comport with the orders as given. For this reason, soldiers who ought to have been in battle remained at the base camp, and those who went forth were dressed for the occasion and carried what they wanted.[6]

Like the enlisted personnel, the officers of the Seventh were attired according to their tastes and in deference to comfort during a warm time of the year. For most of his service on the Great Plains, particularly during the summer months, Custer was inclined to wear buckskin. He did so again during this campaign. He wore his jacket as the weather and the situation dictated, and his buckskin pants were tucked into long Wellington boots. His blue-gray flannel shirt was decorated with the crossed sabers and a "7" in white or yellow silk at the points of the collar, and the breast was ornamented with narrow white braid. His gray-white, low-crowned, broad-brimmed hat—perhaps with the right side turned up and fastened to the crown by a hook and eye—covered a receding hairline, the hair in back cut short for the campaign but now pressing against his collar. In a canvas cartridge belt worn around his waist were two English Bulldog self-cocking, white-handled pistols and a Bowie knife. He carried his Remington sporting rifle with its octagonal barrel in a leather sling fastened to the pommel of the saddle in front of him. He rode either Vic (Victory) or Dandy, the first a light sorrel virtual pure-bred with three white stockings and a bald face and the latter (his favorite) a dark-brown army horse with a little white blaze on the forehead.[7] As one enlisted man recollected: "[Custer's] magnificent bearing was superb. I see him this minute as he stood there, the idol of us all."[8]

Because imitation is the sincerest form of flattery, it is not surprising that Captains Tom Custer and George Yates, Lieutenants William Cooke, Algernon Smith, and James Calhoun, and maybe Captain Myles Keogh and Lieutenant James Porter were also clad in buckskin, to a degree at least. Tom had the buckskin blouse, but he wore soldier pants and a blue flannel shirt. The others apparently also completed their outfits with blue army trousers, blue shirts with the emblematic "7," and high boots. Lieutenant Henry Harrington is said to have worn a blue army blouse and white canvas trousers. Major Marcus Reno and others wore the sutler's straw hats.[9]

The weapons for officers depended on their personal preferences and their resources to purchase the best guns available. Tom Custer used a Springfield sporting rifle, and other officers presumably had at their disposal some make of repeating arm, probably with brass as opposed to copper shells. Even noncommissioned officers had procured, at their own expense, rifles superior to the standard issue. Still, at least some of the officers and their senior subordinates seem to have been content to rely on the single-shot Springfield carbine, an excellent weapon for dealing with an enemy at a distance but one inclined to jam when overheated or otherwise fouled. The government-approved carbine was sufficient for expected eventualities, but when the spent copper cartridges had to be extracted with a knife in the midst of fighting at close quarters, the men would have preferred the repeating weapons used by many of their opponents.[10]

With Custer in the lead, the column moved up Rosebud Creek. The order of march is not known, but a senior captain was in charge of the rear guard and the pack train. According to Lieutenant Edward Godfrey, the packs followed the troop to which they were assigned; however, this is inconsistent with virtually all other testimony, which indicates that the mules trailed the regiment as a whole and were a problem from the outset. "This sort of business wasn't what the mules hired out for," recalled Private Theodore Goldin, "and they soon spread over the country, running hell west and crooked, shaking off their packs and mixing things up generally."[11]

The number of soldiers detached to ride with each company's packs is central to understanding the disposition of forces within the regiment as a whole. Most historical accounts place the size of the detail at one noncommissioned officer and six enlisted men. However, a soldier actually with the pack train said that the complement was one noncommissioned officer and seven troopers, and another equally well-placed trooper stated that the total was two men from each company, for a total of twelve. The commander of the packs, Lieutenant Edward Mathey, indicated that he had about 160 mules and was "supposed" to have "an average of five men from each company," for a total of about seventy soldiers, plus four or five civilian packers. Perhaps the one-and-six or the one-and-seven specification devolved into lesser numbers as the campaign progressed and as it became clear that the troopers in Reno's wing were more adept at keeping the cursed mules in order. In any event, describing the beginning of the march, Godfrey captured the essence of the problem: "Pack trains proved troublesome at the start, as the cargoes began falling off before we got out of camp, and during all that day the mules straggled badly."[12]

The march of 22 June covered, by all accounts, approximately twelve miles. Perhaps the mules were at fault for the little distance covered, or maybe the companies were simply off to a faltering start. Regardless, Custer's initial movement was perfectly consistent with the army doctrine of the time: long marches should begin "moderately," covering no more than ten or twelve miles a day in the early stages and increasing to twenty-five or so miles when the mounts had become "inured to their work." A commander was expected to understand "the rules of management" pertaining to horses: "An ignorant or careless commander will always have broken-down and unserviceable animals." It may be recalled that the first day's march out of Fort Lincoln covered approximately twelve miles, followed by daily advances of twenty miles on the average.[13]

Since no new horses had been added on the trail, presumably all of the animals had become accustomed to their tasks, and those that had displayed obvious signs of fatigue or weakness had been left at the Yellowstone depot. Even though the regiment's horses had endured an extended march over difficult ground since leaving the post, and even though the six companies on Reno's scout had traveled thirty miles a day for more than a week, such arduous treks were customary in military campaigns in the American West. In *My Life on the Plains*, Custer asserted: "Our average daily march, when not in immediate pursuit of the enemy, was about twenty-five miles." Like the men who rode them, some of the mounts may have become jaded, but that was probably more often the exception than the rule, as the available evidence suggests.[14]

At officers' call on the evening of 22 June, Custer told his assembled subordinates that the march would be accomplished in easy stages of twenty-five to thirty miles a day, which was in keeping with the calculations made during the strategic planning session on the *Far West*. In a serious mood, gathered around Custer's bed, the officers were surprised to hear their commander speak in a manner "extraordinary" for him. Much of what he said covered routine business, such as company responsibilities, the cessation of bugle calls while in hostile territory, and the use of fires only large enough to cook coffee for the men. He explained why he had not accepted the offers of a battalion of the Second Cavalry (he thought it would not make a difference and might cause friction) and of the Gatling guns (he thought they might hamper movements at a critical moment). He expressed confidence in the "judgment, discretion, and loyalty" of his officers and requested that they make whatever suggestions they thought fit. As Godfrey remembered, the general spoke in a way "conciliating and subdued," and in that "there was an indefinable something that was *not* Custer." Because Custer was normally curt to his subordinates, rarely inviting them to contribute their ideas, Lieutenant George Wallace saw in this change of behavior a premonition that Custer would be killed.[15]

Custer did emphasize that he wanted all suggestions to reach him in the proper manner. He also stated that he wanted all orders obeyed, whether they came from him or from any other officer to subordinates. He noted that he had heard reports of grumbling to members of Terry's staff about the management of the regiment, and he stated that he would not permit such carping to continue. When Captain Frederick Benteen spoke up to request the identities of the guilty parties so that all would not be lashed for the offenses of one, Custer replied that he would not be "catachised" by the captain, but he said, for Benteen's information, that the captain was not one of the culprits and that in fact he could not recall having heard criticism from Benteen on any expedition. Lieutenant Winfield Edgerly put the best face on this exchange, suggesting that it was not "unpleasant," but Benteen, later describing this episode, displayed his normal preference for treating Custer's remarks as a personal challenge.[16]

This contretemps apparently followed Custer's assertion that of all the regiments in the cavalry, the Seventh was best equipped to whip whatever hostile force might be brought against it, and he wanted his subordinates to work in harmony, without complaint. As Edgerly described the moment, the trip had been generally pleasant, and "everybody was in excellent spirits," their only fear being that the Indians would get away. Edgerly noted, "After a few remarks from Major Reno, the General bade us good-night."[17]

After the meeting, the scout Mitch Boyer approached Godfrey with questions about the coming campaign. He wondered whether Godfrey had ever fought the Sioux and how many Indians the regiment expected to find. Godfrey replied that indeed he had fought the Sioux, that as many as one thousand or fifteen hundred might be found, and that they could be beaten. "Well," Boyer said, "I can tell you we are going to have a damned big fight." In his assessment of the Indian strength, and in his expression of confidence regarding the Seventh's ability, Godfrey was undoubtedly in accord with his fellow officers.[18]

In 1876 Boyer was approximately thirty-seven years old, the offspring of a French father and a Sioux mother. He spoke his mother's tongue as well as Crow and English and was regarded as one of the best scouts west of the Missouri River. He had actually started the expedition with Gibbon's column out of Fort Ellis, but when it became clear that the Seventh would form the strike force up the Rosebud, Boyer and six Crow scouts were detailed to Custer's regiment. The Crows were Curley, Half Yellow Face, Hairy Moccasin, Goes Ahead, White Man Runs Him, and White Swan. These men were said to know the Rosebud–Little Bighorn country thoroughly.[19]

The Crows were a roving people, considered by the whites to be quite handsome and generally good-natured. However, they were fierce in their hatred of their archenemy, the Sioux, who had driven them from their land, whom they feared, and from whom they stole horses in a long history of hit-and-run warfare. Their alliance with the soldiers was therefore one of convenience; they had reasons for disliking the *wasichus* ("people you can't get rid of") as well, since many Crow people had died of white-infected diseases in the eighteenth and nineteenth centuries. Like all other nomadic Plains tribes, the Crows placed a high value on the horse, and they thought that with the army's assistance, they would be allowed to plunder the Sioux herds as partial compensation for their scouting skills. The Crows and Boyer operated under the direct supervision of Custer.

Like the Crows, the Arikara scouts regarded the Sioux as their enemy, but unlike the Crows, these Indians (also known as the "Rees," a shortened form for "Arikaras") tended to live in permanent villages. Although they hunted to survive, they also depended on agriculture, which was disdained and denigrated by the Sioux. The Arikaras were under the command of Lieutenant Varnum, who had recruited forty to fifty of them (as well as a small number of Sioux and the part-Indians William Cross and Robert and William Jackson) before leaving Fort Lincoln. Although not soldiers per se, these scouts were hired at the discretion of the department commander and received the same pay and allowances as the cavalrymen. Custer's favorite Arikara, Bloody Knife, was not a scout but was a "guide" employed by the Quartermaster Department at about five dollars a day, much more than the thirteen dollars a month paid to the quasi-soldier Arikaras. Far less familiar with this territory than the Crows, the Arikaras served as an "eyes and ears" vanguard to the Seventh's advance. Frederick Gerard was the interpreter for this band. By the time the regiment started up the Rosebud, Varnum's scouts had dwindled to roughly twenty-five or thirty, including Cross and William Jackson, the remainder having been dispatched with mail and messages along the way.[20]

The white scout George Herendeen had been loaned to Custer from Gibbon's command, with the understanding that he would carry to Terry the message detailing Custer's examination of the upper reaches of Tullock's Creek, as anticipated in Terry's instructions. Additionally, "Lonesome" Charley Reynolds accompanied the regiment as a guide. Custer's twenty-seven-year-old brother Boston and Custer's nephew Harry Armstrong "Autie" Reed, only eighteen at the time, rode with the Seventh as civilians with miscellaneous quartermaster duties. Young Reed was supposed to have remained on the *Far West*, but he reportedly pouted until Custer relented and agreed to take him along.[21]

Isaiah Dorman, a Sioux interpreter and the only black man with the regiment, was also present. Herendeen thought him "a man of considerable intelligence and a man who enjoyed the respect and confidence of the soldiers." Married to a Sioux woman, Dorman had worked for the army in various capacities, the most recent of which was for the Seventh as interpreter at Fort Rice. Custer had directed that Dorman join the regiment only several days before it departed from Fort Lincoln, probably because Varnum had succeeded in recruiting non-Lakota Sioux scouts. Custer may also have felt that Dorman's skills might come in handy in dealing with the Lakota Sioux whether they were encountered by happenstance or were captured, before any battle or after.[22]

In accordance with regimental orders, the march on 23 June began at five o'clock in the morning. Presumably before that time, Benteen reported to Custer for instructions, either as officer of the day or as the person whose turn it was to direct the protection of the pack train. If, as seems likely, the assignment of rear guard was rotated according to a duty roster, both of those alternatives may have been correct. It is not clear who had the task on the twenty-second, but Benteen clearly had it on the twenty-third, and Keogh, Yates, and Captain Thomas French have all been mentioned as officers who performed the role at one time or another. During the first three days of the expedition, the job of protecting the packs fell to a battalion of three companies commanded by a captain. But after the division of forces on 25 June, Captain Thomas McDougall's Company B would form the rear guard by itself.[23]

In some of Benteen's writing, he claimed that he had been assigned to guard the packs because his soldier-packers had been reported to be deficient by Lieutenant Mathey, who was actually in charge of the train and its cargo. According to Benteen, the other two companies in his rear-guard battalion had also been cited for laxness in looking after their supplies, but this comment probably just reflects Benteen's penchant for portraying himself as the eternal scapegoat.[24] It is true that Custer had asked Mathey "to report at the end of each day's march the order of merit of the efficiency of the troop packers," but Godfrey interpreted this instruction simply as an instrument for deciding future deployments: "It is quite probable that if he [Custer] had had occasion to detach troops requiring rapid marching, he would have selected those troops whose packers had the best records."[25]

Mathey himself indicated that it was not until the night of 24 June that he reluctantly reported to an inquiring Custer that the packs of Benteen's and Lieutenant Donald McIntosh's companies had given the most trouble and that whereas McIntosh took it well, Benteen was angry. The likelihood is that neither Custer nor Mathey was singling out Benteen, certainly not before Benteen had rear-guard duty on the twenty-third, and that Custer was already planning for an inequitable distribution of personnel out of the companies to protect the mule train, with the greater portion of that burden falling on those troops who had been on the Reno scout. As Private Fremont Kipp of Company D observed, "it was some little trouble to learn a new man to pack a mule using the diamond hitch," and officers would be loath to introduce "green" troopers so near in time to a fight. The events of the next two days would further influence Custer's thinking regarding the optimal method of manning the pack train so as to achieve the best chance of rapid reinforcement during any encounter with the enemy. He was using Mathey's reports not to punish companies for their failure to control a situation totally new to them but to establish a record of performance on which he could base subsequent decisions.[26]

While Custer was contemplating future contingencies, Benteen was managing the back end of the mules with his usual flair for self-congratulation.

Discovering immediately that the beasts had a tendency to stray, Benteen devised a strategy for enclosing them so that they would have less opportunity to wander. He simply placed one company on either side of the herd and one behind, thus creating a kind of moving corral. This could hardly be called an extraordinary idea, but it had the desired effect.

In his memoirs, Benteen made much of that practical innovation, probably because it gave him another example of his willingness to confront Custer. First, Benteen conveyed his experience and his improved method to Adjutant Cooke, suggesting that Cooke mention it to the general in the course of their conversations. Benteen would have done this himself, but he recalled Custer's injunction that recommendations ought to come through "proper" channels, and he did not want to be viewed as a "fault-finder." Cooke refused and proposed instead that Benteen take the matter up with Custer directly. When an opportunity presented itself, Benteen did so. He told Custer that "on account of fearing for the safety of the train," he had made an arrangement different from the one that Custer had ordered. In reply, Benteen later stated, "Custer stammered slightly" and said, "I am much obliged to you Col. Benteen, I will direct the officer who relieves you to guard the train in the manner you have done." The idea and Custer's seemingly flustered reaction apparently gave Benteen's starved ego a charge, but it is unlikely that Custer made so much of the situation.[27]

During that day of 23 June, the regiment traveled thirty to thirty-five miles, mostly in the valley of the Rosebud because the surrounding terrain was rough. The pack train still lagged behind, in spite of Benteen's efforts. After the first eight miles, signs of the Indian trail noted during the Reno scout began to appear. Three times the column halted so that Indian camping places could be examined more closely. Such pauses in the march were sufficiently long that knowledgeable persons could study the age of pony droppings and the breadth of lodgepole trails, as well as speculate as to the significance of the many wickiups, the small temporary shelters for individual warriors. All indications were that the villages were large and contained many people. According to the scout Herendeen, the Indians and the pursuing soldiers followed the main buffalo trail up the Rosebud.[28]

By 24 June, rather than a single trail indicating the movements of Sitting Bull and his associates, the Seventh found a virtual network of converging paths made by numerous hunter bands and summer roamers from the reservations. But with the information available to him, there was no way for Custer to fully understand the many merging and separating trails made by unknown Indian groups. Although a large assembly of Indians could not remain together long because of the demands for game and grass, by moving often they could stay mostly intact for about a month, long enough to give Custer all of the action he hoped to find.[29]

Over a distance of some twenty-eight miles, many halts were made on 24 June so that scouts would have time to prowl in advance of the Seventh, looking for additional evidence of the size and direction of the Indian band. As had been the case on the previous day, the march was steady but broken by occasional pauses every hour or so, interludes prescribed in cavalry regulations but driven primarily by the need to investigate the ground and the trail. Early in the day, the regiment discovered a Sun Dance lodge, with scalps of white men inside. In these lodges, Indian warriors proved their courage and worthiness by enduring incredible pain. During these ceremonies the Indian men, suspended above the center of the large tent circle and hanging by mere strips of skin, experienced an agony that produced hallucinations; in a state of near unconsciousness, they dreamed those dreams that defined their manhood and forecast deeds almost universally congenial to their desires. For example, Sitting Bull's vision said that if soldiers were coming, they would fly headfirst into the arms of the Sioux.

At about midday trackers noticed that the main trail split, with one fork leading southwest toward the Rosebud–Little Bighorn Divide and the second heading southeast. In the early afternoon the head of scouts, Varnum, was summoned by Custer, who said that Lieutenant Godfrey had observed such a diversion about ten miles to the rear. Custer ordered Varnum to go back and look for the supposed travois trail, and after "considerable discussion," Varnum did as he was directed, only to discover that the divergent path merged again with the main line of Indian advance toward the Little Bighorn. Varnum had now ridden twenty or so more miles than the regiment, and although he had never believed that the trails separated, he did not complain unduly about Custer's order, based as it was on a company commander's observations.[30]

As usual, the Seventh made camp at about five o'clock that evening. The three days' march had been conducted at a moderate pace, with intermittent pauses or halts and with ample time for the men to sleep, at least on the first two nights. In fact, Benteen remarked that the halts were "frequent and sometimes quite lengthy" and that when he arrived at his camping place, the grass was lush.[31] However, grazing for the horses may have been a bit thin overall, since Indian pony herds probably fed on the same ground. The alkaline water common to the region was likely difficult to swallow, for horses and men alike. Still, small fires allowed the soldiers to cook a little coffee and bacon to go with that least tasty of army staples, hardtack. The last into bivouac were the mule train and the rear guard. The officer of the day and the commander of the battalion that had to eat the dust of the regiment and the mules on 24 June may have been Captain Yates, since Mathey recalled speaking to him several times during this period.[32] Godfrey noted that the trail was so dry and powdery that companies had been required to march on separate paths so that dust clouds would not rise too high.[33]

It might have been as late as seven o'clock by the time all of the components of the column had arrived and any semblance of calm had been established, and even then guards had to be posted and the animals looked after. Lieutenant Charles DeRudio said that the campsite was at a place where the Rosebud was very crooked (near the present town of Busby). The cavalrymen and scouts bivouacked on both sides of the creek, under a bluff furnishing some concealment. As the soldiers settled in for the night, the Crow scouts and probably Boyer continued on to the Wolf (or Little Chetish) Mountains, where there was a high point called the "Crow's Nest" from which they had, on many occasions, watched the Sioux and waited for an opportunity to steal ponies.[34]

Some of the officers gathered to discuss the day's events and to listen to DeRudio's stories. Benteen stretched out on his saddle blanket, warning his companions that they had better get some sleep; he felt—based on one of his presentiments—that there would be a night march. Godfrey and Lieutenant Luther Hare did lie down "to take a nap" at about 9:30, all having been made ready to begin the march two hours later, suggesting that a night movement had already been planned (and thus making it relatively easy for Benteen to see into the future).[35]

Custer likely did not go to bed at all. Normally, he slept little. Probably he was alone, perhaps lost in thought. Captain Yates's wife, Annie, said that Custer had seemed much older during the Civil War but that this was the

99

result of a mask worn by a "boy general" intent on making himself credible in the eyes of other officers and men. Now, at age thirty-six, Custer continued to do everything quickly, from eating to speaking. The "real gold" hair and darting blue eyes recalled by Annie belied the precocious warrior on the threshold of middle age, as evidenced by the last picture taken in the spring of 1876, when the lean and aquiline profile of the Civil War years was displaced by a subtle filling out of the face, by the inevitable rounding of sharp edges.[36]

On 9 June Custer had written to Libbie about another *Galaxy* article just completed and sent off to the magazine. He continued: "As a slight evidence that I am not very conceited regarding my personal appearance, I have not looked in a mirror or seen the reflection of my beautiful (?) countenance, including the growth of *auburn* [Custer's emphasis] whiskers, since I looked in the glass at Lincoln." Full of fun at his own expense, this was another private joke between the two, perhaps referring to the darkening of his golden locks and perhaps hinting at the sneak attack of gray along the fringes of his thinning hair. By the evening of the march up the Rosebud, he was telling Libbie that he was "hopeful of accomplishing great results." And on the morning of the regiment's departure, he wrote his always "dear durl" of the pride he felt because of General Terry's expressed confidence in him. But the pat on the back he really wanted and depended on was several hundred miles away at Fort Lincoln; in separation, the two friends and lovers were still in touch with one another, even as the future was tumbling beyond their mutual control.[37]

The day had been a long one, full of signs that unsettled the Indian scouts, not to mention Lieutenant Wallace, who saw bad tidings when Custer's headquarter's flag was twice toppled to the rear by a stiff breeze coming from the south. In front of the command, the Crows had been unable to make observations from their favorite lookout (the Crow's Nest) because of inadequate light, and they arrived back in camp at about nine o'clock. What they had discovered was that the trail of the quarry turned in a western direction, up Davis Creek, toward the Divide between the Rosebud and Little Bighorn Valleys. As Custer sat in a clump of trees and spoke in low tones with the scouts and Boyer, he was probably not surprised to hear their news and probably experienced no doubts as to his next move.

The regiment was now camped about thirty miles north of where the Sioux and Cheyennes had stalled Crook (an event still unknown to Custer or Terry). Terry's instructions to Custer were that the Seventh should proceed "perhaps" to the headwaters of the Tongue River—about equidistant with the point of the Rosebud fight—even if the trail of the enemy diverged to the west. Because of the broad discretion specified in Terry's order, and because Custer was determined to pursue the Indians in a straight line so as not to lose them, his natural course of action was obvious, at least to him, and with that in mind, he summoned his officers. Over on the Bighorn River, maybe forty miles to the northwest, Gibbon was supposedly telling a fellow officer, "I am satisfied that if Custer can prevent it, we will not get into the fight."[38]

Stumbling through the darkness toward the single candle that marked Custer's tent, the officers assembled to hear words that would not have startled those who expected a night march. While Godfrey's K Troop had apparently made preparations for the move, Benteen took the time to check with his first sergeant to confirm that Company H was ready and so (as usual) was too late for the meeting. What Benteen missed was Custer's explanation that he wanted to march at once in order to reach, before daylight, a point near the Rosebud–Little Bighorn Divide, where the regiment could be concealed and the necessary intelligence gathered in anticipation of an attack on 26 June.[39]

While the company commanders retired to carry out the orders, Custer met with Varnum to discuss the details of the forthcoming scout. Custer said that he wanted an "intelligent" white man to go with the Crows—that is, someone who could assimilate the information gathered by the Crows and who could communicate that information in message form to Custer. Varnum replied, "That means me." Contrary to his reputation for snapping instructions, Custer said that Varnum had already had a hard day and that he did not want to order the lieutenant on such a trip. Varnum responded that as chief of scouts, he objected to sending someone else unless Custer had lost faith in him. As Varnum later recalled, "He thought that was about what I would say, and [told] me to go."[40]

By now, Custer had detailed Lieutenant Hare to serve as an assistant to Varnum, who had ridden harder and farther than any other officer in the regiment and who was determined to retain the confidence of his superior in the wake of the supposedly missed trail earlier that day. Varnum departed for the Crow's Nest with five Crows and Boyer, about a dozen Rees to serve as messengers, and the guide Reynolds, an English-speaking white man with whom Varnum could converse. The entire regiment (including Hare and the remaining scouts) would follow within an hour or so.

At some point between 11:30 and 12:30 that night, the Seventh advanced through impenetrable darkness, climbing in the direction of Davis Creek. The regiment was soon fragmented, groping its way through pitch-blackness, bumping and dividing as men drove forward blindly under a moon completely concealed by clouds. The pieces of the column followed one another by means of lit matches, whistles, shouts, clanking equipment, and barely perceived clouds of dust. Called a "forced" march, the distance covered was only eight to ten miles in about three hours, the pace being a walk for some horses and a trot for others, but in the red-eyed confusion, the particulars of the murky sojourn could hardly have been clear to anyone.

If disciplined soldiers with the means of communication had difficulty ascending through the dark unknown, the pack train was nearly a total wreck. As the officer in charge of the rear guard, Captain Keogh struggled mightily to keep the mules on track, "making the very air sulphurous with blue oaths" and taking an inordinate amount of time to get the beasts across Muddy Creek. With packs falling willy-nilly in the night, Keogh complained to Benteen that he could not make head or tails of the convoy's status, to which Benteen counseled patience, proposing that the missing cargo be retrieved on the following day. In what must have been irritation piled on top of aggravation, Custer sent DeRudio back to tell Keogh to close the pack train up, and after a ride of several miles, DeRudio found Keogh trying to deal with sixteen mules stuck in the mud while the rest had scattered along the trail for some distance. Whereas Benteen's ability to manage the animals in an efficient way had been demonstrated (albeit in daylight), Keogh's temperament was not suited to herding wandering mules through the dark.[41]

Even as the Seventh plunged forward through the night, Custer wanted to be certain that all or part of the hostile Indians had not turned left, or south, up the Rosebud. To that end, he took Gerard and two Indian scouts with him in the most advanced position, their instructions being to look closely for any evidence that bands might have departed from the western direction in which the main camp appeared to be heading. It would have been difficult for the scouts to detect much of anything in the darkness, but with the column moving in fits and starts, and with the pack train falling dangerously behind, there was time enough for them to feel through the darkness for obvious signs of separating trails. However, the scouts were convinced that with a thousand warriors in their front, there was little need to worry about small divergent groups. Nothing of significance was discovered, and the head of the column went into bivouac at about 3:30 A.M. at the point where Davis Creek connects with the Rosebud.[42]

Not yet convinced that the Sioux would be found in the Little Bighorn Valley, Custer decided to camp at a point where he could keep his options open. Additionally, the Crow scouts had informed him that he could not reach the Rosebud–Little Bighorn Divide before daylight. From the moment the trail had first been discovered, several scouts had told Custer that there were many Sioux ahead. His expressed attitude was "show them to me," not because he disbelieved either the obvious signs or the word of the scouts but simply because he had to see them for himself. And if he ridiculed the suggestion that there were more hostile Indians than the Seventh could handle, he did so in the belief that once he had established—through his own senses—the nature of the situation, the regiment could achieve its objective.[43]

The Seventh straggled into the bivouac as dawn broke on 25 June. First Custer, then company after company—men haggard, hungry, and red-eyed—dragged into camp, falling prostrate where they parked their horses, taking only as many minutes as required to slacken saddle girths and slip the bits from the mouths of their mounts before they collapsed from sheer exhaustion, reins wrapped around their arms. Many men were so tired they could not eat and could not even drink the awful coffee conjured up out of salty water and cooked over brief fires. For the next four or five hours, the soldiers would have a chance to catch up on the sleep they had lost the night before. Some must have been deep in slumber by the time Keogh rolled in with the pack mules and the three companies under his command. The tireless Custer had nothing to do but wait for word from Varnum, whose function was not to gather intelligence but to impart it in intelligible form from Crow scouts who had been recruited to scan and make sense of the surrounding landscape.[44]

The Varnum party had reached the Crow's Nest at approximately 2:30 A.M., not long before summer's early sunrise. The lookout was located just short of the Divide, about fifteen miles from the Little Bighorn, and though not the highest point in the area, it provided a good view of the relatively flat terrain bordering Reno Creek, which ran crooked to the river. Below the peak, toward the Rosebud side of the ascent, was a hollow where the Crow scouts usually concealed their horses while on their pony-stealing sorties. Having been without sleep for some thirty-six hours, Varnum lay down to rest until daylight. He was asleep when the Crows came down from the top of the hill to tell him what they could see.[45]

The climb up the buffalo grass slopes to the observation point was steep. Varnum's eyes were sore and inflamed. When the Crow scouts pointed in the direction of the Sioux encampment, Varnum could see nothing except what he would remember as two lodges on a tributary (Reno Creek) leading to the river. The Crows gave him a cheap telescope and told him to look for the pony herd on the far side of the bluffs that blocked a clear view of the main Indian camp. Although Varnum thought his eyesight was above average, he was still unable to see anything, so they suggested he try to pick out "worms in the grass"—that is, an immense pony herd shifting about on the plateau west of the river. Reynolds looked through the glass and nodded, confirming the sightings made by Boyer and the five Crow scouts. Unable to verify the evidence for himself, Varnum had to depend on the Crows', Arikaras', and civilian scouts' judgments that there was indeed a formidable body of hostile Indians out of sight in the valley of the Little Bighorn.[46]

On the basis of the information provided by the scouts, Varnum sent Custer a message stating that "a tremendous village" had been discovered, and he used the Arikaras Red Star and Bull to deliver the note to Custer. Those scouts remaining at the Crow's Nest could see the smoke from the small fires that the men of the Seventh had built to cook their coffee. The Crows were annoyed that Custer would allow his soldiers to reveal their position in enemy territory, but for the Arikaras, the smoke offered a convenient way to identify the Seventh's base, about five miles distant.[47]

As the messengers departed, Varnum and those still at the Crow's Nest detected strangers on the horizon. First, on a ridge parallel to their location, they saw two Indians, apparently herding stray stock and heading in the general direction of the Seventh's bivouac. Varnum, Reynolds, Boyer, and two Crows started off, dismounted, to cut them off, but before the scouts had gone very far they were recalled by the other scouts, who informed them that the pair had changed direction and were now moving away. At the same time, the scouting party noticed six or seven Indians riding along the crest of a ridge over toward the Rosebud, their ponies looking "as large as elephants" against the early morning skyline. Both of these groups soon disappeared, but the watchers were convinced that the regiment had been discovered and that the outriders would report the soldiers' approach to their village.[48]

Meanwhile, Red Star was delivering Varnum's message to Custer. As he neared the Seventh's location, he called out and zigzagged his horse, as a signal that he had found the enemy; he tied up his horse's tail in accordance with Arikara custom to tell his friend Stabbed that the Sioux had been sighted. After a few words with Bloody Knife, Red Star squatted down with a cup of coffee and conversed, by means of signs, for a few moments with the general and Tom Custer. Then he handed over the Varnum note, and Custer bobbed his head in understanding. According to Red Star, Custer said to Bloody Knife in sign language as he pointed to Tom: "Your brother, there, is frightened, his heart flutters with fear, his eyes are rolling from fright at this news of the Sioux. When we have beaten the Sioux, he will then be a man." If Custer did not actually sign his sentiments in exactly that form, these were certainly the kinds of thoughts he would have expressed not only to tease his brother Tom but also to put a brave face on the situation. Since Tom Custer had won two medals of honor and had been in almost as many fights as his older brother, Custer was more likely saying to his Indian friends that even though they might all be afraid, they would together become men again in battle.[49]

Custer climbed aboard Dandy, the chocolate army-issue horse and his first choice of mounts, and after riding through the bivouac to impart instructions to his subordinates, he followed Red Star out of camp in the direction of the Crow's Nest. The Seventh moved forward from its camp near the mouth of Davis Creek within half an hour of Custer's departure. Under the temporary command of Reno, the regiment advanced "without orders or bugle sound," according to Benteen.[50]

Varnum could see Custer approaching, the dust of the Seventh several miles behind. So far, Custer had heard nothing except that there was a large

Sioux village, probably on the Little Bighorn. The bearer of bad tidings, Varnum rode out to meet his commander. "Well," Custer said to his chief of scouts, "you've had a night of it." As the two men were speaking, Tom and his brother-in-law Calhoun rode up, and as Varnum recalled, Custer angrily ordered them to return to the column. Such a reaction tends to support Gerard's testimony that Custer did not want the regiment moved until he had returned from the Crow's Nest, testimony that is consistent with his need to see for himself the location and disposition of enemy forces. Being a dutiful chief of scouts, Varnum must have told Custer, in the early stages of their conversation, that the enemy may have seen the regiment. Varnum's report could not have made Custer happy.[51]

Probably even before Custer departed the camp, Sergeant William Curtiss of Company F was leading a detail on the back trail to recover packs lost during the march of the previous night. In view of Keogh's difficulties with the mules during the night march and Benteen's advice to let the cargo fall off for later retrieval, the packs of more than one unit had likely been left behind.[52] Or perhaps Curtiss, as the noncommissioned officer assigned to his company's mules, had simply noticed the loss of a single pack. Sergeant John Ryan indicated that "some" bundles—at least one belonging to Company M—had been cut loose because they were falling anyway, and Private Goldin thought that Private John McEagen of Company G had accompanied the detail to recover a pistol misplaced while repacking. Whatever the impetus for the ride back, after about four miles the detail discovered an Indian (one of a group) trying to open a box containing cooking utensils and hardtack. The soldiers shot at the thief, but he escaped, providing another reason to worry whether the regiment had been dis-covered. Two hours after it had left, the detail returned to report the unfortunate turn of events, and Godfrey remembered the determined look on Tom Custer's face as he announced that he would report the episode to his brother at once.[53]

As Custer climbed the grassy incline leading to the pinnacle of the Crow's Nest, he was not yet aware of the Indians on the back trail, and he had no way of knowing that none of the sightings would constitute advance warning to the Sioux and their allies. None of the various Indians thus far seen would arrive at the enemy village in time to provide notice of the regiment's presence. The Sioux seen from the Crow's Nest were apparently Oglalas on their way back to the Red Cloud agency, whereas the Indian discovered opening the hardtack boxes was among a group of Cheyennes who would follow the soldiers for a time, then take a roundabout course to the Indian encampment, arriving after the battle was over.[54]

But the cumulative effect of Varnum's intelligence was ominous. Given the circumstances and the information available to him at that moment, Custer must have scrambled up the hill, eager for his first look at the foe. Perhaps the situation reminded him of his Civil War experience down in Virginia as an engineering officer riding a balloon to reconnoiter the Confederate lines, swallowing his fear as he soared above the trees and tents to sketch maps of the surrounding terrain.[55] Now, his thoughts racing, his mind filled with excitement and perhaps a bit of uncertainty, he would find more in the way of opinions than clear and unassailable intelligence. As they had done with Varnum, the Crow scouts told Custer to look in the direction of the Little Bighorn for hints of the herd and traces of smoke rising from the valley some fifteen miles away. Like Varnum, Custer could see nothing of the Indian camp even though he thought he had "mighty good eyes," and the telescopic glass—"a mere toy," according to Varnum—available to the men already on the hill was of no help to Custer, who was clearly frustrated by his inability to see what the scouts had seen.[56]

Probably sensing Custer's distress at not being able to confirm the details discovered by the superior eyesight of the Crows, Boyer remarked, "If you don't find more Indians in that valley than you ever saw together before, you can hang me." Custer jumped to his feet and replied testily, "It would do a damned sight of good to hang you, wouldn't it?" Varnum recalled that it was only the second time he had ever heard Custer curse, indicating the level of the general's annoyance. As they lingered in disappointment, Custer and Varnum discussed the fact that DeRudio had a fine pair of field glasses. They left the hill to rejoin the regiment.[57]

As Custer and the scouting party rode down, the column was seen approaching, dust doubtless rising from their line of march even though company commanders had been instructed to stay off the trail to avoid such telltale signs. The interpreter Gerard described Custer's annoyance at seeing the whole regiment on the march, but it is unclear whether Gerard's account referred to the incident that Varnum had also reported, when Custer had reprimanded Tom Custer and Calhoun. According to Gerard's recollection, Custer expressed dismay that the regiment was being brought forward, and his brother Tom—perhaps riding ahead so that he could relay the bad news obtained from Sergeant Curtiss and his party—explained that he did not know who had given the order. Exactly what time Curtiss departed and returned is unclear, but the evidence suggests that when that party came back, Custer was not available and must still have been at the Crow's Nest.[58]

As for the movement of the command, no one took responsibility. Both Benteen and Tom expressed ignorance of who had directed the advance, and Reno denied having been consulted; Godfrey thought that Custer himself had left instructions for the column to prepare to depart. The most plausible interpretation of these events is that Custer left orders for the column to be ready to move after receiving word from him and that either because of an imperfect understanding of the directive (perhaps poorly expressed) or because of innate nervousness, Reno led the regiment out of its first Davis Creek camp. His denial notwithstanding, Reno was in command during Custer's absence and at a minimum should have been able to explain either Custer's orders or his own independent decision. Instead, at the court of inquiry, Reno tried to place the blame on the aide-de-camp Tom Custer, who was by then, conveniently for Reno, dead.[59]

At that point, the premature movement of the command and Curtiss's report were simply more small annoyances with which Custer would have to deal. By all accounts, Custer called his officers together and advised them of the state of affairs. As Benteen remembered the meeting, Custer noted that the scouts had seen the encampment but that he had not and did not believe they could have. Custer probably did say that. After his first trip to the Crow's Nest, most likely Custer merely relayed the fact that he could not confirm what the scouts had observed, adding that the regiment had apparently been discovered by the enemy and that his subordinates should prepare for a forward movement.[60]

The problem with Benteen's description of events is that it does not reflect the results of Custer's *second* trip to the Crow's Nest, an event not addressed in previous studies of the battle. When Custer returned from his first excursion, he sent Adjutant Cooke around to see DeRudio with the message that the "toy" telescope in the hands of the scouts was not strong enough to see anything and that Custer wanted to borrow DeRudio's binoculars, which had been discussed by Custer and Varnum. According to DeRudio, the glasses had been a gift to him from an Austrian optician, and although DeRudio did not want to lend them, he finally did so, never to see them again. With the improved capability in hand, Custer went off to find himself a target.[61]

While the exhausted Varnum would later maintain that he did not recall a second visit, Lieutenant Hare asserted that "during this halt, Custer *again* [emphasis added] went to the Crow's Nest to look at Indians." In this instance, Hare is more reliable than Varnum, who confessed that after the long day, his attention was occupied with food and sleep. Besides, it is hard to imagine that Custer would have been content with the unsatisfactory result of trying to see the Sioux encampment with his own eyes during the initial survey. The recollections of Red Star support the proposition that Custer did indeed make a return visit to the high ground, at which time he finally made his decision to begin the attack on the enemy during the daylight hours.[62]

Because Red Star was present at both of the visits to the Crow's Nest, his several accounts overlapped and became confused as he expressed himself through interpreters. The most compelling part of his story is that he placed Custer in an extended colloquy with "Big Belly," the Arikara name for the Crow scout Half Yellow Face.[63] In response to a question from Walter Camp, Varnum stated emphatically that Half Yellow Face was not present on the first visit to the Crow's Nest, and the Crow scout Hairy Moccasin confirmed the absence of his compatriot.[64] Since Half Yellow Face was not with the first party, he must have been present during what would be Custer's second visit, confirming the recollections of DeRudio and Hare. Sergeant Daniel Kanipe said that the regiment marched up to the Divide and halted (presumably at the second camp on Davis Creek). He added, "General Custer took the chief trumpeter and two scouts and was gone two hours."[65]

The Red Star narrative is interesting in several respects. First of all, he noted that Custer did see evidence of the Sioux camp through Reynolds's (DeRudio's) field glasses. Also, Red Star recounted in detail how Custer had argued with Half Yellow Face, saying that he (Custer) did not believe the enemy had seen the regiment and that he intended to stick with his plan of keeping the Seventh concealed under the bluffs during the night in anticipation of an attack on the morning of 26 June. The Crows contended that Custer's plan was "bad" and that he should begin the assault at once, capture the Sioux horses, and prevent them from moving rapidly. Finally Custer replied, "Yes, it shall be done as you say."[66]

Also, the Crow scout Curley recollected that Custer went to the high point with two or three officers, one of whom "had a very long beard," an almost certain reference to Lieutenant Cooke and his unique facial hair. Then Custer said, "That's good, we can see the village, and will charge on it."[67]

In opposition to Benteen's contention that Custer did not believe his scouts and did not know the location of the hostile Indians, Lieutenant Godfrey noted in his diary: "General Custer came around personally and informed us that the Sioux village was in view."[68] Lieutenant DeRudio agreed that when Custer returned, he reported having seen "cloud-like objects," which the scouts had described as pony herds.[69] What Custer may not have divulged at that moment was the precise goal he had in mind, although Private John Donoughue recalled hearing the general advise the officers that he would rather attack than be attacked.[70]

When he met with his officers after the second visit to the Crow's Nest, Custer announced that the advance would be by merit—that is, the order of march would be dictated by the sequence in which companies reported their compliance with the orders issued on the Yellowstone relative to proper support for the pack train and to the prescribed allotments of ammunition per trooper. The degree to which individual company commanders actually checked their units is unknown, but according to Benteen's own testimony, he did not even consult with his first sergeant to determine that Company H was ready and in conformance with orders. Godfrey noted that some commanders reported without checking anything and so got the lead. Having ridden almost two days while eating the dust of the regiment, Benteen was obviously determined to assume the advance position, even if that meant shortcutting the commander's instructions. According to Benteen, Custer never expected or desired that he should have the honor of the advance, but Benteen obtained by expediency the position he desired, if only temporarily. Again Custer stammered, "Well, Col. Benteen, your troop has the advance."[71]

Within a short distance, Custer rode forward and informed Benteen that he was setting too fast a pace, at which point Custer took the lead and directed the regiment over the Divide—another source of annoyance for

Benteen. During the time it took the group to traverse the Divide, Custer would decide on a disposition of forces best suited to achieve the objectives he had in mind. It was clear that the main Indian encampment—large by the standards of even the most seasoned frontiersmen—lay behind bluffs that made it discoverable only by surmise. Custer knew that an immense trail terminated in puffs of faint smoke and dark clouds of horse-flesh beyond. It was a powerful circumstantial case, but still he had not seen this great village. What he had seen clearly through DeRudio's Austrian field glasses was what Varnum had observed earlier through naked and bloodshot eyes: tepees on Reno Creek between the Crow's Nest and the Little Bighorn.

Varnum recalled seeing only two lodges while at the lookout in the early morning hours. But Custer must have seen many more tepees during his second visit to the high ground. Apparently at the last halt on Davis Creek, after Custer had returned from that second trip to the Crow's Nest, Private Daniel Newell heard the general say to Captain French: "It will be all over in a couple of hours. I was at their camp last night and they only have ten or twelve tepees." Having seen the large trail, Newell did not understand how Custer could make such a statement. Of course, Custer had not actually been to the Indian camp on the previous evening, and Newell may have misheard (or mistakenly recalled) the exact number of lodges, but the private had no reason to invent such a story. He recollected the essence of that conversation, which was that Custer believed the Seventh might achieve a quick victory by falling on a small Indian village.[72]

Similarly, Sergeant Ryan said that after the regiment had crossed the Divide, the men saw a "few" lodges. In retrospect Ryan, like Varnum, would characterize these tepees as "abandoned," because that was their condition when the column finally reached them. But Ryan concluded: "I think Custer had preparations made to charge that camp, thinking it was an Indian camp." That was precisely the plan, and by the available testimony, the senior personnel in at least Company M comprehended Custer's purpose. As we shall see, the first military objective was known to other officers and men in the regiment, including Reno and Benteen.[73]

The last piece of business left undone before the regiment crossed the Divide was to fulfill General Terry's instructions regarding the investigation of the upper region of Tullock's Creek (also called Tullock's Fork), after which Custer was to send a report of his findings to Terry. The message would be carried by the scout Herendeen, who had been taken along for just that purpose. However, by the time it was feasible for Custer to examine upper Tullock's Creek, the location of the Indian encampment had already been established and sending a dispatch to the commanding general would have made no practical difference.

According to Gerard, the Tullock Creek area was visible from the Crow's Nest, and it was possible to determine from that point—as well as from the direction of the trail—that no hostile Indians were present in that valley.[74] When Herendeen raised the question with Custer after the visits to the Crow's Nest, Custer responded "impatiently" that the Indians were ahead, that the regiment had been discovered, and that the regiment therefore needed to charge the village at once. Although Herendeen believed that Custer wanted to fight the Sioux with the Seventh alone, the scout agreed that there was no use in exploring Tullock's Fork for an enemy whose location was obvious. Varnum also concurred with the scouts that if the regiment was looking for Indians, the Little Bighorn Valley was the place to find them.[75]

Although it may be tempting to ascribe the worst of motives to Custer (namely, that he wanted to keep the Terry-Gibbon column out of the battle), the fact is that sending Herendeen alone through potentially hostile territory even on the fastest horse in the command made no sense at that juncture. Custer did not know exactly where the Terry-Gibbon column was located, but he had no reason to believe that it was closer than the Bighorn River, perhaps forty miles away at best. A rider making good speed over difficult and unknown terrain could not have reached Terry before the battle was nearly over. Had Custer been able to conceal the regiment until the morning of 26 June, as he had originally planned, sending Herendeen immediately would have been in accord with Terry's instructions and the exigencies of the moment.

Custer won at the Washita not by annihilating all of the Indians in a small village that he virtually stumbled across in the middle of a winter night but by taking as many prisoners as possible and then using them to make good his escape through a force of warriors that might have done the Seventh great damage. Custer understood that Indian warriors valued their families above all else and that if he could capture even a small number of dependents or chiefs, bloodshed might be minimized and the Indians might be persuaded to surrender to the desires of the U.S. government.

Speaking of his dealings with the Cheyennes and other tribes during 1868–69, when he not only directed the battle of the Washita but also, through foresight and subterfuge, managed to secure the release of two white women from the Indians, Custer observed in *My Life on the Plains:*

> Indians contemplating a battle, either offensive or defensive, are always anxious to have their women and children removed from all danger thereof. . . . For this reason I decided to locate our camp as close as convenient to the village, knowing that the close proximity of their women and children, and their necessary exposure in case of conflict, would operate as a powerful argument in favor of peace.[76]

A little village would do as well as—even better than—a large one. Conditioned by experiences so central to his being that he had written them down for posterity, Custer must have had in mind the serendipitous Washita as his regiment crossed the Divide to begin an operation that might replicate that earlier success. Although not specifically authorized to negotiate an end to hostilities, it surely occurred to Custer that with captives in his possession, someone in the formidable main Sioux-Cheyenne village just might want to talk.

CHAPTER SIX

WHAT THEY SAW

What Custer had observed from the Crow's Nest was a cluster of perhaps a dozen lodges belonging to Lakota Sans Arc people who had remained behind when the main Sioux-Cheyenne village relocated across the Little Bighorn River. These people were the friends and relatives of a warrior mortally wounded in the fight with General George Crook a week earlier near the headwaters of Rosebud Creek. The warrior was now dead and buried in what would become known as the Lone Tepee, and the people were mourning his loss. Without knowing anything about their identity or their grief, Custer hoped to catch the Indians unaware and, if possible, ensnare some of their number for use as leverage with the inhabitants of the larger encampment.

The ride from the last halt on Davis Creek to the Divide was less than a mile, at which point the regiment began to ascend the relatively low ridge that separated the Rosebud and Little Bighorn Valleys. Moving the horses up the slope at a walk, Custer and his headquarters staff occupied the lead position, followed by Captain Frederick Benteen's Company H and the other troops in the order that their commanders had reported them ready to advance. On the opposite side of the Divide, while still concealed from view, Custer would have to decide how best to align the Seventh so as to achieve his immediate objective of surprising a small enemy camp in broad daylight.

After a trip of several miles, the regiment had passed over the crest of the Divide and was moving downhill, twelve miles or so from the Little Bighorn. Between 12:00 and 12:15 P.M. on 25 June, Custer halted the command so that he could organize the components for the coming assault. As Benteen remembered the terrain at that juncture, there were "hills on every side," and the regiment paused "between the slopes of two hills." There Custer and Lieutenant William Cooke went "a few yards in advance of the column, just out of 'earshot,' and were diligently engaged in talking and making notes on a scratch pad."[1] Lieutenant Winfield Edgerly agreed that Custer and Cooke went off to make the division "with pencil and paper, and then they were announced."[2] It was Adjutant Cooke who went around and notified the battalion and company commanders of their assignments.

Various commentators have maintained that Custer arranged the companies within the wings and battalions so that he could keep his relatives and close associates with him. But even though Custer's brother, his brother-in law, and many of his best friends did finally ride with the general, Custer made some rather simple decisions when he and his adjutant stepped aside to commit a few ideas to paper. Clearly, any order of march that had the overeager and uncooperative Benteen in the lead was inappropriate, but that likely had little to do with Custer's judgment at this point. Rather, he chose to revert to the two-wing structure that had been in place when the Seventh had departed Fort Abraham Lincoln. That scheme may have involved a suggestion of favoritism, but in reality, it paid strict attention to the official pecking order so dear to army officers.

With a single exception, the two-wing formation created at Fort Lincoln was based on officer seniority. That is, rank and the date of grade determined which officers would fall under Major Marcus Reno's right wing and which under Benteen's left, as listed below (the company is indicated in parentheses after the name of the officer and his relative seniority):

Right Wing	*Left Wing*
Maj. Reno: 1	Capt. Benteen: 2 (H)
Capt. Keogh: 3 (I)	Capt. Weir: 4 (D)
Capt. Yates: 5 (F)	Capt. French: 6 (M)
Capt. Custer: 8 (C)	Capt. Moylan: 7 (A)
Capt. McDougall: 9 (B)	Lt. Godfrey: 10 (K)
Lt. Smith: 11 (E)	Lt. McIntosh: 12 (G)
Lt. Calhoun: 13 (L)	

The one deviation from a strict system of seniority is that Captain Tom Custer and Captain Myles Moylan were out of proper sequence, their positions being reversed. There seems no way to account for such a disturbance in the arrangement made at Fort Lincoln except to conclude that Custer made an arbitrary decision—though one consistent with a commanding officer's privilege—to accommodate his brother and perhaps even Benteen.[3] Tom may have asked his brother to revise the wing assignments so that he and his Company C would not fall under the command of Benteen, who might have been expected to treat Tom badly to settle old accounts. Custer would certainly have been sympathetic to Tom's concerns and could have made that judgment so as to forestall future internal squabbles and to promote good order within the ranks. At the Powder River, Custer had made a similar decision when he had allowed Tom to remain behind on the Reno scout. The general had always looked after his younger sibling's interests and welfare, just as President Ulysses Grant and Generals Philip Sheridan and Alfred Terry—among many in a government and an army "full of assiduous nepotists"—took care of their relatives.[4]

The other interesting feature of the wing assignments made at Fort Lincoln concerns Benteen and Captain Myles Keogh, two men who had been promoted to the rank of captain on the same date. The only way that Custer could have decided on Benteen as a wing commander was on the basis of his brevet rank of colonel; Keogh held the brevet rank of lieutenant colonel. In spite of Benteen's belief that his political connections forced Custer's hand, Custer in fact followed military protocol, although he may have been sorely tempted to find an alternative solution.

Since Custer had decided to resurrect the wing structure, and since he planned personally to lead one of the two primary components, it was logical that he would bump Reno down to the left wing and would himself take command of the right wing. Within that wing, Custer now created two battalions, one under Captain Keogh and the second under Captain George Yates. Again, having made virtually all assignments by rank and date of grade, Custer naturally continued in that manner:

Battalion 1	Battalion 2
Capt. Keogh: 1 (I)	Capt. Yates: 2 (F)

Capt. Custer: 3 (C)   Lt. Smith: 4 (E)
Lt. Calhoun: 5 (L)

For the time being, all companies within this wing would march as a single component. Company B under Captain Thomas McDougall was assigned to guard the pack train, but on paper his unit belonged to the Custer wing.

Nominal command of the left wing now fell to Major Reno, but because Custer's plan envisaged a rough encirclement of the satellite Sans Arc camp, that wing was divided into two parts, designed to operate as separate and distinct arms during at least the first phase of the operation.

Battalion 1   *Battalion 2*
Maj. Reno: 1   Capt. Benteen: 2 (H)
Capt. French: 4 (M)   Capt. Weir: 3 (D)
Capt. Moylan: 5 (A)   Lt. Godfrey: 6 (K)
Lt. McIntosh: 7 (G)

The configuration of this wing may have occupied most of the quarter-hour that Custer and Cooke spent scribbling on paper. In the regulation scheme of things, Captain Thomas French should have been with Benteen, and Captain Thomas Weir with Reno, but Custer twiddled their positions for unknown reasons. One possibility for this departure was that Weir and Reno did not get along; another was that Custer intended for his compatriot Weir to look after and perhaps influence the maverick Benteen.

Personalities aside, Custer likely made his decision based on the relative strengths of the companies. Captain French and his M Troop were the strongest component in the regiment in terms of leadership, experience, and numbers, and if Reno was to have the advance, he would need the most capable force available. In deciding to proceed in this way, placing Benteen in his customary reserve role and giving the second-in-command Reno the lead position, Custer chose to consign the fate of the regiment to the vicissitudes of the army's seniority system.

Once again it was Lieutenant Charles Varnum who, in retrospect, provided an insight into this facet of Custer's personality: "Benteen and Reno always hated him. Custer knew this but was considerate of them and was always ready to do them favors."[5] The causes of Benteen's disdain for the regimental commander have already been documented at some length. In Reno's case, the major and brevet colonel had graduated from West Point several years ahead of the young upstart Custer, and in the aftermath of the Little Bighorn fight, he would recall that he had known Custer for a long time and had had "no confidence in his ability as a soldier."[6] Yet this was an opinion expressed by a neophyte, who until this expedition had never served with Custer on the frontier and whose only Indian-fighting experience had been the recent Powder River excursion and a three-month scout in Colorado during the summer of 1870.[7] Supposedly, some men in the regiment had urged Custer to drop Reno from the command of any supporting movement, but Custer was following army procedure, regardless of personal feelings.[8]

The second decision that Custer had to make at the halt after crossing the Divide concerned the composition of the pack train. Up to that point, a senior captain and three companies had provided security for the packs, and six, seven, or even eight enlisted men from each company had accompanied the train, in conformance with a regimental order promulgated at the mouth of the Rosebud. Since that time, Lieutenant Edward Mathey had reported to Custer every evening on the status of the packs, advising the general of those companies that had been deficient in managing their charges. Additionally, Custer himself had observed the poor performance of left-wing packers as they had left the Yellowstone depot and of the entire regiment as it had departed clumsily up the Rosebud under the watchful eye of General Terry. Lastly, and probably decisively, the night march had been a near disaster, not just because fallen packs had revealed the location of the regiment but also, and more important, because the entire train had straggled terribly. The regiment could afford to lose nonessential cargo, cutting it loose if necessary, but the mules carrying the ammunition would have to keep up. The hundred or so rounds carried by each trooper and his horse would not last long in a big fight.

For these reasons, Custer must have made a deliberate decision that the soldiers from the right wing could best provide the kind of support necessary to keep the train closed up, since they had the experience of Reno's extended scout. Besides, if they could perform the function as efficiently as Custer expected, this would free up other men to accompany the advance combat units. As it turned out, a few troopers from the left wing did remain with the packs, but only because they had either shown exceptional proficiency in managing the mules or were detailed to perform some special duty, such as leading an officer's second horse.

If the records of individual soldiers are anywhere near correct, the companies in Custer's right wing were depleted by having the following numbers of enlisted men assigned to the packs: C, eight; E, ten; F, six; I, eight; L, twelve—for a total of forty-four. The left wing's contingents were reduced as follows: A, two; D, none; G, three; H, one; K, two; M, none—for a total of eight. These fifty-two men operated under the authority of Lieutenant Mathey. In addition, from six to ten civilian packers accompanied the mule train. One Arikara was detailed to drive the five pack mules assigned to the scouts.[9]

Counting the approximately forty cavalrymen in McDougall's B Troop who guarded the pack train, some one hundred men pushed the 160 or so mules in the general direction of the objective. The contingent assigned to the packs was roughly comparable to the number of enlisted men who had driven the train of about 150 mules on Reno's scout. However, instead of a battalion protecting the supplies, as had been the case in the early stages of the march up the Rosebud, there was now only a single company.

It is hard to know whether McDougall minded being the protector of this wild bunch, but if in fact he was the last to report when Custer experimented with the march by merit, he may have been content with the task. According to his own testimony, he reported to Custer on 25 June at about 11:00 A.M. "on the divide" for orders and was told that he would be in charge of the rear guard. Since Keogh and Yates had already had turns as keepers of the mules, and since Tom was acting aide-de-camp and as such would probably have been the last captain so assigned, it made sense that the junior captain, McDougall, would be saddled with the least-desirable assignment within the right-wing structure, whether he reported late or not. Whatever the reason for his being stuck with the tail end of the column, there is no evidence that he was discontented.[10]

Having followed the general course of Davis Creek, the Seventh emerged from one of the many shallow depressions west of the Divide and northwest of the Wolf Mountains. The likely order of march over the second ridge in the Divide was Custer and his headquarters detachment, the left wing (with Reno in the advance position), the right wing, the pack train, and the rear guard under McDougall. No orders had yet been given for dealing with the satellite village indicated by the Lone Tepee some eight miles away.[11]

Once the Seventh had passed over that second or lower ridge, Custer was able to see down into the broken plain and to deploy his forces accordingly. Perhaps he had already begun to formulate a plan of attack based on his observations from the Crow's Nest, but only now could he actually point to the lines of march that he wanted his subordinate battalions to follow. Whether he fully explained his intentions is unknown, but Libbie once said: "The general planned every military action with so much secrecy that we were left to divine as best we could what certain preliminary movements meant."[12] At the Washita, he had told his subordinates of his plan, but the Washita was a fixed objective and the target of a synchronized surprise attack at dawn. The Little Bighorn represented a somewhat different situation, and it is not known whether Custer told his subordinates much beyond "preliminary movements." By nature a private person, Custer was less likely than most to open himself to criticism, but in this case he imparted to Reno and Benteen a fuller understanding of the tactical objective—the Sans Arc camp—than they ever admitted after the battle.

According to Benteen, Custer divided the regiment and gave orders for the disposition of forces at the same time. Such a coincidence of events is impossible to believe on several counts. First, Benteen repeatedly stated that Cooke delivered the particulars of the company assignments and the line of march in what was essentially a single order while the regiment was surrounded by hills. Having designated H, D, and K Troops as Benteen's battalion, the commander's tactical directive was that the captain should proceed to high ground to the left, from two to five miles distant. However, if the regiment was enclosed by hills, it would have been totally out of the question for anyone to point to an objective completely out of sight.

Second, Private Charles Windolph claimed that he heard Benteen say to Custer: "Hadn't we better keep the regiment together, General? If this is as big a camp as they say, we'll need every man we have." To this concern, Custer is alleged to have responded, "You have your orders." Windolph was a member of Benteen's Company H and a loyal adherent, and his story may therefore be apocryphal, but if true, it means that Benteen spoke to Custer and did not receive his supposedly senseless orders through the adjutant.[13]

Second in the line of march, Benteen was the first to leave. As he moved to the front, Reno allegedly asked where he was going, and Benteen supposedly replied that he was going to the left with instructions to pitch into whatever lay in the hills. Reno may have been shocked to discover that half of his wing was being detached to perform a function that, he would later claim, was a total mystery to him, but he may also have been given to understand that the components of his full command would eventually be reunited. Later, at the court of inquiry, he asserted that when assigned his complement of companies by Cooke, he asked, "Is that all?" Cooke replied, "Yes." Doubtless Reno expected more—that is, the entire left wing. He added that he "made no further inquiries but moved my column to the *second ridge* [emphasis added]."[14]

In this testimony, Reno did not mention receiving any orders at this point, from either Custer or Cooke. In his official report prepared after the battle, he stated that he "assumed command of the companies assigned to me and without any definite orders moved forward with the rest of the column and well to its left."[15]

Thus it is not certain that Reno received orders directly from Custer after the regiment passed over that second ridge, but Lieutenant Edgerly's testimony at the court of inquiry makes clear that Reno did in fact get instructions from someone:

> Captain Benteen was ordered to move to the left at about an angle of 45 degrees and to pitch into anything he came to, and Major Reno's orders were to move down the valley and attack anything he came to. Those were all the *orders I heard* [emphasis added].

Since Edgerly was second-in-command to Weir in Company D within Benteen's battalion, he could only have heard the orders to Reno before Benteen left to commence his valley hunting. Also, if Edgerly heard the orders given to those two men, it is more likely that Custer announced the orders himself, while the officers were gathered in a group, than that Cooke went around and conveyed the instructions to individual battalion commanders. Unfortunately, at the court of inquiry the nature of the recorder's questions caused Edgerly to compress the creation of battalions and the issuance of orders into a single event, as others had done.

121

The recorder was sufficiently interested in this subject, however, that he recalled Edgerly to the stand for clarification:

> Q: Any impression you might have had with regard to the part Major Reno was to take in those engagements was merely an impression of your own?
> A: That is all, except the order given him to charge *towards the village* [emphasis added], that was the only command I heard given him.[16]

Thus, in his second explanation of what he had heard, Edgerly added the important information that Reno was ordered to "charge towards the village." The only village that was in sight at this point, and the only one that could have reasonably been "charged," was the Lone Tepee encampment some seven miles away, not the fully concealed main Indian camp five miles beyond that. Rather than being forced to move forward without any definite instructions, as Reno contended, he had clear and explicit orders to charge a known military objective. By definition, a cavalry charge in those days was "a direct and impetuous march, the object of which is to strike the enemy." Reno could not have misunderstood or forgotten those orders, except in a deliberate effort to deceive and obfuscate in his official report and while on the witness stand, sworn to tell the truth.[17]

Probably as he planned the attack, Custer expected that Reno's smaller battalion would reach the campsite first and that his own wing of five companies might be somewhat slower. That Custer considered Reno's unit the vanguard is clear from the way it was used subsequently and from the fact that Custer sent two of the three surgeons with Reno. The advance unit was more likely than supporting elements to suffer casualties. Doctors James DeWolf and Henry Porter accompanied Reno while the senior physician, Dr. George Lord, remained with Custer.

No doctor went with Benteen, suggesting that Custer considered that battalion a blocking force to contain the Lone Tepee inhabitants and to guard against any satellite villages among the hills on the left flank. Custer had surely examined those hills while he was at the Crow's Nest, but just as he could not determine from that vantage point how large the main camp was or even precisely how many tepees were concealed among the cotton-woods near the Lone Tepee, he could not be certain whether there were lodges hidden by the high ground to his left, the area that Benteen had been sent to inspect. Sending Benteen there was a mere precaution, taken with little expectation that those three companies would find any Indians to fight, or Custer would have sent a surgeon along.

Benteen had his own explanation for the absence of a doctor among his number. Responding to Dr. Porter's reported remark that Custer had ordered him to join Reno, Benteen argued that such a decision would have been made by Dr. Lord, the senior surgeon. Benteen thought that the question of assigning doctors was somehow beneath Custer and that Dr. Lord made judgments of this kind independent of Custer's plans, opinions, or desires. Again, Benteen could not admit what he knew to be true: once more he had been relegated to a reserve role, his persistent and painful fate.[18]

Besides the instruction for Benteen to search the hills and valleys south of the main advance, he had another mission, as explained by Edgerly:

> The idea I had was if they [the Indians] ran out of the village we would strike them on the left, and if the right, then some other part of the command [would strike them].[19]

If Edgerly had that idea, it likely came from hearing some amplification of the orders, probably given by Custer himself to Benteen. And at that juncture, the directions could only have pertained to the community of mourners at the Lone Tepee.

Edgerly's testimony is decisive in indicating Benteen's primary mission, and if the bystander Edgerly knew this mission, then certainly Benteen did too. And if they both knew, Reno knew as well, just as Captain French and Sergeant John Ryan of Company M knew. No matter how abrupt Custer's orders were, they were clear to all who could hear and all who cared to remember. Sufficient clues were available at the court of inquiry for the truth to have been ascertained, but the recorder, Lieutenant Jesse Lee, never pressed that line of questioning. Custer divided the regiment near the headwaters of Reno Creek, for perfectly sound tactical reasons consistent with a logical battle plan. That decision, in concert with subsequent developments, would dictate the follow-up disposition of forces, which may have already taken shape in Custer's mind as a contingency plan aimed at the main Sioux and Cheyenne village.

Except for the scouts, who had left to perform their duties before the departure of the main body of the regiment, Benteen and his three companies headed out first, at about 12:15. The order of march was Benteen's H Troop, followed by D (Weir/Edgerly), and K (Godfrey). In giving this half of the left wing to Benteen, Custer had been more than fair in terms of assigning combat capability to the battalion.

Whatever his personal shortcomings, Benteen was a capable and energetic leader once committed to a fight. According to the best information available, Benteen's battalion was composed of five officers and approximately 125 enlisted men. Benteen's recollection was that after his unit departed, Reno was "given time" before moving out with his command. Since Reno was operating under orders to charge in nearly a straight line to the objective, it made sense that there was a delay between Benteen's leaving on a roundabout circuit and Reno's departure.[20]

Being given the honor of the advance with just three companies was probably the last thing that Reno wanted. By nature and experience a staff officer, with the voice of a "first-rate drillmaster," he might have been better off training new recruits in St. Louis. When he asked Cooke, "Is that all?" he was almost certainly reaching for that flask on the inside of his blouse to find the elixir that might numb his rapidly fraying nerves. Although he may have had no confidence in Custer's ability as a soldier, Reno likely would have given anything to cling to his commander's buckskin.[21]

As Reno's battalion departed the second ridge, the order of march was Companies M, A, and G, ordered by rank and seniority, as had been the case with Benteen's squadron. At the head of the column, after Reno and his staff, was Captain French and M Troop. Presumably by design, Custer had given Reno probably the strongest single unit in the regiment and arguably the most courageous company commander. "A first-class officer" was how Sergeant Ryan described French.[22]

Reno's battalion consisted of six officers, two doctors, and about 145 enlisted men, far more than the 112 as claimed by Reno and Lieutenant George Wallace at the court of inquiry. Counting Wallace, Varnum, and Lieutenant Luther Hare (plus their orderlies), as well as the Crow, Arikara, and civilian scouts who would eventually accompany Reno down the Little Bighorn Valley, the vanguard totaled around 180 men, not much smaller than Custer's wing of the regiment.

Even though the Custer column had the advantage of above-average leadership in each of its five companies, the ranks had been depleted by detaching men to accompany the packs. Of the forty-four soldiers left with the mule train, five were sergeants and twenty-eight were so-called veterans (nonrecruits). Thus approximately 15 percent of the effective fighting strength of this wing was absent, and more important, the bulk of those performing the essential function of moving supplies of ammunition and rations were men who might also have been valuable in the opening stages of a fight.

Besides the men in the companies of the right wing, the headquarters command included Custer, his brother Tom, Adjutant Cooke, the engineering officer Lieutenant Wallace (until he departed to join Reno), Sergeant Major William Sharrow, Chief Trumpeter Henry Voss, Color Sergeant Robert Hughes, Dr. Lord, and several orderlies, one of whom was Trumpeter John Martin (born Giovanni Martini) of H Troop. Additionally, one noncommissioned officer and four soldiers from Company F may have been detailed to ride with the regimental commander as a kind of honor guard. Also with the headquarters component were Custer's nephew Autie Reed, the reporter Mark Kellogg—who rode his mule as quickly as he could to keep up with the head of the column—and probably Boston Custer. The total number of soldiers in Custer's wing was around 220 before messengers arrived or left and before some men dropped out.[23]

The last to begin the downhill trek was the pack train. The one hundred or so men who guided the mules started forward about twenty minutes after Custer's wing had departed, according to Captain McDougall, who was bringing up the rear with his Company B. He stated that although he was not sure whose trail he was following, he tried to keep the unwieldy caravan near the center of the three columns. Although he later claimed that he had not seen Benteen leave because of straggling mules, McDougall said that he observed that battalion about 700–800 yards away and in motion after the mule train got under way.[24]

Custer's intention at that time was to sneak up in a hurry so as to surprise a small village of Indians, who would bolt at the first sign of an approaching column. Located in a more forward position with the packs, Lieutenant Mathey likely had a better idea of direction than McDougall, although both officers must have recognized the need for concealment under the pressure of time. According to Mathey, after the column had passed the Divide and had gone some distance, Adjutant Cooke came back with orders from Custer to keep the mules off the trail because they were raising too much dust. Later, Cooke returned, and when Mathey asked if there had been improvement, Cooke said yes.[25] At about the same time, Mathey reported that McDougall was urging him to move the mules as fast as possible, but this was difficult because of the continuing need to repack. The frustration of this work was apparent in Mathey's description several years after the battle: "When a mule became unpacked, I would leave two men to pack him and go ahead with the train and leave them to bring up that mule. We pushed along with a good deal of trouble."[26]

In short, the damned mules wandered or faltered, would not retain their cargoes, and were in general a drag on the advance. It was no easy task for either McDougall or Mathey as they followed haphazardly in the wake of Custer's methodical push toward a small but crucial target. The several visits made by Cooke are ample evidence that Custer had neither forgotten nor forsaken the supplies, which might finally prove essential and which in the organization of the regiment properly belonged to the right wing. Keep the mule train closed up, Custer must have said, but do not let them betray our position.

Meanwhile, the scouts had kept the Lone Tepee site under surveillance for an hour or more. The Crow scout Curley said that he, Boyer, and four of his brethren had watched the Sioux with field glasses in the early afternoon before the arrival of Custer's command. Curley stated:

> [The party] lay on a rocky hill *all forenoon* [emphasis added] watching *the Sioux* [emphasis added], and the lone tepee in the Indian camp [was] down under them, to the left.

In a separate statement, he noted that Boyer and the Crows had watched the Sioux through field glasses from a rocky bluff "just opposite" the Lone Tepee. The import of Curley's testimony is that the Lone Tepee was the focus of the Crow scouts' attention for an extended period of time during the 12:00–2:00 P.M. period. Also, they were looking at a body of Indians, not just a single burial lodge.[27]

The Crow scout Hairy Moccasin added:

> I went to *a butte at the head of Reno Creek, from where I could see the village* [emphasis added]. I reported the camp to Custer. He asked if any were running about away from the camp. I said, "No." We *then* [emphasis added] came on down to the forks of Reno Creek.

To his interviewer, Hairy Moccasin stated this as a matter of fact, without reference to it as an event of consequence. It simply occurred, and Hairy Moccasin went on with his story. But from the context of his responses, it is clear that this incident occurred well before the Crows separated from Custer an hour or so later at the junction of Reno Creek and its North Fork. The village to which Hairy Moccasin referred was situated at the Lone Tepee site, and the occupants had not yet begun to run.[28]

The recollections of the Arikara scout Young Hawk help to locate the position of the Crows.

> [The Arikara scouts] went down the dry coulee and when about half way to the high ridge to the right, Young Hawk saw a group of scouts at the lower end of the ridge *peering over toward the lone tepee* [emphasis added]. The scouts he was with slowed up as the others came toward them. Then behind them they heard a call from Gerard. He said to them: "The Chief [Custer] says for you to run."

The Crows had reconnoitered the Lone Tepee for some time and had determined that the residents were still in place, and Custer wanted the Arikara scouts to get out front. The nexus between watching the Sans Arc camp and charging it was established.[29]

Exactly what were the Crows watching, and from where were they making their observations? It is hard to know for sure. According to Private Daniel Newell's remembrance, Custer had seen perhaps a dozen lodges in a late-night or mid-morning visit, apparently with DeRudio's invaluable field glasses—ten more tepees than Varnum could recollect seeing from the Crow's Nest. If a dozen is a proximate number, there were fifty to one hundred Indians paying their last respects to the warrior who had died. They were four or five miles from the Little Bighorn and within a mile or so of the chalky bluffs from which Boyer, Curley, and the other Crows had apparently been observing their activity. The precise point within those easily identifiable white bluffs where Boyer and the Crows lay in hiding is not known.

A week earlier, the entire Sioux-Cheyenne village—less some number of late arrivals—had occupied the ground in a glorious continuation of the Sun Dance summer. A cadre of mostly young men had suffered the pain of initiation and confirmation along the trail up the Rosebud, and the Indians were in good spirits, a confidence born of size and unity and reinforced by Sitting Bull's vision of soldiers falling into their camp. All the way up the Rosebud, Custer and his men had seen the evidence of that celebration, including traces of the many families and bands arriving from the agencies, without necessarily grasping the meaning. By 15 June the growing assemblage of Indians had crossed over the Divide into the valley of Reno Creek and established their village along a narrow strip of generally rolling earth, the whole camp being perhaps two miles in length. Out of this small city had poured about five hundred warriors—including Sitting Bull and Crazy Horse—intent on confronting the body of soldiers approaching from the south, led by General Crook. From this group of valorous Indians who met Crook's column on 17 June, about a dozen were killed, but only one would be memorialized by the burning image of the Lone Tepee.[30]

The warrior who was housed in that richly decorated mausoleum has been variously identified as Little Wolf or Plenty Bears or Old She Bear or Sitting Bear, a Sans Arc and possibly the brother of Circling or Turning Bear. The dead warrior had been shot in both hips, in the bowels, or somewhere else in the midsection. Exactly when he died is not clear, but it may have been as late as the evening of 24 June, and if so, he must have suffered greatly before passing on. The likelihood is that he was still alive when the Sioux and Cheyennes moved their village from Reno Creek to the western side of the Little Bighorn on 18 June and that he died some days after that, causing his relatives and friends to remain at the site, in accordance with customary mourning traditions.[31]

To reach the objective, Custer's wing followed Reno's lead down from the higher ground to the upper end of Reno Creek, a mostly dry streambed that ran to the Little Bighorn River. Custer may have continued to trail behind Reno on the left side for some time, and at least according to Sergeant Daniel Kanipe, they may have stopped once to water the horses in the few pools of water laying stagnant and no doubt alkaline in the easternmost length of the creek. At an unidentified point (perhaps as far as the landmark Morass), the two columns split, with Reno remaining on the left and Custer going to the right of the creek. Whether Custer crossed the streambed more than once is unclear, but since he intended to surprise the inhabitants, he probably hugged the tree-lined banks as long as possible, to within a mile or so of the target.[32]

The two columns were now moving parallel to one another down Reno Creek. Custer's command was separated from Reno's by as little as fifty yards or as much as several hundred yards, depending on the terrain, which tended to be undulating and sagebrush-covered, with occasional stands of cottonwood. Also, the ground was cut up by deep ravines that fed into the creek. Although in the initial stage of the advance neither column had probably moved much faster than a fast walk or a slow trot, the pace was about to increase.

At some point before the Lone Tepee was reached, Custer sent two messages to Benteen, whose column was probably still in sight over to the left while the main body was descending the Divide to Reno Creek. For the contents of those two orders, the historical record is totally dependent on the memory and veracity of Benteen, who presumably did not bother to share the text with any subordinate. According to Benteen, his column had gone about a mile from the Divide when Chief Trumpeter Voss arrived with Custer's instructions that if the battalion found nothing in the designated hills, it should move on to the following line of bluffs. After another mile, or about fifteen minutes later, Sergeant Major Sharrow delivered the message that if Benteen discovered nothing at the second objective, he was to continue until he came to an unidentified valley, to "pitch into" any Indians he encountered, and to notify Custer at once. In short, the original orders and the follow-up messages were essentially the same except that the latter ostensibly extended Benteen's reconnaissance by some distance. Almost certainly Custer's expectation was that Benteen's line of march would take that column to the South Fork of Reno Creek, opposite the Lone Tepee, or—more precisely from Custer's point of view—about three small valleys beyond the starting point.[33]

With Custer's orders and amplifying instructions in hand, Benteen trudged on in search of unspecified valleys and unseen enemies—or so Benteen wanted his later audience to believe. When he realized that Custer was apparently leading the regiment into battle without him (he said he saw the Gray Horse Troop galloping), Benteen became frustrated and angry, and it would now take a very special invitation to move him faster than a walk.[34] A fellow officer (Second Lieutenant Charles Roe of the Second Cavalry) later told Walter Camp what Benteen only hinted at. According to Roe, "Benteen's friends" felt that Custer had sent the captain off to the left in order to keep him out of the fight, a particular slight since Benteen was supposed to have the advance "and should regularly have been with head-quarters." Of course Benteen did not have the advance in any sense of the word except that he left first because he had a greater distance to cover, and if his "friends" believed that he did have the advance, Benteen must have told them so. No matter how wrongheaded, no matter how much at variance with the facts, such sentiments doubtless reflected Benteen's own assessment of the situation.[35]

Enlisted men from top to bottom understood what was taking place. Sergeant Kanipe noted: "Major Reno was to the left and abreast with General Custer and Captain Benteen was to the left of Major Reno. You could tell that the plan was to strike the Indian camp at three places. . . . We went at a gallop. Turning down what is now Benteen's Creek [Reno Creek], we made our way to a crossing and found a vacated camp on the other side. The fires were not all out."[36] Private Francis Kennedy said that the regiment attacked the village from three directions, with Custer taking "the end farthest to the right, Reno the center of the main village and Benteen the left end."[37]

Private John Donoughue went even further, claiming that he actually heard Custer give the instructions. "'Major Reno you will charge down the valley and sweep everything that will come before you; Captain Benteen will take the extreme left. I will take the extreme right myself with five companies.' . . . General Custer here described the point that Major Reno should strike the camp supported by Captain Benteen and his three companies. 'I will strike them on the opposite point and we will crush them between us.'"[38] In the context of the other evidence, and in view of the rest of Donoughue's story regarding an actual charge on the Lone Tepee, his testimony is plausible, although by his reckoning, Custer made his scheme known to his subordinates even before the Seventh crossed the Divide.

Private Jean Baptiste Desire Gallenne of Reno's leading Company M observed that having been organized in "columns of attack," the several parts of the regiment moved forward until they perceived "a wigwam of war and a large column of dust about ten [sic] miles ahead." He added, "We believe[d] it to be the Indians retreating."[39]

Perhaps a mile or so from the Lone Tepee, the Custer and Reno columns began to shift into a near gallop. It was 1:30–1:45 on a sultry summer afternoon. The pressure was on the scouts to provide current intelligence on the strength and disposition of the opposing forces. Trumpeter Martin remembered scouts riding in and out. After hearing from them, Custer would "gallop away a short distance to look around." The Crow Hairy Moccasin had already told Custer that the Indians were not running, but now Boyer and his group were coming in with additional news. For a time, Varnum had been one of those reporting to Custer on what he had seen, but Varnum had long since separated from the Arikaras (who were now with Hare) and was in the process of working his way far in advance and to the left with just his orderly. An exact reconstruction of scouting activities at this point is nearly impossible, but obviously a great deal was happening very quickly.[40]

The experience of Lieutenant Hare is probably a fair indicator of the excitement prevailing during this period. Responsible for all of the scouts in Varnum's absence, Hare was operating in advance with direct orders from Custer to maintain vigilance and to report as soon as Indians were found. Looking behind, Hare discovered that Custer and the command were gaining on him, so he increased his gait. In spite of his faster pace, Sergeant Major Sharrow caught up "in a great rush" and, after presenting the general's compliments, asked why Custer had heard nothing from Hare. The lieutenant returned the compliments and answered that if he discovered any Indians, he would report them. In Hare's mind, Custer seemed to be very impatient. Of course he was.[41]

Custer may have been charging, but it was already too late. The Arikara Strikes Two reached the Lone Tepee first and struck it with his whip. He was followed by his comrades, who rode around the target. Young Hawk then went to the north side of the lodge and cut it open. According to George Herendeen, he helped slash the thin shell of the tepee to see what was inside. The only trophy for the first phase of Custer's battle plan was a man already dead.[42]

The dead warrior was a Sans Arc, dressed in attire appropriate to his standing within the community. In accordance with Indian tradition, he had been supplied with the equipage necessary for his trip into the next world. Whether there was a second lodge standing or knocked over is not certain from the evidence, but one trooper clearly recalled two tepees decorated with elaborate charcoal drawings, and it is at least possible that one of the dwellings was pulled down by the Arikara scouts, confusing the issue in the host of testimony that referred to the site. In any case, the Lone Tepee remained upright.[43]

When Custer arrived, he ordered his men to burn the lodge. Sergeant Kanipe recalled hearing Custer tell his orderly to set the tepee afire. Private Peter Thompson remembered that Custer directed a detail from F Troop to "investigate" the contents of the death lodge and thought it may have been these men who were responsible for the fire. This was an act of desecration, no different in essence from the Sioux practice of digging up dead enemies to fill their bodies with arrows or otherwise mutilating them before they departed for the great beyond. The comparison is not meant to justify Custer's decision or to mitigate the horror of the deed, but on the American frontier, extreme brutality was the special province of no ethnic group, even if the victims were long past caring. Besides, as explained below, Custer may have had another purpose in mind for the little conflagration, which did not entirely destroy the Lone Tepee.[44]

As the burial lodge burned, Reno's battalion appeared from around the hills bordering the creek to the south. Although Reno commanded nominally the advance combat unit, he was hard-pressed to keep up with Custer, not only because Custer was more eager and determined but also because Reno had more difficult terrain to pass over. The ground on the south side of Reno Creek was more broken and hilly and was intersected by a major tributary (No Name Creek) of that stream. Both prongs of the assault force had alternated between a trot and a gallop, depending on the lay of the land, but Reno's squadron had the disadvantage and so arrived some minutes after Custer.

The most vivid description of Reno's approach to the Lone Tepee was provided by Private Donoughue. "Only a short distance ahead we saw smoke, the men calling out 'villages ahead.' Our officers ahead raised their hands and gave the command 'charge.' Then came the throwing away of all surplus material, such as overcoats, haversacks, etc., to make themselves as light as possible and be in fighting trim. Reaching the place where the smoke was seen it was found to come from a lone tepee which General Custer's command set fire to and destroyed."[45]

As Reno appeared in sight, Custer waved him over to the north side of the creek. After all, there was no need for Reno to continue operating on the left, now that they had determined that the Lone Tepee was in fact only a single burial lodge located about where the South Fork connected with Reno Creek, over four miles from the Little Bighorn River. The first phase of Custer's battle plan had reached a most unsatisfactory conclusion.

An assortment of witnesses would later characterize Custer as amiable and depressed, good-natured and gloomy, jaunty and sad, an assortment of conflicted emotions. He had just experienced a severe disappointment, a setback to a plan that envisaged a relatively easy victory, but he retained the initiative. Now he would have to resort to the military dictum of "audacity, audacity," which in real terms meant exploiting the available opportunity with all of the invention, imagination, and flamboyance that he could summon from his highly charged memory banks. Setting fire to the Lone Tepee was the first step in a revised stratagem of trying to cow a superior force, as he had done so many times during the Civil War, almost always with a positive result. As he observed in *My Life on the Plains,* referring to his unorthodox maneuvers to extricate his forces at the Washita: "I again had recourse to that maxim in war that teaches a commander to do that which his enemy neither expects nor desires him to do."[46]

He was perhaps only moments too late to catch some captives. It is not known who alerted the Sans Arc village about the advance of Custer's column, but the messenger may have been the lone Indian sighted by the scouts Herendeen and Boyer. Regardless of the source of the warning, the inhabitants had been startled and were on the scoot, still within sight but beyond the reach of even the fastest-moving of Custer's components. The Sans Arc escapees would arrive in the main village only a short time before Major Reno began his attack on that encampment.[47]

In their wake, the Sans Arcs left evidence of their hurried departure. Sergeant Kanipe said that when Custer reached the Lone Tepee, fires were still smoldering. Private Thomas O'Neill stated that the "small band of Indians" had evidently been surprised and had "retreated to a larger camp on the river." In their rush to leave, they had left "their cooking utensils on the fires."[48] The scout Herendeen called it "a freshly abandoned Indian camp."[49] At the court of inquiry, Lieutenant DeRudio recalled: "The impression was that the Indians had left the village very suddenly not long before."[50] The interpreter Gerard provided a simpler, if somewhat confused, characterization of the event: "The camp we had found was the smaller camp (the larger camp was downstream farther), and was on the way to the larger camp and this led us all to believe that the Indians were stampeded."[51]

Although Custer did indeed charge this site while on his way to the main camp, the flushing of the satellite village was not an accident, a mere incidental occurrence along the path to greater glory. The event was central to his overall intentions, and his failure—through no fault of his own—to grasp that moment and that opportunity would cost more than even he could have foreseen. By the word of officers and enlisted men alike, Custer's purpose was known. He had a plan, the self-serving falsehoods of Reno and Benteen and perhaps other officers to the contrary.

In a letter written a month after the battle, Reno betrayed his knowledge of what had happened: "My battalion was to the left and rear when we approached the village, but [was] brought to the front by Custer." What had been a village was, by the time Reno arrived on the scene, just the Lone Tepee, too minuscule or too embarrassing to be recollected by anyone as more than a landmark en route to short-term disaster and long-term recriminations.[52]

CHAPTER SEVEN

A FATAL SEPARATION

"Here are your Indians, running like devils!" the Arikara interpreter Fred
Gerard shouted, wheeling his horse and waving his hat to draw attention
to his announcement.[1]

Indeed, the refugees from the vacated Sans Arc camp were fleeing over
the broken and uneven ground between the Lone Tepee and the Little
Bighorn. Custer paused in the vicinity of the burial lodge while he absorbed
the information available in the deserted village and received reports from
observers stationed on adjacent elevations. Having driven the inhabitants
of the Sans Arc village in the direction of the main Sioux-Cheyenne camp,
he was relatively close to the dust that marked their trail, perhaps no more
than two miles away. Doubtless he was impatient, but he did not rush. In
a period of ten to fifteen minutes, events were transpiring almost without
discernible sequence.

When Gerard announced his sighting of the skedaddling Sans Arcs, he
was located on a small hill twenty to twenty-five feet high and variously
estimated as fifty to two hundred yards from the Lone Tepee. In his court
of inquiry testimony, he claimed that from that knoll he saw a whole town,
with Indian tepees and ponies, and though in his memory he may have
misplaced the "town" on the far or western side of the Little Bighorn Valley,
in fact what he saw was the satellite village on the run.

The white scout George Herendeen also saw a heavy cloud of dust, as
well as stock apparently on the move. Like Gerard, he would mistakenly
suggest that viewed from the little hill, the retreating Indians and their

135

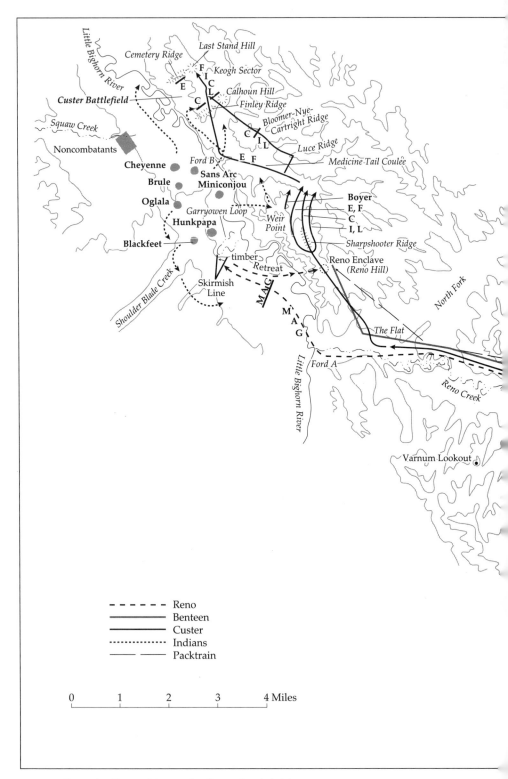

Little Bighorn River

Cemetery Ridge

Last Stand Hill

F
Keogh Sector
E
I
C
C
L
Calhoun Hill

Custer Battlefield

Finley Ridge

Bloomer-Nye-
Cartright Ridge

Squaw Creek

Noncombatants

C
I
L

Luce Ridge

Ford B

E
F

Medicine Tail Coulee

Cheyenne

Sans Arc

Brule
Miniconjou

Oglala

Boyer
E, F
C
I, L

Garryowen Loop

Hunkpapa

Weir
Point

Blackfeet

Sharpshooter Ridge

timber
Retreat

Reno Enclave
(Reno Hill)

North Fork

Skirmish
Line

M
A
C

M
A
G

The Flat

Shoulder Blade Creek

Ford A

Little Bighorn River

Reno Creek

Varnum Lookout

– – – – – Reno
————— Benteen
————— Custer
· · · · · · · Indians
—·—·—·— Packtrain

0   1   2   3   4 Miles

From the Crow's Nest to the Custer battlefield

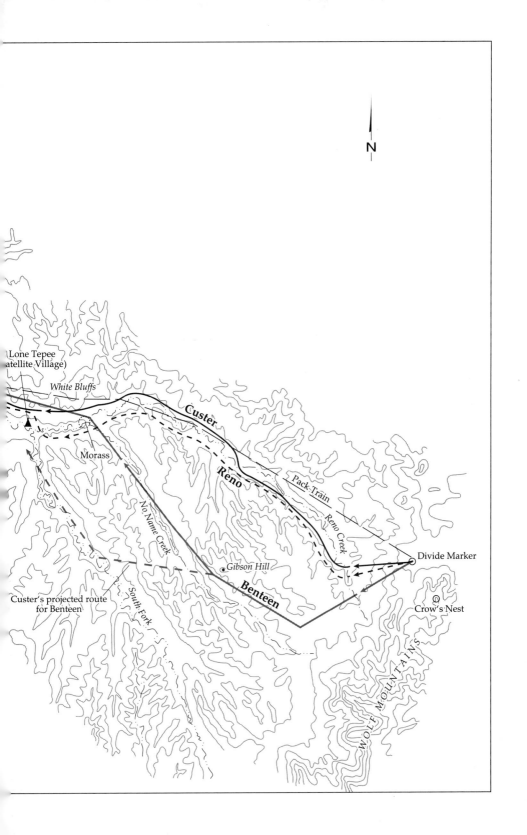

N

(Lone Tepee
Satellite Village)

White Bluffs

Custer

Morass

Reno

Pack Train

Reno Creek

No Name Creek

• *Gibson Hill*

Divide Marker

Custer's projected route
for Benteen

Benteen

South Fork

Crow's Nest

WOLF MOUNTAINS

animals could be seen in the river valley. Only if the ridgeline east of the river could be considered one side of the Little Bighorn "valley," or if he had in mind the North Fork of Reno Creek, would such an account comport with the facts. From that knoll, a person would simply not have been able to see into the low ground bordering the western banks of the Little Bighorn, five miles distant.[2]

The remainder of Herendeen's rendering became more consistent with reality. He noted that he saw "a few Indians on the hills riding very fast, and seemingly running away." He was clear that the sighting of the Indians occurred before the Lone Tepee was cut open. He told those with him that if the regiment did not hurry, the Indians could not be caught, at which point Lieutenant Luther Hare wrote a note to Custer.

Hare recalled that what he had observed from the hill close by the Lone Tepee were forty or fifty Indians on a rise between there and the river. In his opinion, the fleeing band must have "discovered" the presence of the soldiers because they soon disappeared—for the time being, at least. Yet the retreating village was probably moving less quickly than Gerard and Herendeen imagined, since it was surely burdened with noncombatant impedimenta.[3]

While this knot of scouts and interpreters was viewing the departure of the recent inhabitants of the Lone Tepee "town," Custer was approaching at a "stiff trot," the right wing in his wake. Whether Hare actually wrote a note to Custer and whether Custer ever came to the knoll to see the body of Indians for himself (as Gerard thought possible) is not clear from the other available evidence. The latter possibility is unlikely for the simple reason that Hare had remained long enough to see the withdrawing village vanish into the undulating terrain between the small promontory and the river, and he did not mention that Custer joined him on the hill.[4]

The right wing arrived soon after Custer, the cavalrymen in a state of "commotion," probably because they had ridden hard and ready for combat, only to discover that the military objective had vanished, leaving behind one dead warrior and the smoldering residue of the small village's recent departure. At that point, Custer's column stopped near the Lone Tepee while soldiers burned the lodge and while the general organized his available forces for pursuit. Herendeen came down from the knoll to help the Arikara scouts slash open the tepee, and Gerard accompanied him in order to be in a position to hear firsthand what Custer planned to do next.[5]

According to Major Marcus Reno's account of his crossing of the creek, he responded immediately when Custer beckoned by waving a hat, but passing through the dry, tree-lined creek bed proved difficult. When Reno's battalion reached the north side, it emerged in some disorder near the rear of Custer's column.

> I *there* [emphasis added] received an order from Lieutenant Cooke to move my command to the front. When I got there, there was a turmoil among the Indians that were with us as scouts. They were stripping themselves and preparing for a fight. . . . I moved forward in accordance with the orders received from Lieutenant Cooke to the head of the column.

Reno told the court of inquiry that "soon after" this, Lieutenant William Cooke arrived with final orders from Custer, even though there was in fact an interval of at least thirty minutes and three miles between the two events.[6]

In nearly all of his utterances, Reno maintained that he received a single order from Lieutenant Cooke and never spoke to Custer directly. Obviously, the above testimony represented a slight hiccup in his core story, but the inconsistency was never fully developed by the court recorder, Lieutenant Jesse Lee. Of course, Reno conveniently forgot that Custer had given him instructions at the Divide, and he and Lieutenant George Wallace would so muddy the true state of affairs after leaving the burial lodge that Custer's real final orders were subsumed within the body of conflicting and seemingly contradictory testimony regarding the "in-between" directives. Out of all the incidental features of the Little Bighorn cover-up, the concealment of the facts bearing on Custer's orders was central to perpetrating the big lie for the benefit of Major Reno and eventually for Captain Frederick Benteen. If Reno was credible, then it would be impossible to reconcile the testimony of all the other witnesses, each of whom thought that *he* had heard the one and only order given by Custer. To comprehend the disaster at the Little Bighorn, we must distinguish the four separate episodes within which orders were conveyed from Custer to Reno.

At the Lone Tepee, Adjutant Cooke delivered a simple "lead-out" order, and Reno moved his battalion out in front of the Arikaras. These scouts had prepared themselves for battle as the regiment moved over the Divide.

Custer had already given the scouts instructions to ride hard and take Sioux horses, and in preparation for the coming fight, the Arikaras had made good medicine for themselves by spitting on clay carried from their home villages and then rubbing the mixture into their chests. They had tightened the girths and lightened the loads on their ponies long before reaching the Lone Tepee.[7]

Either as Reno was crossing the creek or shortly before, Hare came down from the knoll and talked with Custer. In the course of that conversation, it was determined that the fifty or so Indians who had earlier disappeared into the landscape were visible again. Custer then ordered Hare to take the Arikara scouts and advance, saying that the soldiers would follow.[8] However, the Arikaras showed their good sense by refusing to advance without the soldiers. In his later court testimony, Hare stated: "The Indians refused to go and he [Custer] ordered them dismounted and turned around to Adjutant Cooke and told him, as the Indians would not go ahead, to order Major Reno with his battalion ahead." Hare informed the court that this order from Custer to Reno via Cooke occurred within a hundred yards of the Lone Tepee.[9]

At about the same time that Hare was descending the knoll, Lieutenant Charles Varnum was returning from his scout to the left. According to Varnum, he and his orderly (Private Elijah Strode) had been well out in advance of the regiment, probably a mile or so to the southwest, conducting a reconnaissance. In his memoirs, Varnum stated, "From every hill where I could see the valley, I saw Indians mounted." But at the court of inquiry, he stated that the lay of the land prevented visual access to much of the Little Bighorn bottomland. It is more likely that he saw the Sans Arcs on the move than that he detected any body of Sioux in the valley of the Little Bighorn. "I reported to the General saying I guess he could see about all I could of the situation," Varnum recalled. "'I don't know. What can you see?' said the General. 'The whole valley in front is full of Indians,' I replied, 'and you can see them when you take that rise' (pointing to the right front)."[10]

The only Indians who could be seen over the next rise were the Sans Arcs. By all other accounts there was no gathering of adversaries on the western side of the river—not yet. What Varnum saw was certainly that ephemeral collection of mourners, here and then gone, the group that he was sure Custer must have observed and would again see after he climbed the next hillock to the right-front. None of this surprised Custer, who had already foreseen the relationship between the twin targets, one fixed and one on the move. By burning the burial lodge, he was sending his calling card.[11]

When Varnum arrived, he saw all of the Arikaras "bunched behind Custer's staff." "Lonesome" Charley Reynolds, Mitch Boyer, Isaiah Dorman, Herendeen, and Gerard were still there. None of the scouts or interpreters had yet departed. Having given his report to the general, Varnum told Custer that the Rees had run away from him while he was out on his reconnaissance. Varnum then proceeded to cuss out the scouts "in pretty strong language, saying they were a pack of damned cowards." Varnum later recalled: "Custer said, 'Dismount them all and let them walk and lead their horses.' Gerard then said, 'I think they will follow me, General.' Custer said, 'Try it.' Gerard harangued them in their language and waving his arm, started off at a gallop."[12] Gerard later explained that it was all a misunderstanding. Custer had expected the Arikaras to hurry forward after the fleeing Sioux, but without Reno's vanguard, they were understandably reluctant to proceed, particularly in view of their relatively small numbers. No doubt Gerard's impassioned speech helped to persuade them otherwise, but more important, Reno's battalion was at that very moment marching to the front. The Arikara One Feather responded by scolding Gerard for running off with the soldiers and leaving the scouts without an interpreter, causing them to misunderstand the orders.[13]

And what exactly were Custer's initial "lead-out" orders for Reno, an event that occurred "in the vicinity of" the burial lodge, by Reno's own admission? Reno had just crossed the creek and was apparently waiting to the rear of Custer's position for further instructions when Adjutant Cooke arrived. But what did Cooke say that would contribute to such confusion in discerning the content and sequence of Custer's several orders? Of those who survived the battle, two people in a position to hear Cooke were Reno's orderly and a doctor.

The orderly, Private Edward Davern, recollected that a directive was received perhaps two hundred yards short of the Lone Tepee, while both columns were halted. "The order was, 'Girard [sic] comes back and reports the Indian village three miles ahead and moving. The General directs you to take your three companies and drive everything before you. . . . Colonel Benteen will be on your left and will have the same instructions.'" The reference to Gerard indicates that this message was conveyed after the departing satellite village had been sighted from the knoll near the Lone Tepee. The directive also reminded Reno that Benteen was still on his left, providing a screen under Custer's original concept of operations.[14]

Since Davern must have heard that order when Cooke went back to bring Reno's battalion forward, it is likely that Dr. Henry Porter recalled the same occurrence when he testified at the court of inquiry. He also remembered that Cooke had brought instructions from Custer to Reno "near" the Lone Tepee. "The adjutant came over and told him the Indians were just ahead and General Custer directed him to charge them. He [Reno] turned around and asked the adjutant if General Custer was going to support him. He [Cooke] said Custer would support him. He [Reno] asked him if the General was coming along and he told him, 'Yes,' the General would support him." Later in his testimony, Porter said that after delivering this order, Cooke "rode back" to the command.[15]

Thus, Davern and Porter provided intriguing additional recollections concerning this conversation between Reno and Cooke. That is, specific reference was made to Benteen in the obvious context of a plan, and it was Reno who pointedly asked whether Custer *personally* was going to support him.

Sergeant Daniel Kanipe said that after Reno had been called over (and after the "lead-out" order was given), Reno and Custer "rode side by side and Custer talked to him direct," a tête-à-tête that may have occupied "several hundred yards."[16] During this time, Gerard and Herendeen heard Custer again order Reno ahead, although at the court of inquiry and in almost all post-battle accounts, Reno would deny that Custer ever spoke to him in person. Gerard recalled that Custer said: "You [Reno] will take your battalion and try and overtake and bring them to battle and I [Custer] will support you. . . . And take the scouts with you." Herendeen stated: "I heard General Custer tell Major Reno to lead out and he would be with him. . . . He [Custer] said, 'Take the mounts [scouts] with you, too,' and I supposed that included me and I went along."[17] This was the third order given to Reno, the second near the Lone Tepee, and it was delivered by Custer himself. The question is why Reno would have stopped to speak with Custer after having already received an order, through Cooke, to advance to the head of the column and—as expressed in Davern's and Porter's testimony—to overtake those fleeing villagers seen by Gerard, Herendeen,

Varnum, and Hare. Long after the battle, Hare would concede: "Custer may have later repeated the order [delivered by Cooke] verbally."[18]

From Reno's own pen, we know that he did in fact ride with Custer for some distance and that they spoke. Many years after the battle and shortly before his death, Reno wrote what must have been his last testament on the affair, a document found among his effects. In this narrative, addressing the moments after he had crossed the creek, Reno described Custer as seeming "rather depressed," an impression that scarcely could have been gained while hurrying to get ahead of Custer's wing in pursuit of the Sans Arc band. Continuing, Reno confirmed that he had indeed spent time in Custer's presence.

> I remember, *as I rode back to my command* [emphasis added], the last remark I ever made to him was—"Let us keep together." In his jaunty way he lifted his broad brimmed hat as much as to say, "I hear you." But alas! he did not heed me.[19]

This was not the kind of admission that Reno could have made at the court of inquiry, where he and his attorney were intent on discrediting witnesses like Davern, Porter, Herendeen, and Gerard, whose collective testimony attested to two nearly identical orders given near the Lone Tepee, before Reno started off in self-proclaimed befuddlement to engage the enemy.

At the Lone Tepee, Custer had reason to be disappointed. But when he tipped his hat in that "jaunty way," the act said as much about Custer as did the troubled, sun-burned visage beneath the broad brim. And if Reno did say "Let us keep together"—if those words were not simply a self-serving after-action invention—they tell us more about Reno's state of mind than Custer's auricular capacity. Reno was on his way to the head of the column to lead half a wing into an increasingly risky enterprise. It would have been a daunting prospect for any officer, even someone with more natural courage and a stronger personality than Reno. At that point and under those circumstances, only a truly intrepid soul would have cared for "the honor of the advance."

From Gerard's testimony, however, it appears that the major did not stop for reassurance but that Custer called Reno to his side. According to Gerard, Custer "beckoned with his finger and the Major rode over," at which point the third order was issued. The major was to pursue that escaping village, and yes, he would be supported. Perhaps Cooke had indicated to Custer that Reno seemed a bit nervous about going alone. Perhaps Custer felt that he needed to assuage those fears by speaking directly to the major. As the two men rode together, perhaps Custer said something beyond the hearing of Gerard and Herendeen, possibly an indication of an alternate plan that envisaged a division of the regiment, causing a skittish Reno to utter those fateful words, "Let us keep together." In summoning Reno, Custer must have intended to do more than simply repeat orders already delivered by Cooke.

In nearly every description of his return from the left-front reconnaissance, Varnum stated that Reno's column was pulling out just as he arrived, but this is impossible according to the timing factors and testimony already cited. Varnum said that when he reached the Lone Tepee, Hare had just come in, presumably from the knoll. At that point, the Arikaras were still in place and Reno was about to move forward to the Lone Tepee.

According to the weight of evidence, therefore, events occurred in the following sequence: Hare descended the hill to the Lone Tepee; with the Sans Arc village having been seen again, Custer ordered Hare to take the Rees ahead on the run, but the Arikaras would not go; Custer instructed Cooke to move Reno forward to take up the chase (an order heard by Davern and Porter); Varnum returned and reported to Custer on the results of his reconnaissance, then joined Gerard in reprimanding the Arikaras; shortly thereafter Reno reached Custer, they rode together for several hundred yards, and Custer told Reno what he expected the major to do (an order heard by Herendeen and Gerard); aware that Varnum and Gerard had been successful in their entreaties to the Arikaras, Custer called out for Reno to take the scouts.

Now, seeing that Reno's battalion had pulled away from Custer's right wing, Varnum asked the general where Reno was going. Custer replied that the major was leaving "to begin the attack." Varnum later recalled:

> I asked instruction & he said to go on with them if you want to. Lt. Hare & I and my whole party started at the trot. Lieut. Geo. D. Wallace, a classmate of mine & dear friend & old roommate, was riding at the head of the column with the Genl. He was acting topo-

graphical officer. I called back to him, "Come on, Nick, with the fighting men. I don't stay back with the coffee coolers." Custer laughed and waved his hat and told Wallace he could go & Wallace joined me.

Varnum, Wallace, and Hare (with their orderlies) were then riding together. The Arikaras (including Custer's favorite, Bloody Knife) and the white scouts and interpreters moved forward in fragments, all trying to catch up with the head of Reno's column. The time was approximately 2:15 P.M., and Wallace had ceased being the regimental engineering officer, as indicated by his official report, which ends its account of the Little Bighorn expedition when he went off with Varnum. In three separate accounts of this incident, which effectively saved Wallace from dying with Custer's wing, Varnum proved that Wallace lied repeatedly to the court of inquiry when he said he always rode near Reno.[20]

Reno advanced at a trot while Custer followed at a slightly slower pace. Over the next fifteen to twenty minutes, covering two miles or so, the space and time separation between Reno and Custer increased a bit, although each column remained in sight of the other. When Custer told Reno to take the scouts, Boyer and the six Crows were not included. More than ever, Custer depended on Boyer and the Crows for their superior knowledge of the terrain in the immediate area of the Little Bighorn. Now Custer needed to know in greater detail what lay beyond the bluffs blocking visual access to the river valley.

To obtain such intelligence, he dispatched the Crow leader Half Yellow Face and White Swan to the ridge overlooking the valley, but before they reached their destination, they veered to the left and joined Reno's advance, possibly attracted by Varnum and the body of scouts rapidly filling the gap between Reno and Custer. On the other hand, Hairy Moccasin intimated to Walter Camp that the two Crows were purposely sent with Reno because they "were better informed of the country." Although this is plausible, the bulk of the evidence suggests that the two Crows made an independent decision to join the vanguard, perhaps with the hope of getting in on the pony stealing.[21]

Catching the startled Sans Arc encampment must have been a forlorn hope, but up to this moment, Custer apparently had not articulated any feature of an alternative plan to his subordinates. This is not to say that he had failed to formulate such a second phase. After all, he had seen signs of the main camp from the Crow's Nest, and the trail up the Rosebud foretold a large number of Indians in his front. But Reno remained the lead element in pursuit of remnants of the desperate satellite village, rather than a point unit charged with implementing a revised operational plan.

At the court of inquiry Lieutenant Charles DeRudio recalled that after passing the Lone Tepee, the command had seen Indians: "We supposed they belonged to that village."[22] As second-in-command of Company A, DeRudio was with Reno. After the fact, some recalled seeing clouds of dust along Reno Creek and well beyond the Lone Tepee. Private William Morris of Reno's lead Company M would connect seeing a party of about one hundred Indians before the river was reached with pursuing them across the Little Bighorn and down the valley.[23]

All of them must have considered that the Indians might be engaged in a favorite tactic, certainly for the Sioux and Cheyennes: decoy and ambush. Although the Plains Indians did not use what might be called standard tactics, the decoy-and-ambush gambit was one that had worked well on more than one occasion, most notably in the Fetterman Massacre. Custer himself had experienced the ploy during the Yellowstone Expedition of 1873, when he had declined to be invested by a larger band after chasing a small group of Indians for some distance. Although inexperienced in Indian warfare, Reno must have been aware of the tactic, which may have accounted in part for his insistent queries about support as well as for his later concern that he was being drawn into a trap. More than likely, during their extended ride together near the Lone Tepee, Custer would have reminded Reno of the dangers of such a contrivance. This is one way to explain Reno's plea, "Let us keep together."

Within two miles of the Little Bighorn, Custer acquired intelligence that would solidify the second phase of his battle plan. Whether Sergeant Kanipe was the first to see fifty to one hundred Indians on the bluffs to Custer's right is unclear. By Kanipe's testimony, when he saw the Indians, he informed First Sergeant Edwin Bobo, of his Company C, who reported the fact to the de facto commander, Lieutenant Henry Harrington, who told Tom Custer, who passed on the news of the sighting to his brother. In Kanipe's opinion, this body of hostile Indians was north of where Reno would eventually be "corralled"—that is, at least two miles from Custer's position at that moment. What this told Custer was that although Reno might be on a fresh trail, he was no longer in pursuit of all or even most of the former occupants of the Lone Tepee site. This report called for revised instructions to Reno.[24]

It was probably at about this time that Custer realized that Half Yellow Face and White Swan were not going to complete their mission to the edge of the bluffs. In their place, Boyer and the four remaining Crows started off for the ridge line, which would give them a partial view of the Little Bighorn Valley. At about the same moment, Custer dispatched Cooke—accompanied by Captain Myles Keogh—to deliver new orders to Reno. Those two officers not only would tell the major what to do but also would ride with him in the first stage of an updated battle plan that reaffirmed the division of the regiment and that introduced the concept of hitting the main Sioux-Cheyenne village in alternate thrusts.

As remembered by Reno, the orders delivered by Cooke were as follows: "General Custer directs you to take as rapid a gait as you think prudent and charge the village afterwards, and you will be supported by the whole outfit." This was his testimony at the court of inquiry and was almost exactly what he also asserted in his official report, submitted just a little more than a month after the battle. Regardless of the manner of expression, Custer was telling Reno to be careful—that is, to ride quickly but prudently and to be wary of a trap.[25]

Unfortunately, no one present would survive to corroborate Reno's claim of precisely what Cooke said. By the time Cooke and Keogh arrived, Reno's column was moving at a fast trot over rolling and broken ground and could not have been well closed up. Additionally, a large body of soldiers on horseback moving at an increased speed would have generated a great deal of noise—hooves striking the earth, equipment clanking and creaking, and all the sounds attending a cavalry unit riding rapidly and in some disorder, on the verge of battle. In such circumstances, only Lieutenant Benny Hodgson, Reno's adjutant, *might* have been close enough to listen while Cooke imparted Custer's instructions, although as part of his responsibilities, Hodgson was almost certainly keeping an eye on the entire column of troops, from front to rear. Since Hodgson, Cooke, Keogh, and Custer were all killed in the fight, no one could confirm Reno's assertion as to the full text of Custer's final directive.

One person who claimed to have heard Custer direct Cooke to take orders to Reno was Trumpeter John Martin, Custer's orderly. In an account given long after the battle, Martin telescoped events, but since his comments are pertinent to the question of Custer's orders, they are quoted in full here:

> Just a little off from that [the Lone Tepee] there was a little hill, from which Gerard, one of the scouts, saw some Indians between us and the river. He called to the General and pointed them out. He said they were running away. The General ordered the Indian scouts to follow them, but they refused to go. Then the General motioned to Colonel Reno, and when he rode up the General told the Adjutant to order him to go down and cross the river and attack the Indian village, and that he would support him with the whole regiment. He said he would go down to the other end and drive them, and that he would have Benteen hurry up and attack them in the center.[26]

The first part of Martin's story is consistent with the idea that the tactical objective was the Indians who were running between the Lone Tepee and the river, but the latter portion appears to refer to the second phase of Custer's evolving strategy. Specifically, Reno was to cross the river and begin the assault on the main village, and Custer would support him with a multifaceted plan, one feature of which was the projected involvement of Benteen's unit, an eventuality also reflected in Private Davern's slightly garbled recollection. Unfortunately, Martin mistakenly combined the acts of Custer calling Reno to his side and Custer sending Cooke with the last message.

From the manner in which Custer deployed his forces and from the logic of developments, Martin's remembrance, in all important respects, appears accurate. In delivering the fourth order since the Divide, Cooke had to tell Reno something new. Thus it would have made sense for Custer to convey some idea of what would be expected of Benteen's command, the other half of Reno's wing. Custer must have been distressed that the troublesome Benteen had not yet arrived, and after seeing Reno's nervous condition up close, Custer had to continue to provide the major with a measure of reassurance. Since under the original concept of operations the three columns were to have marched in parallel against the small Sans Arc village, it was surely inconceivable to Custer that Benteen could have become so completely lost.

Two features of Custer's first three orders to Reno, in all of their iterations, are striking. First of all, from the Divide to the Lone Tepee, Reno was told to take the advance and to drive the Indians before him. This continuous instruction for Reno to move to the front was delivered by either Custer or his adjutant, was heard by a variety of witnesses, depending on the circumstances, but was never altered in its essence. Second, in none of the first three orders, no matter where conveyed, was there any reference to following a particular trail, crossing the river at any specific point, proceeding down a valley, or charging into a main Indian encampment. The target of the first three orders was always the Sans Arc villagers.

As already discussed, Reno stated that his battalion was to the left and rear of Custer's column when they approached "the village" (the Lone Tepee). He noted that he was then brought to the front by Custer. However, Reno next combined Custer's repeated order to move forward with Cooke's delivery of the final instructions "five miles from the village," obviously—in his revisionist memory—meaning the main encampment. In Reno's mind, these were "only the usual orders to the advance guard to attack at a charge."[27]

The wonder is that Reno knew where to go and what to charge. Although one could conclude that an officer experienced in Indian warfare might, with caution, decide to pursue clouds of dust stirred up in territory totally unfamiliar to him, it strains credulity to suppose that a man who had never chased an angry Indian in his life would suddenly acquire that faculty. Besides, no one had yet seen Indians in the valley, and in fact there were none. The great Sioux and Cheyenne village had not yet begun to stir in anticipation of meeting Custer's advance.

The mendacity of Major Reno is clear from the record. His several assertions that he never talked to Custer or questioned Cooke closely—that he merely marched in the direction of some unspecified Indians "without any definite instructions or orders"—indicate a pattern of obfuscation and deliberate deception aimed at personal survival and exoneration. From the outset, Reno was deeply afraid. Custer had virtually held his hand as they parted. Be brave and do not be deceived by Indian tricks, Custer must have said to Reno in so many words, and Benteen and the rest of your left wing will be along shortly.

Not long after the fight, Reno described a second purpose in Cooke's mission. "After Colonel Cooke gave me these instructions he rode with me for some time, as also Captain Keogh, and said, in his laughing, smiling way, 'We are all going with the advance and Myles Keogh is coming too.'" In his court of inquiry testimony, Reno added that Cooke merely took a position on his left, after which they supposedly never spoke again. Even though Reno and Cooke rode together for "some time," the major never inquired further regarding Custer's plans, never wondered aloud where the hell they were going. Reno made no further mention of Keogh.[28]

The question is why Cooke and Keogh accompanied the Reno column at all after the last order was delivered. They were not going in with the advance. Both departed before all of Reno's battalion had crossed the river. There is no evidence that they were suddenly recalled at Custer's behest. Was Cooke's laughing remark meant to reassure an unsteady Reno? Was Keogh's presence intended to stiffen the major's backbone? It is impossible to know for sure why these two trusted officers would ride with Reno for nearly a mile, then abruptly leave as the battalion was about to enter into battle. However, as one of the people most familiar with Custer's tactical intentions, Cooke was a logical choice for such a mission, and as second-in-command of the right wing, Keogh would have brought authority to the task. When they eventually left Reno's side and fell back, he took no notice and was not even curious as to why Custer's two close associates would, without apparent explanation, precipitously exit when they were supposed to advance. According to Reno, he was busy getting his battalion across the river and had no time to miss his erstwhile companions. Nonsense!

The body of scouts and interpreters apparently did not reach Reno before his command crossed to the south side of the creek at about where it intersects with North Fork. Varnum said that just after that crossing, he had managed to reach the middle of the column when he was forced off the trail, presumably because hills in the area would not permit the passage of more than one or two riders at a time. Assuming that Varnum was in the lead of the scouting party, others in the group must have left the trail as well.[29]

Hare stated merely that he had been delayed. Herendeen also fell behind, not because the terrain was difficult but because his horse stumbled on the approach to the river. None of the three men caught up with the column until it had begun to traverse the Little Bighorn. Some of the Arikaras also dropped out before they arrived at Ford A, the point at which the battalion crossed the river. Of the thirty or so Rees with the party, about one-third did not join in fording to the western bank, at least some because their mounts had given out. As a result, Varnum's assemblage arrived in considerable disarray at the eastern edge of the Little Bighorn, no doubt trying their best individually to get out ahead of Reno's soldiers.[30]

The path to the river forked around a knoll near the bank. The command passed to the left of the hill, although there was a large trail to the right as well. The river at this juncture was maybe fifty feet wide and stirrup-high on the horses, not a particularly difficult ford to cross except that, as was normal in such circumstances, the column had difficulty keeping closed up, causing some delay. According to several accounts, Adjutant Cooke was on the bank and tried to get the soldiers to tighten their ranks because there was "hot work" ahead. He called out to the soldiers: "For God's sake men, don't run those horses like that; you will need them in a few minutes."[31]

Another reason for the delay in crossing was that at least some men either let their horses drink or could not stop them from drinking. The truth of the matter probably depends on the actions and perceptions of individuals—some had mounts in good shape and some did not, and some let their horses drink and some did not. On the question of watering the animals, cavalry rules were clear: all should be watered within an hour of the last halt; while on the march, none should be watered unless all were watered. According to the evidence Reno, following regulations, allowed time for the men to let their horses take at least a sip of the refreshing river water while the soldiers filled their canteens, if necessary. In any event, there was some congestion and confusion as the battalion crossed the river.[32]

Lieutenant DeRudio also arrived late at the river's edge. He testified that when he eventually caught up, Reno and Gerard were sitting on their horses in the river. He said that Reno was drinking from a bottle of whiskey. Riding a stubborn horse, DeRudio had to force the animal off the bank and into the river, and as man and surging beast hit the surface, water splashed on Reno, who complained, "What are you trying to do? Drown me before I am killed?"[33]

At about the same time, the scouts were shouting, in their own language, that rather than running away, the hostile Indians were coming out to meet Reno's command. Private Thomas O'Neill remembered that some of the Arikaras were located on the small knoll near the edge of the river and that one of the scouts repeatedly gathered blades of grass in his hand and dropped them, indicating that the Sioux were as thick as that. Gerard and Herendeen recollected hearing the scouts call out that the Sioux were going to fight. By this time, some of the Rees and the two Crows had likely crossed the Little Bighorn to get a better look at the tactical situation, since the scouts could not have seen much from that hill. The most cogent explanation is that Gerard was hearing from Arikaras who had crossed the river and looked down the valley, where they saw that the camp had not been struck. They had already seen enough to know that the main village was large, and if it was not moving, they had reason to report the results of their survey with urgency and with more than a little trepidation. After all, Custer expected them to get out front and capture and scatter those Sioux ponies.[34]

Gerard asserted that when he heard the Arikaras' alert, he passed the information to Reno. However, Reno emphatically maintained that Gerard had not relayed such an alarm and that if he had, Reno would not have believed him. Because of what Gerard did next, chances are that he did communicate to Reno the import of what the scouts had seen, even if the two men's mutual dislike would have precluded a protracted discussion. Herendeen heard a similar report from the Crows, and he shouted the warning to no one in particular.[35]

At that juncture, Gerard's attitude was "Hell, Custer ought to know this right away." He started back to share the news that the Sioux were in a mood to fight, that all of the assumptions about Indian behavior under military pressure had been wrong. In his opinion, such information might cause Custer to change his plans. He immediately retraced his steps across the river and up the trail around the knoll on the east side. Within several hundred yards, he met Lieutenant Cooke, who had obviously remained in the area until at least a part of Reno's column was safely across the river and in pursuit.[36]

"Well, Gerard, what is the matter now?" Cooke asked. After Gerard had conveyed the Arikaras' intelligence, Cooke told him to go ahead with Reno. He added, "I will go back and report." Meanwhile, Reno's battalion had plunged through a hundred yards of timber and fallen trees bordering the west bank of the Little Bighorn and was in the process of closing up before charging down the valley. Presumably on the far side of those woods, the entire column dismounted so that men could recinch their saddles and do whatever else was required to get themselves in fighting trim. That done, the cavalrymen climbed aboard their steeds and, forming in column of fours, started at a trot over the flat ground that led toward the main encampment scarcely visible through the dust that had now begun to rise ahead.

The timing is not clear from the record, but Reno must have sent his first messenger to Custer soon after crossing the Little Bighorn, probably while the battalion was wending its way through the timber. The first soldier dispatched was twenty-one-year-old Private Archibald McIlhargey of I Troop (Reno's striker), who carried the message that the Indians were in front and were "in strong force."[37]

However, the only witness who could say with certainty that McIlhargey recrossed the river was Private Davern, Reno's orderly, one of whose functions was to carry messages. When Davern asked McIlhargey where he was going, the messenger replied that he was going to see Custer. Why Davern was lagging so far behind while Reno's body servant carried such an important message is not clear. Sergeant Ferdinand Culbertson also saw McIlhargey going back but did not specify whether he saw the messenger actually cross the river.[38]

Another person who may have seen McIlhargey leaving to deliver Reno's urgent warning was Gerard, but his testimony is ambiguous. In his court of inquiry account, he said that he had not seen anyone coming from Reno's command toward Custer, but he told Walter Camp that after reporting to Adjutant Cooke, he "rode back toward the river" and, before reaching it, "met a mounted soldier hurrying east." The timing and the evidence already cited suggest that the latter statement is the more accurate and that the soldier Gerard saw was McIlhargey spurring his quick horse in the direction of Custer's column.[39]

It was now a little before three o'clock. Within moments of his striker's departure, Reno supposedly dispatched a second message to Custer by way of his cook, Private John Mitchell, also of I Troop. Reno later stated that the reason he sent this second courier with the very same message was because no instructions had yet been received in response to the first notice, carried by McIlhargey. But since the interval between sending those two couriers was only "some minutes," one wonders how Reno could have expected a reply even if Custer was in his immediate rear (within sight, if one cared to look), given the fact that a river and a hundred yards of timber had to be traversed. There is no other evidence that Mitchell was ever with Reno. Mitchell, like McIlhargey, was killed with the Custer wing.[40]

On what basis did Reno send his striker and his cook back with the same message to Custer, the message being that the Indians were strong in his front and were coming out to meet him? To this point, Reno had no sure knowledge of what the Sioux were up to or how many there were. He had only Gerard's interpretation of what the Arikara scouts had reported. Reno claimed not to have heard any such alerts. And after he had crossed the river, Reno had few reliable ways of acquiring additional information from either the Arikaras or the two Crows. Gerard was gone, and according to Varnum, the Indian scouts and the others in his party got out ahead of the battalion as soon as the timber had been navigated. Either Reno was relying on the general warnings provided by Gerard and possibly Herendeen, or he was depending on his own eyesight and a feeling of growing unease. But what had he actually seen by the time one or both of those messengers left his presence?[41]

The answer is, probably not a great deal. Later he would say that because he "had been a good deal in the Indian country," he was "convinced that the Indians were there in overwhelming numbers." His opinion was that the hostile Indians were trying to draw him into a trap, and as he was sending those messengers, he became more certain that his "opinions were correct." However, Reno's expressed concerns were based more on imagination than experience. Had he ever actually fought an Indian, he would have realized that the family-oriented warriors would never have invited the enemy into the middle of their camp as part of a decoy-and-ambush scheme.[42]

Just as Private Morris apparently believed that the battalion had pursued the Sans Arc Indians across the river and down the valley, so Reno perhaps could not disconnect the Lone Tepee episode from Custer's orders to charge the main encampment. Although it does not prove the case, one exchange between Reno and the recorder at the court of inquiry suggests this possibility:

Q: Describe what force you drove down the bottom.

A: I suppose there were some 40 or 50, perhaps less. They were decoys sent out there.[43]

Maybe what Reno really saw was the ghost of Fetterman.

The truth is that at the edge of the timber, Reno was more than two miles from the first lodges in the main Sioux and Cheyenne village. Even as the battalion started the charge down the valley, the most that any other observer could report was that through faint puffs of dust, figures could be seen moving about. Only when they were much closer to that encampment could those witnesses determine numbers of Indians, ranging from twenty to fifty, riding in circles to stir up the dry earth and create a screen for the inhabitants. From all indications, it appears almost certain that those Indians had come out from the village, rather than going into it.

In sending two messengers with nearly identical warnings, Reno may have intended simply to advise Custer that the situation was different from the one anticipated, but the redundancy also suggests another motive. From the moment he had left Custer's side, Reno had been anxious regarding his role as the vanguard of a general attack on a large village. By the time he was across the river and through the trees, he was rattled and was drinking heavily from his flask. He knew that Custer was not going to join him in the advance. He knew that Cooke and Keogh had provided assurances, but the most they could promise was that Custer would not abandon him and that Benteen would furnish direct support once he arrived on the scene. Reno realized that he was alone for the time being with less than a full wing, that he had no experience fighting Indians, and that the sky was falling.

When and where Lieutenant Cooke caught up with Custer to report the latest intelligence regarding Reno's advance is not known. Keogh had likely returned first with word that Reno and his column had indeed marched in the direction of the river. However, Cooke carried the more important information that Reno was crossing the Little Bighorn and was about to be confronted by an undetermined number of Indians.

While Cooke and Keogh were gone, Custer lingered near the confluence of Reno Creek and its North Fork, the so-called Flat, a bit more than a mile from the river. Trumpeter Martin thought that Custer remained at the Flat for perhaps ten minutes, but the right wing probably did not come to a full stop for more than a moment or two. A widespread presumption is that during this period, the Sans Arc villagers were seen on the bluffs and that Custer started at once to pursue them. As Kanipe remembered events, his report of fifty to one hundred Indians caused Custer to turn right immediately and to rush his command toward the high ground, riding at either a trot or a gallop, depending on the version. It is understandable that Kanipe would want his observations to trigger a sudden reaction in Custer, but the evidence does not support such a direct cause and effect, at least in terms of impelling Custer to make a foolhardy chase after a relatively small body of Indians. Once the Sans Arcs had departed the Lone Tepee, Custer's intention was clearly to drive them in panic toward the main camp.[44]

Sergeant Kanipe and the Crow scout Curley agreed that Custer separated from Reno some two miles from the river. It must have been at this point, before Custer even reached the Flat, that the Sans Arcs were seen and that Custer dispatched Cooke with new orders for Reno. Custer then veered to the right, leaving Reno's trail, and drifted across the Flat while he awaited the return of Keogh and Cooke and while he gave Benteen additional time to catch up.[45]

The group of retreating Sans Arc Sioux had now been seen at least three times, and the distance between them and Custer had remained fairly constant. By timing factors, Custer had left the Lone Tepee at about 2:15, traveled some two miles in perhaps twenty minutes (2:35), saw the Sans Arcs and sent Cooke at about the same time, then headed northwest for a mile at an accelerated pace to the Flat (2:45), where he paused for some minutes (2:50). In contrast, the Sans Arcs had to travel a bit over five miles from the Lone Tepee to the bluffs. Assuming that they had departed the site even half an hour before Custer arrived and were dragging their baggage uphill, it is reasonable to suppose that they reached the high ground during that 2:35–2:40 window. Those Sioux spotted by Kanipe had likely been seen by dozens of others, probably by Custer himself, who was always well in advance of the column and who was as alert to his surroundings as any man serving under him. After all, he was looking for just those Indians.

Custer delayed in the westernmost area of the Flat until two intelligence probes had been recovered. From Cooke and Keogh he needed to know that Reno had his orders to cross the Little Bighorn, and from Boyer and the Crow scouts he needed to hear about the disposition of enemy forces beyond the bluffs. What Custer learned just before three o'clock was that Reno had begun to cross the river and that within less than half an hour, the major and his battalion would encounter some number of Indians, possibly a rear guard protecting the main Indian camp. With that information in hand, Custer began his march toward the bluffs on the eastern bank of the Little Bighorn River and, in the course of that advance, picked up Boyer and his scouts, although they had little information to share.

In fact, Curley said that the scouts "could see nothing of the valley where the village was located" and that "Custer's troops were not hurrying—they rode at a walk—probably because they were going up a grade." It certainly makes sense that Custer would have started slowly, then accelerated the pace in easy stages, in contrast to Kanipe's recollection that the column galloped up the slope for more than a mile, at which point they discovered— hardly surprising—that the band of Sans Arcs had disappeared.[46]

The testimony of the Arikara scout Soldier confirms that Custer did not go racing up the hillside and indicates that the arrival of a messenger had a positive effect on the morale of the cavalrymen. "A messenger met the general, and Custer took off his buckskin coat and tied it on behind his saddle. Custer rode up and down the column talking to the soldiers. The soldiers cheered and some tied handkerchiefs around their heads and threw hats away. They gave a big cheer and went ahead, but my lazy horse straggled behind. . . . Stabbed was behind, came up behind me and explained that he had been out with a message to soldiers over to the east." Thus, an unidentified messenger (Keogh, Cooke, McIlhargey, or Mitchell) arrived while Custer's wing was either moving slowly or had stopped. The news brought by that messenger caused Custer to notify the men of its significance, and the troopers reacted by cheering.[47]

We have no way of knowing exactly where and when this sequence of events took place, but we can safely assume that it occurred somewhere between the Flat and the bluffs on which the band of retreating Indians had been seen, a total distance of a bit more than a mile. The first to return, Keogh can be eliminated as the messenger because he had nothing to report except that Reno's column was moving toward the river. Cooke's information was more definitive, detailing the river crossing and the scouts' belief that the Sioux main village had not yet dispersed. But Cooke could not have been this man, because Soldier would not have confused the adjutant with a mere "messenger." When Walter Camp showed Soldier a picture of Cooke, "he kissed it, saying that he [the adjutant] was a lovable man, his very breath being nothing but kindness."[48]

The most logical conclusion is that McIlhargey was the messenger and that, appearing after Custer had left the Flat, he brought word that Reno was deploying for combat and that the Sioux had assumed a defensive position. But Reno saw only billowing dust some two miles in front of him. The major did characterize the opposition as "strong," though not immediately threatening or disruptive to offensive operations. Whatever it was, Reno was preparing to attack it. That was surely good news to Custer, who then shouted to the men in his command that their comrades were about to engage the enemy. They bellowed their approval, if only to summon courage for their own forthcoming intervention.

For all Custer knew at this juncture, the Sioux encampment could have occupied both sides of the Little Bighorn River. With Keogh and Cooke back in the fold, Custer's march to the bluffs on the eastern side of the river might have begun at a walk, then a trot. The reason Soldier was present to see the messenger and to hear Custer encourage the men was that his horse was too slow to keep up with Reno's column. He and other Arikaras were straggling and thus attached themselves to the more deliberate pace of Custer's wing. When McIlhargey arrived with Reno's message, somewhere uphill from the Flat, Custer's wing sped up, and the Arikara scouts fell increasingly to the rear.

If for no other reason than military protocol, the messages from Reno required a response from Custer. His second-in-command had just notified him once, perhaps twice, that contrary to expectations, the Indians were not running but meant to make a stand. Implicit in Reno's messages was uncertainty, possibly hesitation, maybe even a plaintive request for recall. But changing the plan was out of the question, even if Custer had been so inclined, which he was not now that the Indians had been engaged. Even though, by Trumpeter Martin's testimony, Custer had communicated to Reno, through Cooke, how he meant to join the fight, the general may still have been under some obligation to answer Reno's expression of uneasiness. If Custer did send a reply message to Reno, however, it was likely never delivered.[49]

158

After the Lone Tepee gambit had failed, and the large group of Indians was sighted on the bluffs, Custer's experience and instincts dictated a new plan of attack. A simultaneous assault from several directions was out of the question. Rather, Reno's battalion was the first stage of Custer's improvised and purely intuitive plan for a series of staggered thrusts aimed at convincing the Indians that the soldiers were more than they could handle.

The problem is that on the issue of Custer's explicit operational intentions, we are totally dependent on Reno's word, corroborated by Lieutenant Wallace alone. And it is clear from the evidence that Wallace lied under oath at the court of inquiry to protect Reno and in a misguided effort to preserve the honor of the Seventh. Fortunately, other surviving officers told just enough of the truth to escape being branded traitors to the service, and with information furnished by enlisted men and auxiliaries, a sensible scenario can be extrapolated.

Between the Divide and the Lone Tepee, Reno was told three times—twice by Custer himself and once by Adjutant Cooke—what was expected of him as the commander of the advance unit. As confirmed by Lieutenant Hare, the object of Custer's interest remained the departing Sans Arc village as the regiment passed the Lone Tepee. Unless one is inclined to believe that Custer would engage in superfluous exercises, we can conclude that some event caused him to send Cooke with another message to Reno. That occurrence must have been the sighting of the Sans Arcs emerging from low ground and appearing on the bluffs overlooking the river to the north of Custer's position.

The last message, carried by Cooke, conveyed a change to, rather than a mere repetition of, the earlier orders from Custer. The instructions surely gave Reno, who was some distance ahead and who was still under the impression that he was pursuing the flushed quarry, a new direction and a different purpose. To underscore the directive, to strengthen Reno's resolve, and to bring back needed intelligence, Custer instructed Keogh and Cooke to ride with the major as far as the river, which is all they did. Cooke must have said something more about Custer's plans, something that Reno could never admit—namely, that Reno was expected to at least cross the damn river, as Trumpeter Martin's testimony suggests. After which, he was to charge (not into or through anything), to engage the Indians, to bring them to battle. There was a Sioux village of undetermined proportions and disposition in the valley of the Little Bighorn, and Reno's job was to fight it as he found it, moving or standing still. The execution of Custer's last orders was left to Reno's discretion.

Reno nearly always contended that he expected support to come from his rear and that he thought the supporting element would be led by Custer. And yet there is no evidence that Reno ever looked back, ever—even during his cautious crossing of the river—wondered what had become of Cooke and Keogh, let alone Custer's entire wing. In fact, as he ordered the "forward" out of the timber, he already knew that he had been cut loose and was on his own, a terrible and fearful isolation in the face of a formidable Indian village not on the run but poised to resist his advance.

In his official report, Reno acknowledged that he could understand how Custer might have meant to support him by moving down the east side of the valley so as to carry out a flank attack on the village, but in virtually all subsequent statements on the subject, Reno insisted that he expected Custer to support him by following right behind. That is, by looking over his shoulder as he rode down the valley of the Little Bighorn, Reno honestly expected to find Custer with the entire right wing charging in his wake.

Such a dimly perceived expectation showed an abysmal lack of understanding of Custer's military tendencies. Even if we assume that Cooke said nothing about Custer's plans, which strains credulity, Reno ought to have known that the general would not dawdle in the rear while one of his subordinates dashed to glory. After all, many officers in the army believed that Custer was a glory-hunter, ready and willing to sacrifice everything in order to obtain some advantage for himself. If the most pejorative descriptions of Custer as a show-off committed to foolhardy charges were true, he would have ridden over Reno to get to the front of the line, where he might tempt fate, risk death, and capture the headlines once more.

Of course, other signs, unbeknownst to Reno, indicate that Custer never intended to follow his subordinate across the Little Bighorn. For example, when Custer told Reno to take the scouts, Boyer and the remaining four Crows were not included. The value of Boyer and the Crows was that they knew the terrain better than anyone else. If Custer meant to follow Reno in an attack on the main camp, their service as intelligence operatives was no longer required and they might as well have been with their brother scouts, rounding up those Sioux ponies, one of the rewards for participating in this enterprise. On the contrary, Custer sent them to examine the high ground on the east side of the river, far removed from Reno's line of advance.

Finally, there was the pack train. Almost to a man, the surviving officers of the Seventh believed that Custer made a fatal mistake in dividing the regiment. After the battle, these officers conjectured that if Custer had just kept the Seventh together and charged into the Indian village, an expensive victory might have been ensured. None of these men (or later commentators) ever explained how the entire regiment could have been assembled at the southern end of the Indian village while still protecting the pack train, which was at least five miles and a good hour behind Custer's wing even as it paused at the Flat.

As in all military operations in the West, the pack train (the logistical tail, mules or wagons) constituted the real Achilles' heel of the Seventh Cavalry. Accepting the fact that the Lone Tepee was Custer's initial objective, requiring a parallel march of three columns under his concept of operations, he would not have been able to organize his forces for a unified attack from one direction without jeopardizing the mules and their invaluable loads of ammunition. The Sans Arcs were on their way to warn the main village. There was no time for a tidy organization of forces, as might have been possible in a big war against a known opponent using understood tactics.

No, another plan was required, and Custer had an idea—had probably carried it in his head in some nascent shape since crossing the Divide—a plan that in its formulation must have seemed the best that could be devised under the circumstances, designed to threaten the enemy from several directions while still blocking all approaches to the vulnerable pack train. Custer must have felt confident, even without detailed intelligence on the size and disposition of the main village. The Sioux and Cheyenne warriors had not come out to meet the Seventh. Major Reno had been placed in an unenviable situation, but the regiment held the initiative, and within a matter of minutes Custer—retaining the parallel march of columns—would be in a position to show himself on the bluffs, confusing the Indians and possibly throwing them into a panic. The plan might work if only Reno could hold, as Custer had done in a stand of timber along the Yellowstone in 1873, and if only the often late Benteen would finally come, as he had come so gallantly (and in the end so full of himself) at the Washita.

CHAPTER EIGHT

A TERRIBLE FRIGHT

As Major Marcus Reno collected his battalion on the edge of the timber preparatory to charging down the valley of the Little Bighorn, the main Indian encampment lay largely concealed behind dust and trees several miles away. By signs alone, the soldiers knew that the village would be huge, and in the face of this perception, there was reason enough for soldiers to feel fear, for hearts to pump wildly, for adrenaline to run almost amok into already dry mouths and deep sweats. Even for those who might have been called veterans in such matters, being frightened nearly to death before the first shot was fired was natural and understandable.

From where Reno and his troopers sat astride their horses, it was over two miles to what has been called the "Garryowen Loop" of the Little Bighorn, a place where the river swung out into the prairie. The Indian village lay beyond that point, stretching another two miles or so downriver and extending westward from the banks for maybe a mile across the relatively flat bottomland in the direction of low hills. It was a good location for the camp, with plenty of wood and water and with ample room to graze an immense pony herd.

The village was organized into roughly five circles, with each of the primary tribes occupying a space sufficient to accommodate its men, women, and children. From south to north, the major tribes were camped in the following order: Hunkpapa (Campers at the Opening of the Circle), Miniconjou (Planters by Water), Sans Arc (Without Bows), Oglala (Scatters Their Own), and Northern Cheyenne. In addition, a smaller Brulé (Burned

Thighs) camp was attached to the Oglala circle but located closer to the river. A few Blackfeet Lakotas (a hunting party) were included in the Hunk-papa circle, and some Two Kettle (Two Boilings) Lakotas occupied scattered lodges. Here and there were Santee Sioux and Yankton and Yanktonai Sioux who had come out for the great Sun Dance. Five Arapahoes were present through coercion and would remain under guard in a tepee until the fight began.[1]

The actual population of this village remains a matter of some debate. In the years immediately after the event, knowledgeable soldiers and civilians with the regiment provided vastly different estimates of the numbers of people and warriors within the village. Some of the guesses greatly exaggerated the size, probably at least in part because doing so served the interests of the participants or the army or white America. According to this view, the Seventh Cavalry was simply overwhelmed by hordes of Indians. However, even by Indian accounts, the strength of the encampment was impressive. As many Indians recounted after the fact, the village was too large for any complement of soldiers—as understood in their collective memories—to conquer them. If Custer really believed (he may have said so) that the Seventh could defeat all of the Indians on the Plains, the Indians were equally convinced that in the aggregate, they were invincible.

In fact, the white and the Indian accounts vary so significantly from person to person that it is impossible to know how many people inhabited the camp. Excluding the over and under extremes of the various estimates, the village contained possibly 1,200 lodges, plus several hundred wickiups housing individual warriors. The total population of men, women, and children probably reached 6,000 or 7,000 at its peak, with 2,000 of these being able-bodied warriors, including teenage males with sufficient exposure to hunting and fighting to be capable of battling for the life of the tribes.

Although it was fashionable after the fight to overstate the numbers of warriors available for combat, in more recent history the tendency has been to scale down the Indian advantage in manpower, as if it is somehow necessary to level the "playing field." The truth is that by almost any method of calculation, the Indians had at least a ten-to-one advantage over any part of Custer's triad. The Indians were right. They were too many. Custer meant to convince them otherwise, but his plan failed, though not necessarily because it was a bad plan.

Custer had come within half an hour of surprising the Sans Arc mourners at the Lone Tepee site. Once the approach of the Seventh had been discovered and that village had hastily departed for the protection of the main encampment, he had no real hope of sneaking up on his secondary and much more formidable target. Personally impatient and frustrated by the failure to gobble up the little camp, he took up the chase with the caution behooving a cavalry commander obliged by regulation to maneuver a force heavier and more cumbersome than its adversaries. The chief strength of the army was its ability to operate in a coordinated and cohesive manner according to doctrine, in keeping with the training afforded enlisted men and officers alike. Custer could scarcely move faster than the book allowed.

As a consequence, the fleeing Indians were bound to alert the main village before Custer could get into position for a "surprise" attack. How that Sioux and Cheyenne encampment came to be notified of Custer's approach is related in a wide variety of stories told by Indian survivors of the battle, most of them warriors. Some of these accounts are alike in essence, but many vary significantly. None is totally compelling as giving the whole truth of how the Indians first learned of Custer's presence near their village. Such a diversity of testimony is what one might expect from any body of witnesses to a moment of crisis in a swirl of chaos and fright engulfing a virtual city of several thousand people.

A persistent tale is that the initial alarm was given by Indian women digging for turnips on the northern (or eastern) side of the Little Bighorn. That is what He Dog said, but it is not clear that he was actually present with the women.[2] Red Horse supported this story, claiming that he was with the women when one of them called attention to dust "arising in the neighborhood of the camp," soon after which he discovered that the soldiers were attacking. It is clear from Red Horse's several versions that he connected the sight of the dust with Reno's actual assault on the village.[3]

A variation of this event was provided by Moving Robe Woman, a Hunkpapa who related her story nearly seventy years afterward. According to her, it was a sultry day, and she was out digging wild turnips with her pointed ash stick when she saw a cloud of dust beyond the bluffs east of the river. At that point, she looked in the direction of the camp and noticed a warrior announcing that the soldiers were only a few miles away. Thus, the sight of that enigmatic dust to the east (Custer) and not "close by" the village (Reno) was relayed by a warrior riding about and shouting the news that the soldiers were approaching. The question, then, is where that warrior acquired the definitive intelligence.[4]

A number of Indian sources ascribed the first notification to people who had left the camp for the reservations. Respects Nothing (Fears Nothing) said that some Oglalas had started for the Red Cloud Agency and that a slowpoke in the group saw Custer's column and came back to warn the camp. Since Respects Nothing was an Oglala himself, his story carries weight.[5] However, the Hunkpapa Mrs. Spotted Horn Bull claimed that the signal was given by two Cheyennes waving blankets from the bluffs east of the river. These two were part of a group of seven on their way to the Spotted Tail Agency.[6]

The tale with the most variations on a theme concerned two men who had gone out to recover horses and in the process detected the soldiers' approach. The Hunkpapa Iron Hawk described them as simply two Indians, one of whom was killed.[7] The Miniconjou Flying By said they were "some Sioux."[8] Feather Earring (also a Miniconjou) indicated that they were two Sans Arc young men who had gone up Reno Creek to catch a pony wounded in the Crook fight and who, after seeing the soldiers, returned to warn the camp. One (Two Bear) was killed, but the other (Lone Dog) rode his horse from side to side to announce the presence of the enemy.[9]

In addition, some evidence indicates that the two men were in fact a father and son of the Sans Arc Lakotas. The father has been identified as Brown Arse (or some variation thereon) and the son as Deeds (or Plenty of Trouble), a ten-year-old who was killed under unknown circumstances on the way back to the village, possibly by Custer's Indian scouts. Like all of the other individual remembrances, this version lacks sufficient verification to be considered totally reliable, but it does have the advantage of more specificity than most of the others.[10]

It is tempting to conclude that in the Indian memory, the location of these two Sans Arcs was confused and that, rather than providing warning to the main camp, they had in fact brought the first word to the Lone Tepee site. One of them could have seen George Herendeen or Mitch Boyer, causing the Sans Arcs to pull up stakes and head for the hills. However,

Feather Earring was clear that he saw one of the Sans Arcs "signaling that the soldiers were coming" and heard him calling out that the troopers were close behind.

The only evidence from the Sans Arc circle in the main village was provided by Chief Joseph White Bull, a Miniconjou who was living with his Sans Arc wife and her family. Almost sixty years after the fight, he stated that the Indians had known that the soldiers would arrive "that day" because "scouts saw them coming *at the sundance ground* [emphasis added]." In this context, he could have been talking only about the Lone Tepee site, and although Indian witnesses were as apt as their white counterparts to overstate their prescience, like sending scouts, the truth would appear to be that the warning to the main village was first provided by the inhabitants of the satellite Sans Arc village—surely providential, a lucky accident.[11]

The Sans Arc refugees had to furnish the initial notice of Custer's approach. They themselves were on the run, barely beyond Custer's grasp. When they reached the bluffs overlooking the river and the main encampment, Custer was less than two miles behind, marching in place while he sent new orders to Reno and waited for the recovery of his intelligence probes. The Sans Arcs were indeed the key to protecting the village from total surprise. Whether they waved blankets or rode in circles or shouted the alarm, they were by happenstance the unintended sentinels of the Indians' survival. Of course, the irony is that from being mere morsels in Custer's original stratagem, they became the relatively small means of his undoing. They not only provided warning to the village but also caused the general to implement the second phase of a battle plan that included a chase into the unknown.

Common sense suggests that as the Sans Arc colony fled from Custer, some of the fastest riders would have deployed forward to furnish the earliest-possible alert to their compatriots and to the village as a whole. Perhaps one was Brown Arse or some other hero lost in the mists of disremembering. Ten years after the battle, Hunkpapa Chief Gall would recall that unidentified Indians had seen Custer and Reno separate and come into the valley of the Little Bighorn. Incorporated into the amorphous Lakota oral history, the source of these observations could not have been other than the Sans Arc refugees. On the bluffs above the Little

Bighorn, a rear guard of warriors would have allowed the noncombatant impedimenta to pass around Sharpshooter Ridge, down Cedar and Medicine Tail coulees, to the Sans Arc circle at the terminus of the latter depression. That is how Custer went in pursuit of the small band of Indians he could not catch.[12]

However the notification was delivered to the village, the effect was one of surprise, if not disbelief. Custer had caught the encampment off guard, with less than half an hour separating the Sans Arc departees from the right wing of the Seventh Cavalry. Low Dog heard the report of soldiers coming, but he did not take it seriously. Two Moon was watering his horses, Turtle Rib was sleeping, and Wooden Leg was also napping when word arrived that the attack had begun. Kate Bighead was down by the river with many companions as the alarm circulated through the camp that the blue-coats were almost among them.[13]

Within minutes of those earliest and variegated reports of soldiers in the area, Reno began his march down the valley, his battalion's cloud of dust a mirror image of the frenzied to-and-fro of Indians in his front. Reno rode at the head of his 145-man command, organized into three companies. The first in order of march was M Troop, led by Captain Thomas French, followed by A, under Captain Myles Moylan, and finally Company G, commanded by First Lieutenant Donald McIntosh. The troops moved out in column of fours at the trot. Lieutenants Charles Varnum, Luther Hare, and George Wallace with their orderlies were ahead and to the left, as was Private Edward Davern—Reno's orderly, whom the major had released to accompany Varnum—and some of the Arikaras, the Crows, and the white scouts and interpreters. The rest of the Arikaras bore to the right.

As the battalion moved away from the fringe of timber and started down the valley, Captain French ordered First Sergeant John Ryan to take ten men and deploy them as mounted skirmishers to the right of the column. It is unknown whether Reno instigated this precaution, the purpose of which was to explore the woods lining the Little Bighorn all the way to the village in the event that "some Indians might be lurking there." Probably Ryan's ten men included himself, the first two sets of four in M Troop, and another noncommissioned officer. According to Ryan, his group did not go ahead of the main column but remained abreast and some distance off, examining on the run the band of cottonwoods, bullberry bushes, and other underbrush at the river's edge all the way to the Garryowen Loop without encountering a single Indian.[14]

The pace of the battalion's advance accelerated from a trot to a slow gallop. The column did not move forward in a direct line from the ford to the objective but rode in a slight curve that paralleled the general course of the river. Nothing of the village proper could be seen by the main body of the command. In the early stages of the attack, the trees blocked visual access to the camp, and those Indians constituting the "strong force" in Reno's front consisted of shadowy figures—warriors and horses—dancing wraithlike behind a thin wall of dust.

Soon after starting out with the battalion in tandem, Reno may have brought the heads of the companies on a line with an interval of fifteen to twenty-five yards between them. After perhaps a half mile or less, Reno ordered "left front into line," deploying his forces out of the column of fours and into line of battle. As the troopers by the fours shifted in an oblique manner to the left, a single line began to form across the prairie, M Troop occupying the westernmost position with Company A on its right. For the time being, Company G was relegated to a reserve role, riding in line behind the other two units.[15]

Although Reno was not clear on the timing, the battalion could not have remained in this formation long before Company G was brought up in line with the other units. Thus, within a mile of the Garryowen Loop, all three companies were probably aligned across the valley floor: M on the extreme left, A in the center, and G on the right, all riding hard in full gallop, the horses kicking up the powdery gray soil in their wake, creating the cloud by which the Indians would identify the ominous correlative of earlier warnings. Lieutenant Charles DeRudio said the ground was sandy and full of sagebrush, difficult for cavalry to manage.[16]

DeRudio also said that Reno was out in front of the line, "continually checking the men, keeping the line in good order." Whether Reno was *always* ahead of his command is debatable. After all, in an advance of this kind, it would have been extremely difficult—even impossible—to keep a line of 145 horses and men straight. Certainly Reno could not have done so by himself, even if he had been totally absorbed with the alignment of his forces.

And there must have been distractions. Private William O. Taylor of Company A later described the trip down the valley of the Little Bighorn:

> We were nearing the Indian skirmishers on our ride toward their village, the Indians were firing and shouting their defiance, and we had been ordered to charge and some of the men began to cheer when Major Reno shouted out "Stop that noise." And once again came the command "Charge." Charrrage, was the way it sounded to me, and it came in such a tone that I turned my head and glanced backward. The Major and Lieutenant Hodgson were riding side by side in the rear of my company, perhaps 30 or 40 feet away, possibly more but certainly a very short distance. As I looked back Major Reno was just taking a bottle from his lips and passed it to Lieutenant Hodgson. In appearance I should say it was a quart flask, about one half or two thirds full.[17]

Like others, Taylor may have been telescoping experiences, but on the whole his description sounds credible. On the other hand, DeRudio testified that he heard no order to charge and that in fact he could see nothing to charge.[18] But the formation of the battalion from column of fours to line of battle was not just an exercise. An increase in speed from trot to slow gallop to full gallop was not a drill. As the pace increased, as the momentum of the moment accelerated, as greater fear sought refuge in bravado, it stands to reason that "charge" would have been the command and that "cheers" would have been the norm among the men.

Captain Moylan went on to tell the story of a trooper in his company whose horse was misbehaving. Without indicating a specific point in time, Moylan alleged that Reno turned around in his saddle and told the soldier to get his animal under control, "that he [Reno] would give him all the fighting or all he wanted of it before the thing was over." Apparently this episode was meant to illustrate Reno's cognizance of even small matters. First Sergeant Ferdinand Culbertson (also of Company A) recalled a similar incident on the way down the valley, when Reno told G Troop "not to get excited, that they would have hot enough work" ahead.[19]

Another distraction was the sighting of Custer's command on the eastern side of the Little Bighorn. Private Thomas O'Neill of Company G said that after about a mile, he saw Custer and his "whole command" moving at a trot on the bluffs east of the river, a little south of where Reno would later fortify. Corporal Stanislas Roy of A Troop heard some of the men say, "There goes Custer." Private Henry Petring of G also saw Custer and heard his comrades comment: "There goes Custer. He is up to something, for he is waving his hat."[20] Private John Donoughue reported seeing Custer's battle flag on the opposite side of the river.[21] Private Daniel Newell of M recollected a similar sighting.[22]

Regardless of the differences in these accounts, a number of individual soldiers confirmed the presence of Custer's column on the far side of the river and, in their stories, affirmed that the men in the ranks of every company muttered or shouted or pointed to communicate this information from front to back or up and down the line. The wonder is that Reno himself did not hear or see any signal from the soldiers whose behavior he was supposedly managing so closely. Perhaps the sight of Custer was just another cause for the cheering that Reno could not abide.

The line of battle was now spread across the valley floor, flanked on the left by Varnum and his group and on the right by Ryan's squad peering into the trees and brush. For some of the Indians in the village, the sight of the dust plume rising behind the rapidly moving line was the first sign that the soldiers were near. Others would claim ignorance until bullets began to tear through the tepees, snapping lodge poles and igniting small fires and killing the inhabitants.

Between the time the Sans Arc signaled from the bluffs and the time that Reno appeared as a discernible fighting force, probably not more than fifteen minutes had elapsed. It was 3:10–3:15 in the afternoon on a lazy day when Reno's force was first observed approaching. Many of the Indians had partied late into the night before, and so they were swimming or fishing or napping in sluggish disregard at the instant of decision. Not surprisingly, the word-of-mouth alarm spread slowly through the somnolent camp. Some could not believe the truth, some were confused, and some were panic-stricken.[23]

Even that old warhorse and now spiritual leader of the whole Sioux confederation, Sitting Bull, was lying in his lodge when the attack began. Hearing the shooting, he is alleged to have shouted: "Get busy and do something!"[24]

The women screamed, and the children cried. Old people sang death songs. The inhabitants of the village scurried about trying to secure what possessions they could carry. Some lodges were taken down in anticipation of the scattering of the clans, the usual practice when attacked. The noncombatants were hurried northward, downriver, toward the Cheyenne end of the camp. As they became aware of the threat, the warriors collected to form a rear-guard wall between the dependents and the aggressors.

The assault by Reno's battalion struck the Hunkpapa and Blackfeet circle, and warriors from these tribes were among the first to offer resistance. Any warrior with a horse immediately available joined that small blocking force, riding back and forth to create that screen of dust so essential to concealing the general activity in the village. Participation was a matter of individual responsibility rather than an organized defense, but with the soldiers so suddenly and so unexpectedly on the very outskirts of the camp, there was no choice except to fight. By the time Red Horse had returned to the council lodge, the headmen had gathered, but there was no time to consult. The old men helped the warriors dress and paint themselves for battle. Young men sang their war songs.[25]

White Bull thought that the bullets hitting the lodges were too high to hurt anyone, but for Gall, the truth was decidedly different. Gall later recalled, "When Reno made his attack at the upper end, he killed my two squaws and three children, which made my heart bad." From the evidence, those fatal shots into the Hunkpapa circle were probably fired by the Arikara scouts, who had gotten far enough forward to make effective use of their weapons.[26]

As quickly as they could acquire mounts, the Indian men hurtled ahead to confront the enemy. They advanced, and they retreated, trying to buy time for the noncombatants to reach relative safety and for other warriors to obtain horses. While the earliest handful created the dust clouds, the later arrivals filled Shoulder Blade (Box Elder) Creek and rode westward to the low bluffs that overlooked Reno's left flank. Those without ponies filtered into the timber along the river, from which position they could harass Reno's right.[27]

Thus, when Reno sent word to Custer just after crossing the Little Bighorn, the Indians could not have been "strong in his front," except in his imagination. In fact, the Indians were probably worried first about Custer's force east of the bluffs, as reported by the Sans Arcs and as detected by the wild-turnip diggers. Respects Nothing indicated just such a sequence of events: "When the Indian returned and gave warning of the approach of Custer there was a good deal of excitement and a rush was made for the ponies, and before the people could get out, the village was attacked. Reno crossed and came down the bottom of the river to the mouth of the Box Elder and began firing from a clump of woods at that point." The warriors were reacting to a general alarm when they began to gather ponies and disperse the noncombatants in an atmosphere of terror and confusion. Once again, it was simply good fortune for the Indians that some of their number were positioned so as to detect and confront Reno's advance. The Indian force was small, but it was sufficient to stall the soldiers until more warriors could get mounted, which they did, quickly and steadily.[28]

While the Reno line of battle was still in motion, a few of the Indian scouts were working toward the left, trying to reach and capture some of the Sioux ponies grazing on the ground west of the village. Lieutenant Hare remembered seeing a Sioux or Cheyenne—probably gone to gather horses himself—fire at the Rees, but the scouts chased him and managed to collect a number of ponies. The Arikara Strikes Two noted that they were chasing a bunch of horses herded by two Sioux when others Indians came out of the village to help the herders. In his opinion, the village at that juncture "was not stirred up," but in this "little skirmish," he killed one of the enemy.[29]

Other Arikaras drifted toward the right and the timber, from where they observed three Sioux women and two boys on the east side of the river, leaving the village. The scouts began to give chase, with a view to killing the refugees, but when they noticed a herd of several hundred ponies, they ended their pursuit of the Sioux in favor of the horses. Bloody Knife was pleased that the scouts had plundered Sioux booty. That was their function and their reward, and they had made a good beginning.[30]

The importance of the Indian scouts' testimony is not so much that they were performing as expected but that their recollections confirm the likely sequence of major events. Their ability to infiltrate the pony herd and scoop up some number of head, while meeting only light resistance, suggests that not many warriors had made their way to the grazing area. Similarly, the presence of women and children in the vicinity of the southernmost Hunkpapa circle indicates that not much progress had been made in evacuating the noncombatants. If Custer's auxiliaries were responsible for killing Chief Gall's wives and offspring while the women and children remained in their lodge, as seems likely, the obvious conclusion is that Reno's appearance was a total surprise and a counterpoint to Custer's complementary dust cloud.

From the time his battalion departed Ford A, if not before, Reno's disinclination to get caught in some kind of clever Indian trap must have influenced his thinking in favor of a defensive deployment. On that point his testimony is fairly consistent and revealing. He said that from the size of the trail, he knew there was a large number of Indians. It was this "knowing" that caused him to bring G Troop in line rather than leave it in a reserve role. As he neared the village, a considerable body of Indians appeared in his front and in the foothills to his left. Again, "knowing" that no support could be coming, he occupied a point of timber (the Garryowen Loop) "about a mile upstream from the village, sheltered my horses and advanced to the attack, reaching within two hundred yards of the village. The Indians *then* [emphasis added] came out in overwhelming numbers."[31]

Nothing in Reno's orders directed him to charge into the Indian encampment. That option was left to his discretion as commander of the battalion. The only obligation that could have been envisaged in Custer's battle plan, and that would have been reflected in the orders carried by Lieutenant William Cooke, was to attack and engage the enemy. Cut loose from Custer, on his own, Reno was merely cautioned to be "prudent" (avoiding the dreaded decoys). Under those rules of engagement, Reno probably made a wise choice when he headed for the Garryowen Loop. That point of timber offered shelter for the horses and was close enough to the village to represent a threat to the inhabitants. So far, Reno was doing all that had been asked of him and his men.

When Reno's battalion was within perhaps a half mile of the village, he called out for the line to stop, using words akin to the following: "Battalion halt—prepare to fight on foot—dismount."[32] The order was repeated up and down the ranks as Adjutant Benny Hodgson raced to the left to ensure compliance. As Corporal Roy asserted, the skirmish line was "formed in regular order and every commissioned officer in their places and discipline good among the enlisted men."[33] Believing that the transition from mounted to dismounted attack had been accomplished "nicely," Lieutenant DeRudio—the man who later claimed that he never understood what the devil they were charging—would also later contend that his response to Reno's decision was, "Good for you."[34]

Captain Thomas French held a different opinion:

> What made him [Reno] halt and dismount when he did is a matter in regard to which I am equally ignorant. It was not the kind of warfare to which I had been accustomed—and that was this—to be watchful, and prudent and never to take less than an even chance, but when once in to do as is said to be the custom at Donnybrook Fair—"if you see a head, hit it." I thought that we were to charge headlong through them all—that was the only chance.

Why French thought that the battalion was going to "charge" through the village is not known, but at a minimum, in the absence of any other instructions from Reno, he must have been led to believe—by order, by insinuation, or by formation—that such was the plan. French may have been wrong about the merits of charging into a hostile camp of that size, but he also expressed a deeply felt regret that he had not perished there.[35]

For Private George Smith of Company M, the order to halt did not come soon enough. Unable to control his horse, he was carried into the village and was never seen alive again. Also, three members of Sergeant Ryan's mounted skirmish squad rode horses that bolted ahead of the command. Private Roman Rutten said that his horse had been acting up since Ford A because it "smelled Indians," and as he neared the skirmish line, the animal lunged forward and bore Rutten nearer the village. Other observers would say that Rutten actually got among the tepees before he managed to turn his fractious horse and return to the timber. Private John "Snopsy" Meier had a similar experience and was also able to escape Smith's fate, "shooting his way out with his six gun." The last member of this trio was less fortunate. Private Henry Turley—"a very nice young man"—could not restrain his horse and ended up among the Indians, an early fatality of the long-range fracas.[36]

The fact that three of the nine troopers with Ryan lost control of their horses seems extraordinary but suggests that the order to halt and dismount reached this group later than the main body of soldiers. This delay was understandable, since Ryan's assignment involved examining the fringe of woods along the river and since Reno's line would have had to shift slightly left away from the river to create a right angle to Garryowen Loop. The distance separating the two groups would thus have increased, making the relay of instructions more difficult, particularly now that Captain French and Company M were on the extreme left of the line.

Lieutenant Varnum and his group on the left were clearly caught off guard by the decision to suspend the advance. As Varnum recalled events, he, Hare, and Wallace were riding together, advancing rapidly down the valley, somewhat ahead of the battalion. The Indians, who had been retiring before them, suddenly began to come forward, causing Varnum to look around and discover that Reno's line was dismounting. Because the Arikara and other Indian scouts had departed on their pony-hunting enterprises, he had no command and so sought out A Troop, his assigned unit. As he rode across the prairie toward the timber, he saw Custer's Gray Horse Troop moving at a trot "on a high bluff" across the river. Varnum thought that Custer, seeing Reno deployed in a defensive position, "must have been satisfied to proceed."[37]

Herendeen, Fred Gerard, Charley Reynolds, and the two Crow scouts Half Yellow Face and White Swan were also left of the line. This group traveled slightly to the rear of the advancing soldiers, trying to stay out of their way. Herendeen stated that there were no Indians within range—only a number sitting on horses over near the foothills to the west—until the battalion dismounted, at which point the Indians began to come closer. Like the Arikaras who had gone in that direction, Herendeen and his group then moved to the right, toward the timber. The skirmish line, he observed, was then facing the hills. Such a northwestern inclination at that juncture would have made sense, since that was where most of the warriors were located; it is also an additional argument against the soldiers as the source of fire that hit tepee-tops and killed noncombatants.[38]

As the troopers swung out of their saddles, the number fours in each set of four took the three unoccupied horses in hand, probably using a snap device to hold the free reins, and led the unneeded livestock into the woods for protection. The departure of these horse-holders immediately reduced the effective fighting force on the line from about 145 to approximately 110 men. Of course, taking the horses out of danger was in conformance with regulation, practice, and common sense, but the loss of these soldiers represented the first stage of what would be a rapid decline of manpower on the field of battle.[39]

The morale of those remaining in the open was apparently quite good in the beginning. Private O'Neill later said, "The men were in good spirits, talking and laughing and not apprehensive of being defeated." The Indians remained out of range, still kicking up that dust. Lieutenant DeRudio and others confirmed that most bullets appeared to be falling short of their targets, and officers urged the men to take their time and aim carefully. Some of the less-experienced soldiers may have been firing more rapidly than the veterans, causing their Springfield carbines to overheat and making the extraction of spent copper-cased cartridges more difficult, but discipline was satisfactory and the guns were working well enough.[40]

Neither side was doing any significant damage to the other. In spite of evidence that Reno, Hodgson, and others may have made passing remarks to the men about their rate and effectiveness of fire, these officers were themselves engaged in demonstrating their marksmanship at six or seven hundred yards, the approximate distance to the nearest tepee (if the soldiers were even shooting in that direction), or at three to four hundred yards, the distance to the nearest dust-cloud-enveloped and scampering Indian. Whether the officers had the time or the inclination to caution their charges about adjusting the sights of the long-range Springfields is not known. If the soldiers were in high spirits, it was not because they were hitting much. The officers had not yet begun to leave the scene for the comparative comfort of the woods.[41]

As indicated in the Indian testimony and confirmed by the soldiers, the hostile Indians were pouring up dry Shoulder Blade Coulee to the high ground west of Reno's position. Either on horseback or afoot, the Indians moved in small groups of three or four and remained low, creating poor targets. Counting the heads of the enemy was impossible, although almost every witness tried. Lieutenant Hare said Reno could not have seen Indians in the coulee before the command dismounted; Hare could not, and he was in a more advanced position. He said the Indians did not begin to come out of the coulee, located three or four hundred yards in front of the skirmish line, until the advance was stopped.[42]

From the evidence, Reno apparently did not form his line directly opposite the Garryowen Loop but rather dismounted a hundred yards or more short of it. At least part of the soldiers may then have moved forward, most likely the right flank wheeling on French's pivot in order to face the primary threat from the northwest. Corporal Roy of A Troop, situated in the center of the line, was one of those who recollected such an advance. He also recalled that Indians in the timber fired in an oblique direction from woods in the right front. This account is consistent with Indian claims that they infiltrated the timber but differs from the accounts of Herendeen, who saw no such firing, and of DeRudio, who did not think the Indians ever got into the woods. From the Sioux point of view, the soldiers knelt or lay down while they fired, planting guidons to mark unit locations. Some may have used the mounds of a prairie dog town as temporary breastworks.[43]

How long the skirmish line remained out on the plain is debatable. Private O'Neill and Corporal Roy thought twenty minutes or less. Private Edward Pigford of Company M said the line was no sooner formed than it "broke up." Herendeen asserted that the firing on the line lasted no more than five minutes, an opinion generally shared by Gerard. DeRudio guessed about ten minutes. As might be expected, Reno and Moylan set the time at fully half an hour. Of course, the exact number of minutes the men remained on the line depends on which soldiers one is talking about.[44]

With the loss of the horse-holders, the men who could not control their animals, and the doctors and their orderlies, who went into the timber to arrange a first-aid station, the actual strength of Reno's skirmish line probably did not exceed one hundred men after the command was dismounted. For a few minutes, perhaps no more than five, the troopers fired with confidence and little effect at the far-off Indians.

At that point, some unidentified voice called out that the Sioux were turning Reno's right—that is, in the woods. From all accounts, it appears that Reno was the only one who heard that voice. In his court of inquiry testimony, he said that he was near Moylan when "word" came that the Indians were engaged in this flanking action. Moylan said he "understood" that Reno "got information" that Indians were coming up the left bank of the river and threatening the horses. Reacting to Moylan's assertion that the Indians were getting to the horses, Varnum left A Troop, went into the timber, and had the horses moved to afford them greater protection. He saw no Indians. When he emerged from the timber, all or some part of Company G was going into the woods "to attack the village."[45]

The leader of this G Troop contingent was none other than Reno himself. The most reliable source for how much of G departed the line might be Private O'Neill, who was a member of that company. According to him, he went with Lieutenant McIntosh and the "whole troop" to investigate the report, but in a separate account, he estimated twenty soldiers, or roughly a platoon.[46] Reno also suggested that he took the entire body of G troopers. However, Moylan, stationed on the left of that company, said that Reno accompanied the "greater portion" of G, forcing Moylan to fill the gap between the right of his command and the timber or whatever was left of G Troop. In addition, Lieutenant Wallace, relieved of his engineering duties and now reinstated as second-in-command of Company G, averred in his perjured testimony that when the troop left the line, he remained until the ammunition was nearly exhausted. Since corroborative testimony indicates that Wallace was still on the line after G departed, he was either acting as an independent agent or some part of his assigned troop did not go into the timber. The bulk of the available information tends to support the notion that Reno took McIntosh and a platoon-plus of G into the woods to investigate reports that the Indians were turning his right flank, were endangering the horses, or were crossing the river and getting into the rear of his command—or alternatively, that Reno was organizing a force to attack the village.[47]

Whether the entire company or a platoon departed the field is incidental, except that the main body and thrust of the battalion was deprived of just that much manpower. If all of G went into the woods, the force of one hundred soldiers was depleted by about thirty, leaving approximately seventy men still shooting at the ever-increasing Indians; if half of G left, fewer than ninety remained on the field. In any case, the line of battle facing the primary Indian threat was being decimated by degrees.

In an exploration of the flank, occupied by some forty troopers (number fours and others), against attack by "creeping" Indians, one might suppose that Lieutenant McIntosh and all or some part of his troop would have been enough. Why Major Reno felt impelled to "lead" that investigation would constitute a mystery were it not for the law of self-preservation, more pronounced in some than in others. Why he would desert the obviously endangered portion of his command to search out phantom adversaries announced by a disembodied "voice" ought to puzzle, but for his own parting and imploring remark to Custer: "Let us keep together."

Stationed behind the right of the line, where Reno occupied space, Gerard remembered that the major emptied a bottle of whiskey just before he took Company G into the woods. Because Gerard disliked Reno, stemming from their earlier contretemps, the interpreter's observation could be dismissed as the product of bias except that his was the third independent account of Reno's dipping into the sauce between Ford A and the timber. In the course of those observations, the contents of the flask or bottle steadily diminished until Gerard's declaration that the container had been drunk dry. By that measure alone, Gerard's assertion has a high degree of credibility.[48]

Whether Reno was inebriated by the time the battalion reached the timber is largely a matter of perception and interpretation. He was a heavy drinker. After the battle, a charge-account book maintained by post traders showed that Reno purchased seven gallons and two demijohns of whiskey over a twenty-two-day period, an amount approximately equal to the total of that of all other Seventh Cavalry officers who bought spirits at that time. Maybe he threw a party or two, or maybe he was badly stressed from the Little Bighorn experience, but this is still a remarkable quantity for one man to procure. Captains Thomas Weir, Thomas McDougall, Frederick Benteen, and French were at one time or another rumored to have indulged in serious routine or binge drinking, and yet by at least this one record, they could not approach Reno in imbibing capacity. But assuming that all of the officers and men of the regiment who had a taste for the grape stashed a bit on their persons or in the pack train for those exhausted or desperate moments in the field, the available storage space must have been a veritable treasure trove of bug juice. At the court of inquiry, it was readily acknowledged that indeed good officers might without prejudice pack a bit of liquor for comfort while on difficult duty away from the conveniences of the garrison. The similar cravings of the enlisted man were not addressed.[49]

The truth is that Reno needed to drink at all times and especially under pressure. He could not stop being the person he was, and drinking only made him more so. If Reno was drunk, he was not a stammering, staggering, fall-down fool. Rather, as indicated earlier, he was just a very much afraid, Indian-fighting novice who sank increasingly into a dark, no-neck persona incapable of instilling confidence in other men. When Reno allegedly expressed his deep sorrow that his "strange actions" at the Little Bighorn were due to drink, he was articulating an excuse that makes no real difference. To varying degrees, every man who charged down the valley of the Little Bighorn—like the Sioux and Cheyennes who opposed them— was scared beyond the normal human ability to comprehend the concept of fright. Drunk or not, Reno lacked the capacity for intrepid leadership, and from the outset of his orderly march down the bottomland, he was looking for an avenue of escape, preferably toward the bluffs to the east, where Custer and his command had been seen by perhaps half the men in the regiment.[50]

As Reno and the G Troop contingent left the line, Moylan moved his Company A to the right, ostensibly to fill the space left by the departees. Why he would have felt it necessary to make such a redeployment is not entirely clear, since the major threat remained on the left of the line and since such a movement would have forced his men to get up from kneeling or prone positions in order to reset themselves and to realign their sights on the targets flying westward. The repercussions of this maneuver echoed down the line to the last man of M Troop. The skirmish line was shrinking, and the intervals between soldiers were becoming irrelevant. Captain Moylan was getting closer to the woods, where his commander was now safely ensconced, and the enlisted men were bunching behind, trying to touch the timber.

Soon after G had gone, and presumably as his own men were repositioning themselves, Moylan sent some number of soldiers—either a "few" or every other file—from his command into the timber to retrieve additional ammunition from the saddlebags on the horses. Even allowing for the most lenient timing factors, the soldiers could not have been on the line for more than ten minutes before Moylan thought it necessary to dispatch a squad or every other trooper into the timber for resupply. Moylan could not possibly have believed that his men were running short of ammunition after so brief a period of engagement while his company was redeploying. In fact, at the court of inquiry, he said that he only *thought* the men had used up the fifty rounds each carried, and he acknowledged that it would take about forty minutes to use forty rounds. Even for the most junior members of the company, such an expenditure is incredible—while they were on the move. Step by quick step, and in spite of later rationalizations, Moylan was delivering his men and himself to the safe haven of the woods.[51]

As for second-in-command DeRudio, he had no recollection of sending A Troop men into the timber for ammunition. According to him, he simply *followed* a group of five or six cavalrymen into the woods. He later contended that after Lieutenant Wallace said that Indians were getting into the timber, he blithely trailed after some small number of troopers to see what was up. Long after the battle, he would claim that he "took" these men into the woods before the Company G contingent was led off the field by Reno and that his purpose was to "watch" for Indians possibly coming from the north, across the river (the Garryowen Loop). Thus, he apparently intended to do precisely what Reno himself meant to do—heed the call of that disembodied voice.[52]

In his court of inquiry testimony, DeRudio told several different stories. First he said that Wallace's remark (made while they were sitting together on their horses) caused him to go with a half-dozen men to investigate the situation. Then he asserted that he "was all the time with the skirmish line— it withdrew into the woods the same time" he did, which would explain how in a later statement to Walter Camp he could claim that finding Sergeant Charles White wounded, he (presumably after dismounting) picked up the sergeant's gun and fired at the Indians. He had to have been on the skirmish line long enough to go from Wallace (G Troop) to White (M Troop) and back again, all the while regulating the fire of his own unit (A Troop). Finally, DeRudio stated flatly that he followed some number of men into the woods from Company A's position "right at the timber," meaning that the G platoon-plus had already been removed from the line. He added that other men of A Troop were already in the woods and that the "command" (Moylan and the rest of the company) entered with him.[53]

In fact, DeRudio was simply included in a knot of enlisted men who wandered off the line to seek refuge in the timber. Having ridden up and down the companies rather than tending to the business of managing his own men, DeRudio concluded that it was more important to seek out additional Indians in the timber to the right, even as their number increased steadily in the opposite direction, where Captain French and his Company

M had been left hanging. As DeRudio entered the timber, he caught sight of Custer, Cooke, and another man waving their hats from "the highest point" on the other side of the river, only about ten minutes after Lieutenant Varnum had observed some portion of Custer's column moving downriver at a trot.[54]

With the absence of horse-holders and with the departure of half of the remaining soldiers to retrieve ammunition, Company A was now reduced to seventeen men, if we can assume that DeRudio's half-dozen enlisted trailblazers were part of this general depletion within the ranks. By the best of interpretations, A Troop lacked the manpower to fill that all-important gap between the right of the line and the timber except by running after the leaders who had deserted them.

The disposition of Company A at this critical juncture was provided by First Sergeant William Heyn, who was in a position to know whether his superiors were present or not. He told Walter Camp that when he and the last of the A troopers left the line, *there were no officers on it.*[55]

Where had all the officers gone? The meanderings of Lieutenant Varnum provide the best clues to their whereabouts. The peripatetic subaltern had ridden from the left of the line to rejoin his Company A, had gone into the woods to check on the horses, had returned to the field to discover that G Troop was heading for the timber, and had exercised the option of an independent agent to follow the action. When he followed G into the woods, he was under the impression that Reno was going to attack the village. This must have been his conviction because he had just seen for himself that there were no Indians in the nearby timber. It would have made tactical sense to seek an alternate route by which to assault the encampment and to relieve pressure on the skirmish line, and the fringe of cottonwoods and underbrush would have provided ample cover for such a venture. Actually, however, the terrain was not really suitable for the kind of expedition Varnum might have imagined was about to take place.

To reach the wooded sanctuary from the undulating prairie, the soldiers had to descend an embankment several feet high, through narrow openings among the trees that demarcated the two levels. The timber along this second bank was described by Varnum, Moylan, and DeRudio as being quite heavy, so dense in places that finding a path was difficult. Between this fringe and the river to the east was an open area or a "park" about a hundred yards wide, with more cottonwoods and a variety of brush along the banks. The ground of this bottomland was gravelly in places, since in high water it was flooded by the Little Bighorn. To the north was the Garryowen Loop itself, a double band of the river that had to be traversed in order to make an attack in either direction. Whatever Varnum's perception of Reno's plans, this was not a route that offered easy access to the village.[56]

Of course, Reno had no intention of attacking from that or any other direction. Varnum's various accounts are somewhat confused in regard to timing, but they are consistent in stating that Reno was with Company G, apparently deploying the unit in the area north of the park. On the way to find Reno, Varnum thought he might have shouted something like "I am going to charge" as he passed members of the regiment. But when he reached Reno, the major merely confirmed that Varnum had recently been on the skirmish line, then made a request: "I wish you would go back there, and see how things are going on, and come back and report to me."[57] Private O'Neill, a member of the initial G Troop contingent, remembered Reno as "apparently not excited" in the park. Likely that was Reno's demeanor at the time, as he became increasingly self-absorbed. He was not charging Indians through the woods. He was not preparing a defensive position in the event his entire battalion had to retire from the field. The most that can be said is that he was vaguely mindful of the men who remained exposed to a growing threat on the open prairie.[58]

As Varnum left Reno and started back toward the line, he ran into Lieutenant Hodgson, the battalion adjutant and the officer who was supposed to be observing activity outside the timber. Varnum suggested that Hodgson tell Reno what was happening on the line. By the time Varnum reached the edge of the timber, the entire skirmish line had withdrawn from the field. He gave slightly different sequences of events in his various accounts, but the dynamics of the tactical situation had established an irreversible momentum, and no matter how he told the story, the loss of leadership and the breakdown of good order and discipline on the skirmish line were mere harbingers of the wild retreat that would soon follow. The woods were becoming crowded with officers, led by Reno. For all practical purposes, the only officer who had remained on the line for any length of time, directing Reno's primary attack force, was Captain French.[59]

Moylan later claimed that seeing the left of the line being flanked and turned by the Indians, he called for Reno to come and have a look, and that as a consequence of their consultation, the rest of the soldiers were withdrawn from the prairie. According to Moylan, the withdrawal was carried out by a flank movement to the right, his A Troop followed by M, half of which had to face the foothills where the enemy was concentrated. In short, the redeployment was accomplished by a neat wheeling movement, as one might have observed on the parade ground, so that the westernmost unit (M) now became the right of a new line established behind the natural wall at the edge of the woods.[60]

However, Moylan was likely trying to put the best face on a tactical withdrawal that was not nearly so neat. If Varnum was correct, Reno was still in the woods when the line fell back. If First Sergeant Heyn was right, there were no officers present at the time, at least in A Troop, with DeRudio having followed a squad of men into the timber and Moylan presumably seeking guidance from Reno. Additionally, Gerard said that as the Indians turned the left of the line and began to get in the rear of the command, "the men broke from the line and went into the woods. . . . The men ran into the timber pell mell, and all resistance to the Sioux had ceased."[61]

By the most generous estimation, no more than half the command remained on the line before the last rush for safety. Granted, the vast majority of those troopers belonged to M Troop, the largest and strongest unit. But even the best of men had to suffer some degree of demoralization as they watched the right of the line wither, as first G Troop (or some significant part of it) departed with the battalion commander and then as Company A disappeared in small groups, each time forcing the men of M Troop to get up and shift eastward to fill the gaps until a skirmish line several hundred yards in length dwindled to half that distance. The urge to retreat into the woods must have been irresistible. It would have taken the best efforts of Captain French and Sergeant Ryan to get those soldiers out of harm's way with even a modicum of order. In the end, the last of the men on the line surely sprinted for cover, as Gerard and others remembered.

Within fifty yards of the timber, Sergeant Myles O'Hara of Company M was killed, the only fatality suffered by Reno's battalion while on the skirmish line. Private Edward Pigford remembered O'Hara calling out to him, "For God's sake, don't leave me." Maybe someone else stopped to see if O'Hara was really dead. Maybe not. The fact that O'Hara's body was left on the field of battle may have been an indication of the battalion's demoralization. As far as Pigford knew, O'Hara was still alive, so it is a simple matter to blame the young private for not pausing long enough to pull O'Hara to safety. However, whether dead or alive, O'Hara was within easy reach of many of the men at the edge of the timber. The popular noncommissioned officer, only recently promoted from corporal, was the only soldier left lying on the prairie. Maybe his fellows could not see him. Maybe they could. Certainly more than one of them knew that he was no longer counted among their number.[62]

As for the Sioux and Cheyenne warriors, they were busy filling all of the empty space. They circled around what had been the left flank of Reno's skirmish line and effectively cut off the route leading back to Ford A. They were pouring down the hill at the head of Shoulder Blade Creek. In the woods, where there had been no Indians within sight, DeRudio saw them coming. They clambered up the bluffs on the eastern side of the river, giving them some access to the rear of Reno's position. They were confident and angry, but still wary. Having taken extra time to get himself ready, Crazy Horse was on the way.

In the face of only modest resistance to his charge down the valley, Reno had surrendered the combat initiative to an enemy who thrived on fear in the opposition. Except for the horse-holders and surgeons, Reno was the first man off the battle line, taking a significant portion of one company with him to find nonexistent Indians or to begin an attack that was neither feasible nor intended. Through steady attrition, the officers and men followed their leader into the timber, where the battalion commander ought to have been contemplating a defensive strategy.

Moylan—a member of Custer's extended family but soon to be a close associate in Reno's exculpation—later testified: "I know that the command as a whole was not put in the timber for the purpose of defense." He went on to assert that if Custer had seen the battalion deploying in the bottom, the general would not have imagined for a moment that Reno was in danger and that Custer would have been justified in believing that Reno would hold his position. These are odd admissions from a man who would shortly be as eager as Reno to get out of the woods.[63]

A tenable defensive position would not be used to maximum advantage. Those already in the timber simply waited for the last of the troopers on the line to find their way into the bosom of temporary sanctuary, which was actually no more than a holding area for incipient panic. By order or invitation, the race for survival was about to begin.

Brevet Major General George Armstrong Custer, 1865. Photo courtesy of Little Bighorn Battlefield National Monument (LBBNM), Catalogue #16660.

Lieutenant Colonel George Armstrong Custer, 1876. Photo courtesy of LBBNM, Catalogue #333.

Elizabeth Bacon Custer, 1876. Photo courtesy of LBBNM, Catalogue #451.

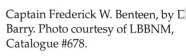

Major Marcus A. Reno, by D. F. Barry. Photo courtesy of LBBNM, Catalogue #7109.

Captain Frederick W. Benteen, by D Barry. Photo courtesy of LBBNM, Catalogue #678.

Captain Thomas W. Custer, circa 1872.
Photo courtesy of LBBNM,
Catalogue #526.

Lieutenant William W. Cooke, circa
1875. Photo courtesy of LBBNM,
Catalogue #7556.

Hunkpapa leader Sitting Bull, by D. F. Barry, circa 1885. Photo courtesy of LBBNM, Catalogue #523.

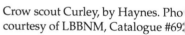

Crow scout Curley, by Haynes. Pho courtesy of LBBNM, Catalogue #69.

CHAPTER NINE

HURRY UP AND WAIT

Cautiously optimistic, concerned but determined, Custer paused near the Flat at the junction of Reno Creek and its North Fork. The failure to scoop up at least part of the Sans Arc satellite camp had been discouraging, but the departees were still in sight, Major Marcus Reno was about to commence the next phase of Custer's improvised tactical plan, and reserve forces were within hailing distance. Besides, the Sioux and Cheyenne warriors had not yet come out to challenge the regiment's advance. To Custer, that fact must have constituted both a wonder and a worry. The regiment had presumably been seen by Indian outriders three hours earlier, the Sans Arc mourners were on the move, the Lone Tepee had been burned, and the dust of the combined Custer-Reno column was surely visible to anyone within ten miles—and still no Indian fighters had appeared.

Custer had told Reno to be "prudent," probably to be wary of being drawn into a decoy-and-ambush situation, although such a gambit by the Indians was unlikely so near their village and its substantial number of noncombatants. Facing a large military force, the Indians usually either broke up their camp and scattered or sent out fighting men to intercept and engage the foe, as they had done with General George Crook a week earlier. In fact, to oppose Crook and a force much larger than their own, they had traveled to the headwaters of the Rosebud, fully forty miles from their village at the site of the Lone Tepee. Of course, Custer was unaware of Crook's withdrawal from the field, but had he known, it would merely have added to the puzzlement of how he could march almost at his leisure without resistance from a huge hostile village only three miles away. Still in possession of the combat initiative, no matter how peculiar and eerily fortunate that may have seemed, Custer was being drawn toward an irresistible objective, his thoughts totally occupied with the second phase of his multifaceted plan to make the Seventh Cavalry appear larger than it was.

Custer's line of march toward the bluffs above the Little Bighorn began several hundred yards beyond North Fork. The time was shortly before three o'clock. Captain Myles Keogh and Lieutenant William Cooke had returned. Riding at a full gallop on Cooke's heels, Private Archibald McIlhargey arrived soon after, bringing Reno's first message as the entire right wing was trotting toward the north. Because the column was moving uphill and needed to save the horses, Custer probably traveled no faster than a slow trot. Besides, the Sans Arc villagers were likely already disappearing on the far side of the ridges that Custer would soon have to navigate and were thus, as they had been for the past hour, beyond the wing's reach, no matter how fast it rode.

While at the Flat, Custer may have adjusted his order of march in a manner best suited for coping with a wide range of contingencies. The only description of that wing configuration was provided by Sergeant Daniel Kanipe, who said, "Custer was trotting and galloping along with companies in columns of twos, *all 5 companies abreast* [emphasis added]." Such a formation offered sufficient flexibility that Custer could rapidly deploy his manpower by individual companies or by the two battalions under the command of Captain Keogh (I, C, and L) and Captain George Yates (F and E).[1]

Thus, the command advanced, spread out, up the slopes almost directly north of the starting point west of the Flat. This route took Custer away from Reno in terms of distance, although their movements were roughly parallel. The intervening high ground prevented Custer from seeing anything of Reno or the main Indian village. He was operating in the blind, and his primary concern was to get to the top of those hills, which were obstructing a view of the Little Bighorn Valley. As soon as possible, he wanted to see for himself the precise nature of his tactical problem, and he needed to show the troopers in the bottom that he had not deserted them.

Therefore, as the command reached the ridgeline just east of the bluffs guarding the valley, the pace may have picked up to a lope or a slow gallop. The five columns were by now traveling on comparatively level ground

194

heading for a hill—later named Reno Hill, the area where the embattled major would later fortify. At about this time, from the valley below, the men of Reno's attacking force saw their comrades, guidons flying and Custer waving his hat, some distance south of Reno Hill, almost exactly opposite the line of Reno's advance. It was now perhaps 3:10, and Custer was making no effort to conceal his intentions. He wanted the vision-and-hearing-impaired Reno—and the Indians—to know where he was and where he was headed. Had Custer meant to sneak up on the village in a surprise flank attack, he had plenty of room and opportunity to slip unseen through creeks and gullies and ditches well east of the ridgeline. Instead, he marched in concert with but slightly in advance of Reno's battalion, trying perhaps to reassure his subordinate, never really leaving the second-in-command to whom he had entrusted the honor of the advance, never breaking faith with the faint-hearted fellow officer to whom he had promised support. As it turned out, Custer doffed his hat in vain.

Just as Custer's advance could be seen from the valley floor, so could Reno's line of attack be observed by the riders on the bluffs. That much was confirmed by Sergeant Kanipe. He said that when Custer's troopers saw Reno speeding northward on the opposite side of the river, they "broke into wild disorder," waving their arms, yelling, and "urging their horses ahead at break neck speed" so that many of the men actually got out in front of Custer, who told them: "Hold your horses, boys; there are Indians enough down there for all of us." The remark reflected Custer's awareness of the magnitude of the problem facing the regiment, even though he had not yet seen the full extent of the village. Kanipe stated that Custer's column did not pause to cheer Reno. On the other hand, it is improbable that Custer intended his command to gallop, because no trooper on a well-traveled government-issue horse could have surged past the general on Vic unless Custer was deliberately moderating the pace of the advance, as his admonishment indicates.[2]

Kanipe was certain that Custer could see Reno's command. Kanipe himself observed it "plainly," and Custer and Kanipe were separated by only about fifteen yards. The sergeant elaborated:

When Custer and his five companies came to the top of the bluffs in sight of Reno and his three companies in the bottom, I did not see any

195

Indians directly in front of Reno, as he was getting too close to that spur of timber that reaches out across the bottom from the river, where Reno dismounted and formed his skirmish line. I saw plenty of ponies moving off to the left of Reno as though they had riders on them, but it was so far that I could not tell, but in the manner they were moving indicated there were riders on them.

Down in the valley, Reno's force was deploying from column to line, still moving at a trot, probably within a mile of the Garryowen Loop, and as suggested earlier, sweeping in a slight arc along the general course of the river in the direction of the open prairie. As yet, there were no Indians in any number or concentration, no skirmish line, and no combat. Seeing what Kanipe saw, Custer had good reason to signal his approval to Reno and the men riding below.[3]

A half mile or so past Reno Hill, Custer brought the wing to a halt. Looming in his front was a promontory that provided just the kind of vantage point that Custer needed to examine Reno's position relative to the village, to assess the location and strength of the Indians, to determine the whereabouts of the fleeing Sans Arcs, and to find out what the hell had become of his lollygagging reserves. It was an almost perfect spot from which to gather the intelligence he desired. Custer climbed Sharpshooter Ridge.

Kanipe did not specifically refer to such a halt, but such an omission is understandable, since he was about to leave on an urgent mission himself. But Trumpeter John Martin, serving as a Custer orderly, did recall the stop. In an interview with Walter Camp, Martin noted that at that juncture, Custer did indeed come to an extended stop and did ascend to high ground. Camp paraphrased Martin's testimony:

> Martin says Custer's trail passed along where Reno retreated to [Reno Hill]. Then Custer halted command on the high ridge about 10 minutes, and officers looked at village through glasses. Saw children and dogs playing among the tepees but no warriors or horses except few loose ponies grazing around. There was then a discussion among the officers as to where the warriors might be and someone suggested that they might be buffalo hunting.

The naivete reflected in this account is typical of many comments made by the young Italian immigrant, a private of two years' service, who had enlisted as a "musician" and whose understanding of the English language— particularly colloquial expressions—was poor at best. Martin may have been regarded as simpleminded, even ignorant, by some of the officers and men, but he was neither blind to, nor uninformed about, the essence of the moment, which must have been a time of great excitement for him. Given those circumstances, his memory was sharper and truer than that of many men who would pass themselves off as his "betters."[4]

In the Camp interview, Martin specified that Custer went to "the high ridge." In a later account, he recalled that Custer "first halted" on "Weir's Hill" to take a look at the village. He gave W. A. Graham an even more graphic description:

> After we had gone about a mile or two we came to a big hill that over-looked the valley, and we rode around the base of it and halted. Then the General took me with him, and we rode to the top of the hill, where he could see the village in the valley on the other side of the river. It was a big village, but we couldn't see it all from there, though we didn't know it then; but several hundred tepees were in plain sight. There were no bucks to be seen; all we could see was some squaws and children playing and a few dogs and ponies. The General seemed both surprised and glad, and said the Indians must be in their tents, asleep. We did not see anything of Reno's column where we were up on the hill. I am sure the General did not see them at all, because he looked *all around* [emphasis added] with his glasses, and all he said was that we had "got them this time." He turned in his saddle and took off his hat and waved it to the men of the command, who were halted at the base of the hill, could see him, and he shouted to them, "Hurrah, boys, we've got them! We'll finish them up and then go home to our station."

When Martin said that Custer climbed the high ridge, he meant not "Weir Hill"—afterward identified as Weir Point or Weir Ridge—but rather the most obvious promontory in the vicinity.[5]

Sharpshooter Ridge was so named, after the fight, in recognition of the Sioux and Cheyenne marksmen who had, from its heights, poured a heavy fire into Reno's eventual position (the Reno Enclave). It is hard to know when the name for that high ground came into common usage, but Sharpshooter Ridge was certainly not identified as such on the Lieutenant Edward Maguire's maps, which were the authoritative military charts during the 1876–79 period. It is clearly an appellation with which Martin was not familiar, because that is the "hill" he and Custer climbed.

Located approximately a half-mile beyond Reno Hill, the ridge blocks direct access to Medicine Tail Coulee and the ground leading to the Custer battlefield. About thirty feet higher than the terrain looming above the river, Sharpshooter Ridge appears from the valley below to be a slight elevation, close enough to the bluffs to be part of them. A natural extension of the irregular incline up from the Flat, and less than a mile in length, the ridge of Martin's recollection was the first high point from which Custer could have satisfied his need for information. To the left of Sharpshooter Ridge (toward the river), the land adjoining the bluffs is upgrade and just wide enough to comfortably accommodate a column of fours; to the right, the ground is undulating and broken but easily accessible to the usual formations of cavalry. As indicated by Martin, the companies were waiting at the base of the hill for further instructions, which came initially as a few words of encouragement from the commander.

In his court of inquiry testimony, Martin said that after leaving the Flat, Custer's command advanced several hundred yards in a straight line (possibly awaiting the return of Adjutant Cooke) before turning right. After another quarter mile, the columns passed around some hills "and went on top of the ridge," which was "very high" and too far back from the bluffline to see the timber on the east bank of the river. On the trip up from the Flat, the wing did not move very fast because of the hills. When asked in court for a more exact location of where he and Custer had stopped to look at the Indian village, Martin actually pointed on the imprecise Maguire map to the place where Sharpshooter Ridge would have been situated—that is, if Maguire had properly pictured that nameless landmark. Martin indicated that the ridge "was on a line leading from Major Reno's position [the Reno Enclave] to the point '7'" on the map. The "7" on the map had in fact been placed there during previous testimony to mark the spot where Lieutenant Charles DeRudio had seen Custer, Cooke, and an unidentified person. What Martin recalled was the *first* time Custer had climbed the ridge, whereas DeRudio was reporting a sighting that reflected Custer's *second* trip up the hill. The two positions were separated by less than a mile and ten minutes of activity, the approximate distance and amount of time occupied by Custer along the length of Sharpshooter Ridge.[6]

The Crow scout Curley confirmed Martin's remembrance of Custer's line of advance and the terrain he encountered. As paraphrased by Camp, Curley also provided a distinction between Sharpshooter Ridge and Weir Point.

> Custer's route from this point [separation from Reno] was directly across the country, on the crest of a long ridge, running to the bluffs and coming out at a point about 500 ft. north of the Reno corral. From here Custer passed along the crest of the bluffs for fully 3/4 mile, in full view of the river and of the valley over across it. Custer hurried his men, going at a gallop most of the time. Reno and his command were plainly seen by Custer's whole command while marching this 3/4 mile. On the first line of bluffs back from the river there are two high peaks marked "A" on the map [Camp's map], now called Reno peaks [Weir Point]. For some distance south of these there is a high ridge [Sharpshooter Ridge] running parallel with the river, not so high as the peaks.[7]

In another of his iterations on this sequence of events, Curley said that he, Mitch Boyer, and the other three Crows had ascended a hill, and when they looked back, they could see Custer coming and Reno crossing the river. At some point after this: "Custer and his brother went to the right of us as we were standing on the hill. Custer turned around as he reached the top of the ridge and waved his hat, and his men at the bottom of the hill waved their hats and shouted. Custer kept on going on the ridge and the men followed him."[8]

Another of the Crow scouts, White Man Runs Him, told a similar story. According to him, when the scouts reached "the ridge," they saw tepees down the valley. Custer advanced slowly, stopping occasionally. They remained in this general area until Reno started firing. Like Curley, White Man Runs Him said that Custer and Tom went to a hill just to the right of where the scouts waited, and there Custer waved his hat, then led the soldiers along the ridge. The scouts had to hurry to keep up.[9]

199

The Crow scout Hairy Moccasin provided supporting testimony. According to him: "Custer yelled to us to stop, then told us to go to the high hill ahead (the high point just north of where Reno later entrenched). From here we could see the village and could see Reno fighting."[10]

Where he sent Boyer and the Crows, Custer followed to see for himself. From Sharpshooter Ridge, at about the midpoint between Reno Hill and Weir Point, Custer encouraged his men to give "the regular charging yell." In the valley below, Reno was telling his troopers to shut up.[11]

At the court of inquiry, Trumpeter Martin asserted that the first group to ascend Sharpshooter Ridge—other than the scouts—included himself, the general and Tom Custer, and their nephew, Autie Reed. Once on the ridge, the first order of business would have been to determine the direction and location of the Sans Arc satellite village. Martin confirmed the existence of such a fleeing encampment by indicating that Custer had turned right after the Flat to follow a trail that "looked like tepee poles had been dragged along there" and from that position had gone to the "highest point" east of the river. Through DeRudio's binoculars, Custer would have searched the landscape north of his position for signs of the villagers he could not bring within his grasp. Beyond that, Custer would have determined that there was no significant camp east of the river, although the several high peaks of Weir Point blocked his vision of the bottomland northwest of his position. Lastly, he would have noted that the terrain in his front (north) was suitable for the kind of tactical scheme he had in mind if his plan was implemented as he envisioned it.[12]

Concurrent with his scan of the ground to the north, Custer assessed the situation on the west side of the Little Bighorn. He knew the relative position of Reno's battalion, even if at that very moment it was out of his line of sight. Martin said that from the ridge, Reno could not be seen, but as an orderly, Martin would have been to the rear of Custer and his aide-de-camp brother, and Martin was not examining the scene through binoculars. The likelihood is that Custer saw more than Martin but not so much as to make any real difference in determining the juxtaposition of principal players in the unfolding drama.

Like Martin, Custer saw hundreds of white-skin or canvas tepee tops extending westward beyond the timber and for some distance to the north. Perhaps through DeRudio's glasses he saw individual riders scampering to recover ponies from the immense herd on the far side of the village, and doubtless he picked out the Indian women and children and dogs seemingly at play on the outskirts of the camp, with Custer perhaps no more able than Martin to define that terror-stricken tableau for what it was. From the evidence, it is understandable that Custer would have wondered aloud about the absence of warriors in Reno's front. By now (3:20), Reno was approaching the place where he would establish the skirmish line. To Custer, it made no sense that only women and their offspring could be seen, that there were no warriors in sight, that there was no shooting. Perhaps his brother Tom did speculate, in an offhand way, that the men of the tribes were out hunting buffalo. It was possible. In any case, Custer naturally concluded that he had caught the Indians "napping"—to Martin, "asleep"—which was very nearly the truth.[13]

The last order of business would have been to espy those reserve units on the back trail. The most that Custer could have seen from Sharpshooter Ridge was a cloud of dust approximately five miles distant. He may have been able to make out sufficient detail to identify the source of the dust, but it is more likely that through experience and instant analysis, he concluded that the size, shape, and pace of that murky body marked the trail of the pack train. For whatever reason, perhaps having to do with expectations as to where things *ought* to be, he concluded that Captain Frederick Benteen's battalion was not a part of that assemblage.

With this initial assessment, Custer flourished his broad-brimmed hat and shouted his optimism to the men waiting expectantly at the base of the ridge. They cheered again, and some of the horses lurched forward at the sudden outburst. If Custer was confident and eager, the troopers followed his lead. Bravery, like fear or any other raw emotion, can be a contagious thing, particularly before the test of its depth, and Custer's honest display of enthusiasm was surely reassuring to the blindly subservient men in the ranks. Most had no choice but to trust the officers who led them, and Custer had a reputation for wanting and daring to win. For all of the troopers, ignorant of strategy or tactics or the latest intelligence, winning meant simply a fair chance of staying alive.

At that juncture, Custer's own state of mind must have been one of suspended disbelief. He might have made brief mental reference to all of the good luck that had passed his way during a lifetime of taking calculated risks, but as fortunate as he may have felt at this moment, the ease with which he was approaching the largest Indian village ever seen with his own eyes had to be unsettling. True, he had managed to strike this formidable Indian encampment before it could scatter, but he had to be troubled by the whereabouts of all those Indian fighters and by when they might arrive on the scene and from which direction. He would not leave this ridge until he had taken another look for himself.

According to Trumpeter Martin, when he and Custer came down from the ridge, they "rode back to where the troops were" near the base of the hill, and Custer spoke to Lieutenant Cooke about what he had seen. Presumably at this time Custer also gave his adjutant instructions to be relayed to the battalion and company commanders regarding the disposition of forces. Simultaneously, Captain Tom Custer left his brother and went directly to his own Company C in search of a reliable messenger.[14]

Apparently Tom intended to select a noncommissioned officer for this important assignment, and the first one he reached—other than First Sergeant Edwin Bobo, who had been serving as de facto second-in-command of the troop—should have been Sergeant (George) August Finckle. At least, Sergeant Kanipe believed that Finckle would have been the choice had not Finckle's horse given out, obliging him to fall back in the line of march. As it turned out, Kanipe was chosen to perform the task and so was spared Finckle's fate.[15]

In his various accounts, Kanipe gives the impression that he received his orders from Tom Custer while the command was marching from the Flat but *after* passing Reno Hill. However, since this was his last contact with Custer's command, and considering the intensity of feelings during those final moments, his remembrance of those circumstances extraneous to his receiving the instructions may have been less than complete. He did not deny that the wing paused near Sharpshooter Ridge while Custer and his brother climbed the hill to assess the situation; rather, Kanipe is consistently silent on the subject. In context, it is simply unreasonable to suppose that anyone would have been sent with a message to units on the back trail while the wing was on the move and before Custer had made a judgment based on a close personal evaluation of their location relative to his physical position and tactical predicament.[16]

When Tom Custer reached Kanipe, he told the sergeant to find the pack train and deliver instructions that the rear-guard commander, Captain

Thomas McDougall, was to hurry the mules straight across country and that if any of the packs got loose he was to cut them off unless they were ammunition packs. Tom added, "And if you see Benteen, tell him to come on quick—a big Indian village."[17]

Thus, Sergeant Kanipe was nominated by happenstance to carry not the last but the most important message sent by Custer. In historical terms, this message would be adjudged just a precursor to the final written directive initiated by Custer, one carried by the very last white man to see Custer alive. That man would be Trumpeter Martin, the undereducated Italian immigrant who later would be criticized for failing to move the immovable. The word carried by Kanipe should have been enough, but he found himself speaking to the deaf and dumb. By the time Martin got his chance, the dye was cast, and the word "urgency" had all but lost its meaning, particularly in terms of Custer using Benteen and the ammunition packs in a coordinated way.

The interesting aspects of Kanipe's message are that McDougall was to bring the pack train directly across country and that the only essential cargo was the ammunition. The message also makes clear that even from the heights of Sharpshooter Ridge, Custer was not certain about the position of Benteen's battalion. Such factors tend to support the notion that Kanipe did not receive his instructions until after Custer and his brother had gone to the ridge, from which point they could confirm, through close-in observation, that there was a big village and that it was possible to bring the packs from the relatively flat land near the Lone Tepee in a more direct route to the high ground.

With the orders in hand, Kanipe turned his horse in the direction of the back trail. Seeing the dust of the pack train, he veered to the left rather than following the route taken by Custer from the Flat. He was heading directly for McDougall and the packs when he noticed Benteen's column off to his right. Driven by Custer's instructions and the best of intentions, he altered his course to intercept the officer.[18]

Custer had to be annoyed that Benteen had not yet appeared within easy recall. After all, Benteen had been on his ancillary blocking assignment for more than three hours. In all that time, Custer had heard nothing from his temperamental battalion commander and was probably beginning to regret that he had not sent someone at the Lone Tepee or the Flat to round up the recalcitrant Benteen. Maybe there was a sarcastic edge to Tom Custer's voice when he suggested that "if" Kanipe saw Benteen, he should tell the captain to "come on quick." As best Custer could determine, Benteen had done nothing quickly, even though Custer's wing had lingered behind Reno's advance, had dallied in the vicinity of the Flat, and had taken some fifteen minutes getting to and assembling at Sharpshooter Ridge. Now, instead of using Benteen as an element in his staggered attack, as indicated in Martin's recollection of the general's last orders to Reno, Custer would have to improvise further, employing his own wing to achieve the same objective while holding Benteen's battalion in reserve, assuming that Benteen would at long last accelerate his pace.[19]

By the time Custer reached Sharpshooter Ridge, he was already committed to a general proposition and a specific plan of attack that envisaged striking the Indian village from several directions—not simultaneously and not at first light, as at the Washita, but openly, at midday, and in alternate thrusts. The advantages of such a strategy were that the enemy would have to divide its forces to cope with the multiple corridors of attack and that the avenues of escape to the east (Custer), the south (Reno), and the north and possibly west (Terry-Gibbon) would be inhibited if not tightly sealed. The disadvantages were that all of the players on all sides would have to behave as hoped or expected and that the failure of any friendly component could doom the whole plan by allowing the opponent, with the shorter lines of communication, to recover and defeat widely separated units in detail. In the face of limited options, and with a confidence in the Seventh and his own instincts unshaken by any piece of intelligence up to and through Sharpshooter Ridge, Custer decided to continue with the somewhat risky venture.

Trumpeter Martin remembered that after Custer came down from Sharpshooter Ridge, he remarked: "We will go down and make a crossing and capture the village." According to Martin, the officers believed that because no warriors could be seen, the encampment of mostly noncombatants could in fact be captured and that the warriors would be obliged to surrender when they returned. From the Lone Tepee and long before, Custer had planned to win by bluff or bluster or subterfuge, using all of the tools at his disposal. Perhaps Custer still believed that he could gather some hostages or perhaps he merely expressed a wish, a boon that might be granted. Just in case he had been deceived by appearances, he wanted the reserve ammunition and, if possible, Benteen.[20]

As Custer and Martin rode back to the command, Tom went directly to C Troop and conveyed the general's orders to Sergeant Kanipe, who started immediately across country. Custer spoke encouraging words to the soldiers, and they bellowed their approval. Turning Vic, Custer started up the ridge again, with some part of his command—now more tightly formed in column of fours—in his wake.

Martin firmly believed that *all* of Custer's command followed the general up and along Sharpshooter Ridge. Although this was certainly possible, a number of factors militate against such a conclusion. First of all, what did Martin mean by "command"? Did he mean simply the head-quarters contingent, of which he was a part? Located at the head of the column, and clearly preoccupied with his duties as orderly, was he even mindful of precisely which units came after? Given the several trails identified after the battle, and in view of other occurrences while the wing was advancing, Martin appears to have been making a general observation. More likely, Custer made an additional division of his forces for tactical and demonstrative reasons.

Sergeant Kanipe, other participants, and most analysts of the Little Bighorn have contended that Custer traveled so near the bluffline that the valley was always in sight. Of course, Kanipe was gone before Sharpshooter Ridge was circumvented, and most others with a personal recollection based their opinions on a trail observed after the fight. On the other hand, Lieutenant Edward Godfrey, basing his conclusion entirely on after-action observations of a trail of shod horses, decided that Custer had gone east of Sharpshooter Ridge. The Godfrey map is clear on this matter. There is also evidence that Custer traveled the length of the ridge with all or some part of his right wing. Even though individual misinterpretations are pos-sible, all three conclusions are likely correct. Custer most probably passed the ridge in a tactical configuration designed to cover a wide swath of ground quickly while at the same time showing his command to those in the valley below.[21]

Almost certainly E Troop traveled west of the ridge. The testimony of Lieutenant Charles Varnum is clear that he saw, from the valley floor, the gray horses moving northward at a trot. He apparently had only a glimpse of the company, but that brief sighting was sufficient to permit a fairly authoritative picture of its passing. At the court of inquiry, he said that he saw "about the whole of the Gray Horse Company," although the head and the rear of the column seemed to be in a kind of "hollow." The ground over which E Troop moved was "uneven and rolling . . . a high bluff," about opposite the skirmish line. In a later account, Varnum repeated: "The conformation of the ground on the bluff was such that I could see only that much of the column." Although not definitive, Varnum's statements would tend to favor a path west of Sharpshooter Ridge rather than a route along its top for the simple reason that from the valley, the ridge appears relatively level, so that neither the head nor the tail of a moving column would be out of sight in the way he described. However, the bluffline to the west dips slightly, with just enough visible space to accommodate Varnum's word-picture.[22]

The testimony of the interpreter Fred Gerard is less specific than Varnum's but is generally supportive in terms of chronology. Gerard said that as he was entering the woods, he observed a "portion" of Custer's column moving downriver "along the hills" at a rapid pace. Since Gerard left the field early, after perhaps only a few shots had been fired, his sighting can be considered nearly contemporaneous with Varnum's. However, Gerard estimated Custer's position to be more to the southeast, closer to Reno Hill, a paradox explained partly by Gerard's poor sense of geography and partly by the fact that his judgment—like Varnum's—was based on a fleeting glance. Interestingly, he did not recall seeing the Gray Horse Troop, which, once seen, seemed to stick in everyone's memory as a totally unique and identifiable entity. However, by Varnum's description, by the presence of a trail of shod horses, and by battalion assignment, it is credible that Company E (the weakest) in the lead and F (the strongest) behind advanced on the west side of Sharpshooter Ridge. What Gerard observed may have been C Troop moving with Custer along the top of the ridge.[23]

Other than Godfrey's recollection of a trail on the east side of Sharpshooter Ridge, few facts support the notion that some fraction of the right wing went that way. But by a process of elimination, we can deduce just such a disposition. The key to this analysis is the proposition that Company C followed Custer's headquarters command over the ridge and that it was the only component to do so, leaving in its wake a full set of four enlisted men. The remembrances of certain Arikara and Crow scouts buttress the plausibility of this thesis.

At some point near Sharpshooter Ridge, four privates belonging to C Troop dropped out of the line of march: Peter Thompson, age twenty-one, enlisted the previous September; James Watson, twenty-six, also showing a September enlistment; John Brennan, twenty-seven, another September enlistee; and John Fitzgerald, a thirty-five-year-old farrier with four years of service in the cavalry. The four soldiers were apparently the last in the C Troop column. Their horses having given out, Thompson and Watson seemingly had a legitimate reason for falling behind; Brennan and Fitzgerald did not have such a reason, as far as is known.[24]

Information on this question comes almost completely from Thompson's narrative, which is flawed in many ways but which is validated in this instance by circumstantial evidence provided by the Arikara scouts. According to Thompson, the relevant sequence of events occurred after the companies were ordered to form into more compact "sets of four," after the village was seen, and after the troopers gave their "regular charging yell." Thompson recalled that a detail of five Company F men was then sent forward to reconnoiter and that at this point he was "gradually left behind" even though he made an effort to keep up with his troop. At about the same time, Watson's horse went down, and Brennan and Fitzgerald disappeared from the scene.[25]

As Watson was trying to get his horse up, Sergeant Finckle—whose own mount had faltered earlier, allowing Kanipe to leave with the message to the pack train and Benteen—arrived and sat "calmly on his horse looking on and making no effort to help Watson in his difficulty. . . . Finally the poor animal gained his feet with a groan, and Finckle passed on with a rush to overtake [the] company." Custer's command was then disappearing over the crest of the hill, and to the west, the Indian village was "all in commotion." In a separate iteration of his experience, Thompson said that while Watson was attempting to get his horse on its feet, Brennan and Fitzgerald were engaged in their "maneuvers" to turn toward the rear. Private John McGuire stated that the latter two soldiers never said anything about their separation from Custer, but the troopers in Company C generally thought that the two men "did not care to enter the engagement with Custer."[26]

The manner in which Thompson described these occurrences leads one to believe that they took place early on Sharpshooter Ridge. The ride uphill would certainly have fatigued already tired horses to the breaking point.

The village had been seen, and the men had cheered. The F Troop detachment (a set of four and a noncommissioned officer) had started forward to perform its advance-guard function with Custer's headquarters unit, as it may have been doing since crossing the Divide. Sergeant Finckle was beginning to make some headway in his effort to catch up with the column. Brennan and Fitzgerald had found the time and the opportunity (before Finckle arrived to chase them back into line) to slip off the ridge and circle back toward the pack train, possibly with the excuse that their mounts were too jaded to continue the pursuit. Lastly, Custer's column was disappearing over the far end of the ridge.

Straggling behind, a group of Arikara scouts were eyewitnesses to some of what Thompson described. The scout Soldier said that at the beginning of the ridge east of the river, they detected signs of Custer's march. Soldier asserted that the trail was plain from the way the grass was trodden down. From this vantage point, they could see the Indian village and fellow Arikara Bob-tailed Bull out at the end of Reno's skirmish line, with many Sioux riding out beyond its left flank. The inhabitants of the camp were taking down some tepees, the first circle (Hunkpapa) already beginning to break up. As the Rees proceeded, they came upon a soldier whose horse had gone down from the heat. The trooper was kicking the animal and striking it with his fist and telling the scouts, "Me go Custer! Me go Custer!" Farther on, they encountered a second cavalryman, who was also angry at his mount, abusing it and calling it a son-of-a-bitch as he indicated by signs to the Arikaras that he belonged to Custer's command. These two men were, apparently, Thompson and Watson.[27]

As already indicated, the Crow scouts had been the first to ascend Sharpshooter Ridge. Curley stated: "Custer saw the camp from the highest point on the ridge to the right of the first [Reno] entrenchment. He saw Reno going down the valley but did not see him come back [the retreat]." Curley also asserted that Custer rode along this "crest of bluffs" for about three-quarters of a mile (the approximate length of Sharpshooter Ridge) "in full view of the river and the valley beyond." The right wing was moving quickly, leaving the Crows perhaps a hundred yards behind, trying to keep up. Curley added, "The soldiers kept marching on the east side of Reno Hill and going down on the west side of the ridge—down a ravine, running northward."[28]

Again, Camp paraphrased Curley's account:

> On the first line of bluffs back from the river there are two high peaks
> marked "A" on the map [Camp's map], now called Reno peaks [Weir
> Point]. For some distance *south* [emphasis added] of these there is a
> high ridge [Sharpshooter Ridge] running parallel with the river, not
> so high as the peaks. Custer's command passed into the valley of a
> tributary of Reno Creek [Medicine Tail Coulee] just behind this ridge
> and peaks and went down it, going in a direction directly north and
> coming out into the bed of Reno Creek [Medicine Tail Coulee] about
> a mile from its mouth at Ford B [also Miniconjou Ford].[29]

The problem with interpreting even eyewitness testimony is compounded
by variations in the names attached to important landmarks. Thus, Curley
may have had in mind one set of names to describe his experience, whereas
Camp obviously used different terms for the same pieces of land and sub-
stituted geographical nomenclature in his notes to comport with his own
understanding of the terrain. For example, Hairy Moccasin used "Custer
Ridge" when his account makes clear that he meant Sharpshooter Ridge.
Taken as a whole, Curley's assertions suggest that all or some part of
Custer's command passed "behind" the ridge that had to be Sharpshooter.[30]

In light of all that we know, a credible scenario is that by the time the
Custer column reached Sharpshooter Ridge, it was formed in column of
twos, with all five companies riding abreast (C, I, L, E, and F, from west to
east). The command halted just short of the ridge while the general and his
party went up to assess the situation. Tom Custer rode back to find a reliable
courier to carry the first message to the pack train and Benteen, and he
returned with the troop over which he had nominal command. Company
C attached itself to Custer and the headquarters unit, perhaps led by the
detachment from F Troop. I and L Troops followed to occupy the right
branch of the advance, then E and F moved out to fill the lane west of
Sharpshooter Ridge. All units were now formed in column of fours, heading
north at a trot.[31]

At the northern end of Sharpshooter Ridge, the three arms of Custer's
advance would have fed down parallel dry drainage ravines to Medicine
Tail Coulee, which in turn led in a western direction toward the Little

Bighorn River and which held in its soft topsoil the pony and rutted lodgepole tracks of the Sans Arc satellite village. When the companies reached Medicine Tail Coulee and stopped, they would, by the order of their descent, have faced west in the following order: E, F, C, I, and L. This alignment is consistent with the weight of available testimony, with the terrain features, with tactical necessity, with battalion integrity, and with Custer's penchant for making use of dramatic effect to achieve his objectives.

The only testimony pertinent to Custer's departure from the ridge was provided by Trumpeter Martin. According to the orderly, the commands "Attention," "Fours right," "Column right," and "March" were given, and the column rode down off the hill, after which "Column left" caused the soldiers to pass down a ravine toward Medicine Tail Coulee. In another version, Martin recalled being "with Custer after he passed the high ground," leaving him "just as the command started down a ravine to get off the bluff, somewhat to the right of highest ground and about 1000 feet from it." Although Martin may have been referring to the place where he left with the message to Benteen, the language is sufficiently vague that one could reasonably infer an earlier separation.[32] Regardless, the fact is that for a brief period of time, the general and Martin were out of touch, and during that interval, Custer returned to Sharpshooter Ridge for his *second* examination of Reno's progress in the valley below.

The conventional view has held that Custer rode to Weir Point after the command had collected in Medicine Tail Coulee, a trip of approximately one-quarter of a mile. At that juncture Custer, his adjutant, and perhaps one other person were seen by Lieutenant DeRudio. However, from the word of those who survived, it is clear that Custer never climbed the several peaks that constitute Weir Point, even though that promontory would have given him a better view of the whole Indian village.

In his court of inquiry testimony, Martin tried, without success, to draw a distinction between the ridge (or hill) and the "high point." He stated flatly that "nobody but the Indian scouts" had gone to the high point (Weir Point), and he emphasized that he and Custer had not visited that place. However, when the court asked Martin who went to the "hill" (Sharpshooter Ridge), Martin—thinking of the first trip, the only one he had made—correctly replied that Custer, his brother (Tom), and his nephew had done so. The inability of the court—including Recorder Jesse Lee—to comprehend Martin's meaning doubtless contributed to the general impatience with the young trumpeter's efforts to tell his story. To them the hill and the high point were one and the same, whereas to Martin the two landmarks were separate and distinct entities.[33]

Similarly, the Crow scout Curley distinguished between the ridge and the two peaks, which he called "Reno Peaks" but which were actually Weir Point. Curley said that Boyer and the Crows stayed to the left of Custer (closer to the river) along the ridge and on the peaks. In an interview with Camp on the battlefield, Curley took Camp to Weir Point and made it clear that Custer *never* went to that location. The other Crows with Custer were generally supportive of the proposition that they and Boyer were on the peaks of Weir Point and that Custer did not come to them.[34]

When DeRudio saw Custer on the east side of the river, the general and his comrades had to have been situated on Sharpshooter Ridge. At the court of inquiry, DeRudio was adamant that he had seen Custer, Adjutant Cooke, and another man on "the highest point on the right bank of the creek [river], just below where Dr. DeWolf was killed [north of the Reno Enclave]." He added that the site was definitely not Weir Point but was rather "one nearer the river and the highest point on that side," a place where the river ran right under a narrow bluff. At that juncture, DeRudio marked a "7" on the imperfect Maguire map to indicate the spot. He went on to say that Custer and Cooke—whom he recognized by their blue shirts and buckskin pants— did not remain on the heights for more than a minute. DeRudio's recollection was clear that he had seen Custer—not Boyer and the Crows—on high ground that had to have been Sharpshooter Ridge, not Weir Point.[35]

As Custer had ridden along the ridge with his three columns running parallel, he may have glimpsed Reno's skirmish line forming in the valley and may have heard the first scattering shots. Preoccupied with advancing the command down the ridge, he would not have stopped to examine Reno's predicament, but once the right wing had cleared the ridge and had started down the coulees, it was perfectly logical—indeed, for a person of Custer's predispositions, imperative—that he went back for a closer study of the obstacles confronting Reno. Also, it made sense that he would have taken Cooke rather than his brother Tom, who was busy serving as the general's alter ego in unknown territory. The third person might have been Chief

Trumpeter Henry Voss or Color Sergeant Robert Hughes, brought along to show the flag. In any case, Custer was almost certainly there, and he might even have waved his hat as a signal of support to the troopers fighting below.

What Custer, sitting on his horse on the northern end of Sharpshooter Ridge, saw of Reno's fight was probably something akin to what the Arikara scout Soldier recalled observing as he ascended the long hill: the skirmish line, with Bob-tailed Bull moving beyond its farthest point and with the Sioux beginning to circle out to the left. Nearly fifteen minutes must have elapsed since Custer had formed his command at the base of the ridge, traveled its length, and then returned for his final look. It was after 3:30, and Reno's skirmish line had been formed long enough for DeRudio to have made his premature departure.

Before leaving the ridge, Custer would likely have taken an instant to check the back trail for his reserves. Looking through his DeRudio glasses, perhaps he saw Kanipe riding hard in the direction of a dust cloud that had to have been Benteen's battalion, now beginning to separate itself from the larger pack train lagging behind. Maybe he even saw his brother Boston chugging across the landscape, full of that Custer energy and determined to get himself back into the game. Custer must have believed that he could at least identify the Benteen contingent some three or four miles away.

By the time Custer reached Medicine Tail Coulee, his command was formed in column of fours facing toward the Little Bighorn River. In Custer's brief absence, the wing had likely closed up and shifted slightly forward so that the middle rested somewhere near Cedar Coulee, the E-F exit point. With the results of his own reconnaissance in hand, Custer's first thought must have been to send another message to Benteen and the pack train. While the right wing advanced on Custer's orders down Medicine Tail Coulee, the general conveyed his wishes to his adjutant and the nearest orderly in the vicinity—Trumpeter Martin.

In one of his recollections, Martin stated that *after* Cooke had written out the order, Custer said: "Trumpeter, go back to our trail and see if you can discover Benteen and give him this message. If you see no danger come back to us, but if you find Indians in your way stay with Benteen and return with him and when you get back to us report." In another rendition, Martin described a different sequence of events and a differently worded order, one more consistent with the text of the message as written: "Orderly, I want you to take a message to Colonel Benteen. Ride as fast as you can and tell him to hurry. Tell him it's a big village and I want him to be quick, and to bring the ammunition packs." Then, perhaps fearing Martin's difficulties with the English language, Cooke wrote out the message "in a big hurry."[36]

At the court of inquiry, convened only three years after the battle, Martin's memory ought to have been better, but since he was treated like an idiot in that forum, there is little guarantee that he was questioned with clarity or that his heavily accented replies were rendered with accuracy for the record. In any case, his testimony differed markedly from the statements cited above:

> General Custer turned around and called his adjutant and gave him instructions to write a dispatch to Captain Benteen. *I don't know what it was* [emphasis added]. Then the adjutant called me. I was right at the rear of the general. He said, "Orderly, I want you to take this dispatch to Captain Benteen and go as fast as you can." He also told me if I had time and there was no danger in coming back to do so, but if there was danger or there were any Indians in the way not to come back but to remain with my company. . . . The adjutant told me to follow the same trail we came down.

Martin was doubtless telling the truth when he said that he did not know the precise text of the written message at that time. On the other hand, if he was as close to Custer as he claimed, he probably heard Custer express his wishes in language very much like that in the written message.[37]

As the last known order from Custer, the Cooke scribble has become a significant relic of the Little Bighorn fight. Short and to the point, it reads as follows: "Benteen—Come on. Big Village. Be quick. Bring packs. W. W. Cooke P.S. Bring pacs [*sic*]." Scratched out in great haste, the message is noteworthy in several respects. First, it is not an invitation. It is a terse and peremptory order for Benteen to get off his butt and move. In tone and abruptness of expression, Cooke was a faithful echo of his friend and commanding officer. Having just learned that the village was *not* "napping," and possibly believing that an earlier courier in the person of Sergeant Kanipe ought to have reached Benteen, Custer was undoubtedly in a foul mood with respect to his slow-poking subordinate, whom the general had intended to use in some phase of his staggered attack.[38]

The second feature that deserves mention regarding the Cooke message is the adjutant's obvious failure to specify *ammunition* packs. Trying to capture the essence of Custer's orders, aware that the column was beginning to move away from him, Cooke was clearly preoccupied, distracted, and in a rush. Additionally, Cooke was instructing Martin in careful terms to follow the trail back to Benteen (not to *look* for Benteen) and to return only if it was safe to do so. Realizing that he had neglected to identify the ammunition packs in the body of the message, Cooke tried to correct the oversight in a postscript. Unfortunately, the adjutant simply repeated himself.

The confidence engendered by Custer's first visit to the ridge had been supplanted by more unsettling intelligence just ten or fifteen minutes later. This was not a sleepy village open to the kind of pincer movement that had been planned for the small Lone Tepee encampment, an easy squeeze that might disgorge a body of hostages for use in extorting the surrender of unwilling warriors. When Custer returned from his second trip to Sharp-shooter Ridge, he knew that he would have to implement a variation of the more aggressive and dangerous plan that must have taken shape in his mind as early as his last trip to the Crow's Nest and no later than reaching the Flat. He had ordered Reno forward on the basis of the broad concept, and though he had shown his right wing on the bluffs for all to see, he would have preferred that Benteen's battalion had arrived in time to fully execute the idea of ostentatious waves. Now the angry Indians were filling the vacuum in his wake—as he must have known they would from his brief observation at the northern end of the ridge and as demonstrated in his final instructions carried by Martin, which recognized that the kith and kin of those gamboling children had awakened from their naps.

When Martin left Custer and Cooke, the column was perhaps a mile from the Little Bighorn. Martin's accounts of his departure from Medicine Tail Coulee and his ride back to Benteen are fraught with minor inconsistencies. In one iteration, Martin said that the column was within half a mile of the river, from which point the southern end of the Indian encampment could be seen; in another version, he asserted that this part of the village was *not* in view. At the court of inquiry, he specified a spot on the Maguire map that was at least a mile from the river. The upshot seems to be that although he could point to the place at which he left, he had difficulty describing it or estimating its position relative to other landmarks. In sum, probably neither he nor any other member of the command could see any significant part of the village from their location in the coulee.[39]

Martin did positively remember that in his journey out of Medicine Tail, he traveled directly uphill and cross-country rather than seeking out the ravines used by elements of the Custer command in their descent from Sharpshooter Ridge. In that sojourn, he would encounter participants of some consequence to the story of the Little Bighorn while totally missing others. It is amazing that there were not more intersections on the back trail of Custer's advance, especially since the time frame for such encounters probably did not exceed five minutes. Either there were gaps in participants' memories or the land was large enough to contain the routes of many travelers. With a historic message in hand, Trumpeter Martin was wearing emotional blinders, resulting in a paradoxical view of the events transpiring in his backwash.

It had to have been 3:35–3:40 when Martin climbed out of the broad ravine and started for Custer's trail along Sharpshooter Ridge. Perhaps halfway between Medicine Tail Coulee and Sharpshooter Ridge he encountered Boston Custer on his way from the pack train to join his brothers. The youngest sibling asked Martin whether or not the general had begun the attack, and the trumpeter answered no. Martin indicated the approximate location of Custer's command and suggested that Boston beware of Indians in the area. In turn, Boston alerted the orderly to the fact that his horse had been wounded in the hindquarters, apparently as a result of enemy Indian fire from along the bluffs.[40]

A bit farther up the hill, Martin met a soldier he recognized as belonging to C Troop, presumably either Thompson or Watson, both of whose horses had played out along the trail. This trooper also inquired as to the location of the command, and Martin answered, suggesting that the soldier ought to fall back to the pack train. The soldier instead went on, and the trumpeter resumed his ride to Benteen.[41]

His horse jaded and gimpy from the gunshot, Martin reached Sharpshooter Ridge within a few more minutes. From that point, he could glance back and see much of the terrain over which Custer would move, as well as the valley west of the river. Martin clearly testified that he never took more than a hasty "glance" in any direction except straight ahead, toward the end of his assignment. At the court of inquiry and elsewhere, he said

215

that he last saw Custer's column in Medicine Tail Coulee, but in some interviews he embellished his look back to include a Custer ride toward the battlefield and Indians waving buffalo robes at the river's edge. He may have glimpsed some part of Custer's wing climbing out of Medicine Tail toward ridges north of the coulee, and he may have captured a fleeting impression of Indians along the banks of the Little Bighorn, but by timing and logic, at least part of his reservoir of information was likely filled by after-action ingestion.

Likewise, Martin said at the court of inquiry that while on his journey to Benteen, he saw Reno engaged in the valley, but "paid no attention to it." Such an attitude is consistent with the single-mindedness of purpose that must have driven the young Italian immigrant—riding a damaged mount—to complete the most important mission in his life. In later statements, he elaborated on that recollection: "It had been not more than ten or fifteen minutes since the general and I were on the hill, and then we had seen no Indians. But now there were lots of them, riding around and shooting at Reno's men, who were dismounted and in skirmish line. . . . The last I saw of Reno's men they were fighting in the valley and the line was falling back." At best, Martin could have gathered only a faint notion of what was happening with Reno's command in the valley, but by timing, this was an accurate observation. Reaching the north end of Sharpshooter Ridge, as he glanced back to take in Custer's situation, he may also have seen the last gasps of Reno's skirmish line, with Sergeant Myles O'Hara falling and M Troop scrambling for the timber. In that ten-minute ride along the ridge, he may have seen the Indians shutting off the escape route to the south and closing in to block Reno's retreat path to the river. Whatever he saw by way of rapid glances was the death knell of Reno's advance, seen through those ubiquitous gray-brown clouds of dust, beyond the finger of timber that so far defined the high-water mark of Custer's plan of attack.[42]

In the bottomland east of the river, a handful of Arikaras were herding Sioux ponies prior to driving them up the bluffs. It was perhaps 3:25, and Reno's skirmish line was just beginning to form, while on the ground above, Custer's E and F Troops were moving downstream near the edge of the bluffs east of the river. As Little Sioux recalled, the Rees were starting up the hill when soldiers fired on them and wounded Boy Chief's horse. Warriors from the village were right on the heels of the pony-captors. Caught between these opposing forces, an Arikara removed his hat and motioned for the troopers to stop firing so that he and his fellow Rees could escape the angry Indians following close behind. Little Sioux said that the cavalrymen shooting "were the rear of a body of soldiers going downstream on top of the hills." Since Sharpshooter Ridge does not provide line-of-sight to the river, let alone the right bank, the troopers who mistakenly fired at the Arikaras were likely from Company F, second in the column riding nearest the bluffs. As the soldiers rode on, firing a few random shots, the Arikara scouts drove their purloined livestock to high ground, out of immediate danger.[43]

Up on the bluffs, Soldier and other Arikara stragglers traveled in Custer's wake, making note of the two troopers whose horses had gone down. At the suggestion of Stabbed, they followed Custer's trail along Sharpshooter Ridge toward the north end, but before they reached that point, Sioux warriors were coming up and getting around them. As the Arikaras retreated, they saw two soldiers afoot on the side of the hill. Soldier thought that these troopers would not be able to evade the gathering Sioux. If the two men were Thompson and Watson, they did in fact survive. Soldier and the other stragglers joined the pony herders, and together they headed back toward the Lone Tepee trail.[44]

Meanwhile, the Crow scouts accompanied Boyer to Weir Point, from where they could obtain the best-possible view of the entire valley. According to Curley, before they reached their destination, Boyer instructed Goes Ahead, White Man Runs Him, and Hairy Moccasin to remain behind and to watch the Indian camp for any indications of danger in Custer's rear. However, Goes Ahead said that they left Boyer because of the Crows' understanding with Custer that they would bring him to the enemy but that they need not go into the fight. In any event, the three withdrawing Crows paused long enough on the bluffs to fire several shots into the village.[45]

From the moment Custer passed over and around Sharpshooter Ridge, he was committed to a course of action that would permit no easy way out. Within a period of fifteen minutes, eager optimism would thin to a slender hope. Where there had been few fighting Indians, there were now many. More bad news was on the way. High expectations were on the verge of being cut to the bone, skinned down to a narrow margin of choice, where many lives might have to be sacrificed unless Custer's old and persistent foe came on the run.

CHAPTER TEN

UNREADY RESERVES

Once again, in Captain Frederick Benteen's mind, Custer had given him the hard work to do—the unrewarding work—even the dirty work. Feeling that he was being denied the opportunity to share in Custer's push for glory, Benteen went off in a pout to perform the bare necessities of duty. His annoyance at being left out of the main line of attack doubtless increased as his column plodded through terrain unsuited for Indian encampments and as his growing frustration with Custer's seemingly useless orders fed an overactive imagination. In the end, visions of Custer and Major Marcus Reno dashing to victory made him deaf to clear entreaties and impaired the judgment of an otherwise capable officer.

At about a quarter past noon on 25 June, as the Seventh Cavalry halted on the western side of the Divide, Custer summoned Benteen to give him the following instructions, as described by Benteen himself: *"He told me, pointing to a line of bluffs* [emphasis added], *to go to that line of bluffs, or at first to send an officer with five or six men to ride rapidly* [emphasis added] to that line of bluffs . . . and if I came across anything before I got to that line of bluffs to pitch into them and send word back to him at once." If Benteen found nothing, he was to return to the main trail. Benteen claimed at the court of inquiry that these were "exact orders, requiring no interpretation."[1]

However, in communications outside the court, Benteen changed the nature of his assignment from reconnoitering the hills for signs of Indians to endless valley hunting. Before Benteen had gone very far, Custer supposedly sent two follow-up messages by way of Chief Trumpeter Henry

Voss and Sergeant Major William Sharrow to the effect that if Benteen discovered no Indians at the first line of bluffs, he was to continue on to a second group of hills, then to a third. Whether those messengers actually conveyed such instructions can never be known with certainty. It does seem strange that Voss and Sharrow would have carried identical directives when one message "to keep on going" would have done as well, but the historical record is stuck with Benteen's word, however tainted by his lack of candor on a host of other issues.

To some extent Benteen gave the game away in letters to his wife shortly after the battle. Without admitting directly the existence of a Custer plan, Benteen hinted at the truth, which he would subsequently stretch into a pointless excursion. "I was ordered with my battalion to go over the immense hills to the left, *in search of the valley, which was supposed to be very nearby* [emphasis added]—and to pitch into anything I came across,—and to inform Custer at once if I found anything worthy of same." Obviously, if there were lines of bluffs to be investigated, there were valleys between them, and those valleys might conceal Indian encampments, but nowhere except in Benteen's subsequent rationalizations did Custer's orders entail a search for the valley of the Little Bighorn.[2]

When Custer pointed to the hills several miles in the distance, he knew two things for certain: the main Indian village lay concealed in the Little Bighorn bottomland some twelve miles away; and there was a smaller encampment a bit more than half as far from the place where he stood on the downslope of the Divide—or, to use Benteen's language, "nearby." That smaller Sans Arc satellite village was the first military objective. Lieutenant Winfield Edgerly heard Custer tell Reno to advance toward that village. Since Edgerly was a subordinate in Benteen's battalion, and since he heard those orders to Reno, the likelihood is that Benteen heard them also. But more important, Edgerly understood that the mission of Benteen's unit was to engage those Sans Arcs if they attempted to escape to the left, or south. Although collateral in nature and undertaken without surgeons, Benteen's task formed an essential part of the overall plan to attack that Indian encampment and, if possible, to take some prisoners. It is inconceivable that Benteen was not privy to at least that much of Custer's thinking.

And Benteen did understand the potential value of acquiring some Indian captives, as he told his wife. He noted that if Custer had not disobeyed

General Alfred Terry's orders, such an outcome might have been realized. "Had Custer carried out [the] order he got from Genl. Terry the command would have formed a junction exactly at the village—and have captured the whole outfit of tepees, etc, and probably any quantity of squaws, pappooses, etc. etc. but Custer disobeyed orders from the fact of not wanting any other command—or body to have a finger in the pie."[3] Benteen used a similar expression to his wife several weeks later, when he criticized General George Crook for failing to join Terry after the Little Bighorn fight so that the combined columns could chase the Indian survivors. Benteen believed that Crook "had held aloof from it—he wanting all the pie for himself." Everyone, it seems, wanted to swipe Benteen's slice of dessert.[4]

With Custer's initial orders in hand, Benteen moved out in a southwestern direction toward the range of hills several miles away, as indicated by Custer's pointing finger. The exact route Benteen followed is not known, but after a ride of perhaps two miles, he veered to the right or nearly straight west, moving roughly parallel to a winding Reno Creek. In the early stages of that movement, the Custer and Reno columns probably remained in Benteen's sight, at least in glimpses, just as some in Custer's command could recall seeing Benteen's battalion here and there. At that juncture, for perhaps the first mile or two down Reno Creek, the three lines of march were in rough synchronization.

The terrain encountered by Benteen's battalion was naturally more difficult to traverse than the ground traveled by Custer and Reno. Benteen called the landscape "rugged," forcing the command to go "through defiles and around high bluffs."[5] Lieutenant Edward Godfrey agreed that the squadron "marched over a succession of rough steep hills and deep valleys."[6] Edgerly also called the bluffs "very high," and he concurred that care had to be taken lest the horses became fatigued. Edgerly also noted that the Seventh Cavalry was "a very fast walking" regiment, able to do about four miles in an hour. As difficult as the ground may have been, however, for at least portions of the trip, the main body of the column was marching among the highest hills, not over them.[7]

The speed at which Benteen's battalion moved was controlled not only by topography and animal husbandry but also by the need to explore the territory indicated by Custer's orders. To satisfy the requirements of his instructions, Benteen selected Lieutenant Francis Gibson to lead a contingent of six enlisted men charged with actually examining the hilly country for signs of Indians. Gibson's own understanding of Custer's orders to Benteen is telling. "If he [Benteen] found any Indians trying to escape up the valley of the Little Big Horn [sic], to intercept them and drive them back *in the direction the village was supposed to be* [emphasis added]. . . . Should he find nothing he was to pick up the trail again and follow it on." In accordance with Benteen's instructions, Gibson thought at first that he had actually gone far enough in advance to see into the valley of the Little Bighorn. With the aid of Benteen's field glasses, Gibson initially believed that he could see that far. However, he could not detect the village because of a sharp bend in the river, he recalled. Seeing nothing in the valley, he hurried back and reported to Benteen, who immediately returned to the main trail.[8]

Gibson would later admit that, on further reflection, he had only gone "far enough to look down on the valley of the south fork of Sundance [Reno] Creek." The Lone Tepee was located at the junction of Reno Creek and its South Fork, the point at which Custer, from long-range observation, almost certainly expected Benteen to emerge.[9]

In fact, Benteen never advanced farther westward than the headwaters of No Name Creek. The highest elevation in the area is here, and it was probably from this promontory that Gibson took his last look for the valley they were supposed to be hunting. During most of the trip, Benteen's column was from one to three miles from Reno Creek, on both sides of which Reno and Custer were marching, but since Benteen was moving through low ground with many hills blocking his view, there would have been few opportunities for him to catch sight of the other commands. Given this disadvantageous position, Benteen probably never saw the Gray Horse Troop in rapid motion, as he claimed. "I thought of course they had struck something," he would say later in feigned innocence regarding his watching the men of Company E ride to the attack at a gallop. At that moment and afterward, he must have been overwhelmed with the associated feeling of being ignored: "None of us too desired to be left out of the fight." Instead, Lieutenant Gibson almost assuredly delivered the disheartening news that Custer was in the attack mode, further poisoning relations between Benteen and Custer and eventually between Benteen and Gibson.[10]

The total distance covered in Benteen's trip from the Divide to the hills and back to the main trail was likely a bit more than seven miles, taking about two and a half hours. Rather than hustling the fast walking horses forward at four miles an hour, which was suggested by various officers and which would have been closer to Custer's order to move rapidly, Benteen's battalion traveled at under three miles an hour—a brooding pace even after allowance is made for the terrain and possible delays while Gibson made several trips to the peaks of nearby hills. Benteen later declared under oath that the gait of his fast walking horse was five miles an hour. "That accounts for getting over so much ground in so short a time," he insisted. His command went in "hot haste" both ways, he contended. However, by way of comparison, the Custer and Reno columns had covered essentially the same distance in an hour less time.[11]

At about the moment Custer started his acceleration toward the Lone Tepee site, Benteen was below the high point near the headwaters of No Name Creek, about three miles from Reno Creek, a separation caused by an extreme northward loop of that stream. Although Benteen would also later claim that the battalion kept moving during the entire operation—never even pausing while Gibson went hill climbing—and that he and his orderly were often in advance of the scouting party, Gibson denied that this was the case. Regardless, when Gibson came back and reported that no Indians were in sight but that the Gray Horse Troop was rushing forward, Benteen ordered a right turn down the narrow valley of No Name Creek toward the main trail.[12]

Benteen later repeatedly asserted that his own "pre's" (presentiments), not Gibson's report, had caused him to depart the bluffs in the direction of Custer's line of march. At the court of inquiry, he stated that it was "entirely" his own idea to leave the hills, that he thought it was his "duty" to do so, and that it was just "providential or accidental" that he heeded his instincts. Further, in his opinion, when he returned to the trail he was violating Custer's instructions. He "shouldered the responsibility" for terminating the mission even before he had found one valley, he said with manly pride. But by pressing westward for less than two miles to South Fork, then by marching an equal distance down to the Lone Tepee, he would have been in compliance with Custer's orders and might have saved the better part of an hour.[13]

In only one of Benteen's explanations was there even a passing reference to Custer's having given him broad latitude in the conduct of the mission.

In a statement given to the *New York Herald* two months after the battle, he admitted that the messages delivered by the chief trumpeter and the sergeant major indicated that Benteen should use his "own discretion" in the execution of the assignment. Naturally, Benteen could not concede that Custer had used those very words himself, even though that is precisely what Custer should have done and probably did do, if only because Custer would later give just that kind of authority to Reno.[14]

Neither could Benteen agree with the recorder at the court of inquiry that in sending follow-up messages, Custer was attempting to influence, if not control, the movements of Benteen's column. The frustrated court recorder recognized the flaw in Benteen's often entertaining but illogical retorts and wondered aloud whether there was anything in Custer's orders that might have caused Benteen to believe that he *should not* return to the trail if he found no Indians. Benteen replied: "I don't think General Custer would have told me that. He would have known that I would come up." It was perhaps the most sober moment of Benteen's appearance—an acknowledgment of Custer's implicit trust present nowhere else in Benteen's arrogant and disingenuous testimony.[15]

It was a little before three o'clock when Benteen's battalion emerged near the mouth of No Name Creek, at which point the column was about four miles behind the separated Custer and Reno components. A hard-riding courier could easily have overtaken Custer in less than an hour, but Benteen was in no mood to chase the man who had left him behind. Rather, after a short ride down Reno Creek, Benteen decided to water the horses.

In the mostly dry land, it was incumbent on Benteen to provide succor to thirsty animals fatigued by a dusty march of almost three hours through hilly country. Along the full length of Reno Creek, there were not many places where such relief could be found. The Morass (as it was afterward known) was one such place. Variously called a watering hole or a spring-fed hollow, the highly alkaline Morass must have been sufficiently large that it could accommodate a number of horses at one time, though the water level above mud could not have been great.

For perhaps as long as twenty minutes, Benteen allowed the horses to suck bad-tasting water out of that Morass. Benteen himself provided an almost playful description of his own mount's determined efforts to get at that borderline muck. While watering his horse, Benteen tied tricky old

Dick to a stump to keep the fractious horse from getting away. It seems that this mount, like its master, had a mind of its own and, once loose, would rejoin the troop when it was good and ready.[16]

Some of Benteen's subordinates were apparently less amused by the lengthy stay at the water hole. Amplifying on testimony given at the court of inquiry, Godfrey told Walter Camp that Benteen remained at the Morass for so long that some of the officers began to grow uneasy. One unidentified subaltern wondered why the "Old Man" was keeping them for such a long time. Captain Thomas Weir especially became impatient with the delay and suggested to Benteen that the column "ought to be over there," indicating the direction from which firing could be heard. According to Godfrey, Weir started out with his company even though he was normally second in the line of march. Seeing Weir depart, Benteen ordered the rest of the column to advance.[17]

If any of the men did actually hear shooting while at the Morass, its origin is unclear, but two enlisted men in H Troop confirmed that such firing could be heard. At this time, roughly 3:15–3:20, the only sources of gunfire were the opening shots of the Arikara scouts and their several Sioux opponents, about seven miles distant. Given Weir's penchant for following the military dictum "to go to the sound of the firing," perhaps a faint shot or two stimulated his independent movement. Or perhaps he was simply upset by the perceived waste of precious time while the bulk of the regiment was operating out of sight. But if gunfire was heard ahead of the battalion, then Benteen is even more guilty of dereliction of duty than is obvious from the record.[18]

As Benteen and his column moved away from the Morass, the pack train occupied the vacated space, the mules driving headlong for the shallow pool of water. The frenzied animals lurched forward to satisfy their thirst, and at least one of them became completely mired in the mud while several others sank ankle-deep in the soft edges of the hole. Extracting the mules proved to be a nuisance for the civilian packers and the soldiers with the train; Lieutenant Edward Mathey stated that during this period, packs were once again "very much scattered from front to rear." Still, most witnesses agreed that the pack train was not at the Morass for more than twenty to thirty minutes.[19]

Considering that the pack train had traveled only about a mile less than Benteen and had started from the Divide nearly half an hour later, its progress was satisfactory. By the clock, the whole train maintained a good pace of three miles an hour, even with some loads coming off and having to be repacked. The train remained at the Morass about as long as Benteen's battalion had, even though it was a larger component, had mules mired, and had to recover packs.

At about the time the train and Benteen's battalion met on the main trail, Boston Custer departed to overtake his brother's command. It is generally believed that Boston was always with the packs and that, as a free agent—accompanying the regiment as either a "guide" or a quartermaster employee—Boston simply took off so that he could be with his brothers and Autie Reed when they went into action. Such was likely not the case. Captain Thomas McDougall said that he talked to Boston "when he came back to the pack train," suggesting that the youngest Custer rode back to the train possibly to retrieve a fresh horse. According to Edgerly, Boston rode by on his mount as Benteen's column was emerging from No Name Creek. "He gave me a cheery salutation as he passed, and then with a smile on his face, rode to his death." Thus, McDougall remembered Boston coming back, and Edgerly saw him leave, but there is no firm evidence of where he was supposed to be located as a matter of course.[20]

At the time of the battle, Boston was twenty-seven years old. He had always been something of a frail boy, and having come West several years earlier to join his brothers, he had adjusted well to life on the frontier, much to the satisfaction of Armstrong. It is difficult to believe that Boston would have remained with the packs while the general's eighteen-year-old nephew Autie Reed advanced with the right wing. At the mouth of the Rosebud, Reed had pouted his way into the company of his uncle, and Boston would surely have done the same, if necessary, to get himself included in the opening action with his siblings. The more likely scenario is that Boston rode with the headquarters unit until the first military objective (the Lone Tepee) had been passed, at which point he returned to the pack train to get a fresh horse, his own having given out. For such an assumption to work, Boston must have left the column after Custer and Reno departed the Lone Tepee but before they separated. This is certainly feasible, and it makes more sense than that he was left behind from the outset, an option that would not have suited Custer and Tom any more than Boston.

The remarkable feature of Boston's ride is that he knew where to go. He must have gone in nearly a direct line to where his brothers were located, a noteworthy accomplishment unless he understood where he might expect to find them or unless he saw them stationed for a few moments atop Sharpshooter Ridge. In contrast, within the hour, Benteen would stand perplexed at the separation of trails, scratching his head over the two choices open to him. In any case, Boston undertook the dangerous mission with little more than determination and a fair share of that Custer pluck— foolhardiness, some might say. Apparently no one, not McDougall or Edgerly or anyone else, had the presence of mind to request that Boston convey their regards to the commander of the regiment, and there is nothing in the record to suggest that Benteen chose to use him as a courier. Nonetheless, the runt Custer would carry information to his hero siblings and, more than that, would constitute in his very person another dreadful burden for the general of the family to bear, at a moment when military options were few.

As Boston Custer vanished into the undulating landscape, and as Benteen's command and the pack train connected for a few minutes at the Morass, General Custer was on Sharpshooter Ridge examining the ground in every direction to determine his tactical situation. Unable to distinguish Benteen's battalion but perhaps glimpsing riderless mules on the dusty backtrail, Custer came down from his first visit to the ridge at about 3:15–3:20 and instructed his brother Tom to find a messenger while he himself organized the companies for the next stage of the advance. The messenger selected by Tom was Sergeant Daniel Kanipe, who hurried to the rear in search of the pack train and, with luck, Benteen.

Kanipe's testimony is slightly distorted by the difference between his seeing his objectives and his actually meeting them. As Kanipe departed the area just short of Sharpshooter Ridge, he saw in the distance a dust cloud that he—like Custer—believed to be the location of McDougall and the pack train. Instead of going back on the trail that led to the Flat, Kanipe started across country toward the dust, traveling downhill with as much speed as his mount could make. When, off to his right, he saw Benteen's unit, he veered in that direction so as to intercept the column and deliver the secondary set of instructions.

In one version of his story, Kanipe said that he first sighted Benteen when the horses were being watered. It seems unlikely that Kanipe could have reached such a conclusion as he began the descent from the bluffs; rather, what he detected was probably the separation of Benteen's command from the pack train at the Morass around 3:15. Clear identification of the group likely occurred to the courier gradually as he raced over broken and uneven ground toward the first body of soldiers within his vision. That is, his ability to draw a nice distinction between Benteen and the packs may have been an afterthought based on what he finally found.[21]

With an unhappy Weir in the lead, Benteen's command probably made good time from the Morass to the Lone Tepee, a distance of about a mile. Benteen said the column moved at a "stiff walk." Reaching the burial lodge, Benteen dismounted to examine it. The structure had been set afire more than an hour earlier, and still Benteen could describe it as "a beautifully decorated tepee of buffalo hide," in which was housed a single Indian "on a scaffold or cot of rude poles," indicating that Custer's firing of the lodge had done little more than create a temporary smudge pot. After a brief visit, the column resumed its march toward the Little Bighorn, with Benteen back in the lead.[22]

Kanipe was consistent in stating that he actually met Benteen about a mile west of the Lone Tepee. It was now 3:40–3:45, about the time Trumpeter John Martin was riding hard along Sharpshooter Ridge bearing Custer's second message to the rear components of the regiment. Galloping in the direction of the column that Kanipe may now have recognized as Benteen's, the sergeant removed his hat and waved it, in response to which the battalion turned to the right to meet him. Kanipe recalled that the command was marching in column of twos, without any separation.

The encounter between Kanipe and Benteen could not have taken more than a moment or two. As directed by Tom Custer, Kanipe informed Benteen that the train was to be hurried along straight across country, cutting off loose packs unless they contained ammunition. He added, "They want you up there as quick as you can get there—they have struck a big Indian camp."[23]

That uncomplicated message by itself might have prompted Benteen to hurry his command with mules carrying ammunition in a direct line to Custer, but unfortunately for all, Kanipe conveyed another and inadvertent impression. Understandably excited, Kanipe was bringing word from the front to men at the back end of the enterprise, and he could not refrain from saying more than he knew for sure. All that he could have reported with certainty was that Reno's command was advancing toward the Indian village and that Custer's column was about to move out in a northern direction. He had seen no more than that. However, natural optimism had an inordinate influence over his tongue, and in the flush of completing one part of his assignment and wanting no doubt to encourage his comrades, he told them what they surely wanted to hear: "We've got 'em!"—echoing Custer's own disposition as he had ridden down from his first visit to Sharpshooter Ridge.[24]

The primary source for Kanipe's extraneous comments is Lieutenant Godfrey's several descriptions of the event. Besides reporting the exclamation that the advance units had "got 'em," Godfrey quoted Kanipe as saying, "They are licking the stuffing out of them." From these kinds of comments, Godfrey concluded, those present inferred that Custer had captured the village. Such an interpretation of Kanipe's spoken words and animated body language was obviously wrong, but if Godfrey was really convinced of that point of view, then Benteen—the man who mattered most and who was all too ready to think the worst of Custer—was a willing receptacle for the notion that his natural enemy had already won the day without him.[25]

The depth of Benteen's petulant funk was demonstrated by his immediate dismissal of Kanipe without enough conversation to ascertain Custer's real situation and by his later unwillingness at times to even admit that Kanipe had brought him orders. The arrival of a buoyant Kanipe confirmed what Benteen had suspected since Custer had sent him on that pointless valley-hunting exercise: Custer wanted to keep him out of the fight. If Custer did not need him engaged in the main event, Benteen knew how to dawdle, fishing pole at the ready. For an officer as seasoned as Benteen to have refrained from interrogating Kanipe at length is proof enough of Benteen's mood. He could convince himself that the instructions were not intended for him, and besides, McDougall's Company B—and by extension, the pack train with its ammunition—belonged to Custer's right wing.

The messenger's assertions aside (that he bore orders for Benteen to "come on quick"), Benteen stated to the court of inquiry that Kanipe carried only instructions to the commanding officer of the mule train to hurry up the packs. Benteen told the sergeant that he had nothing to do with that and that Kanipe could find Captain McDougall and the pack train some "seven miles" in the rear. "He simply had verbal instructions to the commanding officer of the pack train and I did not consider that an order to me," Benteen said again of Kanipe's brief visit. Benteen attested that the sole message meant for him was delivered later, by Trumpeter Martin.[26]

The truth may be that except for Benteen's forced treatment of the subject at the court of inquiry, he was in denial regarding the seminal importance of Kanipe's visit. Kanipe was emphatic in his claim that he had carried a directive from Custer for Benteen to hurry and that he had delivered those instructions to Benteen in person. Benteen's contention that he received no such order might carry equal weight were it not for the fact that Kanipe diverted from his path with the obvious purpose of seeking out the captain to convey the instructions as Tom Custer had spoken them. Kanipe was guilty of saying too much to a prideful officer in a snit, but in sending the noncommissioned officer packing in search of the train, Benteen was forecasting his attitude toward a similarly effusive Trumpeter Martin.

Kanipe did not need Benteen's help in finding the pack train. He had had it under observation since he had started downhill from the position just short of Sharpshooter Ridge. The packs were not seven miles in the rear, as suggested by Benteen, but were only a mile or so back and were closing on the Lone Tepee. Assuming that Kanipe continued to ride at a courier's pace, it probably did not take him more than ten minutes to reach his destination, although he later indicated that the time seemed closer to twenty minutes. Kanipe claimed that after delivering the orders to Captain McDougall, he "rode at the head of the pack train and brought them back as near as" he could to the route he had followed in coming from Custer— that is, across country, as instructed.[27]

While Kanipe furnished no record of his conversation with McDougall, surely the core meaning of Tom Custer's message to the senior officer with the packs was repeated: bring the mules quickly in a straight line to Custer, and disregard the loss of packs unless they contain ammunition. Kanipe may have displayed some of that ebullience that had seemingly distressed Benteen, but it is hard to believe that even a happy courier could have been misunderstood regarding the heart of the matter, particularly since the pack train had been prepared for just such an eventuality.

In his court of inquiry testimony, however, McDougall testified that he received no notification to hurry the pack train. He thought that perhaps

Lieutenant Mathey, who was actually managing the mules, got the orders and conveyed them to McDougall, who in turn directed Mathey to accelerate the pace. McDougall indicated that the front mules were then moving at "a sort of dog trot," while those in the rear "were being pulled with lariats and whipped with black snakes to get them along." For his part, Mathey said that the only orders he received came from McDougall. Thus, apparently neither the senior officer nor the person in charge of the mules could recall Kanipe or the message he delivered.[28]

The wonder is that some twenty years later McDougall would be able to summon up sufficient memory to recognize Kanipe's heretofore forgotten contribution. "On the afternoon of June 25th, 1876, when the entire country was full of hostile Indians, Sergeant Kanipe brought me an order from General Custer 'to bring the pack train across the way' where I found Major Reno. The Sergeant was probably one of the last men to see General Custer alive, and I take great pleasure in giving him this small certificate of merit." In this testimonial, McDougall left no doubt who received Custer's orders by way of Kanipe.[29]

Thus, Kanipe apparently carried Custer's order directly to McDougall, who passed the word to Mathey while Kanipe went to the head of the train to assist in guiding it to Custer. However, rather than making a beeline for Sharpshooter Ridge, the train ambled toward the Lone Tepee, before perhaps angling slightly in the desired direction. The civilian packer John Frett said the mules went only as fast as mules could walk, rather than trotting, as McDougall thought. At the Lone Tepee McDougall, like Benteen before him, dismounted so that he could look inside (claiming to see "three dead Indians"), in spite of the instructions to rush those ammunition packs forward.[30]

The importance of the ammunition had been known from the start. Assigned to the pack train, Private Francis Kennedy of I Troop recalled that when the regiment was divided at about noon, orders were given to bunch the mules together, "with the exception of the ammunition mules, which were taken on ahead."[31] Somewhere between the Divide and the Morass, the horse of Private John McGuire (Company C) went lame, and the young enlisted man was sent back to the pack train. At that time, probably after the Lone Tepee attack had gone bust (and about when Boston may have returned to the train), the orderly for Lieutenant Henry Harrington (acting commander of C) appeared with that officer's extra horse, and McGuire was informed that he should remain with the packs. The orderly further conveyed another directive: "If it was found impossible to keep up with the command we were to cut away all the packs but the ammunition and make all possible haste to keep up." Such an obvious understanding regarding the ammunition must have been common throughout the ranks.[32]

At the court of inquiry, the civilian packer Benjamin Churchill stated that about a half mile past the Lone Tepee, the orders were "to take the ammunition mules out and go ahead with them." He added, without clarification, that similar instructions had been issued during other parts of the march. Likewise, the packer Frett indicated that the pack train "had several reports . . . which did not prove to be true" until finally Sergeant Kanipe arrived with orders that the train "should hurry up, that General Custer was attacking the Indians." The only conclusion is that keeping the ammunition mules in the advance was *always* the intention, in all likelihood on the basis of orders issued by Custer at the outset of the march down Reno Creek. It is also plausible that a "heads up" regarding the ammunition packs was received when Custer began his assault on the Lone Tepee and again after the first phase of the battle plan fizzled—thus, those other reports that Churchill and Frett remembered.[33]

The extraordinary feature of this continuum is that McDougall and Mathey could have been so dense about what was expected of them. By the time Kanipe reached them, had they shuffled the ammunition mules forward so often that they were numb to the exercise? As experienced officers, did they fail to grasp the importance of the moment? Were they simply tired, so tired that McDougall especially would be inclined to dip into the alcoholic contraband hoarded by scrounger Mathey? Was the good captain making another astronomical observation through the bottom of the tumbler, as Benteen liked to characterize him? If so, it is little wonder that McDougall saw three dead Indians where there was only one in a burning burial lodge.

While Kanipe was guiding the pack train over precisely the ground he had covered on his way from Sharpshooter Ridge, not directly across country as he later recollected, Trumpeter Martin arrived to deliver Custer's final message to Benteen. It was almost four o'clock. Reno had begun his retreat from the valley, and Custer was lingering in Medicine Tail Coulee, waiting for word from Mitch Boyer before dispatching the ghostly, larger-than-life gray horses down the gully to sow indecision in the minds of his adversaries.

After Godfrey's report of hearing gunfire while at the Morass, there was apparently no further evidence of a fight in progress, even though the Benteen column had moved at a steady pace of five miles an hour toward Reno's noisy withdrawal from the field. At about this time Trumpeter Martin arrived with Custer's last call for help. The mystery is that based on the trumpeter's report, no senior officer among Custer's reserves had the curiosity to investigate the true state of affairs or the gumption to take unsure steps in the direction of the action.

In one of his accounts, Martin said that he—like Kanipe—waved his hat as he raced downhill to intercept Benteen's column, with the commander himself riding at a fast trot in the lead. Weir and the rest of the battalion were several hundred yards to the rear. Responding to Benteen's request for Custer's location, Martin said that the Indians were running and he supposed that by then Custer had charged through the village. Martin meant to tell Benteen about Reno being in action as well, but before he could continue his story, Benteen changed the subject by noting that Martin's horse had been wounded.[34]

In none of his renderings did Martin ever indicate that he pointed in the direction Custer had gone. Neither did he answer in words Benteen's understandable question about the regimental commander's location. In short, Benteen asked *where*, and Martin answered *what*, and that *what* was more than the orderly could have known positively. In everything that he said or did, Martin unintentionally created a false impression, but in truth, it would have been improper for any enlisted man to volunteer information to an officer. It was Benteen's responsibility to inquire into the matter until he was satisfied, but apparently he did not. Rather, with Custer's message in hand and with the Kanipe and Martin unintentional impressions in mind, Benteen was content to let his athletic imagination leap to the only possible conclusion: his "pre's" had been right again, and Custer had deliberately gone off in search of glory alone.

Benteen agreed that he met Martin about two miles from the river and some two and a half miles beyond the Lone Tepee, in the vicinity of the Flat. For a full mile (the distance from the Flat to Reno Hill), Benteen had seen the lone rider that was Martin approaching, appearing and disappearing down the rolling slope. That is, within about fifteen minutes of Kanipe's departure for the pack train, Benteen observed another courier hurrying down from the bluffs on the east side of the river valley.

Captain Benteen always contended that the orderly had used the word "skedaddling" to describe what the Indians in the village were doing, but Martin denied ever having employed such a term. Whether Martin used that expression or not, by his own admission he had suggested to Benteen that the Indians were running. The truth was probably encapsulated in a Benteen remark at the court of inquiry: "My impression from Trumpeter Martin was that the Indians were skedaddling." This may have been Benteen's word for what Martin had told him.[35]

In one of his narratives, Benteen described Martin as "a thick headed, dull witted Italian, just about as much cut out for a cavalryman as he was for a King." Benteen's low opinion of the trumpeter-orderly may have been the consequence of daily dealings, but Benteen may also have held him responsible for a distorted report at a critical moment, just as Benteen probably faulted Lieutenant Gibson for an incomplete intelligence report during Custer's assault at the Lone Tepee site. Additionally, Martin's badly garbled testimony at the court of inquiry, especially if the trumpeter had been coached, probably did not endear him to Benteen.[36]

Big village. Come quick. Bring packs. That was the essence of the message written out by Adjutant William Cooke and delivered by Martin. Nothing in the text or the postscript specified hurrying the ammunition packs forward, even though, as indicated, enlisted men and civilian packers knew that this cargo was so special that it needed to be kept out in front. Following the abbreviated conversation with Martin, Benteen read the message and handed it to Captain Weir, who had by this time ridden up to the head of the column. Weir also read the note and supposedly offered no comment, nor did Benteen ask any questions of his subordinate. The message was unambiguous in stating that Benteen was to "come quick" with the packs, but the quandary for the bewildered Benteen was how to do both things at once.[37]

The slow-moving mule train was still more than a mile behind, and if Benteen waited, he could not "come quick"; if he went back to get it, precious time would be lost; if he continued forward at a rapid pace, the distance between the two components would increase. At the court of inquiry,

Benteen argued his case on just such grounds, and it is hard to fault his logic, even though his argument was laced with a fair amount of rationalization and ended up sounding more like an excuse than a reason. He went on to explain that another courier (Kanipe) had already passed by with instructions for McDougall and the train to come straight across country. Although he recognized that it was his duty to bring up the packs after receiving the order by way of Martin, Benteen said that after the orderly had conveyed his "skedaddling" comment, "there was less necessity for . . . going back for the packs." In fact, Benteen added, Martin gave the impression that Custer had not only attacked and scattered the Indians but was "in possession of the village."[38]

Like Custer before him, Benteen felt that he could advance without waiting for the packs because any enemy force would have to get through his battalion in order to reach the train. "Well!" Edgerly quoted him as saying, "If he [Custer] wants me in a hurry, how does he expect that I can bring the packs? If I am going to be of service to him, I think I had better not wait for the packs."[39] In his official report Benteen said, "It savored too much of 'coffee-cooling' to return when I was sure a fight was progressing in the front."[40] Or as he told the court of inquiry, "I couldn't waste time in going back, nor in halting where I was for them." Finally, Benteen insisted that he had not sent Martin with any message to McDougall.[41]

Late in his life, Martin stated flatly that he did not carry any instructions to the pack train. When he reached Benteen's position, the packs were in sight, but as the battalion sped up, McDougall's command and the packs faded to just another dust cloud. The problem with this version of Martin's recollection is that it totally contradicts the very detailed testimony he gave at the court of inquiry.[42]

He told the court that as he approached the train, the packs were pretty well closed up and McDougall was riding 150 yards to the rear of the column. Martin informed McDougall that Benteen "sent his compliments and wanted him to hurry up the packs." Martin then rode back and took his place on the left of his assigned company (H) in Benteen's battalion. This testimony is compelling because it was given under oath and included particulars such as McDougall's position in the column and the language of a courier delivering instructions. Additionally, this was what Benteen ought to have done in order to be in compliance with Custer's orders.[43]

On the other hand, Edgerly claimed that he heard Martin speak to another cavalryman behind Benteen. Martin was laughing and seemed very much elated, saying that it was the biggest village he had ever seen and that Reno had charged and was killing all of the inhabitants. Edgerly supposed that Benteen heard Martin's overzealous and wrongheaded excesses. At a minimum, Martin did not leave immediately with a message for the pack train.[44]

The evidence is skimpy and conflicting, but the probability is that Martin did not carry a message to McDougall and the pack train. Instead, he was given another horse and joined his company and rode on, no doubt continuing to babble excitedly to his comrades about his singular experience. If we therefore accept Martin's disavowal of his court of inquiry testimony, one is left to wonder what might have prompted the young enlisted man to deliberately lie under oath. Martin claimed that the court record was a mistake, but on this issue the questions were too precise and Martin's replies too fulsome to reflect mere errors in transcription.[45]

And so Benteen apparently started forward without sending any additional notification to the pack train. His subordinates agreed with him. As Edgerly said, "The remark was made by someone, either by Captain Weir or myself, that he [Custer] could not possibly want us to go for the packs as Captain McDougall was there and would bring them up." Although Edgerly wanted to go faster, he concurred in the deliberate gait in order to keep the horses in good condition. Godfrey thought that the command marched at a walk or a trot, depending on the terrain—the same ground over which Custer's column had advanced without apparent difficulty and, more important, over which Reno's battalion had moved toward the river at an overall speed of a fast trot.[46]

Instead of turning north toward the bluffline from which Kanipe and Martin had come with messages from Custer, Benteen pushed forward in a western direction until he reached a trail separation, which was not that far from where Custer had ceased following Reno some two miles from the river. Godfrey and Gibson agreed that at this point, Benteen became confused. "Here we have the two horns of a dilemma," Gibson quoted Benteen as saying. Exactly what occurred at the juncture is uncertain.[47]

Shortly after the perplexing trail problem, some of the officers began to hear firing. Edgerly said that the firing was not very heavy and occurred when the column was about a mile from the river. To Godfrey, the shots were scattered in the battalion's front, and the pace increased to a trot. As the gunfire became more pronounced, the command began to gallop, pistols drawn. But in which direction? Toward what? Godfrey also remembered that there was firing to the right and that Weir departed at once with his company in pursuit of that activity while Benteen and Godfrey continued forward toward the river until they had advanced far enough to see Reno's retreat through the trees.[48]

What Benteen later claimed to have seen was downright amazing. From the east side of the river, perhaps on a slight elevation, through stands of timber, he saw a dozen dismounted troopers in skirmish order being charged and recharged by nine hundred Indian warriors—no closer than two miles from where he stood! Yet there is no evidence that even three soldiers stood together in good skirmish order to hold off such a number of Indians while the entirety of Reno's battalion ran for its life. True, about a dozen men ended up in the timber after Reno's retreat, but they arrived in small groups and with only one man wounded. Additionally, it is absurd to think that Benteen could have seen that much over that distance through the dust and the smoke and the trees.[49]

Benteen added that he believed that he had discovered the whole regiment in the valley and that it was getting whipped. In the end, he decided that he should remain on the east side of the river because those twelve soldiers were being mauled by the horde of Indians. Neither Godfrey nor Gibson saw any of that. If Godfrey was correct, Weir was already heading north, and that initiative could have dragged Benteen behind Weir, as it had done before and would again. However, Gibson said that he was the one who suggested the righthand trail and that this was the direction H Troop took, with Godfrey in its wake. Godfrey said the Crow scouts told them which way to go. Every officer had a story. Only Weir kept moving, at the risk of being cited for insubordination.[50]

Soon after turning right, the Benteen command encountered the three Crow scouts released by Boyer. The Crows spoke no English, and no one with Benteen could communicate with the scouts except in pidgin or by signs, but if one is to believe the various accounts of this meeting, volumes were spoken. As recalled by the soldiers present, the Crows referred to the large number of Sioux, indicated the direction of the fighting, and alluded to Reno's withdrawal. Hairy Moccasin, one of those scouts, later said that he had stated: "Do you hear that shooting back where we came from? They're fighting Custer there now." But who was there to interpret? No one spoke Crow. The evidence is cloudy as to whether Weir was long gone. It was now perhaps five or ten minutes after four in the afternoon, and Custer was about to begin a desperate, no-win march down Medicine Tail Coulee.[51]

Meanwhile, the pack train continued to trudge along, with Kanipe in a lead position. The logistical nightmare was well past the Lone Tepee, having already passed the half dozen or so Arikara scouts hurrying their booty of fewer than twenty ponies eastward, whooping their self-congratulation and kicking up much dust, trying to escape the clutches of very angry Sioux. Still following Kanipe's downhill path, the train probably veered slightly north of west to begin the climb toward the bluffs east of the river. According to McDougall, he saw a good deal of smoke in the distance and sent word to Mathey to halt for a few moments so that the column could close up and prepare for action. Mathey in turn notified McDougall that he would wait while the back end of the train was driven forward. From front to rear, the long line of mules stretched for perhaps eight hundred yards. No more than three miles from Reno Hill, the entire entourage paused for about ten minutes. Seeing black objects on the high ground of Reno Hill, McDougall put one platoon of his Company B in the front of the packs and one in the rear, and the men in the command drew their pistols. To their right, two volleys of carbine fire resounded along the bluffs guarding the valley of the Little Bighorn. It was 4:30. Custer was engaged.[52]

The recorder at the court of inquiry tried to get Benteen to admit that when Custer had sent messengers, he must have expected that Benteen was within communicating distance of the pack train. To such questions, Benteen replied that Custer could not have known where to find him. Of course, Benteen had no idea what could be seen from the high ground. He had no concept of DeRudio's glasses, which from a distance had allowed Custer to espy Benteen's tardiness.[53] "Custer galloped away from his reinforcements," Benteen said, "and so lost himself."[54]

It is hard to imagine that Benteen did not get Martin to tell him on which side of the river he might find Custer's command. Such a lame excuse for not going directly toward Custer ought to have gotten Benteen laughed out of the court of inquiry, but it did not. An ordinarily inquisitive person would have extracted more information out of Kanipe and Martin than did this supposedly experienced officer, for whom current and reliable intelligence ought to have been a fundamental concern. Beyond that, both of these enlisted men were within easy recall for use as guides had not Benteen's wounded pride blinded him to their potential value. Instead, he merely marched forward until faced with a dilemma, in a situation almost as comical—if it were not so tragic—as his patently ridiculous assertion that he was confused because Martin had failed to point him in the right direction. Custer sallied forth on an unknown trail, said Benteen, "and in a direction that we never guessed that he had gone until so informed by Chief Gall ten years after the occurrence of the battle."[55]

The only valid presentiment probably experienced by Benteen was his decision to retain the original copy of Custer's orders, as written out by Adjutant Cooke. In a letter sent to his wife two weeks after the battle, Benteen suggested that she preserve the note—as well as the letter itself—"as the matter may be of interest hereafter, likewise for use." He knew then that someone would have to answer for the debacle at the Little Bighorn, and he was already beginning to prepare his case. Those letters to his wife constituted the framework on which he would later construct his defense, and the hastily written and poorly worded note was the exclamation point for his persistent denial of all responsibility.[56]

By making himself tiny in the total scheme of things, Benteen was in fact able to avoid any official culpability for what happened to Custer and his command. Strictly speaking, he was *not* responsible for the pack train, even though it must have been widely understood that on the verge of battle, additional ammunition was the only cargo of any possible use to forces about to be or already engaged. The men with the packs knew that, Kanipe confirmed it, and the subject was implicit in Cooke's note—a realization that must have come to Benteen soon after the fact, for which reason he retained the note.

As adept as Benteen may have been in anticipating future difficulties, he was equally expert in analyzing contingencies after the fact. According to one of his correspondents, the illustrious captain later said that after the regiment reached the Little Bighorn, all packs except those carrying ammunition were of no further use. At that point, said Benteen, it would have made sense to abandon the mule train. This would have released 170 men for combat and, combined with Benteen's battalion, would have constituted a force of 290 soldiers. Benteen's numbers were wrong, but as he believed, such an assembly of forces could have cleared the valley had Reno held out in the timber.[57]

Unfortunately, such a plan did not occur to Benteen when the occasion called for action, when everyone in the body of the regiment understood that projecting the ammunition packs to the forefront at critical junctures was an operational imperative, and when repeated messages from Custer expressed just that need. Of course, Benteen's purpose in proposing such a commonsense plan after the fact was to blame Custer for not thinking of it and to highlight Reno's cowardice. But the messages delivered by Sergeant Kanipe and Trumpeter Martin offered the perfect opportunities for Benteen not only to implement his ingenious afterthought but also to obey orders received from his commander.

Like Lieutenant Edgerly, Benteen understood his role in at least the first phase of Custer's battle plan, and Benteen probably knew that his battalion fell under Reno's left wing in any subsequent action. In all respects, Benteen possessed sufficient knowledge to have done the right thing, to have at least made some effort to provide assistance—with the ammunition—in a timely fashion to units already committed to battle. But for all the men who failed in ways that Benteen could fathom clearly in hindsight, he had only clenched teeth, a slightly curled lip, and scurrilous sniping in post-battle correspondence. One suspects that Benteen did sneer a little when he saw Boston Custer racing across the landscape to catch up with his older brothers before the fight began. The unbridled exuberance of the younger Custer, a receding figure swallowed by the tortured landscape, was the innocence lost on Benteen's march to the left.

CHAPTER ELEVEN

CHARGE TO THE REAR

Over the period of some twenty minutes out in the open, Major Marcus Reno's skirmish line dissolved by fractions until the entire command found sanctuary in the woods bordering the Little Bighorn River. Reno's failure to make any provision for defense had allowed the Sioux and Cheyenne warriors flanking his force on the prairie to filter into the timber and others to occupy space on the eastern bluffs of the river. The number of Indians in the immediate vicinity was not great, but the battalion of soldiers was in such disarray that it required only a small spark to undermine any idea of security and to ignite a disorderly and headlong rush for the rear. In Reno's mind, this movement was to be a charge, but even to many who countenanced his rapid withdrawal from an untenable position, it was a demoralized rout, with every last man on the jump to save his own skin.

As the remnants of M Troop tripped, skidded, and scrambled down off the plain, some of those who had preceded them into the woods were already searching for their horses while others were firing an occasional shot at the Indians on ponies flashing across the rolling landscape to the west. Sergeant Myles O'Hara lay mortally wounded among the sagebrush and the prairie dog mounds. Sergeant Charles White had also been hit, and another soldier may have been shot, but all in all, the battalion had escaped virtually unscathed from its initial contact with the enemy.[1]

The place of temporary refuge contained features providing a natural fortification, not necessarily secure from every direction but with obstacles protecting all sides from onslaught by massed opponents. To the west, the position was protected by a drop-off from the plain to the alluvium of the old riverbed. From the Garryowen bend of the stream to its southern extremity, the wall extended for perhaps several hundred yards, at heights ranging from a foot to several times that. Along and behind that cutbank, trees furnished additional cover, and with the undergrowth, the verdure was sufficiently thick that entry and exit had to be sought through paths made by animals.[2]

To the south, the timber extended from the prairie to the river's edge, then thinned to a fringe running downriver on the eastern side of Reno's predicament. Farther east, across the river, the bottomland—lower than Reno's position—consisted mostly of heavy underbrush and a few fallen trees. Above the bottomland loomed the steep bluffs that framed that portion of the Little Bighorn Valley.

Northward, the vista was open, but the lower bench abutted against the westward thrust of the Garryowen Loop, with a fall of some ten feet to the river's edge. The gap in the tree line was perhaps fifty yards wide, but beyond the twists of the stream, the timber again filled in to provide adequate protection for small numbers of fighters. In short, this direction was the unobstructed end of the Reno defensive "horseshoe."

In the center of these physical barriers was a kind of "park" measuring maybe fifty yards wide and a hundred yards long. This relatively flat area was covered with prairie grasses and bushes, none so large that they offered any significant protection. Having failed to organize any plan of resistance, Reno occupied this empty land and, in a moment of blind terror, formulated the scheme of extraction and salvation for himself, first and foremost, then for those who cared to follow in his wake.

Could Reno have held in the timber? Opinions offered after the fact were many and varied. Some of the survivors thought that if the battalion had remained only half an hour longer, those who did survive would never have gotten out alive. Some considered the position sufficiently defensible that Reno could have held it for as long as his ammunition lasted, perhaps several hours. Still others thought the area was a "splendid" place for defense and that as a natural fortress, it was far superior to the ground Reno would later occupy on the bluffs.[3]

Naturally, Reno stood by his decision to leave the enclave, claiming that he lacked the manpower to protect its perimeter, even though there is no evidence that he ever undertook a close assessment of that option. Even some of those who felt he might have held for another hour or more were equally convinced that he had made the right choice in departing. Yet the overwhelming body of evidence reveals that the position in the timber was excellent for defense, if Reno had cared to organize his forces for that purpose. Captain Frederick Benteen's testimony on this point is particularly persuasive. He called the timber a "number one defensible position," which Reno might have held for five or six hours. Granted, Benteen was not present at the valley fight, but had he been given the task of leading the initial charge and had he retired to the woods, one suspects that he would have made a better showing.[4]

The civilian frontiersman George Herendeen later recalled having been caught in similar situations and surviving against great odds. Even certain military critics could point to Major George A. Forsyth's defensive triumph at Beecher Island in 1868. Here, Forsyth and about fifty citizen scouts stood off several hundred Cheyenne warriors for more than a week before being rescued. Of course, Forsyth's party consisted of experienced fighters, the kind of "resolute, determined men" that Fred Gerard must have had in mind when he insisted to the court of inquiry that Reno could have held out as long as his ammunition and provisions lasted.[5]

As for the Indians facing Reno, their testimony about the valley phase of the battle tends to be brief and unspecific. After the shock of finding soldiers on their doorstep, the warriors dispensed with these invaders in relatively short order. Only during the actual retreat to the river was there any sort of direct engagement, and since Reno reached the opposite side of the river with most of his command intact, the fight was such that it might be called inconclusive. Besides, those who questioned the Indians afterward were chiefly interested in the combat on the Custer battlefield.

Insofar as they did comment, the Indians—like their white counterparts—tended to split in their opinions regarding the wisdom of Reno's decision. Mrs. Spotted Horn Bull bluntly stated: "The man who led those troops must have been drunk or crazy. He had the camp at his mercy, and could have killed us all or driven us away naked on the prairie."[6] The Cheyenne Brave Wolf observed, "I could never understand why they left it [the timber], for if they had stayed there, they would have been all right." Soldier Wolf shared this opinion, adding that if Reno had held his ground, the Indians could not have killed his men.[7] On the other hand, the Lakota Iron Hawk felt that the command could not have lasted long in the woods.[8]

Such after-action comments are inconsequential, of course, because the fact is that Reno chose to leave the timber—and in a great hurry. How much rational consideration he actually gave to his predicament is unknown because he apparently spoke to no one about his decision to depart, and his own self-serving testimony sheds little light on the subject. After only a few minutes on the skirmish line, Reno entered the timber with some portion of Company G to look for Indians or to organize an attack on the village. As noted, there were no Indians then in the woods, and it was neither feasible nor intended to assault any occupied part of the encampment. While waiting in his sheltered location, Reno is known to have done nothing more than inquire as to how things were going out on the plain. No living person claimed to have spent any time with Reno while he presumably sat on his horse in the park, as the line crumbled and the men left the prairie "like a bunch of sheep."[9]

Following G Troop, Lieutenant Charles DeRudio and half a dozen men from Company A drifted into the timber and toward the northern rim of the redoubt to see if they could find any Indians. At the same time, other soldiers from A were sent to the woods—on Captain Myles Moylan's orders— to procure additional ammunition. Moylan apparently continued to make that call after the last of his command had left the line, expressing the concern that Indians might get between the horses and his men. To assist Moylan, Lieutenant Charles Varnum rode southward through the trees to summon the horse-holders closer. He spoke only to the A men, but he "supposed" that the other companies followed. He saw no Indians. As this was happening, some of the retreating soldiers may have paused at the cutbank to provide covering fire for the withdrawal of Company M from the prairie.[10]

Having furnished what assistance he could to A Troop, Varnum went to the right of the line that had formed along the cutbank facing west. There he hunkered down with Gerard and Charley Reynolds. Varnum asked how it was going, and the two men responded that things looked mighty bad. Gerard had a half-pint flask of whiskey and suggested: "Let's take a drink. It may be our last." According to Gerard, the men fired a few shots at the Indians over on the hills. He observed that Reynolds had never been so "depressed and discouraged" in all of his life, possibly sensing the fulfillment of a premonition that had nearly kept him from accompanying the expedition.[11]

Meanwhile, perhaps as the last of Company M came spilling over the cutbank, the scout Herendeen noticed that the firing of the soldiers had ceased. Located on the south of the line, he went to find his horse and discovered that all of the mounts except his own were gone. He observed that at this time Indians—perhaps twenty in number, in small groups—were in fact approaching downriver through the trees. He remarked that ten or so troopers might have held the line in this direction, but no steps were taken to inhibit the advance of the warriors.[12]

Out in the clearing, Herendeen found Reno sitting on his horse in front of about a company of troopers, apparently aligned in an eastern direction toward the river. Herendeen thought that all or most of these men were from Company A, but from a quick glance he could not be sure. Having lost his straw hat in the charge down the valley, Reno was wearing a red handkerchief wrapped around his head. The Arikara scout Bloody Knife was close by but reportedly in front of Reno as Herendeen rode up to within six feet of the two men. According to Reno's court of inquiry testimony, he was trying to learn from Bloody Knife "by signs where the Indians were going," even though Reno was not equipped to engage in such a nonverbal communication with an Indian scout who would have guffawed in his face at the very question.[13]

In his official report, Reno said that while in the timber, he made some "headway" toward the village but soon realized that his "only hope" was to get out of the woods before he was surrounded. At the court of inquiry, he amplified on this rationale by noting that he thought the Indians were creeping up on him, using the trees for cover. "I left the timber sending orders to Captain French by Lieutenant Hodgson," he said, "and giving the order in person to Captain Moylan and Lieutenant McIntosh to mount their men and bring them to the edge of the timber where they could be formed in column-of-fours." Reno stated that he remained in the park for ten minutes, during which time the scout Bloody Knife was shot and killed. At a later point, however, he said that while the officers were organizing their men, he rode out onto the prairie to see what the Indians were doing, presumably because Bloody Knife was too dead to be of much assistance. According to Reno, Moylan was near at hand, and when Moylan—and only Moylan of the company commanders—reported the column ready, they moved. In another reply, Reno observed that as he went out on the plain Moylan was with him and that this was *before* Bloody Knife was killed. With Reno in the lead so that he could rally and re-form the men once they reached the eastern bluffs, the column charged forward at a "rapid" gait, Companies A, G, and M in order behind.[14]

Only if Reno had meant to assault a few vacated lodges that had housed agency Indians on the east side of the river could he have made "headway" toward the Sioux and Cheyennes. And the evidence is overwhelming that he and his horse never left the middle of the park once they had occupied that spot. The rest of Reno's assertions were a series of contradictory inventions conjured by the major to excuse his headlong retreat.

During his testimony, Moylan explained how he got his A Troop together. As the last of the soldiers came off the skirmish line, Reno gave instructions to mount up the companies. Because it was difficult to assemble the soldiers in the timber, Moylan told his men to mount up "individually" (did he go to each soldier, or did he insist on only one man per horse?) and to move to the edge of the woods, where they might be formed more easily. This was accomplished under his and Major Reno's supervision, he said. Then Company M came up and occupied the space to the left at an interval of perhaps twenty yards. Company G was a "little late," he noted, but it managed to get in column before the entire formation reached the river.[15]

Within weeks of the battle, Moylan wrote to Fred Calhoun, the brother of Lieutenant James Calhoun, who would die with Custer. He said: "Most of the men [had] mounted and in fact all of them that I could see, having been *among the last to leave the woods myself* [emphasis added], on account of some of my men having been wounded." Such effrontery to the truth apparently came easily to a man who saw only precision in the collapse of the skirmish line and in the wild escape from the timber.[16]

First Sergeant William Heyn remembered the scene as he mounted up some part of Company A and rode to the south side of the timber: "There he [Heyn] saw Moylan and Reno just in the edge of the timber with cocked revolvers, ready to ride out. The men straggled out and started across the flat without any particular command, and no bugle being blown, the officers digging spurs in their horses and every man for himself." It was a sight recalled by many who had no vested interest in concealing the truth.[17]

Such are the broad outlines of the experience in the woods, from the disintegration of the skirmish line to Bloody Knife's death, the supposed cause of Reno's withdrawal. But as already indicated, Reno's fear probably began much earlier—at the Divide when he was directed to take the point with only half his wing. It increased to near-panic when he separated from Custer to begin the chase after the Indians right into their camp. He expected to die, and from the moment his battalion crossed Ford A, he was looking for a place to hide and, after finding that hiding place, for a place to run. Succumbing to that crush of fear, he sought out the hindquarters of the only person who might save him: Custer, whom Reno could not have failed to see at every blatant interval along the bluffs. Maybe Reno thought he could explain. Maybe in intoxicated numbness he no longer cared.

No, this was not a tidy affair in the timber. In no more than five minutes after M Troop came off the line, over a hundred impressions were formed. There was no happy chronology for the manner in which crazed, dazed, and bewildered individuals stumbled, struggled, and raced to save their separate souls. Companies by the letter may have left the timber in order, but for many of the real soldiers who filled their ranks, it was mostly a run by the ones and twos, all of their stories overlapping even as they struggled to retain their identities.

Private Thomas O'Neill of G Troop claimed that as Moylan was mounting his Company A, Lieutenant Benjamin Hodgson asked the captain where he was going. Moylan replied that he was going to charge. If we assume that O'Neill's memory was accurate, Hodgson—the adjutant who was supposed to be notifying Captain Thomas French of Reno's planned withdrawal—was in the dark at that juncture. Like most of the officers and men of this battalion, Hodgson may have learned of the skedaddle simply by seeing it happen. O'Neill also heard Reno give the order, "Get to your horses, men." As this occurred, the soldiers stopped firing, and during the lull, the Indians pressed closer through the trees.[18]

In the park, as the scout Herendeen approached Reno, a volley resounded from the direction in which he had seen the infiltrating Indians, and he "saw Bloody Knife . . . throw up his arm and fall over." At the same time, an enlisted man went down, calling out, "Oh! my God, I have got it." Both were killed. Later, Reno would tell Herendeen what happened when Bloody Knife was shot: "His blood and brains spattered over me."

Immediately Reno shouted for the men to dismount and then, just as the soldiers' feet hit the ground, ordered them to mount again.[19]

The men in the last unit off the line, M Troop, likely rushed at once to their horses, and at least a portion of the company pushed into position behind Reno in the park. First Sergeant John Ryan said that as he mounted, he looked back and saw Indians filtering through the timber on horseback. He supposedly said to Captain French that the Indians were getting in the rear, to which the company commander allegedly replied, "Those are Custer's men."[20]

It is incredible that French would have thought that Custer was providing support by charging at that moment through a heavy grove of trees. Indeed French had a slightly different remembrance of his knowledge and his involvement.

> What made Major Reno run away when he did I cannot positively know, and he did not tell me.... To turn ones back on Indians without being better mounted than they is throwing away life. When he started to that hill [the eastern bluffs] he had told me, *not one minute before, that he was going to fight—this was in reply to a question of mine* [emphasis added].

Since French was apparently talking to Reno at the moment of decision, it is unlikely that Adjutant Hodgson—who at that time was asking Moylan where he was going—ever needed to provide notification of the retrograde movement to French, as Reno later claimed.[21]

Rather, as Lieutenant George Wallace asserted, the order to retreat just "passed down the line." Unable to find Lieutenant Donald McIntosh, Wallace mounted the Company G men that he could find, and they followed after the other two units. Although Wallace attested that he heard the retreat order from a voice he supposed to be Reno's, G Troop got out so late that Wallace could say only that the first two companies were "moving off, apparently in column-of-fours, at a gallop."[22]

Although Reno and Moylan both stated that they had consulted at the edge of the timber regarding the objective of their "charge," Herendeen testified that this would not have been possible because he was right on their tails. He had seen Bloody Knife killed, and when Reno left, Herendeen followed right after him. In getting out of the woods, Herendeen had to compete with the individual soldiers for access to the small paths that led to the open prairie. He noted that they were passing him. "All were going as fast as spurs would make an American horse go." Within 150 yards of the egress, Herendeen's horse went down, and he returned to the timber.[23]

At the other end of the timber, Gerard heard the order: "Men! To your horses! The Indians are in our rear!" He was sure that Captain Moylan had given this order, and his reaction was, "What damn-fool move is this?" Nevertheless, his friend Reynolds thought that they ought to go, and so they went out. Reynolds was killed shortly after leaving the timber, and Gerard was forced back into the woods.[24]

When Lieutenant Varnum heard the cries of "Charge! Charge! We are going to charge!" he said simply, "What's that?" After retrieving his horse, he left the timber, well behind the general flow of the retreat. Near Varnum, Gerard, and Reynolds, Lieutenant Luther Hare heard no order of any kind. His only notification came when his orderly brought his horse and told him that the command was departing. Even though he left after the clutch of folks at the north end of the cutbank, Hare later asserted that as he entered the plain, he could see through the dust that the three companies were well closed up in a triangle, with A Troop flanked by G and M—an observation so at variance with the evidence that one wonders how so good a soldier could utter the words.[25]

Even farther north, Lieutenant DeRudio and his squad of Company A troopers had been watching Indians creep forward from that direction for fully ten minutes. The ditch was too deep for the Indians to do much damage, but DeRudio was conscious of their presence in small but threatening numbers. Interrupting DeRudio's concentration on the enemy, Trumpeter David McVeigh arrived with his horse, explaining that the command was "going out." According to his testimony, DeRudio protested that he did not want his horse, but his little band of subordinates mounted their animals and would not heed his commands to stay. As they had led him into the wilderness, so they led him out. From DeRudio's point of view, the left of the line (to the south) was leaving in what appeared to be a panic. He paused to recover the company guidon, which had been left behind. The soldier responsible for the flag supposedly said, "To hell with the guidon, don't you see the Indians are coming in?" As DeRudio testified, he picked up the unit banner and held it across his lap, but when the Indians fired at him, he dismounted to make his way out, only to be separated from his horse by more hostile shooting. He remained in the woods, with or without the guidon.[26]

Also uninformed as to Captain Moylan's intentions was Corporal Stanislas Roy of A Troop, who was looking for his horse when he met Lieutenant Wallace leading a portion of Company G out. Roy asked Wallace where he might find his horse, and Wallace answered, "Grab any horse you can get and get out of here." Shortly after, Roy encountered Private John Gilbert—twenty-two years old and with less than a year of service—leaving the timber with four horses, one of which was Roy's. Roy noted that he was very late in getting out and that A and M had been gone for some time even before he met Wallace. Roy managed to arrive at the river, but without his carbine.[27]

Lieutenant McIntosh, the commander of G Troop and an officer to whom Reno had supposedly spoken personally about the imminent departure, was also wandering among the cottonwoods in search of his horse. Unable to locate the animal, McIntosh took the mount ridden by Private Samuel McCormick of G, who surrendered his means of escape with fatalistic resignation, reportedly commenting that he was a dead man whether he rode or walked.[28]

Private O'Neill of Company G was in the act of mounting when his horse was killed, so he grabbed another, only to have it claimed by Corporal James Martin, who was killed in the retreat. O'Neill followed on foot. Private Henry Petring of the same unit discovered that his horse had also been killed, so he took one belonging to Trooper Eldorado Robb, but when that mount was slain soon after he left the woods, Petring went back and caught a horse running loose. His company had been gone for some time, he said, and he was confused as to which way it had gone, but he finally did reach the retreat crossing.[29]

As McIntosh exited the timber, he met O'Neill and asked where the command had gone; thus McIntosh probably emerged after Wallace had left with a small part of Company G in pursuit of the Reno-Moylan lead. Continuing back into the timber, O'Neill met Private John Rapp, McIntosh's orderly, leading his commander's horse. Among the last out of the woods, Rapp asked for "Tosh," and O'Neill presumably told the orderly where he had last seen the lieutenant. The picture of the loyal Rapp in search of his nicknamed commander, himself floundering and forsaken in a desperate situation, is as heartrending as any other in the gallery of ironies that make up the Battle of the Little Bighorn. Rapp and McIntosh were about to die at the hands of the Indians, whereas the dismounted O'Neill and McCormick would survive.[30]

Reno's orderly, Private Edward Davern, thought that very few of G Troop got mounted. Davern found his own horse plus an extra, which he gave to a sergeant in that company. While Davern and others were still coming out of the woods, men were in the process of crossing the river, he said. Released by Reno even before the valley fight began, the orderly—like Adjutant Hodgson—was too far behind in the retreat to be of much use to the battalion commander, who throughout had been attending to his own needs. According to Lieutenant Hare, his orderly—Elihu Clear, who had brought Hare's horse so that he might escape—was killed shortly after leaving the woods.[31]

One of the men wounded in the timber was under the care of Acting Assistant Surgeon Henry Porter. This man may have been the unidentified horse-holder remembered by Gerard early in the withdrawal from the skirmish line, although in his court of inquiry testimony Porter indicated that he was looking for the man when he heard Reno's retreat order and saw the commander ride out of the woods. Shot in the left shoulder, the soldier was dying, in Porter's opinion. The doctor tried to treat the man for a moment or two, but Porter's orderly with his supplies had already left with the others. The wounded trooper implored the physician not to leave, but Porter told the man that he had to go and instructed the soldier to lie still in the bushes so that the Indians would not find him. With that, the unarmed surgeon mounted his big black horse with some difficulty and, pressing forward against the animal's neck, held on for dear life. Like so many others, Porter was very late in getting out of the woods.[32]

Hodgson must also have been stuck in the forest for a few minutes after the initial sprint for the rear. The young lieutenant, whom Reno would call "my adjutant and a great favorite and friend of mine," was not so prized that the battalion commander took much notice of his absence. Lieutenant Varnum thought that Hodgson left the timber after him, and the timing of Hodgson's near escape and ultimate death suggests that he was not anywhere near the front of the backward march. In that light alone, Reno's later chest-thumping lamentations over the loss of his adjutant ring false.[33]

Although Varnum started out moments after the quickly moving vanguard, he rode a thoroughbred horse that was able to catch up with the head of the column before it reached the river. But even before his departure from the timber, he may have tried in vain to stop the stampede. Private O'Neill recalled hearing him call out: "For God's sake, men, let's don't leave the line. There are enough of us here to whip the whole Sioux nation." Herendeen heard an officer petition futilely: "Halt men! Let us fight them!" In the context of Herendeen's movements, that officer could have been Varnum.[34]

Varnum was more modest regarding his protestations. By his recollection, it was not until he reached the front of the retreating command that he shouted to the men that they could not run away from the Indians. "We must get down and fight," he said. Varnum's humility aside, O'Neill and Herendeen could not have heard him make such statements later than the departure from the timber because both of them were absent at the retreat crossing. As they had been since the withdrawal started, Reno and Moylan were riding in the lead. At the court of inquiry, Varnum indicated that halfway to the retreat ford, he might have said something like: "This won't do, this won't do. We have got to get into shape." Whatever Varnum's words, Reno notified the chief of scouts to back off, saying that he was in command. Clearly he was not in control.[35]

Lieutenant Hare would recall that Varnum still tried to manage the enlisted men on the far side of the river. Dr. Porter also said that as the survivors scaled the bluffs, he heard Varnum plead: "For God's sake, men, don't run. There are a good many officers and men killed and wounded and we have got to go back and get them." Either Varnum tried, all along the line of withdrawal, to bring some semblance of order to the sprint for survival, or individual witnesses misplaced Varnum's single call for discipline; in either case, Lieutenant Varnum strove alone to apply a tourniquet to a general hemorrhage.[36]

Out on the plain, Captain French was simply attempting to get himself and his Company M back on track. As Lieutenant Hare emerged from the woods, he noticed that French and his Company M were traveling south in a straight line back toward Ford A, the point at which the battalion had entered the valley floor, rather than forming one side of a neat triangle, as

Hare had suggested elsewhere. Private Daniel Newell thought the company was trying "to get back to the place where [it] had forded" but was cut off by Indians in the timber to the south. French himself had become separated from the unit and was being chased by three or four Indians, said Hare. To French, it seemed that he was fighting the whole Indian force as, for nearly a mile, he held off a horde of attackers single-handedly, killing one in the process—by his own words, remaining ready and willing to forfeit his own life if necessary. A perplexed and angry French, with his band of soldiers, swung to the left and plunged into the cool water of the Little Bighorn soon after Reno's advance party.[37]

In the early stages of the withdrawal, the safest place for any soldier was in the front, since the Indians had been caught off guard by the sudden emergence of the attenuated and scattered column from the cover of the cottonwoods. Walter Camp paraphrased Private (M Troop) Roman Rutten's description of how the scene appeared to him:

> As Rutten left the timber, a solid line of Indians, as many as 200 . . . rode up on his right and had stopped or nearly stopped, and were doing some very loud yelling as the soldiers were getting out of the timber. A few of these Indians were firing into the retreating soldiers, but most of them were giving vent to a variety of Ha Ha's and Haw Haws, apparently being about as badly excited as the soldiers and apparently undecided as to what movement the soldiers were about to execute.

From Rutten's account, it is not clear exactly when he came out, but from other circumstances mentioned, he must have left soon after the start of the run for the rear. Also, he was probably riding alone rather than with his own company or with Reno's group.[38]

Rutten added that as he advanced, he noticed only a few of the enemy in his front and more riding parallel to the general flow of the retreat. As Varnum recalled, the Indians galloped along the flank, their repeating Winchester rifles resting on their saddles as they pumped bullets into the fleeing soldiers. He said there were no Indians in his front by the time he reached the head of the column halfway to the river. Other soldiers would remember that the Indians hung over the far sides of their ponies as they shot so as to protect themselves from the return fire. From all indications, the soldiers engaged in the mad run for the river did little harm to the Indians. Except for French and the men on foot, probably few of the soldiers hit an opponent until the river was reached.[39]

A short distance south of the timber, Reynolds's horse was shot soon after he parted company with Gerard. Herendeen said that he had warned Reynolds not to leave the protection offered by the trees even as the experienced guide was climbing up on his mount. Reynolds covered about 150 yards before he was unhorsed. Gerard thought that Reynolds had been cut off by the Indians and possibly wounded, perhaps without a weapon and with his leg caught fast under the animal. However, Lieutenant DeRudio recalled seeing the scout on one knee, firing a dozen shots at the Indians before they killed him. Corporal Roy also remembered seeing Reynolds dismounted and wounded but standing still and fighting with a pistol.[40]

Perhaps a bit earlier, and not far from where Reynolds went down, the Sioux interpreter Isaiah Dorman also lost his horse to an Indian bullet and was seen by several witnesses holding his ground. The most detailed account of Dorman's last moments was provided by Private Rutten, who reported that the black interpreter was also "down on one knee, cooly firing his sporting rifle." Rutten added, "Isaiah and I were intimate acquaintances, and as I passed him he looked up at me and cried out, 'Goodbye Rutten.'"[41]

From the cover of the cottonwoods, Herendeen saw Indian women pounding Dorman with stone hammers. Afterward, it was discovered that Dorman's legs below the knees had been shot full of bullets (perhaps while he was still alive), that he had been ripped open, that his testicles had been fixed to the earth by an iron picket pin driven through them, that his penis had been cut off and stuffed in his mouth, that his chest had been shot full of arrows, and that his blood had been drained into a coffee pot and cup carried by Dorman. Called "Teat," he was married to a Hunkpapa woman, and it is possible that Her Eagle Robe of that tribe finally killed him. The extent of the mutilation reflected the animosity felt toward anyone who was thought to have betrayed relatives, the placing of the penis in the mouth being the ultimate Indian insult.[42]

Thus, during this intermediate phase of Reno's sudden withdrawal from the timber, considerable courage had been displayed by men like Varnum and French, Reynolds and Dorman, and the many enlisted men who worked through the chaos, often alone and unled. Under the circumstances, it is surprising that there were not more documented signs of weakness in the ranks and that these undertrained, mostly very young men did not simply sit down and weep themselves to death. In much of the recent analysis of the battle, scholars have posited that the soldiers with Custer's right wing came completely unglued, that they became victims of group psychosis, that they bunched and froze, that they hunkered down in place or shot themselves. But in Reno's battalion the enlisted men—whether fresh or venerable—did everything possible within their puny powers to survive the ordeal even as they had the presence of mind to save that last bullet for themselves. According to the remembrances of those who were there, most of the soldiers who had no chance simply stood their ground.

It is similarly astonishing that the Indian warriors did not inflict even more carnage, given their significant advantage in number, firepower, mobility, and group cohesion. They did back off when Custer showed himself at the other end of the village and when Benteen finally appeared to reinforce Reno's battered command, but because the Indians did not do more harm to the front of the column or to the many individuals who trailed behind, Reno's unexpected run to the river may actually have confounded the warriors to the point that they could not comprehend its real meaning. In the end, and all other considerations aside, Reno could proclaim with pride that he had got away with his charge to the rear, suffering—by his narrow reckoning—an acceptable level of attrition.

One soldier who had difficulty catching up with the head of the command was Lieutenant McIntosh. On the horse surrendered by Private McCormick, "Tosh" rode alone through the dust clouds in pursuit of the column and possibly his own company, now led by Lieutenant Wallace. Private Rutten asserted that McIntosh was by himself, trying to urge on the horse, which seemed to be bothered by a dragging lariat. Within sight of the river, McIntosh was surrounded by twenty or thirty Indians who were circling in for the kill, said Rutten. Private William Morris was sure that McIntosh was only a short distance from the water, "sitting as calm as a deacon at service" on his horse, knowing that he had no chance. The ever-charitable Benteen, who was not there, later told his wife that McIntosh might have lived had he "divested himself of that slow poking way which was his peculiar characteristic."[43]

Seeing McIntosh's predicament, Private Rutten "tore right across the circle of Indians" and, veering to the left, jumped his horse over stumps and fallen timber to the river's edge. Men and horses already in the river were struggling to find a way up over the high bank that guarded the far shore, until "finally the mob of horsemen made for a narrow trail cut by buffalo in going for water." Like other soldiers, Rutten was avoiding that lemming-like crush that had followed in a direct line after Reno and Moylan; as a result, troopers were entering the river all along the western bank in groups and individually.[44]

Caught in the river, apparently to the left of the mob, Private Petring found himself facing several Indians on the far bank. Without aiming, he fired his rifle, possibly hitting one of the warriors. Jumping off his horse, Petring waded through chest-deep water downstream and back toward the western side of the river, where he found safe haven among some willows. He considered shooting himself, but before long he was joined by a dozen other troopers who would—with Herendeen—make up the last large group to escape the timber.[45]

Probably Lieutenant Hodgson was hit as he jumped his horse into the river. So said Private Davern, and Private William Slaper agreed that Hodgson was standing in the water when Trumpeter Charles Fischer of M Troop rode by and offered a stirrup, which the lieutenant grabbed. He was thus pulled to the other side, where he was shot again and killed. However, Private Newell thought that Hodgson and Private John ("Snopsy") Meier had gone for the same loose horse, that Meier had mounted, and that Hodgson had clung to the stirrup for the crossing. Unfortunately, Reno's adjutant did not live to identify the man who may have tried to help him.[46]

And what of the lachrymose Reno, whose crocodile tears for his lost adjutant would be a factor in locking him in place on the bluffs for a good hour after he was safely across the river? In his court of inquiry testimony, Reno said that he had wanted to give the men the best chance of saving themselves and that he had led the charge so that he would be present on the bluffs in order to rally the troops. Except for noting that he had lost his dear comrade Hodgson in the process, Reno asserted nothing of consequence in connection with the terror-filled crossing of the Little Bighorn River. He did observe that Moylan's Company A was in front during the withdrawal, and that this troop suffered the most wounded. But he failed to mention that perhaps only half of Moylan's company was present when the two senior officers darted for safety out of the timber—front and center, where they were able to breeze through the startled Indians.[47]

As for Moylan, he acknowledged that though there had been no provision made for defense in the timber, the movement to the rear was "entirely on the defensive." He could not bring himself to utter the word "retreat." Still, he insisted, the companies had gone to the river "almost on a line." He said that this was *not* a "run" to the Little Bighorn, even though all of the evidence indicates that it was not only a run but a rout, with enough stragglers to represent fully two-thirds of the battalion. Moylan asked the court to believe that midway in the sprint to the river, he dropped back from the head of the column to check on his men, a statement that has the same degree of credibility as his claim that he was one of the last out of the woods. He added that on the far side of the river, he tried to get his company together, since it was "found there were a good many missing." The fact is that Moylan had fled the timber with probably no more than half his command and that he never looked behind even after he reached the top of the bluffs, on the heels of Major Reno.[48]

Meanwhile, troopers were struggling to make their way up the buffalo trail that cut into the bank several feet high on the far side of the river. Sergeant Ryan said that the gap was just wide enough to accommodate soldiers riding in single file. The opening was so steep that the riders "were obliged to lean forward in the saddle, and grab the horse's mane, to keep the saddles from sliding back." At some point, a fallen horse blocked passage to this shrunken avenue of egress from the river, but it was soon pulled aside, and soldiers pushed up the drainage areas that led to the bluffs looming some one hundred feet above. After plunging through fifty feet of swiftly flowing, stirrup-deep water, there was probably not a man or horse that was not fatigued. And still the Indians were taking their toll.[49]

Lieutenant Varnum had remained on the eastern bank as the troopers drove their mounts onto the flat bottomland that intervened between the river and the ascent to the bluffs. He saw Adjutant Hodgson get hit again and fall, mortally wounded. Then he assisted his orderly, Elijah Strode, who had been shot through the thigh and whose horse had gone down. Varnum dismounted, caught a loose horse, and with the help of Sergeant Ferdinand

Culbertson, put Strode on the new mount. Varnum and Culbertson also assisted Sergeant Heyn, who had taken a bullet in the knee.[50]

Varnum intended to climb the sides of the bluffs through a ravine to his left, and he had started in that direction when he heard some of the soldiers shouting something. As they did so, Acting Assistant Surgeon James DeWolf—scaling the slope along the line that Varnum intended to follow—turned around and was killed in his tracks by Indians located on the high ground. The soldiers sounding the alarm had apparently seen the warriors in position above, and they were warning Varnum and others pursuing that course to enter a ravine to the right of the one taken by DeWolf and another trooper, who was also killed.[51]

It was after four o'clock when the last of the soldiers (except those left in the timber) managed to exit the river at the retreat crossing and its environs. How much after is difficult to calculate. Assuming that Company M rolled off the skirmish line at about 3:40 and that the Reno-Moylan skedaddle began five minutes later, the beginning of the retreat started at about 3:45, no later than 3:50. Given the confusion in the timber, probably another five minutes passed before the last of the soldiers was able to find a horse and get out. Recognizing that there were many variables within the whole set of individual experiences, the Reno vanguard was certainly across the stream and up the bluffs by four o'clock, with the tail end of the strung-out caravan of men arriving by 4:10–4:15.

Not including the time consumed in covering the mile to the river, Reno had actively engaged the enemy for less than half an hour. In that period, he lost about a man a minute. Few of those casualties had been suffered while on the skirmish line or in the timber. According to the best evidence available, one trooper died on the line, and maybe three or four were mortally wounded during those five or so minutes in the woods. The overwhelming majority of those lost were effectively abandoned to their fate during the withdrawal phase of Reno's engagement with the Indians. Besides the officers (McIntosh, Hodgson, and DeWolf), some thirty enlisted men, three Arikara scouts (Bloody Knife, Little Brave, and Bob-tailed Bull), and two civilians (Reynolds and Dorman) were killed.

From the moment Reno formed his skirmish line, the Indians had begun to do what they did best: they filled all of the vacated territory and took advantage of any signs of hesitation in their opponents. Thus, they both faced and flanked Reno's line, and when in the early stages of combat the fairly composed soldiers began to inhale the scent of panic and fall victim to the tug of command collapse, the Indians smelled the opportunity for eventual enclosure and perhaps victory, if only in allowing their noncombatants to get free. By the time Crazy Horse and his coterie entered the woods north of Reno's "park" position, other warriors had seeped into the timber south of the battalion, and small groups of Indians were occupying ground on the heights east of the Little Bighorn. Explaining the situation as he had experienced it, Captain Moylan told the court of inquiry that the Sioux and Cheyennes had "not actually" driven the command out of the timber but had "virtually" done so. Indeed, because of Reno's inaction, the warriors had been permitted to very nearly surround the entire command, even though the noose was not so tight that all avenues of escape had been closed to desperate men.[52]

At about four o'clock, Custer's wing appeared opposite the northern end of the village, saving Reno's command from far greater attrition, possibly even destruction. Couriers arrived, said the Miniconjou Red Horse, and advised the warriors engaging Reno "that the women and children were in danger of being taken prisoner by another party of troops." In a more expansive version of that moment, Red Horse explained: "A Sioux man came and said that a different party of soldiers [Custer] had all the women and children prisoners. Like a whirlwind the word went around, and the Sioux all heard it and left the soldiers on the hill and went quickly to save the women and children." Even the warriors on the heights nearly all disappeared, leaving the way open for Reno to rally his troops on the bluffs.[53]

Those men of Reno's command left in the timber were doubtless grateful for the diversion. Herendeen had been joined in the timber by a dozen troopers, including the near suicide Private Petring, all of whom had been left behind in the Reno withdrawal. Half had horses and half were afoot, and there was plenty of ammunition, enough to hold off the Indians for a long time. For approximately an hour, Herendeen encouraged the troopers with the thought that he had been in just this kind of "scrape" before and that they could survive. Herendeen advised the soldiers with mounts to release the animals. When the coast was clear, the intrepid scout left the secreted position, leading the party—except for two of the troopers, who elected to remain and who died for their decision. Encountering a small body of Indians as they crossed the river, Herendeen fired a shot to clear the path to safety. By about 5:30, Herendeen and his fledgling frontiersmen had crossed the river and joined Reno on the bluffs.[54]

More troubled but no less fortunate was another group of men trapped in the backwash of Reno's retreat. Lieutenant DeRudio first found himself in the company of Private O'Neill, and before long the two were joined by Gerard and the guide Billy Jackson. Gerard and Jackson were mounted; their compatriots were not. For twenty-four hours, these four individuals wandered upriver and down in an effort to extricate themselves from a seemingly hopeless situation. By the night of 26 June, all four men were safe with Reno's command.[55]

Such tales of endurance have value in themselves, but more important, they prove that for an hour after Reno's withdrawal from the valley, there was very little Indian residual power at the retreat crossing. The Indians had indeed gone north, or else Herendeen and his followers could not have passed to the east without much more significant hindrance.

Also, the participants in this adventure disclosed that the Indians had set fire to the woods from which Reno had departed. As Private Petring recalled, the enemy set the timber ablaze, but the wind changed and blew the smoke away from the soldiers hiding there. The likelihood is that the still-green underbrush caused the fire to smolder and that the wind blew billows of smoke away from the intended victims of the conflagration. From the Indian point of view, this tactic—possibly employed as early as Reno's charge down the valley—served the dual purpose of concealing their movements as well as driving any soldiers out of the woods. It was probably smoke from this scorched-earth ploy that Captain McDougall and the pack train saw from several miles away.[56]

Lastly, the Herendeen and Gerard groups recalled hearing the sounds of Custer's fight downriver. In one account, Herendeen asserted that while he and the enlisted men crouched in the timber, he heard "nine volleys at intervals," followed by heavy scattered firing for almost an hour. His testimony at the court of inquiry and later was generally consistent, even though it tended to be general, such as "a great many volleys."[57]

Gerard provided the additional information that the shooting at the opposite end of the village began about half an hour after the retreat from the timber. To his ears, it first sounded like general firing, then two volleys seemed louder, with the whole episode continuing for approximately two hours. Private O'Neill, who was with Gerard, thought he heard three volleys. Lieutenant DeRudio reported hearing "immense volleys of firing" while in the woods with this group.[58]

If we average these slightly divergent accounts, it would appear that the firing at the Custer end of the field began at perhaps 4:30 and that a more distant and sporadic sound of gunfire persisted until as late as six o'clock in the evening. By that time, all of the men on the northern front of Custer's advance were probably dead.

At the court of inquiry, Recorder Jesse Lee managed to wheedle out of Lieutenant Edward Mathey words ascribed to his fellow officer Lieutenant DeRudio after the battle: "If we had not been commanded by a coward, we would have been killed." In a continuation of his hearsay testimony, Mathey claimed that he had heard officers say that Reno had "lost his head." In point of fact, no officer at the court of inquiry would assert that Reno had displayed any signs of cowardice. The possible exception was Godfrey, who, without being in the thick of the valley fight, felt that Reno—perhaps in the context of his total deportment—had displayed "nervous timidity."[59]

From the military point of view, the word "coward" connotes more than simply embarrassment or disgrace to the service. To display fear in the face of the enemy ought to have been an unforgivable sin, especially if the culprit was an officer—and beyond that, an officer trained in the art of war at the U.S. Military Academy at West Point. The word "coward" was too strong for the officers who testified at the court of inquiry, but the hard evidence is that Reno "cut and ran" from the outset of the fight in the valley and that he cared more for his own survival than for that of the men who served under him or of the regiment as a whole. Not even the appeal to intoxication could finally spare him from his poor performance as an officer.

In a letter written to Godfrey nearly thirty-five years later, Private William O. Taylor captured the essence of what must have been a general feeling among the soldiers, even those who blessed Reno for his unmilitary inspiration.

> Reno proved incompetent and Benteen showed his indifference—I will not use the uglier words that have often been in my mind. Both failed Custer and he had to fight it out alone. . . . Among the several

things that impressed me greatly, one was the general demoralization that seemed to pervade many of the officers and men, due in great measure, I think, to Major Reno. When an enlisted man sees his commanding officers showing greater regard for their personal safety than anything else, it would apt to demoralize anyone taught to breathe, almost, at the word of command.

So many years after the event, Taylor still could not bring himself to use the word "coward" when writing to an officer about another officer, although this was likely one of the "uglier words" that crossed his mind.[60]

In purely military terms, Reno's decisions to stop the initial charge and to form the skirmish line were sensible and in full accord with his instructions. The withdrawal of the line from the prairie to the woods was defensible as a tactic in the face of superior forces able to outflank and virtually envelop the battalion, although the repositioning was accomplished more by accident than by well-considered command and control. One could even argue (as was done at the court of inquiry) that the retreat itself was a military necessity and that, with the information available to him, Reno was justified in pulling his men out of harm's way and heading for the hills.

Unfortunately, however, there is not a single instance of courage in Reno's behavior from first to last in the valley, nor is there any evidence that he took one step to look out for the soldiers dependent on his leadership. Supposedly he told Captain French that they would fight, but he instituted no measure for defense in the timber and in fact was seemingly frozen in place in the park until driven to action by Indians infiltrating almost to the center of his position. Then he ran—leading, led by, or in harness with Moylan, without a bugle ever sounding assembly or retreat and without any personal involvement in organizing his dispersed and confused troopers. He left many to fend for themselves, so that even officers like Varnum, Hare, and DeRudio—and maybe McIntosh and Hodgson—were notified by happenstance and had to chase after the head of the column. At no point from the timber to the river crossing did Reno make any effort to provide cover for the men in the rear.

Maybe Reno believed that his charge to the rear had saved the battalion and that he had actually foreseen the tolerable human losses that might occur in such an aggressive extrication from near disaster. But in truth, men survived by small, individual acts of ingenuity, bravery, and perseverance and by the selflessness of their comrades—not to mention a fair share of good fortune. Never did Reno acknowledge that Custer's appearance at the north end of the village had saved him by drawing off nearly all of the warriors. Rather, Reno and most other survivors were content to applaud Benteen for his timely arrival, since it was Benteen's own opinion that he had saved the day.

And so Custer provided the support he had promised, in time to save at least a few of the soldiers who had fought in the valley. Had Reno been able to hold out in the woods for another half an hour—as he should have done, as Benteen would have done, or as Captain Myles Keogh or Captain George Yates or Captain Tom Custer would have done—such support might have meant more, not only to those in the valley but also to the two hundred men who were about to feel the full and awesome brunt of the Sioux and Cheyenne wrath.

Lieutenant Godfrey summed up his feelings in a memorandum written many years after the battle:

> As it turned out I think Custer did make a mistake in going in with a divided force, not that the division of itself would have been fatal, but because Reno failed to hold a leg even if he couldn't skin.[61]

That conclusion is not only colorful but apt.

CHAPTER TWELVE

CALLING FOR COURAGE

The end was near for Custer and every soldier in the right-wing formation. Prospects that appeared so positive were about to take a sudden and unexpected turn for the worse. But there would be no going back.

Twice Custer had summoned his reserves, including the extra ammunition carried on the pack mules. They were lagging farther behind than he wanted, but once they had his orders in hand, surely they would accelerate their pace. Also, he had committed his vanguard, and it had engaged the enemy. On his last visit to Sharpshooter Ridge, he had seen Major Marcus Reno's battalion fighting the Indians in the valley of the Little Bighorn. That had clearly pleased him. Eschewing a secret passage to the lower end of the village, Custer had broadcast his own presence to the Indians in so bold a manner that they must have seen him. The whole idea was to convince the enemy that the soldiers were too many. Now it was time to throw the second audacious wave at the flanks of the hostile encampment. If those Indians had not seen the gray horses of E Troop moving across the bluffs above the river, they would soon observe the horses in circumstances that could not be missed or misunderstood.

Unfortunately, Custer was about to receive news from several quarters that would defeat his battle plan even before its critical phase had begun and would so shake his general purpose that tactical fine-tuning would be driven more by blind hope than by logical expectation. A brave man by nature, he would need all of the courage and faith he could muster to go forward with the knowledge that Reno was in retreat and that not all

TO HELL WITH HONOR

of the pieces of the original plan were in place. Hard choices were in the offing.

As Custer came down from Sharpshooter Ridge, he joined the rest of the right wing formed in Medicine Tail Coulee, about opposite Cedar Coulee and over a mile from the Little Bighorn. He immediately dispatched Trumpeter John Martin to Captain Frederick Benteen with a message to "come quick" and to bring the packs. The column started to move in the direction of the river and the crossing point afterward known as Ford B. It could not have advanced very far before Boston Custer arrived, dusty and tired and full of Custer spunk, perhaps trying to conceal an impish grin—the kind that accompanied family practical jokes—as he faced his increasingly concerned brother Armstrong.

If Boston was supposed to have remained with the pack train, his appearance could not have made things easier for Custer at this tension-filled juncture. If (as seems more likely) Boston was simply returning with a fresh horse, the general and Captain Tom Custer would have been relieved at his safe arrival, it being their shared understanding that brothers would go up or down together. Possibly their nephew Autie Reed smiled and winked, quietly pleased that his kin and pal had taken the chance and succeeded in completing the family circle during a time of great adventure. In any event, what Boston had done was just a Custer thing, a bit reckless perhaps but still fearlessly loyal.

As the first order of business, Custer would have quizzed Boston briefly on the position and status of the reserves. Peering through Lieutenant Charles DeRudio's binoculars twice while on Sharpshooter Ridge, Custer himself had doubtless looked in the direction of the formations on the back trail, but he would have seen little more than dust and indistinguishable shapes moving between the Morass and the Lone Tepee. Boston had been there and could therefore tell the general more, even though he had departed well before Sergeant Daniel Kanipe's and Trumpeter Martin's arrivals. Still, Boston could inform his brothers that the mules continued to straggle, that the whole train was struggling, and that Benteen was plodding toward a water hole. Some of the men in Benteen's column had waved him a hearty good-bye. Boston may also have reported that as he passed Trumpeter Martin, he had noticed bullet wounds in the orderly's horse, confirming that the enemy had infiltrated the bluffs in Custer's wake.

264

Maybe Custer believed that his orders would fix that sluggish pace by obliging Benteen to sort out the dozen or so mules carrying ammunition and to hurry forward in support of the attack on the big village. But even if Custer believed that, he also knew that those needed reserves could not arrive in less than half an hour, maybe longer. As much as Custer might have wanted to use Benteen's battalion for the second thrust into the Indian camp, such a notion had long since become an utter impossibility, and the general would have to use the resources at hand to accomplish the objective. From the moment of his first trip to Sharpshooter Ridge, he must have recognized that the perfect instrument for inspiring awe in the natives was the Gray Horse Troop, a looming and ghostly presence, accompanied by as much noise as might be made.

Without witnesses, of course, the nature of the conversation between Custer and Boston is simply surmise. As unsettling or as comforting as Boston's arrival may have been, the next episode and the news it engendered would be even more disquieting, and for that there was a witness.

In the immediate aftermath of the battle, the Crow scout Curley told a story that captured headlines, in large part because he was the last "friendly" to see Custer alive. His initial tales were credible to a public eager to understand how the "boy general" had met his fate, but over time, as Curley continued to attempt explanations, a growing number of experts became more skeptical, chiefly about Curley's escape from the field. Also, the more Curley spoke on the subject, the more inconsistencies appeared in his accounts, until finally authorities in the study of the Little Bighorn battle dismissed him altogether as a totally unreliable source of information. His fellow Crow scouts did not help matters by insisting that Curley had "disappeared" well before the battle began, even though they themselves had left the scene before Custer's descent into Medicine Tail Coulee and were therefore not in a position to verify Curley's whereabouts.[1]

Like all of the other Indian testimony relative to the battle, Curley's accounts were filtered through a variety of interviewers and interpreters over a long period of time. As such, his perception of events was subject to the predispositions of his interlocutors and to the quality of his translators, not to mention his own reshuffled memory, with the loss over the years of an exactitude of recollection that the passage of years exhausts. Nonetheless, taken in its entirety, Curley's central idea of what happened in the penultimate phase of the Little Bighorn fight is persuasive because it makes sense in the context of the right-wing movements and of enemy Indian testimony.[2]

As Custer was positioning his forces in Medicine Tail Coulee for another thrust toward the Indian village, the scout Mitch Boyer and the young Curley remained stationed on Weir Point. The Crow scouts had been authorized to depart, and three of the four did so. From the moment Custer ascended Sharpshooter Ridge for the second time, he had no further need for scouts, but following his departure from that promontory, he did require a sentinel to signal the progress of the Reno fight on the valley floor. That was Boyer's assignment, and from Curley's testimony, the half-blood scout performed as expected, even if the messenger would finally deliver a message that would crush Custer's heart.

The intelligence was conveyed in two parts. In an interview with Walter Camp, Curley indicated that as the scouting party reached Weir Point, Boyer directed the three Crows who were leaving "to watch the Indian camp in the valley opposite and any movements of Indians in Custer's rear." The three Crows remained in the vicinity long enough to fire several shots into the village, then withdrew in the direction of Benteen and the pack train. From their vantage point on Weir Point, Boyer and Curley watched the progress of Reno's battle. "At the sight of this, Boyer could hardly restrain himself and shouted and waved his hat excitedly for some little time," Curley said.[3]

The waving of the hat must have been the semaphore that Curley referred to when he told Camp in a separate interview that at the sight of Boyer's enthusiasm, "Custer and Tom Custer returned [the] signal by waving [their] hats, and [the] men cheered." However, because of the nature of Camp's questions, Curley connected this display of jubilation with the sighting of Reno's retreat, when in fact these were two separate events requiring entirely different kinds of signals.[4]

In terms of timing, Boyer's demonstration of positive news had to have occurred after Custer had left Sharpshooter Ridge (where he had seen for himself what was happening in the valley) and after he had arrived in Medicine Tail Coulee (where he became dependent on Boyer's eyes and ears). This hat-waving episode therefore took place at about 3:40–3:45, as the last of Reno's battalion was withdrawing into the timber, some men still firing as they went. Five minutes later, Reno began his run for the river, and Boyer was obliged to convey another message to Custer, this time in person.

To meet Custer's advance down Medicine Tail, Boyer and Curley angled northeasterly down a ravine leading from Weir Point. The two scouts intercepted the Custer column while it marched toward the river, and Boyer delivered the bad news. As Curley remembered: "Boyer probably told Custer [that] Reno had been defeated, for Boyer did a whole lot of talking to Custer when he [Boyer] joined him and kept talking while they were riding side by side." It was four o'clock, and the plan of action that had seemed so promising half an hour earlier withered under the hot afternoon sun. No doubt stunned and incredulous, Custer must have questioned Boyer closely as to whether he was certain that Reno had retreated. A brief report was not adequate to deal with this unexpected turn of events. There had to have been a conversation, an interrogation, at the conclusion of which Custer— resigned to acceptance of a reported catastrophe that he was unable to personally verify—stopped the column to consider his options.[5]

Custer likely found it hard to wrap his mind around the idea that Reno had left the field. From Boyer's words, Custer must have learned that Reno went into the timber, then out, and that there were many Indians circling the prairie—shooting, kicking up much dust, war-whooping their defiance. Without particulars, Custer could not pass judgment on Reno's decision, but he must have been stunned. Nevertheless it was done, and there was no changing it. Custer held to the maxims "don't cry over spilt milk" and "don't cross a bridge till you come to it." He was a man who operated primarily in the present.[6]

For an instant at least, he surely entertained the thought of taking his own relatively small wing out of action, of delivering Boston and Autie Reed and the newspaperman, Mark Kellogg, to a safer place because they were not professional soldiers or scouts. One drawback to such a course was that in any retrograde movement, Custer risked turning his back on the Sioux and Cheyenne warriors—always a bad idea and anathema to his predilection for a cavalry charge toward the opposition—and chanced surrendering the initiative. Additionally, a retreat might jeopardize the pack train and its precious cargo of ammunition by actually dragging the Indians into the midst of the slow-moving caravan. Lastly, Custer did not know the final status of Reno's command, including the number of casualties.

From his own observations and from Boston's report, Custer knew that the packs could not be closer than three or four miles away. At this very moment, Benteen might be hurrying forward with the ammunition, but surely Boyer advised the general that he could see no sign of reserves near at hand on the back trail. Optimistically, Custer could not expect assistance before 4:40–4:45, likely later even if Benteen came quickly, because the mules would have to be driven at no more than five miles an hour over rough terrain. All other considerations aside, as every last trooper knew, protection of that reserve ammunition was of paramount importance if the regiment as a whole was to survive.[7]

This weighing of alternatives probably did not occupy more than a few moments as Custer's mind raced through the host of variables, including the likelihood that Indians would accumulate between the reserves and his own right wing. Perhaps he consulted briefly with Tom and Adjutant William Cooke, not expecting and not getting opinions at variance with his own conclusion that the situation was serious but that leaving the field was not an option. Almost certainly his thoughts harkened back to the Washita, where he had boldly and purposefully marched toward his Indian enemies and away from his wagons in order to protect his supplies from attack. All he needed was the regimental band playing "Ain't I Glad to Get Out of the Wilderness" to duplicate that intrepid performance, which had worked then and might again. But he had no band to play, to make the noise he had in mind, to create the magic that he might have recalled wistfully from Civil War glory days and so often since. Not the kind of man to live with regret, he would have lingered in such a reverie for only an instant before jerking himself back to reality.

Since withdrawal was out of the question, Custer had no choice but to advance in accordance with his original plan. Using a little imagination and some sleight of hand, maybe he could still trick the Indians into believing that the bluecoats were as many as the blades of grass on the prairie. The arrival of Benteen and the packs might then enhance the desired impression.

During the halt in Medicine Tail Coulee less than a mile from the river, the soldiers dismounted to rearrange their saddles and otherwise prepare for battle. At this time, Custer held a brief conversation with one of the soldiers riding a sorrel-roan horse, then handed the trooper (possibly a member of Company C) a piece of paper. The courier departed toward the north or east, away from the battlefield and presumably with the intention of reaching the column of General Alfred Terry and Colonel John Gibbon. Since no messenger ever reached General Terry, we have no way of knowing the contents of the dispatch, but likely it was a succinct note describing the dire situation facing the regiment.[8]

Then, as Curley remembered, Custer went to the commander of the Gray Horse Troop and gave him orders. Lieutenant Algernon E. Smith commanded Company E, and although he was probably present, Custer would have spoken instead to Captain George Yates, who was in charge of the battalion, which included Yates's own F Troop. The two-company unit departed immediately toward the river, with Company E in the lead. Custer "had all the bugles blowing for some time," Curley said, "the purpose of which I did not understand." It was some minutes after four o'clock in the afternoon.[9]

The sustained flourish of bugles may have mystified young Curley, but to Custer, the brassy cacophony was an essential accompaniment to the charge. It was not the regimental band playing "Garry Owen," but it would have to do, as valid as the Rebel yell or the Indian battle cry, as likely to stimulate the friendly forces as to intimidate the opposition, as ancient a psychological weapon as the ram's horn. Combined with the phantasmagoric front presented by the E Troop horses, the effect was meant to startle and perplex—if only momentarily—Custer's intended audience.

Mrs. Spotted Horn Bull recollected the moment: "From across the river I could hear the music of the bugle and could see the column of soldiers turn to the left, to march down to the river to where the attack was to be made."[10] To this Sioux woman, the sound in afterthought was "music" rather than raucous forewarning. As for the Gray Horse Troop, many Sioux and Cheyennes marked its presence and would remember it from first to last. The Cheyenne White Shield stated that because these animals were "pretty white," they "could be seen a long way off." Thus, although the Custer sound and sight show had the intended dramatic impact, the effect of the bugles and the gray horses was finally muted as Yates stopped his battalion well short of the river.[11]

Not many Indians were immediately available to deflect the arrival of the Yates battalion. When Reno had attacked the upper end of the village, most warriors had rushed to defend the southern perimeter while women and children had sought escape routes to the north, the west, and even the east. According to some Indian testimony, noncombatants had crossed the river into Medicine Tail Coulee and were situated there when Yates's command started down the dry drainage area. Certainly a great number from the upper village had headed toward the protection of the western bluffs, away from Reno's gunfire, but from Indian accounts, it appears that the vast majority of Cheyenne and some Sioux refugees had gone north, running parallel with the river toward a depression known as Chasing (or Squaw) Creek. Such a dispersal of noncombatants was consistent with Indian practices when threatened.[12]

The problem for the inhabitants of the village was that they did not know which way to run. The Sans Arc mourners had arrived from the east, down Medicine Tail, and women digging for wild turnips had spotted dust on that side of the river. Then Reno struck from the south, and as his skirmish line was forming on the prairie, Custer made portions of his wing visible along the bluffs above the Little Bighorn. The Hunkpapa Moving Robe Woman remembered those events as essentially coincident—that is, the sighting of soldiers on the bluffs occurred at the same time as Reno's sudden appearance.[13] The Cheyenne Little Hawk said that when the Indians saw a lot of other soldiers coming, they left Reno in order to engage this second group.[14] Similarly, the Cheyenne Wooden Leg claimed that while the Indians were fighting Reno, a companion pointed out a body of soldiers on the eastern side of the river, at which time part of the warriors departed to intercept what was in fact Custer's wing.[15] Even White Shield's comment that the Gray Horse Troop could be seen a long way off may have had reference to such sightings.

It is little wonder, then, that the totally surprised villagers would have been thrown into terror by Reno's assault, then become confused and disoriented by an additional attack on the lower end of the camp. That is precisely what Custer's plan envisaged. He had created a situation in which individual Indian fighters had to choose a portion of the village to defend, and in theory at least, he had stretched the encampment's line of defense to more than two miles. But Reno did not maintain his position.

The Sans Arc circle was located nearly opposite the mouth of Medicine Tail Coulee. A short distance downriver stood the lodges of the Cheyennes; to the west were the tepees of the Brulés and Oglalas. Given the proximity of these tribes to the crossing point designated Ford B, they should have had better and earlier visual access to Yates's arrival than those situated farther south, Indians who were more immediately engrossed with fighting Reno's men or with collecting their most precious possessions and escaping. Unfortunately there is no Sans Arc testimony available, but there are sufficient Cheyenne, Brulé, and Oglala eyewitness accounts to conclude that Yates's battalion did not get closer to the river crossing than several hundred yards. Such a conclusion is buttressed by information gleaned from interviews of those Indians who had begun to gather in Custer's rear—that is, on the bluffs to the south of Medicine Tail Coulee.

The Brulé Two Eagles confirmed that the fight with Custer (Yates) began opposite the Sans Arc tepees. He said that the soldiers did not reach the river and that the battle in that locale was brief.[16] The Cheyenne Tall Bull thought that the soldiers came down close to the river and that they fought for quite some time. White Shield believed that the Gray Horse Troop got "pretty close" to the river and dismounted before both sides began to fire.[17] The Oglala Lone Bear said that when Custer (Yates) was approaching Ford B, the troopers were dismounted and were leading their horses, adding that the Indians started after the column before it reached the river. At that point, Lone Bear went back to his lodge, and when he returned, the battle had proceeded to its next phase.[18] The Cheyenne Soldier Wolf added that the soldiers got down to a level area near the mouth of the dry creek, where the shooting lasted awhile.[19]

It is impossible to know exactly how near Yates got to the river, but certainly the soldiers did not get closer than three hundred yards. Any nearer than that and the members of the battalion would have been easy marks for the increasing number of Indians gathering on the west side of the crossing. The notion that several troopers went all the way to the river so as to test the feasibility of fording at that point seems most unlikely. Even a few Indians—let alone twenty or fifty—with guns stationed on the west bank, with an open field of fire across fifteen yards of water, would have annihilated a squad of soldiers dipping their toes or walking their horses in order to fathom depth. Yates probably did suffer casualties at the river, but those losses had nothing to do with trying to cross into the Indian village.[20]

In this connection, we should bear in mind what Custer knew when he dispatched the Yates battalion down Medicine Tail Coulee. He knew that

Reno had been defeated. He knew, from his own observations during the last trip to Sharpshooter Ridge, that the Indians were innumerable and that the village was vast. He knew that a battalion of eighty or so men had no chance of succeeding with an impetuous charge (the popular perception) into an encampment so like an anthill that the Indians themselves would use the metaphor to describe their reaction to the intrusion into their nest. Such an offensive gambit was out of the question now that Reno had withdrawn from the field. All of the warriors were free (indeed, they were invited) to concentrate on Custer's column, and he knew that too.[21]

Probably Yates and Smith rode together as the battalion hurried down, bugles blowing, along the northern rim of the gulch so that they might be visible to the Indian village, stopping when the Little Bighorn came in sight. The sudden lurch into halt several hundred yards short of the river may have caused at least two soldiers to be propelled forward, their horses out of control, as had happened in the Reno charge. A soldier on a gray horse rode across the river and into the village, Curley said, "like a man that wanted to die." By Curley's description, he was a soldier with stripes on his arm. In a separate account, Curley remarked that several troopers rode into the river and that one of them actually crossed the river only to reappear again on the other side, just as Privates Roman Rutten and John Meier had managed to escape certain death when they had lost control of their horses during Reno's attack. In July 1876, before Curley had a chance to incorporate collective memories into his accounts, he was reported as saying simply that two of Custer's men were killed and fell into the river.[22] The Cheyenne Soldier Wolf confirmed that two soldiers were killed near the river and were left there, presumably beyond recovery by members of Yates's battalion.[23]

Based on interviews with some Sioux and Cheyenne warriors several years after the battle, Lieutenant Oscar Long of the Fifth Infantry learned that the Indians had killed an "officer" where Custer had made his first "stand," nearest the river. This soldier carried binoculars and a compass in a wooden box.[24] The Indians could not have identified the man as an officer except by his position relative to the rest of the soldiers, but in a separate account, a Lakota named White Cow Bull, who was visiting the Cheyennes at the time, reportedly stated: "The soldiers came down to [toward] the ford led by one with mustache and buckskin jacket on sorrel." The young warrior shot the officer while his companion hit a trooper carrying a guidon. The buckskin jacket, the field glasses, and the compass certainly suggest an officer, and that officer could have been Lieutenant Smith, whose body would be found on Last Stand Hill, not with those of his Company E after the fight. Stationed out in front of his company, he would have made an inviting target at several hundred yards.[25]

As Yates moved his battalion to within a few hundred yards of Ford B, some Cheyenne and Sans Arc fighters on the western bank apparently opened fire with whatever weapons they had at hand. The men and horses in the narrow front of the column may have taken a few hits, and some troopers unlucky enough to ride frightened mounts may not have escaped but may instead have been dragged into the village for further mutilation. Immediately, Yates dismounted some men, perhaps the first two sets of four, to return the fire, unleashing a couple of volleys into the brush that guarded the far side of the river. Indian witnesses recalled that some part of the column dismounted to fire toward the western bank and the village, causing negligible damage. After about ten minutes or so, perhaps with Smith and others down as casualties, the battalion commander ordered the men to remount and, motioning with his right hand, led the column northward across the strip of higher ground separating Medicine Tail and Deep Coulees. The ineffectual bluff was over.[26]

Meanwhile, the Indians were accumulating. Those on foot were supported by an increasing number of warriors on horseback. "The Cheyennes were already fighting," Red Feather was quoted as saying. "The Oglalas acted as reinforcements." Along with other tribes, he might have said, since all of the fighters were pouring north from the Reno battle. As they arrived, the warriors splashed across the river in the wake of Yates's withdrawal, doing what they did best, pushing their advantage from the rear, heartened to a near frenzy by the defeat of Reno. But as eager as they must have been for the chase, the sight on a distant ridge surely gave them pause.[27]

"As I looked along the line of the ridge, they seemed to fill the whole hill," the Two Kettle Runs-the-Enemy recalled. "It looked as if there were thousands of them."[28]

The Cheyenne Two Moon used his fingers to demonstrate how the soldiers "rose all at once" on their horses in column of fours as they came over a hill to the east.[29]

What these Indians saw was Captain Myles Keogh's battalion, under the overall leadership of Custer, emerging from the upper reaches of Medicine Tail. From another point of view, the Hunkpapa Gall noted the progress of the Custer command. Gall had started off with some of his warriors to cut off Reno's retreat, but while he was en route, Iron Cedar hailed him— perhaps from Weir Point, recently vacated by Boyer and Curley—with word that more soldiers were coming. As Gall and three other Indians watched, the column of soldiers filed slowly along Medicine Tail, becoming increasingly cautious as warriors became visible on the hills south of the coulee. The leader of the column lingered and waited for his command to come up. "I saw the big chief riding with the orderly before we attacked," Gall said. "He had glasses to his face."[30]

Gall likely saw Custer trailing behind Yates and watching through DeRudio's field glasses for E and F Troops to show themselves to the village inhabitants before turning right to form the parallel march thus far favored by the general. Satisfied that Yates had begun the required maneuver, Custer led the Keogh battalion northward, actually angling away from Medicine Tail Coulee and toward the northeast and those high ridges where the Indians would see the seemingly immense soldier presence.

Besides Gall, Iron Cedar, and Thomas Disputed, Indians from other circles were diverting from their intended flanking of Reno's withdrawal. The Miniconjou Feather Earring said that many warriors crossed the river south of Ford B in an effort to get around behind Custer and cut him off from Reno, thus preventing a junction. The Oglala Red Hawk noted that while going up a high hill in the direction of Reno, the Indians turned to assail the leading division of these other soldiers, more likely—from his perspective—the Custer command than that of Yates.[31]

Almost certainly Custer remained with the Keogh battalion. Soon after the battle, Curley recalled that after the Yates column "left us," the rest of the right wing turned north, crossed the dry stream (Medicine Tail Coulee), and moved into the hills. In his later interviews with Camp, the construction of the questions and Curley's answers create the impression that Custer himself led all five companies to the mouth of Medicine Tail, but that probably has more to do with Camp's predisposition to believe in such a deployment than with Curley's memory.[32] Similarly, in his July 1876 account, Curley insinuated the separation of the two battalions by stating that "a portion of the command" was dismounted and thrown toward the river, where the soldiers returned the fire of the Indians. This Curley story also implied that the entire wing was engaged in this move, but by the weight of all other evidence, such was not the case.[33]

Besides Curley's clear statement that the gray horses left the main body of the command, including the headquarters unit, Custer's prior behavior and his concept of operations virtually dictated that he would remain with the Keogh battalion. As overall commander, he needed to place himself in a position to view the disposition of subordinate elements and, based on the results, to be so situated that he could revise tactics to deal with unfolding events. He had not gone in with Reno, and it is hard to conceive that he would have accompanied Yates in a maneuver that represented nothing more than a show of force.

Tracing Custer's strategy employed since the Divide, we see that he chose to move in parallel columns toward his military objectives. First Custer, Reno, and Benteen moved in parallel columns in the direction of the Lone Tepee, after which the Reno battalion was sent at almost a right angle to begin a new side-by-side line of march. Then Custer and Reno rode in parallel columns on either side of the Little Bighorn; next Custer and the three parts of his wing moved in parallel columns along Sharpshooter Ridge, after which Yates was thrown toward the river to repeat the pattern. The purpose of such a strategy was always to make the regiment seen larger than its numbers, to baffle and unnerve the enemy by attacking or appearing to attack in unsynchronized waves. The burning tepee, the early assault by Reno (with nearly all the civilian and Indian scouts and two physicians), the flashing of columns on the bluffs, and the use of the gray-horse facade and blaring bugles were simply devices aimed at aiding the overall objective of scaring the villagers into submission. In hindsight, the proposition that brave men and women could be cowed by such a battery of gimmicks might be perceived as foolhardy, but judged by the testimony of those Sioux and Cheyennes on the receiving end of Custer's failed legerdemain, the pieces of the plan were less flawed than their execution.

Custer stayed with Keogh's supporting component so that he could continue to direct his scheme. Although Custer's band of approximately 120 may have looked like "thousands" to some of the Indians in the camp, the warriors that were increasing in the rear of Keogh's battalion were several times the soldier strength. Some of the Indians had come over the bluffs from Reno's fight, but many more were pouring up Medicine Tail Coulee. To slow the advance of those mostly Sioux men testing the tail of the battalion, Custer stopped the column shortly after emerging from the waterless ravine so that several volleys could be fired into the Indian ranks.

The area where Custer chose to pause has since become known as Luce Ridge. The precise spot where he stopped likely lies on the western portion of that high ground, roughly opposite Weir Point. This ridge was named for Edward Luce, who, as superintendent of the Custer Battlefield during the 1940s and 1950s, here discovered dozens of empty cartridge cases from the cavalry's trapdoor carbines; the cases were found in piles, suggesting some kind of skirmish order. Luce's discovery of forty-eight shells at almost regular intervals suggests that the column engaged in massed firing, mounted or dismounted. Company L—last in the line of march—was exactly forty-eight strong, including officers, and was, by numbers and experience, the most formidable in the Keogh battalion. Assuming that the men fired alternately by platoon, two volleys of twenty-four were discharged to send the Indians scurrying for cover.[34]

Farther north, on a distinct elevation later identified as Blummer-Nye-Cartwright, another one hundred or so Springfield shells were discovered during the 1930s, indicating another period of firing, probably by L Troop as well. The number suggests two or four volleys, perhaps directed toward the rear or south, but possibly a volley or two was fired toward the southwest to cover the withdrawal of Yates's battalion. The soldiers of Lieutenant James Calhoun's company expended, in total, only three cartridges each if the unit was formed in line to deliver the salvos.[35]

Thus, within a distance of perhaps half a mile, Custer had deployed a rear-guard unit twice to fend off the approach of Indians from behind. As Red Hawk recounted, "The soldiers delivered volley after volley into the dense ranks of the Indians without any perceptible effect on account of their great numbers." In the beginning, of course, the Indians were not so numerous, nor were they likely formed in a compact body; by the evidence, some ponies and perhaps a few warriors were hit by the long-range fire. At this stage of the action, the Indians were chiefly concerned with providing a screen for the village, and to this end they dismounted so that they could harass the rear of Custer's column from a safe distance. As Custer continued northward, the warriors crept closer on foot, using the network of inter-connecting gulches for protection.[36]

In the Indian mind, the real battle did not begin on this part of the field until the right wing had reunited on what is today known as Calhoun Ridge. The Keogh battalion arrived first. The primary cause for stopping at this juncture was to receive the Yates battalion back into the fold, but within minutes Custer would have another important reason to choose this relatively open high ground for fighting it out to the last—namely, some wounded soldiers.

Calhoun Ridge lies roughly on an east-west line at a right angle from the river. The highest point on the ridge is Calhoun Hill, located at the eastern terminus, the whole hump then tending westward toward the Little Bighorn through another landmark area designated Finley Ridge and terminating at Greasy Grass Ridge. From about the middle of Calhoun Ridge and running northward is Custer Ridge, with the last knoll in that direction called Last Stand or Custer Hill. The general landmass between Calhoun Hill and Last Stand Hill inclines toward the river over rolling and broken ground for approximately half a mile.

As Custer halted the command on Calhoun Ridge, Companies C, I, and L followed his headquarters unit in the order of march, as had been the case since the column had departed Sharpshooter Ridge. There is some tenuous evidence that the F Troop squad detailed to accompany his headquarters had made a sweep to the right, perhaps to conduct a reconnaissance in advance of the battalion. If the party of five soldiers did make a survey of a possible blind spot, the time spent doing so would have been brief, and the squad would have returned well before Custer deployed his battle lines along Calhoun Ridge.[37]

When the column reached this point, Curley said, there was "a hurried conference of officers." By this time, Boyer was wounded and had "lost" his horse (presumably killed). He told Curley that the officers were discussing the feasibility of making a "stand" somewhere, with the expectation that the rest of the command would come up and relieve them. "Personally, Boyer did not expect that relief would come, as he thought the other commands had been scared out," Curley said. From his own observations, Boyer certainly knew that Reno had been "scared out," but he probably did not know of Custer's two messages to Benteen.[38]

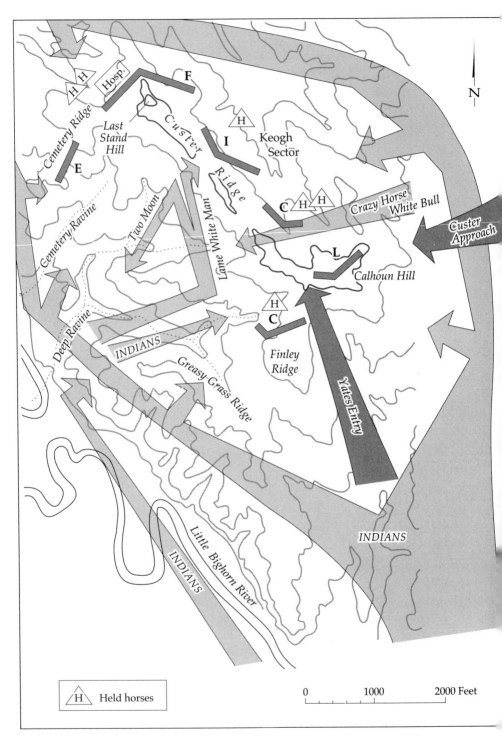

H H

Cemetery Ridge

Hosp.

F

Last Stand Hill

Cu s t e r

H

I

Keogh Sector

E

R i d g e

Cemetery Ravine

Two Moon

Lane White Man

C   H   H

Crazy Horse
White Bull

Custer Approach

L

Calhoun Hill

Deep Ravine

INDIANS

H

C

Greasy Grass Ridge

Finley Ridge

Yates Entry

INDIANS

Little Bighorn River

INDIANS

H   Held horses

0   1000   2000 Feet

The Custer battlefield

Either shortly before or while the officers were addressing the wing's predicament, Custer directed the first platoon of the lead company to form a dismounted skirmish line facing south-southwest, generally toward the river. With Lieutenant Henry Harrington in command, some twenty men of C Troop fell out to comply with the orders. Riding the short distance to the spot later marked "Finley" on the map, the troopers got off their animals and turned them over to the horse-holders, who likely retired to a more protected position on lower ground, leaving fifteen or so men to fire volleys in the direction of the Indians gathering in the space between the ridge and the river.

The area is designated "Finley" because Sergeant Jeremiah Finley's body was found there after the battle. Not far away to the east, Sergeant George Finckle's body was discovered. The fact that the bodies of these two non-commissioned officers were found in this locale makes it more than likely that the soldiers were led by Lieutenant Harrington, whose remains were never identified. As indicated earlier, the de facto second-in-command of Company C was First Sergeant Edwin Bobo, but his body was discovered in what has become known as the Keogh sector of the battlefield, and it is most improbable that the only three sergeants in the unit would fall out with one platoon. Thus, the most logical conclusion is that Harrington led the first platoon, with noncommissioned officers Finley and Finckle to assist with command and control, while Bobo remained with the second platoon, the function of which was to provide support to Calhoun's L Troop.

Again Custer was trying to parcel out small parts of his command to deal with tactical realities. That he placed a platoon rather than a full company at Finley is supported by ample evidence, particularly by the distribution and identity of bodies found after the fight. In addition, the size of his column relative to planned and still undetermined objectives required an economical use of manpower. The primary purpose of the fifteen men at Finley was to provide covering fire for the Yates battalion, which was feeling its way uphill from the river, perhaps encumbered with wounded.[39]

According to Curley, the Yates battalion rode parallel with the Little Bighorn "for some distance and then struck out for higher ground in column of fours, going direct to the point where markers are found at the southeast point of the battlefield," the Calhoun-Finley area.[40] Such a movement is consistent with Indian accounts. Thomas Disputed said that the

Indians chased the soldiers up a long gradual slope away from the river.[41] The Miniconjou Lights recollected that the cavalrymen rode in company formation from Ford B to Greasy Grass Ridge, apparently in good order. There was not much fighting between the two points, he said.[42] The Cheyenne Soldier Wolf asserted that the soldiers retreated slowly, "face to the front," as they "fell back up the hill until they had come *nearly to where the monument now is* [emphasis added]." This memory was shared by Tall Bull.[43] Some of the troopers in Yates's battalion may have been dismounted, providing rear-guard protection to the withdrawing unit.

In the early stages of the battle, Indian responses to the appearance of Custer's command were naturally tentative, and their observations were distorted by the need to deploy for resistance. As soon as Yates left his position opposite Ford B, indicating a line of march and opening the way for an enemy backfill, the available warriors began to cross the river at many points. Although Ford B and another crossing farther north are usually cited as the major avenues to the eastern bank, both Indian and soldier testimony reveals that warriors were able to cross almost anywhere except where steep cutbanks blocked access. And they did so, in increasing numbers, individually and in small groups.[44]

To shield the noncombatants, the Cheyenne warriors hurried north on both sides of the river, keeping abreast of Yates's column. The firing by the opposing forces was occasional and desultory. The soldiers apparently suffered no significant casualties on the trail from Medicine Tail to Greasy Grass Ridge, the upgrade on the north side of Deep Coulee, which the Oglala, Brulé, and Sans Arc warriors were beginning to fill. Wherever there was low ground to offer sufficient protection, the Indians went on foot; even those with ponies dismounted so as to escape the danger of bullets coming from Finley Ridge. Scurrying through the gullies to the west and southwest of Yates's withdrawal, the warriors may have paused to send hundreds of arrows showering down on the soldiers waiting to receive their brothers of the inconsequential feint.

By ten or fifteen minutes before five o'clock, the Yates battalion was reunited with the main body of the right wing. In the last stages of his well-paced march to Calhoun Hill, Yates had been pressed by Indians to his left and rear and, to a lesser extent, by warriors who had followed the Keogh battalion. At the last, he slipped between the troopers who had been stationed at Finley Ridge and the line of soldiers that Custer had posted to guard the backside of his advance. In addition to the two soldiers killed when their horses carried them across the river and perhaps several troopers wounded, perhaps Custer's old friend "Fresh" Smith fell into his arms, thus complicating a situation already fraught with complications.

From Curley's accounts, it is clear that the first complement of soldiers was deployed to Finley Ridge, after which Custer placed Lieutenant Calhoun's Company L along the ridge that would thereafter bear his brother-in-law's name.

> At first the command remained together, but after some minutes fighting it was divided, a portion deploying circularly to the left, and the remainder similarly to the right, so that when the line was formed it bore a rude resemblance to a circle, advantage being taken as far as possible of the protection afforded by the ground.[45]

Subtracting the horse-holders, L Troop had roughly thirty-six men available to form a skirmish line along the ridge—a larger number if a horse-holder tended more than four mounts. As it had done twice before in the northward march from Medicine Tail, the company fired volleys in the direction of the Indians, who were now bobbing and weaving through natural trenches on all sides of the right-wing rear guard.

Curley remembered two such volleys, and he thought they must have been some kind of signal. By now, however, the Keogh and Yates battalions together had fired some eight or ten volleys—the nine or so heard by George Herendeen or the "immense" number recalled by DeRudio. Because there was no large mass of Indians at a point opposite any part of the command, the volleys were probably meant to serve as a notification of the soldiers' firepower (the rough equivalent of cannon or Gatling gun discharges). Beyond being just another show of force, the shooting in unison may well also have been intended as a signal of distress, blasts of noise meant to reach Benteen or any other part of the regiment within hearing. In fact, some or all of those volleys were heard by many of the officers and men gathering on Reno Hill.[46]

Curley said the Indians were on all sides, even in the front, but at that time, the front was toward the northwest, where mostly Cheyenne warriors could be seen moving around Greasy Grass Ridge and slipping downriver in growing numbers. Boyer apparently thought that Custer would continue to charge in this direction—that is, toward the Little Bighorn—thus driving the Indians until the command could find more favorable ground. However, such a move was not made, presumably because the enemy had begun to turn what Curley called the "corner" at Calhoun Ridge. Perhaps one unproductive charge on foot was made by the first platoon of C Troop at this "corner," but if these men made such a movement to drive warriors from ravines near Finley Ridge, the increased gap created between them and Calhoun's line must have been fatal. The "ten or fifteen" soldiers at Finley Ridge were cut off and killed, Curley asserted, although he probably did not actually observe the demise of this contingent.[47]

At about this time, after speaking with the general and Tom, Boyer came to Curley and told him to leave. Go to Terry, Boyer continued, and tell him all the soldiers are killed. Boyer supposedly pointed at Custer and proclaimed, "That man will stop at nothing." This might have been rendered in translation just as correctly as *that man will let nothing stop him*, if the scout said anything like that at all.[48] Curley departed, taking advantage of the terrain and the confusion to sneak through the hostile Indians, who had not yet formed a cordon around the command. From a hill well east of the battlefield, he may have watched until nearly the end, after which he rode back to the *Far West* and tried to convey what he had seen.[49]

One of the last things Curley saw as he left Calhoun Ridge was the Gray Horse Troop leading the way toward the rise that is today called Last Stand Hill. He said the gray horses were keeping well together while the rest of the animals were bunched, an impression endorsed by virtually every Sioux and Cheyenne witness in a position to observe it. As Companies E and F passed through the funnel formed between C and L, they likely stopped momentarily on the back side of Calhoun Hill while Yates reported to Custer. After a brief conference (possibly the one alluded to by Curley), the column continued in the direction of Last Stand Hill, the order of march being the headquarters command, followed by E, F, the second platoon of C under First Sergeant Bobo, and Keogh's I Troop. Likely Custer remained behind to position Captain Keogh's unit along the north-south ridgeline in support of Calhoun's Company L and Lieutenant Harrington's endangered platoon. To the south of Keogh some little distance, Bobo and his platoon were dropped off. Having seen to these dispositions himself, Custer quickly joined the van of the right wing on Last Stand Hill, where Dr. George Lord would have already begun to set up a first-aid station to care for the wounded.[50]

The exact topography of the ground along Custer Ridge is not clear from the maps of the time, but likely there were dips within the length of the hogback, and certainly it was not nearly so broad or flat as it appears today. Lieutenant George Wallace described Custer Ridge as "a series of hills" rather than a continuous hump. The horses of L and I Troops, as well as C's second platoon, were located behind this rolling ridge. One suspects that Harrington's first platoon kept their mounts closer at hand, to the rear of Finley Ridge.[51]

After Custer had decided that he could not retreat toward the pack train with the ammunition or toward Reno with his probable wounded—and after the general had decided that he could not simply push northward and abandon the field of battle—he chose the best available high ground for further maneuvering. He must have felt that even under these most desperate circumstances, nothing could stop him from trying to manufacture a miracle against the longest of odds. One seemingly small thing, like Benteen arriving with 125 more men, might be enough. However, the hour was late. The rear echelons of the wing were under serious duress. The Indians were everywhere, except in front of the pounding hooves of the Gray Horse Troop.

By the time Custer arrived on Last Stand Hill, Dr. Lord had probably established his field hospital on the far side, perhaps in the direction of Cemetery Ridge, the next long and probably rolling elevation to the north-west of Custer Ridge. The gray horses and Yates's company of bays had wound down off the main thoroughfare to collect willy-nilly in the low ground beyond, where they were somewhat protected from the steady stream of Indian arrows and bullets coming from the main line of the Indian advance to the south and southwest.

"They rode over beyond where the monument stands, down into the valley until we could not see them," said Two Moon, who viewed the scene with other Cheyennes to the southwest, then the west.[52]

"Before the fight started," He Dog noted, "we drove him [Custer] up a slope to a ridge and over to the other side of it."[53]

Custer had deployed his forces to cope with that primary thrust coming from the village, groups of Indians moving from south to north. As he looked along the ridge, he saw squads of men from Companies C and I pop up to fire over and between the mounds at quickly disappearing feathered heads. At the far end of the ridge, Harrington's platoon was being engulfed, leaving Calhoun's right flank exposed. The "corner" was being turned and was in danger of being assaulted from every quarter. The ground sloping toward the river seemed so smooth, as it had from Sharpshooter Ridge, when in truth it was subtly tortured by deep and shallow cuts, all sufficient to conceal the uninterrupted creep of the enemy.

It was terrain with which Custer was familiar as a military tactician. In *My Life on the Plains*, that veritable manual of lessons that defined Custer's thinking about war on the frontier, he had noted:

> To an unpracticed eye there seemed no recess or obstruction in or behind which an enemy might be concealed. . . . Yet such was not the case. . . . These ravines, if followed, would be found to grow deeper and deeper, until after running their course for an indefinite extent, they would terminate in the valley of some running stream. These were the natural hiding-places of Indian war parties, waiting their opportunities to dash upon some unsuspecting victims. These ravines serve the same purpose to the Indians of the timberless plains that the ambush did to those Indians of the Eastern states accustomed to fighting in the forests and everglades.

The sum of Custer's experience was present at the Little Bighorn and would find expression again and again in his long last ride—from the Divide to the Lone Tepee to the instructions that, with a final fateful word of precaution, he must have given Reno.[54]

Soon after arriving on Last Stand Hill, Custer ordered the Gray Horse Troop, possibly under the command of Lieutenant James Sturgis, to occupy Cemetery Ridge and from that position to fill, with shot from Springfield carbines, the deceivingly flat land east of the Little Bighorn. In theory at least, Custer had gained possession of all the high ground in the area and, from those positions, could control the fields of fire in every direction. Unhappily for him, the Indians held the upper hand in numbers, firepower,

CALLING FOR COURAGE

and the ability to act in highly individualistic ways consistent with the goals of their community. The terrain favored their unconventional warfare tactics by allowing them to intrude near enough to fire, effectively from cover, at an enemy posted on promontories without any kind of natural protection. In the beginning, the many arrows launched in soft arcs toward the soldiers' positions probably resulted more in creating terror than in inflicting actual casualties. As the fighting progressed, however, the numerous repeating rifles available to the warriors must have begun to take their toll on the troopers exposed at Calhoun Hill and at Finley and Cemetery Ridges.[55]

As in a buffalo hunt, when the Indians knew not to get in front of the herd, so the Indians had avoided getting ahead of Custer's column while it was riding north. However, once he had clearly stopped at Last Stand Hill, the Cheyennes in particular hurried to take possession of that downriver terrain. Similarly, as long as Custer represented a threat to the village, the noncombatants had gone in every direction away from the avenues of assault, which in the beginning was south and east of the encampment. When Custer began to move north, then stopped at Last Stand Hill, the women and children were not about to wait in a depression while he carefully maneuvered his troops to encircle their position. The Indians may have had reason to fear such an eventuality, but they were too clever to huddle like a bunch of sheep while Custer fiddled around in search of a ford in the expectation of capturing some of their number.[56]

According to the evidence and all that is rational, whatever portion of the village had been scurrying north to find sanctuary from the Reno attack must have come to a halt, then returned upriver against the grain of Custer's advance. After the Lone Tepee episode, Custer had no other realistic opportunity to capture any part of the population, a fact that he could have determined from where he stood on the high ground, if he had had the time for such niceties of observation.

From the Sioux and Cheyenne point of view, Custer's column was formed along the main battle ridge, with the horses congregated primarily in the depression to the east. As the Miniconjou White Bull noted, the warriors kept themselves between the soldiers and the noncombatants. To create this barrier, which was certainly not solid, the Indians gathered in knots of fighters between Greasy Grass Ridge and Deep Ravine, using the

285

coulees for concealment and protection while they looked for opportunities to isolate and destroy portions of the Custer command. The first such opportunity probably occurred at Finley Ridge, where Lieutenant Harrington had deployed with the first platoon of C Troop.[57]

He Dog stated that in fact the fighting had started at Finley, and Tall Bull recalled hearing the first volley at that location "at the beginning of the fight." That is also what Curley remembered before he departed to the east, where there were few hostile Indians early in the conflict. In addition, the C Troop platoon was the most exposed of the wing components, having been deployed as a salient terminating nearly at the center of the Indian concentration. Not far away, Calhoun Coulee offered a splendid avenue of approach for warriors trying to assault the soldiers. An abbreviated charge by any of these troopers on foot likely had little effect on Indians holding the superior defensive position and, on the contrary, probably tended only to debilitate the energy and morale of the soldiers. On the other hand, the later discovery of fifteen or so bodies of Company C men—including two sergeants—in this vicinity is testimony to the unit's cohesion and to a stout, if brief, resistance.[58]

One oddly connected with the annihilation of this platoon is the absence of Lieutenant Harrington's body. In fact, his remains were never found anywhere on the battlefield. His body may have been so mutilated that it could not be identified among the group at Finley, but since the burial parties made an extra effort to find the remains of all officers, it is tempting to conclude that he escaped the platoon's extermination, only to die elsewhere, outside the battlefield proper. The Sioux warrior He Dog said that one man on a very fast horse escaped toward the north from Calhoun Ridge, before Custer was surrounded. This soldier shot himself, intentionally or not; one warrior said that the soldier was whipping his horse forward with his revolver.[59] Respects Nothing told a similar story, although in his version, the soldier was a long way off when he was killed by pursuing warriors.[60] The Indian accounts include many such tales, all sufficiently different to preclude easy reconciliation. Regardless, Harrington was not found with his command. Without too much strain, we can imagine that the still-mounted Harrington hurried north toward Last Stand Hill and, unable or unwilling to stop his powerful mount, broke free through a gap in the ridges into the open prairie as yet unoccupied by the enemy.

Private William O. Taylor thought that Harrington—who rode a very large and powerful horse and who therefore might have had the means to escape—was the man who killed himself.[61] Like Harrington, Corporal John Foley of Company C may have perceived a similar escape opportunity, but to the south (it is not out of the question that Harrington went this way as well). His body was found here, north of Medicine Tail Coulee.[62]

The destruction of Harrington's platoon left the right flank of Calhoun's Company L hanging. Drawn up in a line to resist pressure from the south, Calhoun may have wheeled part of his command to confront this new threat from the west. With a quarter of the manpower available to Custer, L Troop was the floodgate that protected the rest of the wing from the deluge. To the east, the Indians had not yet assembled in numbers sufficient to overwhelm Calhoun in a rush, but even his thirty-five to forty troopers (not counting horse-holders) would have been inadequate to deal with the growing infiltration from three directions. The bodies of Calhoun and his second-in-command, John Crittenden, were found to the rear of their company, with enough cartridges nearby to suggest a determined struggle.[63]

But the battle along Custer Ridge did not occur in neat little increments. While Harrington's platoon was falling and while Company L was being decimated by fractions, Custer was deploying the Gray Horse Troop to cope with the Cheyenne and Oglala warriors gathering opposite the head of the column. Some of these Indians had traveled up the right side of the river, but many others moved along the west bank to block the soldiers' access to what was now the rear of the noncombatant retreat toward the village. Seeing that Custer had stopped his forward movement, the Indians did what was perfectly natural: they began to circle north toward the front they had heretofore avoided, with a view to eventually surrounding the blue-clad forces assembled on Last Stand Hill. Custer dispatched Company E along Cemetery Ridge to confront this threat.

The Indian testimony is consistent in observing that the Gray Horse Troop was in the lead as Custer's command moved from Calhoun Ridge to Last Stand Hill, although Companies E and F probably disappeared for a time on the eastern side of the high ground. As already indicated, Lights said that the grays formed the "fighting front" until the cavalry reached Keogh's position midway along the ridgeline. After that, Lights noted, the gray horses were "mixed in" with the other colors.[64] Virtually all the other

Indian witnesses confirmed that once the Gray Horse Troop reached Last Stand Hill, it remained there. Because that unit's horses—not necessarily its men—were located in the vicinity of Custer's final position, many of the Indians came to believe that Company E was among the last to fall. But the Indians did not know one company from another without their horses. By the time the grays reached the temporary shelter behind Last Stand Hill in the company of horse-holders, these horses had ceased to have any permanent connection with the men of Company E and became instead, in the Indian mind, the most visible reminder of the final episode of this battle.[65]

In fact, the men of the Gray Horse Troop were killed before the drama played out on Last Stand Hill. Whether Company E deployed westward along Cemetery Ridge on horseback or on foot is not clear from the Indian testimony. The Cheyenne Wooden Leg recalled a troop of cavalry galloping from the ridge toward the river, causing the Indians gathered in that direction to disperse.[66] Kate Bighead, who was riding on the outskirts of the battlefield, recollected a similar event, but she added the important information that these soldiers dismounted "along another ridge, a low one just north of the deep gulch."[67] Presumably, her "deep gulch" was Deep Ravine, to which the Cheyennes and Oglalas had retreated with the approach of the soldiers. A lower ridge to the north of Custer Ridge is consistent with Cemetery Ridge. If Company E rode into position, the horse-holders returned the mounts to the concealment behind Last Stand Hill several hundred yards away, where the grays commingled with the other colors until near the end.

If the Gray Horse Troop rode down Cemetery Ridge, and if roughly every fourth man departed with his consignment of animals, Company E was left with approximately thirty soldiers to fend off Indian attacks on Custer's right flank. Archaeological discoveries support the notion that extensive cavalry fire originated along Cemetery Ridge, and the later burial of twenty to thirty E Troop bodies to the south of this position confirm their detachment as a discrete unit from the headquarters and Company F components, most of which were found on Last Stand Hill. Whether Sturgis led E Troop is not certain; his body, like Harrington's, was never found. However, blood-stained clothing belonging to him was recovered afterward in the village.[68]

Probably for some minutes the Company E contingent was able to inflict some significant damage to the Indians who had collected between Cemetery

CALLING FOR COURAGE

Ridge and Deep Ravine. However, even though the unit occupied high ground and even though the cross fire with those stationed along Custer Ridge may have been momentarily effective, the E Troop position was finally untenable. With the nearly unhittable Indians scampering for cover to the south, and with their numbers growing to the north, the twenty-some men of Company E must soon have found themselves dangerously exposed on the heights.

Pressed hard from the rear (that is, to the north), Company E abandoned the high ground for the relative safety of the broken terrain to the south, from which the Indians had been cleared. The soldiers did so in remarkably good order, if we can believe the after-action accounts of the burial parties who found bodies of the men of this troop in almost a skirmish line. Lieutenant Luther Hare helped bury the men of E Troop, and according to him, these soldiers were found in "skirmish order," at about "skirmish intervals." Lieutenant Wallace thought he saw the men of E "lying in skirmish order."[69]

The Hunkpapa Iron Hawk recollected that these soldiers were so scared that they did not know what they were doing. "They were making their arms go as though they were running very fast," he said, "but they were only walking. Some of them shot their guns in the air." Other Indians remembered that the troopers shot wildly or randomly, as though there was something wrong with them. Perhaps they were drunk, some of the warriors thought.[70]

What Iron Hawk saw was men hurrying downhill, trying to keep their balance, their arms moving faster than their small tentative walking steps. As they slid and skidded off Cemetery Ridge, quick-stepping down the slippery slope, they surely emptied their revolvers aimlessly in every direction, particularly over their shoulders toward the Indians chasing them. At the base of the ridge, they tumbled into Cemetery Ravine, still together as a company. They began to dig in for what would prove to be a fight of short duration, the covering fire from Last Stand Hill still formidable but finally insufficient to save the erstwhile riders of the grays.[71]

"Some of the soldiers made a rush down the ravine toward the river," said Runs-the-Enemy, "and a great roll of smoke seemed to go down the ravine. This retreat of soldiers down the ravine was met by the advance of Indians from the river."[72] Again, because the Indian accounts lack common terms of reference, their meanings vis-à-vis specific geographical locations or unit activity are hard to assess. Indeed, the historian Robert Utley correctly noted that the Indian stories tended to be "a disconcerting jumble of ephemeral non-chronological impressions."[73] For example, Two Moon recalled that five men on horseback and forty on foot started for the river, a soldier with black hair and mustache and dressed in a buckskin shirt shouting orders all the while. This leader supposedly rode a sorrel horse.[74] Likewise, Lieutenant Long learned from his informants that while Custer was making his stand, forty men—"*letting their horses loose* [emphasis added]"—made a break for the river. These sources thought that there was no officer present, presumably because none of the men were mounted.[75] Were they talking about E Troop's dismounting to fight on foot or Company C's abortive charge at Finley, or did all of the horse-holders behind Last Stand Hill release the animals for which they were responsible so that the men could run on foot to the river? Unless they were deploying to fight, what group of soldiers would relinquish their means of a fast getaway in order to hoof it into oblivion? These very different reports most likely point to the dismounting of the Gray Horse Troop.

The evidence is persuasive that twenty-some members of Company E did advance along Cemetery Ridge toward the river, that they fired for some time at Indians located on the flats to the south, that this maneuver drove the enemy deeper into the coulees, and that the soldiers in turn were finally forced downhill into the first ravine at the base of the ridge—that is, Cemetery Ravine. One problem with seeking cover in these natural trenches was that the troopers were thus deprived of the elevation and angle necessary to sight and fire on the Indians, who were using these ditches as infiltration routes to reach fixed objectives. In short, the men of Company E fell into a temporary safe haven, which eventually became a mass grave.

Captain Thomas McDougall felt that the troopers had "used the upper sides of the ravine as a kind of breastwork, falling to the bottom as they were shot down."[76] Sergeant John Ryan remembered finding men in a ravine. "I also saw marks in the embankment, made by the toes of their boots, where they tried to get up, and were shot, and fell back," he said.[77]

Maybe some of the soldiers attempted to get out. Maybe some tried to dig in. Maybe some pushed with the toes of their boots to brace and steady themselves along the upper edges of that natural but inadequate breastwork, searching vainly for something to shoot at. With no more ammunition than they could carry, maybe some climbed out of the coulee to make an open fight of it, possibly one or two even faintly hoping to return in the direction of Last Stand Hill or to flee toward Deep Ravine or Greasy Grass Ridge. Whatever the individual intentions of the men, the twenty-some bodies that belonged to this company and that were found together may indeed have looked like a kind of skirmish line, half in the hole and half out, most of them shot in the side.[78]

The Indians who attacked and eventually eliminated E Troop were mostly Cheyennes. In her circumnavigation of the battlefield, Kate Bighead confirmed that her fellow Cheyennes were concentrated primarily in the northwestern sector. As she rode from south to east, she saw only Sioux in warrior society bands. It was not until she got around to the west that she found Cheyenne and some Oglala warriors crawling through the deep gulches between Custer Ridge and the river. A leading warrior chief of the Cheyennes was Lame White Man, who lay in hiding near where a small party of soldiers (presumably E Troop) dismounted. Other Cheyennes located in the vicinity were Two Moon and Wooden Leg.[79]

Like Kate Bighead, Wooden Leg thought that the long-range firing continued for quite some time, during which period the Indians lofted countless arrows toward the soldiers and their mounts, causing the horses to squeal and plunge in pain and fear. All the while the Indians were creeping closer to the soldiers. As Company E approached along Cemetery Ridge, the warriors withdrew and scattered, but Lame White Man called out that the Cheyennes could kill them all. After the troopers had been surrounded and annihilated, the Indians took the soldiers' arms and remaining ammunition, "which they turned against the rest of the soldiers on the ridge *above* [emphasis added]."[80]

Two Moon said that he led the Cheyennes up the ridge running from the valley (presumably Cemetery), "blocking the soldiers." The warriors broke this line and went over the ridge, firing and advancing, suffering significant casualties themselves. Two Moon noted that his group then tried to assault the position occupied by the gray horses (Last Stand Hill), but they could not break the line at that point. As he bore to the left, heading north, the soldiers and the group following Two Moon exchanged fire. Two Moon apparently meant to convey that he had run the gauntlet along Custer Ridge, but his various versions are muddled, and in Wooden Leg's opinion at least, Two Moon was "a great liar."[81]

Two Moon probably did not lead this Cheyenne contingent but rather followed after Lame White Man, who by all accounts did attempt to cut through the soldiers' position along Custer Ridge and lost his life in the process. For Lame White Man and his warriors to have made this run, E Troop had to have already been eliminated as a fighting force, opening the way from Deep Ravine to the Finley-Calhoun sector through a series of coulees. Emerging opposite the southern end of the Keogh sector, Lame White Man and his band would have had a relatively short ride to the gaps between the hills forming Custer Ridge. The Cheyenne chief charged the soldiers near Calhoun Ridge, said Little Wolf, and "chased them to Keogh." When Lame White Man was killed on the western slope of Custer Ridge, Two Moon and the others must have turned to the north, then to the west, circling back to their starting point.[82] After Lame White Man's death, Two Moon did assume a leadership role, but before that, he was more likely merely a member of the wild, brave ride into the center of the bluecoat line. From the opposite direction, Two Moon suggested, some of the Sioux were attempting a similar reckless charge. In the van of that invincibility test may have been Crazy Horse and White Bull.[83]

By about 5:30 the C Troop salient had been engulfed, and the Company L formation was collapsing under a persistent assault from three sides, causing the men of that unit to splinter in nearly every direction. With Calhoun and Crittenden dead on the line, the survivors of L were falling back into the Keogh sector of the field or seeking other avenues of escape, as was probably the case with First Sergeant James Butler, who from the evidence sold his life dearly several hundred yards to the south. To the northwest, the men of the Gray Horse Troop were in their death throes within the shadows of Cemetery Ridge. Wherever the Indians could approach close enough, chiefly east of the Calhoun position, they were waving blankets to spook the held horses, many of which broke free from the men trying to tend them and thus carried hundreds of rounds of ammunition into the hands of the enemy.[84]

Aiming to demonstrate their own brand of courage, Crazy Horse, White Bull, and some of the "suicide boys" rushed through the gap created by the defeat of Harrington and Calhoun, between the undulations of Custer Ridge. It was probably at such defining moments that every warrior whipped another man's pony into the onslaught as leaders cried out that it was a good day to die. With as much noise as they could muster, the warriors defied the desperate fire coming from the miscellaneous units gathered under the falling banner of Captain Keogh. The valley of the Little Bighorn was shrouded in dust and gunsmoke, and within the heavy gray clouds, figures half human and half horse darted out of sight or out of range. Visibility was so bad that some of the Indians shot their comrades by mistake.[85]

As portrayed by White Bull, Crazy Horse painted his face with a red zigzag line and white dots, representing lightning and hail, the revered symbols of the thunder beings. He wore a single eagle feather tip down on the back of his head. The court of inquiry recorder, Jesse Lee, said that there was no Indian braver than the taciturn Crazy Horse. About five feet six inches tall, with a slight and wiry build, he was inclined to a melancholy expression. He hated whites. He gave no interviews to white men. To the best of the available information, he had no pictures taken. Everything that is known about Crazy Horse has come secondhand. Thus, in terms of the fight on the Little Bighorn battlefield, White Bull's story is critical to understanding the participation of this leading Oglala warrior.[86]

From White Bull's various accounts, it appears that like many of the other Sioux warriors, White Bull joined the fight to the rear of Custer's column, keeping himself between the soldiers and the village noncombatants. Concealing himself in the network of troughs to avoid being hit by fire from Calhoun Ridge, he worked his way to the east, where he joined a group of Indians who were beginning to drive the soldiers. From this position and throughout the battle, White Bull claimed that he "counted coup" (touched an enemy living or dead) seven times, an extraordinary achievement for a warrior in any single engagement.[87]

As indicated on White Bull's map of the fight, his first coup definitely occurred to the east or southeast, possibly between the Calhoun and Keogh sectors, where horse-holders were beginning to lose control of their mounts. In this case, White Bull counted coup on a soldier who had been knocked off his horse, after which the Miniconjou warrior took the trooper's weapons and ammunition. According to White Bull, Crazy Horse counted "second coup" on this cavalryman. If so, Crazy Horse began his participation on the east side of Custer Ridge, rather than with the many Oglalas who had gone with the Cheyennes to the west and north.[88]

White Bull also maintained that, possibly following another coup or two, he and Crazy Horse (apparently leading) charged into the soldiers and through to the west side of Custer Ridge. Neither of these men was hit in this daring ride. They were likely the Sioux that Two Moon saw coming from the east, meaning that their charge was nearly coincident with Lame White Man's thrust from the west. Of course, circumstances had to be favorable for such feats of derring-do to succeed, and the ability of these Sioux on swift ponies to split Custer's forces depended on more than powerful medicine. Many of the Indian warriors were courageous, but they were not stupid. On the other hand, some of the bravest clearly did not survive the gunfire coming from Custer's hard-pressed troopers.[89]

For the many hundreds of Sioux to the south and east of Custer Ridge who did not care to make an extraordinary show of courage, there was ample opportunity to simply push forward, eliminating the remnants of the right wing by bits and pieces. In the Keogh sector, the soldiers were feeling the crush of the Indian weight coming up the broad swale on all sides. White dust covered everything. Their one-shot carbines mostly useless now, the soldiers were unloading their revolvers quickly and in some cases aimlessly until their twenty-four bullets were gone. Against repeating rifles in the hands of too many capable fighters, the men of the Seventh had little chance, although enough stood their ground in the face of the inevitable that Indians would afterward speak with admiration of the resistance on this part of the field.

There was a desperate stand at the Keogh sector, Standing Bear said. The soldiers fell back, leading their horses.[90] The longest fighting was at Keogh, asserted Lone Bear, adding that as the troopers withdrew, they used their horses as shields.[91] The soldiers were not running but simply giving way, noted Lights.[92] Of course, many of the mounts had long since broken away from the horse-holders and run into the hands of the Indians. Thus, a number of the Sioux witnesses agreed that the soldiers had fought courageously, if futilely.[93]

In the midst of the long line of bodies leading toward Last Stand Hill lay that of Captain Keogh. Nearby were the corpses of First Sergeant Frank Varden, Sergeant James Bustard, and Trumpeter John Patton. Apparently one of the bullets that had hit Keogh's horse, Comanche, went on through to fracture the leg of the I Troop commander. Doubtless these key men of Company I had resisted together till the end. Along the route also were the bodies of First Sergeant Bobo and troopers of his Company C, as well as refugees from the Calhoun collapse. The Indians had rolled up the reserves and had forced the few survivors to seek refuge on Last Stand Hill, which was now under assault from all sides. Perhaps another totally forlorn volley or two was fired from this hill, not with the intention of catching the attention of anyone in particular (too late for that) but rather for the purpose of demonstrating the power (already wilted, thudding weakly, more a popgun than a cannon) of the soldiers. It would have been a death knell, far off and barely audible to an audience of puzzled troopers several miles away.[94]

CHAPTER THIRTEEN

WITHIN HEARING, BEYOND REACH

"Major," Dr. Henry Porter said as Major Marcus Reno's battalion clamored up the bluffs after the disaster in the valley, "the men were pretty well demoralized, weren't they?"

"No," Major Reno replied, "that was a charge, sir!"[1]

Indeed, Reno had led his command in a charge out of danger, through a phalanx of Indians so dumbfounded by his tactics that they did not begin to ride down his soldiers for several moments. By the time the warriors recovered to wage an attack that was more like a buffalo chase than like anything that would occur later on the Custer battlefield, Reno was safely across the river and up the bluffs. Behind him lay more than 30 dead and dying members of his 145-man component, plus another 15 to 20 hiding out in the woods lining the Little Bighorn. In spite of an ordeal that would last two more days, almost all of the survivors blessed Reno's expressed determination not to be killed by a "damned Indian," even as they must have pronounced him, in their heart-of-hearts, a coward of the first order.

The evidence is convincing that Reno was the first man over the bluffs above the river. Reno later explained that he needed to be in the front of the withdrawal so that he could re-form the men on the hill and put them in proper skirmish order. When the men reached the bluffs, they tended to keep on running, Dr. Porter said. Still trying to control them, Lieutenant Charles Varnum was shouting, "For God's sake, men, don't run, we have got to go back and get our wounded men and officers!" From the woods to the high ground, Varnum's pleading to go back had fallen largely on deaf ears, and the wounded in the valley would finally have to fend for themselves. But the soldiers on the hill did stop, many of them throwing themselves on the ground for a moment's respite. Everything must have been confusion until more officers and noncommissioned officers arrived to restore a measure of order. Nearly everyone who had crossed the river reached the ridgeline by about 4:15.[2]

At approximately 4:20 Captain Frederick Benteen reached the scene. Whether Benteen was the first of his battalion to arrive is debatable in view of reports that Captain Thomas Weir had initiated the movement toward Reno Hill. Regardless, Benteen's unit as a whole came trotting up to investigate the commotion visible on the rolling tableland above the river, and when Reno rode out to meet the unexpected saviors of the day, Benteen was the one to whom he spoke.

When Benteen met Reno several hundred yards from what would later become their final position (the Reno Enclave), the captain's role as an independent battalion commander ceased—not simply because Reno outranked him but, more important, because Custer's own organization of the regiment dictated that in any combination of forces, Benteen would become second-in-command of the left wing, headed by Reno. From this moment forward, Benteen's blindness to duty was subsumed within a structure ordained by the general himself—with unforeseen consequences, of course. When Custer had sent messages to Benteen, he had believed that the senior captain was still an autonomous component within the overall scheme of things, but once Reno surrendered his position as the vanguard and the two battalions of the left wing were conjoined by circumstances, Benteen was no longer capable of uninhibited decision-making. Possibly Benteen was relieved by this turn of events, since he would in hindsight be quite comfortable with renouncing virtually all responsibility for the pack train and the rear-guard Company B, which by order belonged to Custer's right wing.

So when he handed Reno the note written by Adjutant William Cooke, Benteen surrendered the obligation to abide by its contents. The unequivocal injunction to "come quick" and bring the packs (by ordinary understanding, the ammunition packs) no longer applied to him. The quintessential company commander was now in a perfect position to second-guess the judgments of his superiors, including Reno, an officer quite overcome by events. In addition, Reno's overriding authority as left-wing commander allowed Benteen to claim that nearly every initiative he took thereafter was beyond the scope of his responsibility—that is, was something special, even though he was second-in-command of the wing. As he put it at the court of inquiry, "I was looking after things probably more than it was my business or duty to do."[3]

By most accounts, Reno—still wearing a handkerchief tied around his head—was in an "excited" state when he rode out to meet Benteen. Lieutenant Winfield Edgerly remembered that as Reno approached Benteen's column, the major turned and discharged his pistol in the direction of Indians about a thousand yards away, about nine hundred yards farther than a revolver could effectively fire. Edgerly thought the futile demonstration was "a sort of defiance of the Indians." Likewise, though for entirely different reasons, Lieutenant Varnum did the same on Reno Hill: crying, hatless, a white handkerchief around his head, he fired at the few Indians still lingering along the downriver bluffs.[4]

As Benteen gave Reno Cooke's note, he asked the major where Custer was, and Reno replied that he did not know. Close at hand, Trumpeter John Martin might have helped the two officers locate the general, but no one bothered to ask him. Martin recalled Reno saying, "For God's sake, Benteen, halt your command and wait until I can organize my men." Or, "Well, I have lost about half of my men, and I could do no better than I have done."[5]

In a surprising admission, Benteen noted in one of his later narratives that Reno "had seen nothing of Custer and knew nothing of his whereabouts, but had heard some firing down the river, and supposed he was in that direction." Reno, in his official report on the battle, stated that firing was heard downriver and that the command "knew it could only be Custer." Within ten minutes and for at least an hour after that, virtually every person on Reno Hill would hear volleys coming from the direction of the Custer battlefield, and even though at the court of inquiry both Reno and Benteen would deny ever hearing those volleys, they were clearly deaf by choice and not by disability.[6]

After their brief conversation, Reno and Benteen moved forward with Companies H, D, and K to the Reno Enclave, on the bluffs. By this time, some of the men in Reno's command must have deployed to shoot at the few Indians in the vicinity, although Lieutenant George Wallace would later suggest that in the midst of this extraordinary confusion, "the first thing done was to get the companies together, organize them, and then . . . count off again and dismount so as to make another stand." And this was done in spite of Wallace's assertion that he could find no more than a half-dozen men belonging to G Troop. Captain Myles Moylan may have helped direct activities on the hill, but he himself said he was preoccupied with his wounded. Sergeant Ferdinand Culbertson heard Moylan say he would not sell his horse for anything. As Lieutenant Edgerly recollected, Moylan said, "For God sake, give me some water!"[7]

Benteen's depiction of Moylan was typically uncharitable but probably accurate. Arriving on the hill, Benteen noticed Moylan: "The first thing which attracted my attention was the gallantly-mustached captain of Troop 'A' blubbering like a whipped urchin, tears coursing down his cheeks." Benteen had thought that Moylan had some "nerve," but he noted: "The bottom tumbled out—and all the nerve with it."[8]

Except for Reno's understandable state of denial, all of the officers and men of the battalion who had fought in the valley knew that they had been badly thrashed, and many said so. For Varnum, that defeat had sowed bitterness and anger in his brave soul, and he wept. A gallant man by nature, Lieutenant Luther Hare was happy to be alive. As he said to Lieutenant Edward Godfrey, he was "damned glad" to see his friend; "they had had a big fight in the bottom and got whipped like hell." Trying to be clever, Moylan would tell Reno's counsel, Lyman Gilbert, at the court of inquiry that he would rather have been "dejected on the top of the hill than dead anywhere." Pressed by the court recorder, Jesse Lee, Moylan had to admit with some embarrassment, "Very few men but would prefer to die in the timber than to be on a hill degraded." When asked by Gilbert whether he had felt degraded on the hill, Moylan replied, "Not particularly."[9]

Although Hare believed that Reno's men had ammunition left in their saddlebags, Benteen's troopers shared what they had with those in need. In spite of claims by some at the court of inquiry that men in Reno's battalion had little or no ammunition, Reno delayed the decision to send anyone back for any part of the pack train until he—now the wing commander with responsibility for the entire force on the bluffs—could locate his adjutant's body.[10]

Sergeant Culbertson informed Lieutenant Varnum about Lieutenant Benjamin Hodgson's fate, presumably shortly after they had arrived on the hill. This information must have been passed to Reno, because he soon came to Culbertson and asked whether the sergeant could find the deceased adjutant. When Culbertson said he could, Reno told the sergeant to get some men and accompany him down the steep bluffs to the river. According to Culbertson, Reno had another objective: "He said he was going to find some water and I should go along with him."[11]

The latter, rather peculiar purpose—requiring the presence of the officer-in-charge—was corroborated by Lieutenant Godfrey, who asserted that when Reno went to look for Hodgson, he took men along with canteens to get water. Godfrey added that the effort was fruitless because of fire from Indians on the west bank, but such was certainly not the case. Reno, Culbertson, and about a dozen soldiers did find Hodgson on the bench east of the river, and were sufficiently unhampered that Reno had the time to remove Hodgson's West Point class ring and some keys from his pockets and then reclimb the bluffs, taking in tow a G Troop soldier who had been hiding in the brush along their path.[12]

It is hard to accept Reno's behavior as a sincere expression of grief, since he had left Hodgson behind in the retreat and since he failed to evince a similar level of concern for Lieutenant Donald McIntosh or Dr. James DeWolf or the thirty enlisted men lost in the rush for sanctuary on the high ground. When Reno returned from his bizarre excursion away from the center of unit activity, his first order of business was to name Lieutenant Hare his new adjutant, then send Hare back to hurry up the pack train, directing that the ammunition mules be cut out and driven ahead. It was 4:45, about the time Custer expected to see his reserves come into view, even if they were struggling with the packs over rough terrain. During the twenty minutes of Reno's absence (4:25–4:45), those remaining on the hill began to hear the sound of volleys downriver.

One of the first to hear the firing was Lieutenant Varnum. He was near his old chum Lieutenant Wallace. As Varnum told the court of inquiry, the sound he heard was not exactly a volley but more like a "crash, crash," and he heard it only one time. He said, "Jesus Christ, Wallace, hear that! And that!" It is not known what Wallace replied, but he told the court that he had heard no firing from the direction where Custer was afterward found.[13]

Perhaps the sound noticed by Varnum was the firing heard by Private Edward Davern, who told the court: "I said to Captain Weir, 'That must be

General Custer fighting down in the bottom.' He asked me where and I showed him. He said, 'Yes, I believe it is.'" By Davern's reckoning, the time was approximately 4:30–4:40, and Weir did nothing at that time, probably because Reno had gone in search of Hodgson.[14]

On the other hand, Sergeant Culbertson recollected hearing the volleys while sitting with Lieutenants Edgerly and Varnum, a few minutes *before* Reno came to get him for the Hodgson recovery mission. "At first it was a couple of volleys," Culbertson said, "very heavy, after-wards it was lighter and appeared to be more distant. Lieutenant Varnum made the remark that General Custer was hotly engaged."[15]

Likewise, Lieutenant Edgerly heard "heavy firing by volleys" downriver soon after Benteen's battalion arrived on the hill. In a moment or so, Weir came to Edgerly (his second-in-command) and suggested that Custer was engaged and that they ought to be down there. Edgerly and First Sergeant Michael Martin of D Troop agreed. At that point, Weir "went away, walking up and down rather anxiously." In about ten minutes, Weir returned, and the firing that Edgerly had heard "plainly . . . had almost ceased." Weir asked whether Edgerly would go with just their company if he could get permission from Reno or Benteen, and Edgerly said he would. In a later account, Edgerly said the firing he heard when he had first arrived on Reno Hill lasted fifteen or twenty minutes.[16]

Edgerly was correct. The *initial episode* of gunfire from the direction of Custer's advance can be placed with certainty in the 4:25–4:45 time frame, before Reno left to find Hodgson's body and until his return. That is precisely when Custer was directing volley firing from the Luce and Blummer-Nye-Cartright Ridges. Even the stubbornly evasive Benteen admitted to the court of inquiry that although he recalled no volleys, he had heard "15 or 20 shots" in the direction of Ford B soon after his arrival on Reno Hill. At about 4:35, Captain George Yates and his battalion were beginning to turn away from the river, and Lieutenant Algernon Smith may have taken a disabling hit.[17]

Some minutes after returning from the bottom of the bluffs, Reno launched Lieutenant Hare on his way to the pack train, then supposedly went an unspecified distance away to examine the Custer trail. Reno said that an unidentified person brought his attention to ground that was presumably torn up by a number of shod horses and that he "went to see it" not far from the hill. In the next breath he contended that he had disregarded Custer's order to "come quick" because he "was absorbed in getting those packs together, and did not intend to move" until he had "done so." And he was not about to let any part of his new 350-man command leave either.[18]

Captain Weir was determined to go to the sound of the firing, and he must have paced himself to a fever pitch before he approached Reno to argue in favor of that understood military obligation. Lieutenant Edgerly stood ready to depart as soon as Weir obtained permission to leave with at least D Troop. A member of that company, Private John Fox, later claimed to have been within hearing distance when Weir's conference with Reno occurred. According to Private Fox, the following conversation took place:

> Weir: "Custer must be around here somewhere and we ought to go to him."
>
> Reno: "We are surrounded by Indians and we ought to remain here."
>
> Weir: "Well, if no one else goes to Custer, I will go."
>
> Reno: "No, you cannot go. For if you try to do it, you will get killed and your company with you."

The above sounds like a reasonable approximation of what must have transpired, including Weir's statement that he was prepared to go alone. Fox thought that Reno was somewhat intoxicated as the two men spoke. The private added that Moylan and Benteen were present and that "they did not seem to approve of Weir going and talked as though to discourage him."[19]

Weir did leave, without saying much to anyone and without even motioning for his command to follow. He simply called his orderly, both men mounted, and together they started off, apparently to investigate the source of the volleys. Believing that Weir had obtained permission to advance, Edgerly directed the soldiers of Company D to climb aboard their horses, and within moments of Weir's departure, the whole troop followed their leader. It was some minutes after five o'clock, and on the Custer battlefield Yates's battalion had already entered the gap between the protective fire provided by Company L and a C Troop platoon along Calhoun Ridge.[20]

Many years after the fight, Edgerly explained: "[Weir] told me later that he concluded he had better take a look ahead before asking Reno [for permission] so he mounted and started to the front with only an orderly." Of course, if Private Fox's recollection was correct, Weir had not asked for permission from Reno but had asserted that he intended to go by himself if the whole left wing chose not to advance. Driven by the sound of volleys—by those possible signals of distress—Weir was determined to "show his smartness" (as Benteen said) by going far enough forward to glimpse the situation beyond the intervening hills. Besides the mere fact of Weir's gumption to get up and go, he deserves a large measure of credit for doing so without implicating the rest of his command in an action that might have been grounds for a court-martial.[21]

When Reno realized that Weir had departed with the whole of Company D, he did the sensible thing: he usurped the idea as his own. At the court of inquiry, Reno said that Benteen had told him of Weir's sudden exit, although it defies belief that Reno could have missed two riders churning up dust in the distance, followed within five or ten minutes by forty horsemen filling the landscape to the north. Nevertheless, Reno now considered Weir's command the "advance guard" of the left wing, and shortly the redoubtable major would reinforce the wisdom of his original nondecision by adding to Weir's responsibilities. "I did not think that any one man could go through [to what?]," said Reno, "but I thought he [Weir] could cut through [to what?] with his command." So when his newly appointed adjutant, Hare, returned from the trip back to the pack train, Reno had Hare ride forward with word that Weir was to open communications with Custer, the man who, for Reno, had vanished without a trace from the face of the earth. Before Reno could dispatch Hare, however, he had to ensure that the wounded had been cared for and that the entire pack train had been brought up. During this additional delay, Hare apparently heard more volleys downriver.[22]

Hare's testimony on the volleys is conflicting. At the court of inquiry, he said that just after Benteen arrived, Lieutenant Godfrey called his attention to firing downstream. Hare claimed that he heard "two distinct volleys" before he started for the pack train, in which case his recollection falls within the 4:25–4:45 episode. However, he told Walter Camp many years later that he had heard no firing before he started, that he was gone about twenty minutes (until a bit after five o'clock), and that only then did he hear gunshots coming from the direction of Custer, although he was informed by others that firing had been heard while he was away.[23]

The hard-of-hearing Lieutenant Godfrey recalled only two volleys, but he noted that the firing down the river lasted "a long time." He stated, "We were satisfied that Custer was fighting the Indians somewhere, and the conviction was expressed that 'our command ought to be doing something or Custer would be after Reno with a sharp stick.'" Godfrey said that he had detected "two distinct volleys" a long way off, followed by scattering shots. However, he insisted that this firing had occurred after Hare returned from the visit to the pack train. In spite of Godfrey's sometimes defective memory (and hearing), his corroboration of when he and Hare discussed hearing the distant volleys must stand, marking the beginning of a *second episode* of firing, which occurred during the 5:00–5:30 time period. Still, it is possible, even likely, that Hare also heard volleys before he left to hurry the packs.[24]

Apparently two mules carrying ammunition moved faster than the rest. The civilian packer Benjamin Churchill drove one of those mules. After receiving Reno's order by way of Hare, Churchill managed to cover a distance of two miles in about ten minutes, he claimed. He told the court that soon after reaching Reno Hill, he heard volley firing downriver—four or five not very plain volleys, he said. Even if Churchill's travel time was closer to twenty minutes, he arrived on the hill by a quarter past five at the latest.[25]

Not far behind him came Captain Thomas McDougall, with his rear guard deployed around the remaining packs. As soon as he arrived on the hill, he informed the court of inquiry, he notified Reno that he had heard two volleys to his right as he ascended to the high ground. Reno replied: "Captain, I lost your lieutenant, he is lying down there." Of course, Reno was referring to Hodgson, who had served with B Troop before being detailed as left-wing adjutant.[26]

Like Hare, McDougall told a slightly different story to Camp. In this later version, McDougall asserted that he heard the firing downriver soon after arriving on the hill and that he mentioned it to Godfrey, who acknowledged hearing it. McDougall told Godfrey that they "ought to be down there with him [Custer]," then went to Reno and Benteen and repeated his concern.

As McDougall recalled the scene, Reno did not appear to comprehend the seriousness of the situation. The B Troop commander added that when the pack train arrived, Company D was still in sight.[27]

Obviously, incident and timing factors within this body of testimony are murky at best. If McDougall could still see D Troop when he arrived, Edgerly took more than a few minutes to assemble the company and move out. If McDougall actually spoke to Godfrey, Benteen and the rest of his battalion could not have departed before 5:25–5:30, after the pack train arrived on the hill. However, the particulars of these events are less important than the fact that for over an hour, the remnants of the regiment under Reno took only small incremental steps to move in the direction of Custer and the sound of his desperate gunfire. Even the impatient and fiercely loyal Weir required more than thirty minutes to act on his instincts and risk insubordination.

From Reno Hill, Weir and his orderly bore slightly to their right, following—whether they knew it or not—Custer's trail toward and eventually over Sharpshooter Ridge. Historians have long supposed that Weir headed directly along the bluffline in the direction of two peaks later named for the captain—that is, Weir Point. However, like Custer, Weir must have been eager to arrive quickly on the highest ground in the vicinity so as to assess the situation; Sharpshooter Ridge served that purpose for both men. Sergeant Thomas Harrison of D Troop provided a clear distinction between the two landmarks. For Camp, the sergeant described a "sugarloaf" east of the "two peaks" as the place where Company D conducted its maneuvers. The "sugarloaf" is almost certainly Sharpshooter Ridge, whereas the "two peaks" are Weir Point. Other testimony supports this proposition.[28]

At the court of inquiry, Edgerly said that Weir stayed on the ridge while Edgerly and D rode down "in a sort of valley." In later accounts, he said that with Weir on the high ground, he went around to the right and, after receiving a signal from Weir, circled to the left in front of his commander. Edgerly then marched the company ahead along the ridge, dismounted the men, and returned the fire of Indians. According to Edgerly, Weir never got as far ahead as he did, confirming Sergeant Harrison's impression that Weir stopped well before Edgerly on the "sugarloaf."[29]

Because warriors had been active along the bluffs above the river, it made sense for Edgerly to use Sharpshooter Ridge as a shield for his advance in support of Weir, who proceeded along the hump of earth until he saw all manner of Indians filling the terrain between Medicine Tail Coulee and the Custer battlefield proper. Receiving Weir's signal to cease his forward movement, Edgerly swung to the left and climbed the hill, then advanced a distance that would have been possible only on Sharpshooter Ridge, as suggested by Harrison. Besides, three other companies were about to arrive on the scene, and it is impossible that all of them could have joined Weir, Edgerly, and Company D on the small amount of ground available on the twin peaks.

Since Weir left no direct testimony on his participation, it is unknown what he actually saw when he first reached his most advanced position on Sharpshooter Ridge. Assuming that he and his orderly galloped as far as the ridge, they probably slowed to a trot, then a walk, as they traveled the crest, becoming more cautious as they penetrated deeper into unfamiliar territory. It was perhaps 5:15–5:20 when they saw something that made them halt, and that something must have been Indians in great numbers to the north and northwest. At that point, Weir was not far enough along the ridge to look directly down into Medicine Tail Coulee, so that what he must have seen were ragged arcs of warriors and perhaps women shrouded in dust and pressing closer along the length of Calhoun Ridge, stretching back in random clots of frenzied horsemen nearly to the limits of his vision. His first thought was to signal Edgerly and Company D out of the valley into which they were blindly and rapidly advancing.

Edgerly led D Troop along the ridge, maybe all the way to its northern slope, and there dismounted the men. Corporal George Wylie said that the horses were led to the low ground between the twin peaks and the hill, and the soldiers formed across the hill, east to west.[30] Edgerly stated that when he got up on the ridge and looked off in the distance, he "saw a good many Indians riding up and down and firing at objects on the ground." In a separate account, he noted that one part of a hill on the field was black with Indian men and women standing there.[31]

Since Weir was not with his company, it was perhaps Edgerly whom Corporal Wylie had in mind when he stated that, seeing individuals on horseback with guidons flying, Weir (or Edgerly) supposedly said, "That is Custer over there." Then Sergeant James Flanagan suggested that the officer look through binoculars because those figures were in fact Indians carrying company banners. Wylie's story may be apocryphal, or at least garbled, since none of these soldiers could have seen much farther than Calhoun Ridge, some two miles away, where Company L and the C platoon had been overrun, having fired their volleys. Less than a mile beyond that, beyond swirling dust and smoke and the rolling hills of Custer Ridge, was Last Stand Hill, still occupied by about fifty men with less than half an hour to live.[32]

On several occasions Edgerly said that D Troop's long-range exchange of fire with a small number of nearby Indians lasted about thirty minutes. During that half hour of unproductive sniping (5:20–5:50), the rest of Reno's left wing was finally moving forward. The first man out of the Reno safe haven was Lieutenant Hare, who dashed forward at about 5:20 to notify Captain Weir that he was to open communications with Custer. As Edgerly looked back, he saw Hare arrive and speak to Weir. Hare, his mission completed, then wheeled about and rode back until he ran into the van of the left wing's supporting movement.[33]

Besides delivering Reno's face-saving afterthought, Hare was able in his round-trip ride to visually compare the routes taken by Weir and Reno and, in that comparison, later confirm that Weir had indeed taken the Sharp-shooter Ridge path. Hare testified that there were "two divides" and that Weir followed along the one to the right, whereas Reno took the one to the left "a little further downstream." Using the flawed Maguire map, Hare's placement of the relative positions is somewhat distorted, but the above word-picture—plus his reference to a small ravine (possibly Cedar Coulee) between the two locations—virtually ensures that Weir rode the ridge and that Reno hugged the bluffs.[34]

If all of this is a true reading of the evidence, separate components of Reno's wing followed the three trails made by Custer's command—Edgerly on Keogh's trail, Weir on Custer's, and Reno on Yates's—without a single individual being able to assert with certainty, soon after the fact, that he had seen a track made by the general's several columns of shod horses, four riders abreast. This is purely an academic consideration, however, since Reno had multiple sources of information on Custer's course and predicament.[35]

The order of Reno's belated march down the bluffline above the Little Bighorn was M (Captain Thomas French), K (Lieutenant Godfrey), and H (Captain Benteen). So said Edgerly, Hare, and Godfrey. In Benteen's warped view of events, he was out in front and in total disobedience of orders as Reno had his trumpeter toot the halt, but this claim is preposterous. Not until French peeled off to form his company behind Edgerly and D on a spur of Sharpshooter Ridge, and not until Godfrey had followed, did Benteen gain the advance position on Weir Point, where he supposedly planted a guidon to attract Custer's attention.[36]

Benteen was now indeed farther forward than anyone else, but as he himself stated to the court of inquiry, he was only there "two or three minutes" before Indians began to appear in great numbers and he withdrew. In that brief period of time, he insisted, he had deployed French and Godfrey, and although he was sure that the Custer battlefield could not be seen, he had stuck the guidon in the ground in the hope that "by its fluttering or by the point of brass on the end," it might attract the attention of the general. Benteen confessed limply to Recorder Lee that the guidon and its brass tip would have been less visible than horses. Three miles away, the soldiers remaining on Last Stand Hill were trapped in a powdery fog, hardly in a position to care a fig for a flapping flag.[37]

Benteen could not have reached Weir Point much before 5:45, and by his own admission, he did not stay long before he left to confer with Major Reno, who was far enough in the rear that he could not see much of anything, including the disposition of his forces. As Benteen was withdrawing, he may have passed Lieutenant Varnum, who was hurrying forward to participate in the abortive attempt to reach the sound of the firing on the Custer battlefield. Varnum had been delayed because as the last of the Reno column had been preparing to leave, he had left to bury Lieutenant Hodgson, in accordance with orders given by Reno.[38]

Actually, Reno had instructed Varnum to lead the burial party earlier, but Varnum had successfully resisted performing the unhappy task until the mule train came up so that he might obtain the necessary tools. Then, with the spades in hand, Varnum went with several enlisted men to find Hodgson's body. As Varnum was going down the steep slope, he saw the scout George Herendeen and about a dozen soldiers on their way up the hill. Operating under Herendeen's experienced leadership, the soldiers had remained hidden in the woods for an hour and a half after Reno's retreat, then had crossed the river, chased off a handful of Indians, and walked to safety. Varnum was only part of the way down to the bottom when he was recalled by Lieutenant Wallace to join the belated advance. By the time Varnum got back to the top of the bluffs, all of the Reno column had departed northward except Captain Moylan and his A Troop.[39]

After Companies D, M, K, and H had gone, the order of Reno's march was probably the commander himself, Wallace and G Troop, and then some mix of McDougall's B, the pack train, and Moylan. The reason Moylan went last was supposedly because of his "large" number of wounded, ranging from four to ten, depending on the source of the information. Also according to various informants, four to six men carried each of the wounded in makeshift stretchers, the whole operation so encumbering Moylan's advance that he was obliged to request assistance from McDougall, who sent back a platoon of soldiers from Company B to help. Sergeant Culbertson said that six men were needed to carry each of the "four" wounded soldiers, "and the rest to take care of and lead the horses"—an unorthodox use of manpower at that juncture.[40]

Nowhere in any of the testimony is there significant mention of the wounded in Company M, which was now near the front of the advance toward the Custer battlefield, or in G, though surely neither company escaped the valley fight with only dead men to mark their late and ragged trail. In fact, Lieutenant Wallace made a point of remarking at the court of inquiry that he had only seven men belonging to G as they moved toward the Custer battlefield. In an even more ludicrous vein, writing to Private Theodore Goldin, Benteen painted a dramatic picture of how he had instructed Wallace to place the men of G in the Reno Enclave an hour later. By this time the company had shrunk to two men![41]

In any case, Varnum did not waste much time mounting his horse and completing the mile-and-a-half trip to the northernmost end of Sharpshooter Ridge, where he found D Troop engaged. No matter the speed of Varnum's animal, he could not have reached his destination much before 5:50, about the time Benteen was leaving his forward position on Weir Point. Varnum's memory of his late arrival is telling. He told the court that he rode to "the far point of the ridge downstream," where he found Weir's Company D firing at scattered groups of Indians perhaps seven or eight hundred yards away, probably well protected by the rolling terrain between Sharpshooter Ridge and Medicine Tail Coulee. In all likelihood, these warriors were positioned to provide a rear-guard shield against the soldiers who had been chased up the hill. As Varnum calculated the time, it had been two hours since Reno's retreat, a surprisingly accurate estimate.[42]

In one of his later accounts, Varnum described what he saw when he arrived at the D Troop position:

> We moved to a point that overlooked where Custer's fight took place, but it was covered with Indians riding in every direction. *A considerable firing was heard but there was no body of troops in sight* [emphasis added]. I saw some white objects that I thought were rocks, but found afterwards they were naked bodies of men.[43]

Unlike Varnum, Private Edward Pigford of M Troop was not the most reliable of witnesses, but he was presumably in a position to see what he later described to Camp, who summarized:

> Says at first when looked over toward Custer Ridge the Indians were firing from a big circle, but it gradually closed until they seemed to converge into a large black mass on the side [of the] hill toward the river and all along the ridge. He thinks what they saw was the last stages of the fight.[44]

By Pigford's testimony alone, it is impossible to fix exactly when he saw the reported tightening of the cordon, but considered in the context of Edgerly's and Wylie's observations—and especially in light of what the tardy Varnum saw and heard—his sighting almost certainly falls in the 5:40–6:00 period.

Except for chasing down a few refugees from Last Stand Hill, the Indians had finished with Custer and his soldiers by six o'clock. Then, perhaps drawn by bone whistles and the shouts of war chiefs, the whole mass of triumphant warriors must have wheeled in some slow-motion about-face to begin the three-mile charge in the direction of the soldier scoundrels pecking at their backside. As the warriors whipped their ponies forward, they picked up brothers at intervals along the way, until the whole valley seemed filled with caterwauling horsemen.

The sight of those countless Indians streaming south is something that virtually every soldier witness recalled. The companies of Weir and French kept up their fire in an effort to stem the tide, although Weir himself appears to have crossed the ravine to meet with Reno and Benteen on the upriver side of the twin peaks. Lieutenant Godfrey, whose Company K was on the eastern slope of the ridge, thought that the whole command might make a stand in that location, with Sharpshooter Ridge, Weir Point, and the bluffs themselves furnishing protection in what he called a "hollow."[45] However, according to Lieutenant Hare, Reno and Benteen were discussing the situation half a mile to the rear of the lead elements, and when Benteen suggested that they fall back so as not to be surrounded, Reno agreed.[46] Reno testified that he immediately headed for the front (or rear) of the column—that is, on the upriver side of Moylan's staggering advance—so that he could once again be in a position to deploy the wing when it returned and to arrange "for the shelter of the men and horses."[47]

Precisely who gave the order for the withdrawal of advance units, and who delivered that order, is typically unclear. Reno claimed that Hare had simply come back and reported that he, using Reno's name, had directed the withdrawal; Hare denied ever having said or done that.[48] However, Hare and Weir may both have been close enough to the Reno-Benteen conversation to understand the general scheme, and with or without specific orders, they may have delivered the news to the separated components of the command. Godfrey recalled that Hare brought the word to him; it is certain that Hare remained with K Troop during the retreat.[49]

Over on the Sharpshooter Ridge sector, Captain French came forward and advised Edgerly that an order had been received to fall back. Edgerly said that he thought not. But within five minutes, French mounted his troop and began to withdraw. Edgerly started to follow, but he had considerable difficulty mounting his horse, which was spinning in circles as the Indians began to fire in their direction, Edgerly's orderly inexplicably smiling as the bullets kicked up dust in their vicinity. Still, Edgerly said the engagement to that point was "general but not heavy," and the Indians did not drive the soldiers from their most advanced position. With no persuasive evidence to the contrary, it is possible that Weir came close enough to signal the retreat to French, because it was almost surely Weir who led Company D away, with Edgerly thrashing about in its wake.[50]

As Godfrey and Hare were leading K Troop dismounted and at a walk away from the twin peaks, Companies M and D came tearing off

Sharpshooter Ridge toward the Reno Enclave, near Reno Hill. Following closely behind, Edgerly encountered another cause for delay at the base of the sugarloaf. Farrier Vincent Charley of Company D had been hit in the hips and was crawling toward the rear. As Edgerly passed, Charley called out that he was wounded. Edgerly dismounted and, stooping over the disabled trooper, suggested that Charley crawl into a ravine and remain quiet. Edgerly promised that he would return shortly to get him.[51]

Catching up with Weir, Edgerly repeated what he had promised the fallen trooper, but Weir stated that the command was under absolute orders to withdraw and that, though he was sorry, nothing could be done to honor Edgerly's promise to the farrier. The only soldier lost in the withdrawal, Charley would later be found dead, with a stick jammed down his throat. The Reno side would make much of this episode at the court of inquiry, to the detriment of the dead Weir's reputation, though little was said about the many helpless cavalrymen left to the Indians during Reno's retreat from the bottom.[52]

The conversation between Edgerly and Weir may have occurred as Companies M and D paused to cover the retreat until the command was within several hundred yards of the Reno Enclave. At that point, Godfrey took the initiative to deploy his K Troop to hold back the Indians who were continuing to advance, thus allowing M and D to make their way to the rear. Edgerly said that Godfrey performed this action "in the most brave and fearless manner." As in all things positive having to do with the Battle of the Little Bighorn, Benteen claimed that it was he who directed the disposition of forces during the advance and the withdrawal, but Godfrey told a different story. He noted that as he was taking further steps to discourage the Indians, Benteen sent word by way of Varnum that Godfrey was to send his led horses to the rear, then withdraw his entire company. Shortly after, a trumpeter arrived with Reno's compliments, telling Godfrey to fall back. Godfrey did so. Company commanders could still do almost as they pleased, a fact of cavalry life that Benteen understood too well, even as he tried again to attach himself to all acts of courage, large or small.[53]

With Reno once more at the head of a retreat, the pieces of the left wing fell into the horseshoe-shaped depression near the hill that would later bear the commander's name. Toward the westward side of this oblong saucer, the packs were deposited, with a circle of animals tethered as tightly as possible near the fringe of the makeshift supply depot. Around the circumference of the low ground, the seven companies took their positions, by order or improvisation. Reno indicated that Benteen should take the southern rim of the Reno Enclave while he would command the line to the north. Reno thus occupied the front facing the enemy, but he assigned the most exposed position to Benteen, whose H Troop would suffer grievously from Indian fire.[54]

By approximately seven o'clock, the warriors had begun to shoot in earnest from the high ground surrounding the soldier's enclave. For the next two hours, the attackers would play havoc with the nerves and the flesh of cavalrymen. But the long-distance assault did only moderate damage, and the vast majority of Reno's new command was still alive. The Indians fired until after dark, but finally the torturous day ended. Late on the evening of 25 June the warrior marksmen stopped shooting from the crest of Sharpshooter Ridge (thus its name) and other surrounding heights and returned to their village.

The first night after the big fight must have been a long one for the soldiers. The enlisted men grumbled, some of them wondering what had become of Custer and why he had left them. Down in the valley, the Sioux and Cheyenne men and women were whooping it up, their fires lighting up the sky while tom-toms thumped out the rhythms of both joy and grief, the two totally inseparable by white cognizance. To soldiers with overactive imaginations, the heathens were peeling skin or shrinking heads, skimming the last measure of life out of army compatriots, known by their surnames or not at all. Given their predilections and their predicament, wondering about their own fates, the troopers of the Seventh Cavalry simply could not believe that alien and savage adversaries would celebrate the capture of scalps even while families of the slain mourned their losses. Those "redskins" were up to no good, the soldiers thought, and Custer had left the bulk of the regiment to look out for itself.[55]

The officers and men of Reno's battalion were particularly exhausted. Having slept little in the past twenty-four hours, they had been in what were essentially three separate engagements with the Indians in the past six hours. They had galloped in attack, run for their lives, climbed hills, started and stopped, and held off the enemy till after dark. Even before they could shut their eyes, some of the men busied themselves digging shallow foxholes with whatever implements they could find while others stacked hardtack and bacon boxes along the open eastern end of the horseshoe where Moylan and A Troop were located. Benteen opted against shoring up the defenses on his side of the line.

By perhaps ten o'clock, Reno decided to catch a bit of sleep himself and directed Private Davern to wake him by midnight. Probably at some point after Reno fell asleep, Captain Weir—who had assented to remain awake to command the downriver side of the Reno Enclave—crawled over to Lieutenant Godfrey's position, ostensibly to discuss the disposition of forces. During this tête-à-tête, the two officers discussed other matters. First Weir asked, "Godfrey, suppose there should be a clash of opinion as to what we should do, as between Major Reno and Captain Benteen, whose judgment would you follow?" Godfrey replied that he would side with Benteen, and Weir apparently agreed. As Godfrey observed in a contemporaneous diary entry, he and Weir felt that Reno "carried no vigor or decision, and his personal behavior gave no confidence in him."[56]

Godfrey and Weir also discussed moving the regiment that night: "We had fewer casualties there to take care of than we would have in the future." Under the circumstances, this was not a totally unreasonable idea, but it is unlikely that the weary officers considered the full range of ramifications, particularly pertaining to the logistics of packing up and moving 350 soldiers—wounded or not—very far in the four or five hours of darkness left that night. At first light (about 3:00 A.M.) the Indians would surely return, catching a crippled half-regiment on the limp, burdened with some number of mules and still within easy reach.[57]

The intriguing aspect of this rather innocent conversation is that a casual and nonbinding idea may have circulated like a bad joke through the leading gossip-monger in the regiment to become a piece of fiction that would in later years flabbergast Lieutenant Godfrey. In the days immediately following the Battle of the Little Bighorn and for the next five years, Benteen led Godfrey to believe that he (Benteen) had "secret" information, the gist of which—when finally divulged—was that Reno had proposed abandoning the wounded and heading for the hills under the cover of darkness.[58]

The sad thing is that for most of his life, Godfrey had no comprehension that the story that would so dumbfound and outrage him was one he had helped create. The unworkable idea may have been broached to Reno, and there is some independent evidence that it was, but Reno had plenty of military and personal reasons for rejecting it. As for Benteen, he must have taken perverse delight in dangling that artificial lure in front of so overeager a fish as Godfrey. Some commentators would commend Benteen for standing up to Reno, whereas Benteen himself surely snickered that once again his goose had shit with impunity on the truth.

By midnight Reno was up again, whether he had actually slept or not. At that point, as he later admitted to the court, he finally took a sip from his quart or pint flask. Numerous witnesses testified that he had had his face in the flask all the way from Ford A, and there is evidence that there were at least a half-dozen demijohns of liquor among the packs, but still Reno would insist that not until the bewitching hour did he have his first nip. It must have been during this period that the apparently drunk Reno had a run-in with, and slapped, one of the civilian packers.[59]

The event was inconsequential but is yet another example of what was happening on the night of 25 June to the esprit de corps within the residue of the Seventh Cavalry. Naturally, cracks were present. Men were fatigued, frightened for their lives. Otherwise loyal officers spoke of a virtual mutiny. Some soldiers slept fitfully while the wounded in body and soul cried out for a measure of relief. If not now, then in the early morning hours the besieging enemy would reappear to do significant damage not just to the edge of the Reno Enclave but to its core.

The Indians did resume their virtually unmolested work at about the break of dawn, with enough warriors stationed in every quadrant to ensure a persistent pinging of the soldiers trapped in the shallow bottom near Reno Hill. Committed to an approximately eight-hour workday, the Indians operated in shifts along the rims of high ground opposite the Reno Enclave, though few of the warriors usually got much closer than four hundred yards. The puffs of smoke from Indian rifles seemed almost continuous, with many of the bursts coming from the same type of long-range Springfield carbines that were possessed by the troopers.

Private Pigford said that the Indians tied a stuffed dummy in buckskin on a pony, then set it loose, trying to draw the fire of the soldiers. As Private James Boyle of G recalled, the warriors also waved a blanket to attract the attention of the soldiers; when the soldiers raised up to fire, the Indians shot at the point of discharge. Several enlisted men and civilians were killed as they lifted their heads above the level of the ground to get a bead on a target. Although some soldiers thought that they hit their marks, the Indians had the advantage of elevation, relative safety, and leisure, and they were not seriously hurt.[60]

In a story told by Corporal Stanislas Roy and confirmed by Private William O. Taylor, the civilian packer Frank Mann was firing over a three-foot-high breastwork when he went quiet and remained so for some twenty minutes. Someone then remarked, "Something must be wrong with the packer." Indeed, he was dead, shot through the temple, his head still in position to sight his gun.[61]

Likewise, Corporal Wylie recalled the case of Private Herod Liddiard (twenty-five years old and born in London, England) of the Gray Horse Troop. Liddiard had been saved from that unit's fate by his assignment to the pack train. Benteen was pointing out some potential targets to his command when Liddiard, who was a good shot, took aim, still talking as he did so. He stopped talking, and the men near him noticed "blood running around the rim of his hat." He was dead.[62]

For Private Andrew Moore, the only way to fire for best effect was to stand up. Private Hugh McGonigle warned his Company G comrade to kneel at least, but Moore would have none of it and, when he rose to fire, was hit. The "gallant" and "likable" Moore was taken to Dr. Porter's makeshift hospital, where the gut-shot trooper waved away the attention, suggesting that the surgeon direct his efforts to those who had a chance to live.[63]

Besides the soldiers killed and wounded on the perimeter of the Reno Enclave, the Indian bullets were taking a toll on the inside, where the horses and mules were corralled around the bulk of the provisions and ammunition. As animals fell, their legs were used as posts to tether more securely the remaining livestock. Southeast of the trapped and shifting and whinnying herd, Dr. Porter had established his first-aid station. Porter performed "in a most superb manner," a later judgment universally confirmed.[64]

At some point on 26 June, the mule "Old Barnum" escaped the corral with a load of ammunition. In spite of Indians circling in the area, Sergeant Richard Hanley mounted his horse and headed after the mule, determined to shoot the animal if it did not turn back. The mule was driven back into the Reno Enclave. For this courageous act, Hanley was awarded the Medal of

Honor. Private John McGuire claimed to have joined in the chase on foot after the unruly mule, and there is supporting evidence that McGuire may indeed have done so, but it is impossible now to gauge the value of his assistance.[65]

As always, Captain Benteen claimed to have brought the hard-headed mules to heel. He later told Private Goldin that he had returned two ammunition-loaded mules, which he "had personally caught while they were hell-bent on getting to the blue water which was so plainly in sight." After that, he gave Lieutenant Mathey, who was in charge of the packs, a "cussing out." That Mathey, he said in a letter to his wife, was given to "gossiping away like an old lady over her tea" rather than tending to business. Maybe there was more than one incident involving ammunition-laden mules.[66]

From the testimony provided by nearly every witness located within the Reno Enclave, Benteen had no need to puff up his contributions. All agreed that he showed exceptional courage, and in the opinion of Godfrey and others, Benteen "was exercising the functions principally of commanding officer." This was particularly true on 26 June as Benteen's part of the line was in danger of crumbling.[67]

As already noted, Benteen's company was situated along the southern wall of the horseshoe. In that exposed position, it was being punished severely from Indian fire coming from the north. The men of H Troop were expending great amounts of ammunition, and the increasing casualties had apparently caused some to seek refuge among the packs at the center of the corral. At the same time, a few of the more foolhardy Indians were crawling nearer, so close that they could pitch rocks and arrows into the ranks of the soldiers.

To cope with the disintegrating situation on his side, Benteen went to Reno and requested assistance in dealing with the threat. An uncertain Reno eventually gave in to Benteen's insistence and released Captain French and his M Troop to reinforce the upriver line. As Benteen returned to his position, he gathered up more ammunition and collected those men of his company skulking among the packs. Then Benteen led a charge over the rise to scatter the half-dozen warriors who had crept near enough to constitute a nuisance and a potential danger.[68]

Following this action, Benteen went back to the north side of the line and suggested to Reno that it would be wise to drive the Indians in that direction as well. Although apparently reluctant to give the order himself, Reno simply stared at Benteen for some time, then said, "Can you see the Indians from there?" When Benteen replied that he could, Reno asserted, "If you can see them, give the command to charge." Benteen shouted, "All right, ready boys, charge and give them hell!" The men went up and over the top, charging about fifty yards before they were driven back.[69]

Edgerly was surprised that Benteen was not "riddled" with bullets as he remained, smiling, in an exposed position throughout the ordeal. Godfrey remembered Benteen saying "something about the bullet not having been moulded yet to shoot him, that he had been through too many dangerous places to care anything about their shooting." The men all admired him, and Reno in his official report commended the captain for his "conspicuous services," which deserved recognition by the government. Nevertheless, Edgerly put the matter in perspective by noting that except for the charges, "all the walking that [Edgerly] saw the gallant Benteen do was from his line to Reno's and that lasted but a few moments."[70]

As for Reno, Godfrey described for the court an occasion when he and the major were going from the northern to the southern side of the horse-shoe. The Indian fire was heavy, and Reno was dodging the bullets. Godfrey noted that Reno said, in a laughing way, that he was "damned if he wanted to be killed by an Indian, he had gone through too many fights." Except for his possible participation in Benteen's charge over the northern rim of the redoubt, there is no persuasive evidence that Reno ever risked death for the benefit of his command. His fear of dying at the hands of the savages, in a war that did not matter enough, was first expressed at Ford A. Given that fundamental fear, Reno was no more equipped for field command in the American West than were the clutch of like-minded staff officers and perpetual coffee-coolers hunkered down in the offices and corridors of the War Department and various army headquarters.[71]

Even more pathetic was the case of Captain Moylan. Worse than suffering the criticism of fellow officers, Moylan was apparently the laughingstock of the enlisted men. Private John Burkman said that Moylan was called "Aparejo Mickie" because he never the left the protection of the packs that guarded his A Troop position.[72] In a variation on this theme, Private Goldin noted that Moylan was designated "hard tack Mick" because he remained behind the bacon and hardtack boxes until the night of 26 June. Convinced that Moylan had remained behind the bacon boxes for the duration of the fight, the men of the regiment thereafter would "squeal like a hog" whenever the captain was nearby. Again, according to Goldin, Moylan was "cordially detested by every enlisted man in the regiment" because he was, even to the members of his own company, "the meanest, most inconsiderate officer," one who may have remained so close to the boxes for fear of being shot in the back.[73] Private Francis Kennedy asserted that Moylan was not seen from the time the battle at the Reno Enclave started until it was over.[74] For whatever it adds to the proof, Benteen thought that Moylan showed the "white feather" during the fight.[75]

During midday on 26 June, some troopers volunteered to go down to the river for water, which was much in demand, especially by the wounded. With Indians still in the area, the first several trips were perilous. There were no fatalities and just a few serious injuries. Based on subsequent claims and references to men who supposedly participated in the water parties, roughly fifty soldiers took part, but only fifteen received the Medal of Honor for bringing relief to the wounded. Another three (all from Benteen's H Troop) were awarded the medal as sharpshooters providing covering fire for the water parties.

Late that afternoon, Lieutenant Varnum went to Reno and offered to leave with a message requesting assistance. By this time, the Indian fire had slackened markedly. After some hemming and hawing, Reno refused to let Varnum leave because he was too good a shot. When Varnum persisted, Reno went silent for a while, then said at last, "Varnum, you are a very uncomfortable companion." Varnum left the area where Reno and Weir were located, but after a time, Weir came and said that Reno had agreed that Varnum could pick some Indian scouts to attempt the breakout. The Crow scouts and several Arikaras consented to go, and Reno wrote out four copies of messages. Varnum afterward concluded that the scouts did not attempt to leave. For his trouble, and because he had supposedly added material to Reno's notes, Varnum was later punished by being assigned to lookout duty while the dead on the Custer battlefield were buried. Thus Varnum was not permitted the opportunity for a last visit with those dead soldiers, many of whom were his friends of long standing.[76]

The question of sending messages soon became largely academic. That evening the Sioux and Cheyennes broke camp and began to move away.

The components of their movable village stretched for several miles in length and perhaps a half-mile wide, by some estimates. The immense parade of warriors, women, old folks, and children rode or walked south toward the Bighorn Mountains. Their many wounded warriors were strapped to travois or were mounted precariously on their ponies. Some of these warriors would later die. Lodgepoles scarred the soft earth, kicking up that inevitable dust, while the vast pony herd filled the landscape farther west, smothering the horizon with the thin powder upheaved by their shuffling gait. To the men of the Seventh who watched from the bluffs, the scene was all a mystery, slowly revealing itself like some unfathomable miracle. The Indians were apparently leaving, and for troopers who had come to expect death, the good fortune oozed into badly frayed nerves not quite free from the nagging fear that the warriors might return to finish their work.

The warriors would not return. The Indians had discovered that the column of General Alfred Terry and Colonel John Gibbon was approaching from the north. In any case, the Sioux and Cheyenne chiefs had already decided that the tribes had suffered enough in the Battle of the Little Bighorn, and they were not prepared to take more casualties by trying to drive entrenched soldiers from Reno Hill. If Terry and Gibbon had not been approaching, they might have tried to starve the bluecoats out, but now there was no need to hazard more injury. Many coups had been counted, many scalps and many guns had been taken, and the army of the United States had been taught a lesson. It was time to move on, to end the Sun Dance season, and eventually to break up and scatter for what remained of the summer. A significant number would go back to the reservations.[77]

That evening the soldiers moved their enclave to the south to escape the stench of dead horses and mules. While on Reno Hill, eighteen soldiers had been killed. Fifty-two had been wounded, and several of these men would die before they could reach Fort Abraham Lincoln. By midnight, Fred Gerard and Billy Jackson came in, and within hours Lieutenant Charles DeRudio and Private Thomas O'Neill arrived safely at the redoubt, all having the most harrowing tales to share regarding their experiences while in the river bottom. But for most, it was a good night to sleep, their first sound sleep in many days.

Several miles away, the troopers of Custer's right wing were sleeping the deepest sleep of all.

CHAPTER FOURTEEN

HONOR BOUND

As Captain Thomas Weir sat astride his horse on the summit of Sharp-shooter Ridge, he must have burned with frustration, anger, and bitterness. It was about 5:15 on 25 June. The first man out of the position along the bluffs after Major Marcus Reno's retreat from the valley, Weir remained alone for some minutes, no doubt trying to comprehend what was occurring two miles away. All he knew for sure was that Custer was fighting, but Weir could do nothing to help. The manner in which the Indians were streaming northward suggested perhaps a rout, with rear-guard units of Custer's right wing engaging the hundreds of warriors scrambling to maul the backside of the soldiers' retreat.

Several days would pass before Weir could get close enough to see what he had actually been watching for better than half an hour. Those peculiar white clumps, glistening like pale rocks in the distance, were dead men, stripped and dispossessed of all their earthly belongings. Then there was no way to get clean, no way to wash into oblivion the enormity of the failure, not Custer's alone but Weir's and Reno's and Benteen's—and theirs more than Custer's even because at least the general had died on the field. So it must have seemed to Weir, as the shock of the realization metamorphosed into a deep and inescapable melancholy, a depression that would either kill him outright or drive him to death's door.[1]

Except for perhaps Captain Thomas French, the other officers who had listened to the Custer battle from the safety of Reno Hill, and had then gone near enough to see some portion the fight, fared better than Weir in suppressing the sickening reality or in rationalizing the outcome. Their own two-day encounter with the Indians must have done much to mitigate whatever guilt they felt, and their nearly universal judgment that Custer had made a fatal mistake in dividing the regiment further exculpated them. A good field commander or not, Custer had died, in the end, through his own fault. And yet those volleys must have rung in their ears for many years after the event. Looking down on those bloated bodies scattered around the Custer battlefield, some of the more sensitive surviving officers must have had difficulty disconnecting those dead men from the persistent thuds that had echoed through the hills for fully an hour, like intermittent and fading heartbeats.

By the time that most of Reno's command reached Sharpshooter Ridge on the evening of 25 June, Lieutenant Henry Harrington's first platoon of Company C had been destroyed and Lieutenant James Calhoun's L Troop had been scattered, leaving the unit commanders dead, in their proper places in relation to the line of their men who also fell dead there. The horse-holders to the rear had also been decimated, causing some to escape alone, some to leave with their animals in tow, and most to lose control of their charges altogether, the horses bucking their way to freedom as the number fours were pulled down by the Indians and killed.

With the elimination of the L and C rear guards, and with the quashing of the E Troop salient, the way was open for the warriors to crush Captain Myles Keogh's Company I and First Sergeant Edwin Bobo's platoon and to roll up the valley to Last Stand Hill—but not without a fight that nearly all of the Indian warriors would recall with admiration and respect. The clash of arms in this sector likely did not last longer than ten minutes or so in its decisive phase, but it was without question a fight, face to face and perhaps hand to hand. In addition to the evidence provided by the grouping of bodies, Indian witnesses said there was a stand made here, one of sufficient duration to stick in their memories.

After Keogh and his senior enlisted personnel were killed, a "buffalo hunt" commenced as what remained of unit cohesion in I Troop—along with the men from L and C—dissolved. According to the Cheyenne Little Hawk:

> The soldiers ran and went along the straight ridge where they [the warriors] chased them like buffalo, and as long as they had their backs

toward the Indians, the Indians rode right in among them. At the knoll where the monument stands [Last Stand Hill], the soldiers turned and that is the last place [I] saw them.[2]

The long line of markers in the Keogh sector is testimony to the truth of what Little Hawk said. For a distance of several hundred yards the white stones define a trail of soldiers' bodies, primarily men who, on foot, had attempted to run for the safety of Custer's command at Last Stand Hill, about a quarter of a mile distant. The Indians mixed in with the soldiers, inhibiting the covering fire coming from Custer's position. Nonetheless, a few warriors must have died in this melee.

The fact that the bodies of First Sergeant Frank Varden, Sergeant James Bustard, and Trumpeter John Patton were found with that of Keogh indicates that the "buffalo hunt" did not begin until they were disabled or dead; otherwise, the bodies of these senior personnel would likely have been dispersed all along the trail of the chase. Likewise, the hunt ended with the last cluster of markers, probably because of the gunfire coming from Last Stand Hill, allowing some number of soldiers to "turn" (in Little Hawk's recollection) and deflect the advance of the warriors. In the course of this chaotic and disjointed retreat, soldiers may have shot themselves, killed each other, gathered in little knots of petrified terror, froze with their fingers on their triggers, or discarded their weapons and offered to surrender, begging in vain for mercy. The Indians spoke of such occurrences; the extent to which they happened in the Keogh sector is unknown, but unhappy events like these surely took place, after a brief and valiant stand by some significant part of the seventy or so troopers whose bodies were found on this line after the battle.

Some soldiers, probably including horse-holders and others who had managed to hold on to their mounts, headed west between the hillocks defining Custer Ridge. Two Eagles described how eight soldiers followed just such a route, but there must have been others, accounting for the many bodies found in the area of Deep Ravine. For men seeking any way to escape, the deceptively flat and empty ground in the direction of the river was surely inviting, although that terrain was neither level nor free of Indians.[3]

Initially, Custer may have posted Captain George Yates's F Troop along the perimeter of Last Stand Hill, feeding down the eastern slope to provide cover for Keogh as well as stretching westward in the direction of Cemetery Ridge to furnish support for Company E. In the most sheltered position, northwest of the hill—with Cemetery Ridge to the west and with the held horses of F and E serving as a shield to the rear—Dr. George Lord likely established his hospital, where he could attend to early casualties. By order of the general, the nonmilitary personnel—Boston Custer, Autie Reed, and the newspaperman Mark Kellogg—may have been located in this hollow as well, so as to afford them maximum protection.[4]

The escapees from the Keogh sector to Last Stand Hill probably did not amount to more than a dozen men, all on horseback. From Custer's point of view, the pressure was originating on his flanks—along the series of hills that would later bear his name and along Cemetery Ridge—instead of from the relatively open ground enclosed by his original disposition of forces. Such avenues of attack conformed with the common-sense tactical approach used by the Indians, who thus avoided direct confrontations in favor of oblique assaults on the most exposed points susceptible to an eventual surround. Much the same tactic, on a smaller scale, had been used against Reno's skirmish line in the valley.

Faced with the Indian advance, Custer shifted Company F troopers from the eastern to the western slope of Last Stand Hill. The Oglala Lone Bear asserted that the soldiers made a stand on the top for a short time but were then "forced over the hill."[5] Now all of F Troop was located on the northwestern slope of the summit. As soon as the men from the Keogh sector arrived, Custer had the soldiers shoot a half-dozen horses to construct rough arcs of barricades near the crest of Last Stand Hill facing west. The evidence is that these animals were mostly sorrels, indicating mounts belonging to Company C and possibly delivered to the scene by horse-holders. For perhaps five minutes (5:45–5:50), there may have been an eerie silence as the soldiers went about getting ready for the final onslaught.[6]

Again Custer may have relied on those maxims he had articulated in *My Life on the Plains,* the eternal verities of his own experience. "There is nothing an Indian dislikes more in warfare than to attack a foe, however weak, behind breastworks of any kind," he had said. But Custer had never seen so many Indians, and his breastworks did not amount to much.[7]

Runs-the-Enemy (a Two Kettle) recollected that once Custer was surrounded, there was at first no firing from either side. Then the Sioux charged from the rear (presumably east) but were driven back by strong resistance, resulting in the loss of many ponies. Runs-the-Enemy moved to a position north of the hill and from there saw hundreds of Indians moving through coulees around Custer. He and some thirty warriors charged from this direction, firing as they went, "and captured a lot of Custer's horses and drove them down to the river," probably making a trail of shod animals along the far side of Cemetery Ridge. If accurate, this action resulted in the scattering of the E and F mounts and removed the barrier protecting the back side of the first-aid station. Other Indian accounts indicate that the gray horses were the last ones released by their attendants.[8]

More than 80 horses were being held in the area to the rear of Last Stand Hill, with the remaining 120-plus having been retained near Calhoun Ridge and in the Keogh sector. As suggested, the horse-holders in the latter positions had already been splintered, with some men being shot or pulled from their mounts while the remaining riders headed for Last Stand Hill or passed over Custer Ridge or took their chances by heading for apparent gaps in the Indian lines. The horse-holders located in the vicinity of Last Stand Hill had fewer options open to them. With warriors occupying the Custer and Cemetery Ridges and with a cordon now complete to the east, the survivors would have had little choice but to dismount and join the force on Last Stand Hill or, in at least some instances, to break through the low ground between the ridges and head for the river. Under this scenario, fifteen or twenty troopers riding grays and bays and horses of other colors may have fled the holding area and headed toward Deep Ravine, where they would have been cut down by Indians concealed in the many ditches and, in the process, would have joined the dead soldiers from E and the refugees from C, I, and L already collected there.

Within the next ten or fifteen minutes, the Battle of the Little Bighorn was effectively over. During this period, Lieutenant Charles Varnum heard the "considerable firing" coming from the direction of the field, so far away that it was a sound without identifiable origins. The circle seen by Private Edward Pigford was closing. The dead-horse barricades were insufficient to prevent a terrible enfilading from well-armed warriors along Cemetery Ridge, along the rolling ground of Custer Ridge, in the hillocks to the east, and in ravines in every quarter. Many hundreds of guns were being discharged, and arrows continued to rain down on the unprotected position occupied by Custer and what was left of his command. The dead and barely living soldiers were shrouded in gray, the Indians said, as the fine particles of the battle's awful disruption settled back to earth.

How did the battle on the hill end for most of the soldiers there? The Indian testimony speaks of some hand-to-hand fighting, but if this occurred, it was mostly with disabled or stunned men. More likely, the word of warriors like Lone Bear and White Shield is closer to the truth. These Indians suggested that after nearly all the soldiers had been killed from a distance, the Indian men and women moved in to dispatch the rest—the wounded—with "hatchets, arrows, knives." Had the Indians been on Last Stand Hill in any great numbers earlier, several of Custer's men could not have gotten up and run on foot almost to the river. Rather, the evidence is persuasive that the warriors did not venture onto the hill until the shooting stopped. At that time they had reason to conclude that the troopers were out of ammunition, when in truth the soldiers were all dead or almost so.[9]

There are many Indian stories about the late departure of men from Last Stand Hill. The usual number given is four or seven men, but figures as high as fifteen or twenty were mentioned in various Sioux and Cheyenne testimony. The only way to reconcile the arithmetic of these diverse tales is to conclude that the larger group was horse-holders and that the smaller body consisted of the very last survivors. One plausible explanation derives from the location of certain bodies discovered after the fight.[10] According to eyewitnesses who visited the site after the engagement, and by the weight of subsequent research, the bodies of Dr. Lord, Kellogg, Mitch Boyer, Trumpeter Henry Dose, and Sergeant Robert Hughes (who carried Custer's battle flag) were all found quite a distance from Last Stand Hill, toward the river. The bodies of Boston Custer and Autie Reed were discovered about a hundred yards west of the knoll. None of these men were located where one might have expected to find them.[11]

Is it reasonable to hypothesize that Lord, Kellogg, Reed, Boston, and perhaps Boyer emerged out of the suddenly exposed hospital area at the last to make a run for safety in the only direction in which escape seemed practicable? Is it sensible to suppose that the youngest Custer brother and Custer's nephew, Autie Reed, would have been found near Armstrong and Tom unless an opportunity arose for escape from the scene of certain destruction, perhaps with the general's or Tom's blessing and even urging?

The Indian testimony is that these unidentified people, however many were involved, were shot from behind or were ridden down and beaten to death. That a number of this last-gasp group came out of the hospital enclave seems a fair conclusion.

And so, by six o'clock, Custer's command was finished. By Indian reckoning, the defeat had required no more time than a person might need to consume a hearty meal, or as long as it would take for the sun to travel the width of a lodgepole. It was a brief, small struggle in a war few people wanted, in which men mostly unknown to one another clashed and died on barren and broken ground fit for little else. The Sioux chiefs would later claim that they did not know it was the great "Long Hair" they were fighting, even after they had killed him, but some Cheyennes would insist that they remembered him from the time of the Washita. Only in hindsight would the joyful victory be even greater than the Indians imagined—if, in the context of subsequent events, it was a triumph at all, regardless of the exhilaration the survivors and their offspring might experience in the recounting of real, mystic, and mythic memories.

Unfortunately, actual people died, and bodies were counted. Trudging over the Custer battlefield several days after the event, members of the army burial parties arrived at different figures for the total number of men killed. Lieutenant DeRudio tallied 214; Captain Frederick Benteen supposedly saw 212. By this author's estimate, the fatalities during this episode included 193 enlisted men in five companies, 3 troopers attached to the headquarters unit, 12 officers, 1 scout, and 3 civilians. Added to the soldiers killed in the various stages of Reno's involvement, the total losses for the Seventh Cavalry at the Battle of the Little Bighorn amounted to approximately 265 men, not counting the lives afterward forfeited by the trauma of the event.[12]

The Indians must have had even more difficulty estimating their losses. Two Moon said thirty-nine Sioux and seven Cheyennes were killed and about one hundred wounded. Among the Lakotas, Moving Robe Woman claimed that over sixty Indians were killed, Lone Bear thought thirty-five, and many others gave totals in the thirty-to-fifty range, with significant numbers dying later from wounds received in the battle. The Miniconjou White Bull is generally credited with the best list, presumably because he could name the twenty-seven Indians who had died and in which phase of the battle. However, unless White Bull followed the various circles immediately after the great camp broke up (he did interview members of tribes or bands fifteen years after the event), his numbers are no more reliable than those of Indians who suggested mortalities in the hundreds. Based on all sources, and with no means of verification, perhaps forty or fifty Indian warriors were killed in all phases of the battle, with maybe half that number dying later from wounds received.[13]

The extent of the carnage inflicted on the Seventh Cavalry was discovered on 27 June, with the arrival of General Alfred Terry and Colonel John Gibbon's column, which had struggled up the Bighorn River. The first man to inspect the Custer battlefield was Lieutenant James Bradley, who commanded a scouting party consisting of mounted members of the Seventh Infantry. Wending his way to the south, Bradley—an "old friend" of Lieutenant Edward Godfrey's—reported finding 197 bodies on the way to Reno Hill, an amazingly accurate count, under the circumstances. Later that day, General Terry himself reached the killing ground. By all accounts, almost everyone wept, most of the troopers with Reno simply glad to be alive. Perhaps unable to accept that Custer had not skipped out, Captain Benteen immediately asked for and was given permission to see the dead for himself.[14] "There he is, God damn him!" Benteen supposedly said as he looked down on Custer's body. "He'll never fight any more."[15]

Openly happy to hurl Custer and his family into perdition, Benteen would suffer his own kind of purgatory for nearly the next twenty years, telling and retelling the same tired and untrue tales until the day he died. He could never quite disgorge the bone that he himself had picked and had been forced by pride to swallow after the Battle of the Washita. Even if he did not say the words ascribed to him, Benteen's congenital bile must have felt the tug of a counterflow as he peered at Custer's cadaver: a worthy adversary had died bravely.

"The flower of the American army is dead," General Terry allegedly stated. Terry had considered Custer's services "indispensable" to the expedition, and in spite of misguided efforts on the part of Terry's minions to expiate their boss, Terry was too good a man to speak ill of a fellow officer—especially Custer—under those circumstances and until it became absolutely necessary. Again, the quotation may not be exact, but the words probably capture the truest sentiments felt by Terry at that moment, before the irresistible urge for self-preservation began to infect the highest ranks of the U.S. Army.[16]

According to some after-action accounts, the dead Custer looked as if he were taking a nap, descriptions that probably had more to do with sparing Libbie's feelings than with telling the truth. Regardless, the officers and men who saw the swollen body and famous face (now bearded, with blood congealed where mustache and whiskers met the corners of his mouth) were able to recognize the corpse as Custer's. Located near the crest of "a narrow ridge not wide enough on top to drive a wagon on," Custer was stretched "across two or three soldiers, just a small portion of his back touching the ground." He was naked except for maybe a sock and the bottom of one boot, the Indians having taken the upper part for use in making moccasin soles. Like the other corpses on the field, his body was doubtless bloated from lying in the sun and the intense heat for two whole days.[17]

Lieutenant Godfrey cited a report by the interpreter Fred Gerard: "He found the naked bodies of two soldiers, one across the other and Custer's naked body in a sitting position between and leaning against them, his upper right arm along and on the topmost body, his right forearm and hand supporting his head in an inclining posture like one resting or asleep." Godfrey asserted that Custer's facial expression was perfectly "natural," an impression shared by virtually everyone who saw the body. Corporal John Hammon, who helped bury Custer, added that Custer's right hand was "twisted as if something had been wrenched from it."[18]

These accounts provide no more than an idea of how Custer fell. Every dead cavalryman had been stripped. Therefore, unless the Indians had a gift for removing clothing without disturbing the relative positions of bodies, Custer and his two companion troopers did not go down exactly as portrayed. At a minimum, Custer was rolled or dragged into the config-uration remembered by the several witnesses, although he may well have died near the two enlisted men.

In other respects, the soldiers' recollections of Custer's appearance may not have comported with the facts, especially regarding evidence of mutila-tions. Almost all of these eyewitnesses indicated that Custer had not been scalped or brutalized in any other way. But even though his short and receding hair had not been lifted, there is some belated and suspect testimony that one thigh had been slashed, an arrow had been shot into his genitals, and a finger had been cut off, apparently to remove a ring.[19]

The wounds that resulted in Custer's death are not in doubt. He had been shot once in the lower left breast, somewhere in the rib cage, with a second and possibly related wound in his right forearm. The chances are that Custer survived these injuries, with sufficient residual strength to cling to his pistol. The bullet that sped from one side of his head to the other—from one temple to the other—was certainly fatal.[20]

The nature of these wounds raises the question of whether Custer killed himself or whether he directed his brother Tom or Lieutenant William Cooke or someone else to end his misery. Possibly an Indian put a bullet in his brain as a kind of coup de grace, but given the indignities imposed on the other near-dead on the Custer and Reno battlefields, such a nice dispatching seems most unlikely, especially since in all other respects Custer was spared the worst of mutilations. Neither does it seem probable that a random Sioux bullet could have hit a mortally wounded man precisely above the ear.

Nearly all of the soldier witnesses insisted that there were no powder burns around the wounds in Custer's head. Again, besides the question of their competency to judge such a matter under those extreme circumstances, all of the men of the Seventh were undoubtedly considerate of Libbie's feelings. Sergeant John Ryan agreed that there were no powder burns, but he wrote Walter Camp that the bodies had begun to turn "very black" after three days in the elements.[21] Given the peaceful expression on Custer's face, in contrast to that of many others on the field who evinced terror in the throes of death, it is fair to wonder whether he gave a command similar to one of his earlier injunctions. Previously he had ordered that if Libbie was about to be captured by Indians, his subordinates should shoot her. As she herself observed, everyone felt the "terror of capture."[22]

Without question, on other parts of the field, individual troopers—like those, already discussed, involved in Reno's retreat—considered shooting themselves or weighed asking comrades to assist in their deaths. Kate Bighead and Wooden Leg stated that nearly every soldier on the battlefield killed himself or a mate, an exaggeration of actual events they may have observed. Whether Custer committed suicide or benefited from the help of a friend will never be known, but as the consummate frontiersman, he understood very well the importance of saving the last bullet for oneself.[23]

Tom Custer and Cooke lay within five or ten yards of the general, near the crest of the knoll. Yates and Lieutenant William Van Wyck Reily rested farther down the hill with the bulk of their Company F. Found face-down, Tom was unrecognizable to nearly everyone when he was rolled over. His head had been bashed in by hammers or tomahawks, his stomach had been cut open, he had been scalped, his arm had been broken, his body had been mutilated in other ways, and arrows had been shot into his back. According to Godfrey, he knew it was Tom only because of the initials "T.W.C." (with pictures of the goddess of liberty and the flag) tattooed on his arm, although Private O'Neill, who helped with the burial, said he recognized Tom by looking at his face. Cooke suffered comparatively minor humiliations, including the removal of one side of his whiskers.[24]

All over the field, soldiers were mangled beyond recognition. Heads, legs, genitalia, and arms were cut off. Skulls were smashed, and other bones were broken. Flesh was slashed in every conceivable way. Some men were propped up on their knees and elbows, and arrows were fired into their rear ends. Private George Glenn recalled finding former bunky Private Tom ("Boss") Tweed of L Troop with his crotch split by an ax, with one of his legs thrown up over his shoulder and arrows in both eyes. Assuming that it was true that Indians did not deign to touch men who had taken their own lives, there were fewer suicides than Kate Bighead and Wooden Leg claimed.[25]

The burial parties did not take long to perform their sad and distasteful task. After a special effort to locate the bodies of the officers (Lieutenants Harrington, James Sturgis, and James Porter were not identified), the internments began. There were too few tools, and the soil was both too hard and too powdery to allow for more than a gesture of respect. Into shallow depressions the bodies were shoved or slung, with just enough earth and meager vegetation thrown after to conceal the carcass nearly out of view. Stakes were barely driven into the baked ground to mark the skimpy graves.

The officers got a bit more attention, but not so much as to make any real difference. In Custer's case, special care was taken to mark his inadequate grave. According to Private O'Neill, after Dr. Henry Porter had removed several locks of the general's hair, Lieutenant George Wallace wrote Custer's name on a piece of paper, then inserted the rolled-up reminder in an empty cartridge shell, which someone pounded into the impermanent post at the body's head. The hole that held the general's body was apparently only a bit deeper than that provided for the enlisted men, although more debris may have been heaped above the ground to protect him from the scavengers.[26]

A year after the battle, an expedition under the command of Lieutenant Colonel Michael Sheridan and Captain Henry Nowlan of the Seventh returned to the field to recover the remains of the officers who had died there. They also reportedly restaked the graves of the enlisted men. Accompanying that mission, the scout George Herendeen recollected that out of the hole supposedly housing Custer's body, they recovered no more than two handfuls of small bones. The natural conclusion was that coyotes and other predators had dragged the cadaver out of its inadequate grave and scattered the parts.[27]

What was true for Custer's remains was at least doubly so for all of the others, buried under inches of powder, easy pickings for the ravenous wildlife that must have descended on the burial grounds soon after General Terry's command left the area. How much of Custer's skeleton was removed from the field is impossible to say, but if Herendeen was correct, the remains did not include all of his skeleton. Colonel Sheridan is alleged to have remarked: "Nail the box [containing Custer's remains] up; it's all right as long as people think so." Therefore, although the essence of Custer may reside in his memorial sepulcher at West Point, the bulk of his earthly presence probably helped to fill the mass grave now forming the base of the obelisk on Last Stand Hill. If the coyotes were as reckless with the remains of Tom and Cooke and Yates, pieces of these loyal officers' corporeal afterlife may also rest with the random residue of the general and the others who served with him.[28]

Soon General Terry's attitude began to shift away from tearful good-byes to bureaucratic self-interest. His official report of 28 June was decidedly neutral in its treatment of events, but on 2 July he addressed a "confidential" dispatch to General Phil Sheridan. Doubtless influenced by input from Reno and Benteen, Terry now took the position that Custer had deviated from the plan devised aboard the *Far West* and that, as a consequence, he had made errors that the ex-lawyer euphemistically attributed to "a misapprehension" of the situation. In effect, Terry was saying that Custer had disobeyed orders, then had compounded the problem by tactical failure. Terry said disingenuously that he had not submitted this secret report "to cast any reflection upon Custer" but that he felt that the plan "must have been successful had it been carried out." The dispatch is couched in such slippery language that Terry must have feared for his career and his reputation even though, by the record, he had no need for such a cleverly contrived escape hatch. Nevertheless, his attempt at avoidance was carried on by members of his staff with total moral turpitude for many years afterward.[29]

General William Sherman and General Sheridan received Terry's confidential report while they were attending the Centennial Exhibition in Philadelphia, where the nation was celebrating one hundred years of independence while basking in the glow of national progress in diverse industrial and scientific fields. Some of the inventions (e.g., the telephone) demonstrated at that exhibition would contribute significantly to shrinking the thousands of miles between the east and west coasts of a country proud of its growth and pleased with its accomplishments. The two senior officers were stunned and incredulous at the army news, unable to accept that Custer and his command were dead. Perhaps while in this shocked state, they allowed the confidential dispatch to fall into the hands of a newspaper reporter, who ensured that word of Custer's defeat would reach the public in the worst possible light.

Shortly thereafter, General Sheridan wrote to General Sherman: "I deeply deplore the loss of Custer and his men. I feel it was an unnecessary sacrifice, due to misapprehension, and a superabundance of courage—the latter extraordinarily developed in Custer."[30] Picking up the theme that had been bubbling up the line, President Ulysses Grant pronounced to the public that he regarded Custer's defeat "as a sacrifice of troops brought on by Custer himself, that was wholly unnecessary—wholly unnecessary."[31]

Also during that week Libbie Custer and other dependents at Fort Abraham Lincoln learned that their loved ones would not be coming home. Wrapping a shawl around her slender shoulders, the brave but grief-stricken wife of the late "boy general" accompanied the post notification team from residence to residence, bringing the sad word to the families of the slain— families that had lost as much as she, some more. Her sister-in-law Maggie Calhoun lost a husband, three brothers, a nephew, and dear friends. But it was Libbie who symbolized the cruelty of the blow, not just then but for all of her life. From the beginning of her marriage, she had shared the general's achievements and dangers, his highs and lows, his playful and troubled moods. Now widowed and childless, alone in the world, she would tap her memory to write books attesting to a devotion that seemed never to waver while he lived or after.

A widow at thirty-four, she endured for fifty-seven years as one of the "women who weep"—a woman narrowly proscribed by the Victorian age, untrained for any task beyond being the wife of a once renowned soldier. Possibly she was comforted for the remainder of her life by a justifiable conviction that the general's last thoughts were of her and his personal God. When she died in 1933, over ninety years old and still loyal to her husband's memory, the marvels of the Philadelphia exhibition had been advanced exponentially, and the way west from Bull Run to the Little Bighorn (then to Hollywood) was marked by ever-increasing signs of civilization's inexorable push. Libbie had traveled extensively throughout the United States and the world, but she could never bring herself to visit the ground where Autie had died.[32]

For President Grant, whose administration had been racked by corruption and malfeasance, the debacle on the Little Bighorn—on top of Crook's earlier repulse on the Rosebud—further undermined his two-pronged Indian policy. Those in favor of using force to solve the Indian problem were now furnished with additional popular support for their cause. Grant had reason to be annoyed by the turn of events, but like Generals Sheridan and Terry, he based his rushed judgment regarding Custer's role and responsibility on the flimsiest of evidence. Still, as has already been discussed, even when the army did attempt a detailed investigation into the affair three years later at the court of inquiry, Reno was excused, and the hasty conclusions of Terry, Sheridan, and Grant were effectively vindicated.

In his brilliant summation of the case against Major Reno, Court Recorder Jesse Lee concluded: "General Custer died a death so heroic that it has but few parallels in history."[33] Working his way through a labyrinth of premeditated falsehoods and deliberate evasions, Lee got closer to the truth than the observers in attendance might have expected or wished. At least a few of the officers in the courtroom must have squirmed in their seats as he recounted his findings with logic so sharp and insightful that the razor edge of his voice might have brought blood had the players been real and the courtroom more than a stage. His information was limited and tainted, but he was right, without knowing entirely why. Likewise, even with its exploitative timing and technique, Frederick Whittaker's hero-worshiping and widow-sensitive narrative (*A Complete Life of General George A. Custer*, written in 1876) got closer to the real essence of Custer and the Battle of the Little Bighorn than the politics of history could abide.

In 1897 Lee wrote to Libbie that he had "tried to be honest and fair-minded and allow nothing but *facts* [Lee's emphasis] to make an impression" on his mind. He asserted that as a result of "what was said [to him] by witnesses *before* they went on the stand, and in light of *much* of that testimony on the stand," as well as what he learned later from Indian survivors and others, he had concluded that Custer's fame would "shine with unceasing splendor, while jealousy and prejudice" would be "surely relegated to oblivion." He came to understand "how the living could extol themselves for *prudence* [Reno] and *delay* [Benteen], and condemn the *dead* as *rash* and *impetuous* [Custer]; how authority, though inexperienced, sought to evade responsibility through the loophole of escape [Terry]."[34]

Certainly Libbie Custer deserved to hear the truth, and although she must have felt betrayed by the behavior of some of the officers, she was eventually reconciled to the manner in which her husband had died. His business was to make war and keep the peace, and the pursuit of that career entailed risks if one preferred action in the field to comfort in the corridors of power. Heroism and popular acclaim are not things to be counted on, no matter how intensely one might think about them and hope to conjure them. Many officers believed that there was no glory to be had in the Indian Wars. Although Custer had been hurt by President Grant in early 1876, there is no persuasive evidence that he wanted to do more than spend that summer in the field and make a good report. He may have had visions of great success, but realizing that significant victories had rarely occurred against the Plains Indians especially, he must have been content to know that Generals Sheridan and Terry wanted him to lead the regiment.

To suggest that Custer had some grand designs for after this campaign is nonsense. In her last letter to her husband, Libbie hinted that the subject of employment after the army had been discussed within the family circle, as it must have been in 1866 and 1867 and maybe in 1870. She wished his career interests had fallen along literary lines, then added: "I wouldn't have you anything but a soldier." The prospects for job possibilities outside the military were pedestrian in nature, not the glamorous alternatives imagined by some.[35]

But this book is an analysis of the conflicting evidence relative to the Battle of the Little Bighorn, and a recounting of the essential facts and reasonable assumptions is the best test of Custer's style, skills, and intentions.

For the column assigned to find the Sioux, that summer's operations had begun late and in some chaos. Besides the leadership question, finally resolved in Custer's favor, there were too few horses for all of the Seventh, either at Fort Lincoln or at the Powder River depot, resulting in the absence of a hundred soldiers, many of them veterans—though in the context of the small number of cavalry expeditions conducted in any soldier's five-year hitch and the even rarer hostile encounters with Indians, there were few real "war veterans" with Custer.

Additionally, the regiment was burdened with a large mule train, the management of which was not at all familiar to the men. By the time Custer's command departed the mouth of the Rosebud, the troopers of the Seventh had been on a hard march over hellish terrain for nearly a month, and all, particularly the soldiers of the right wing, were as tired as men— and mounts—got on any extended scout. With orders in hand to pursue the Indians according to his own discretion, Custer pushed the column up the Rosebud in accordance with the strictures of cavalry doctrine: twelve miles, then twenty, then thirty, still with the prospect that the men would have to eat horse or mule flesh before the chase was done. Two days away from Terry, Custer's pursuit encountered the converging trails of the primary Indian encampment and the splinter groups in the process of joining the great summer festival.

Therefore, except for the mule train and the fact that the Seventh Cavalry was acting as a unified regiment for the first time since its creation, this was a typical excursion conducted in a highly military manner, up to the point when Custer made his second trip to the Crow's Nest. Of course he knew that the main Indian village lay beyond the bluffs guarding the Little Bighorn River. But even more important, he could not miss the dozen or so Sans Arc lodges eight miles and two hours' riding time from the Divide that separated the Rosebud and Little Bighorn Valleys.

The evidence is indisputable that such a satellite village existed and, further, that it contained Sans Arc inhabitants fixed in place by the obligation to mourn the death of a warrior in the Crook fight. Custer's subsequent disposition of forces confirms that this small camp was his first military objective. Possibly remembrances of the Washita battle flitted through Custer's mind. The potential psychological ramifications here offered many tempting parallels to the earlier fight. If he could overwhelm one comparatively undersized portion of a larger conglomerate, he might not only achieve significant physical damage (lodges and other possessions burned, ponies slaughtered, warriors killed) but also so unnerve the rest of the Indians that they might scatter or parley, either of which would allow Custer to claim victory.

Attendant to such a plan was the idea that some number of prisoners—noncombatants in particular—might be taken. The Indians feared that prospect to such a degree that in retrospect they would in their oral histories assign that intention to Custer all the way to Last Stand Hill, when it was far beyond his power to accomplish such a feat and far beyond their power to see into his mind. Perhaps the Sans Arcs' memories fed the amorphous tales, passed from generation to generation, that Custer meant to snatch women and children, cramping if not crippling the ability of warriors to act.

On the verge of starting his assault against that Sans Arc village, Custer organized his forces into two wings on the basis of officer seniority, not favoritism. His organization of the regiment was impersonal and trusting and elastic enough to accommodate a variety of scenarios. He detailed experienced men out of his own wing to accompany the pack train, since only those troopers had been exposed to the rigors of managing the mules on an extended scout into hostile territory. For at least the first phase of his operations, his tactical intelligence was adequate, if not complete. All that remained was for Custer to point his forces in the right direction and to send them forth with clearly articulated orders.

The problem with trying to ascertain the directions that Custer furnished his subordinates is that both Reno and Benteen were inveterate liars. Additionally, Custer probably did not say more than was necessary, leaving much to the discretion of his primary officers, as General Sheridan had done, as General Terry had done, as field commanders in many wars had done and would again. In this kind of unconventional warfare, individual initiative and imagination would be crucial. What we know for sure is that four times between crossing the Divide and reaching the Little Bighorn, Reno was told to take the advance and to engage the enemy. Twice Custer gave the orders directly to Reno, and twice Adjutant Cooke delivered the instructions. The first order could have pertained only to the Lone Tepee; the other three related to the second phase of Custer's battle plan, with two orders involving pursuit of the Sans Arcs and with the last instruction, delivered by Cooke, directing Reno to cross the river and indicating eventual participation by Benteen as a reserve force supporting either Custer or Reno, depending on circumstances. At that point, Reno surely knew that Custer would not be following him.

As for Benteen, we have only his word as to what the messengers from Custer said while the illustrious captain was engaged in his self-proclaimed valley hunting. However, according to Lieutenant Winfield Edgerly's testimony, Benteen had knowledge of the Lone Tepee plan, and we can reasonably surmise that the follow-up orders must have pertained to his role as a component of Reno's wing and as the left-flank shield for the general attack. The first of those messages must have been meant to ensure that Benteen went far enough to the southwest to get opposite the objective, whereas the second perhaps provided amplification on what he was to do once he got in position. In retrospect, and without witnesses to the content of the orders, Benteen would be able to compress them into meaningless mush about an endless and pointless reconnaissance that might have taken him to the Pacific Ocean except for his prescience and manly willingness to risk insubordination.

But Custer's Lone Tepee gambit failed. Its meaning within the general's total scheme has been obliterated partly because Reno and Benteen could not admit that their commander ever had a plan and mostly for everyone else because the inconsequential first phase was subsumed within the larger drama, the consciousness-numbing Battle of the Little Bighorn proper, the end of Custer at Last Stand Hill. The obsession with his final words or thoughts masks his purpose at the outset, which from an army point of view might well have been adjudged as skilled and from the Indian perspective as considerate for a white man at war with them. The beginning of the denouement occurred at the Lone Tepee, when Custer finally and irretrievably surrendered command and control of his several independent commanders and, therefore, of events.

Thunder was not enough if there was no lightning. When Reno's charge down the valley of the Little Bighorn collapsed, the game was up. Gray horse phantoms and noisy bugle songs were thereafter not nearly adequate to spook true warriors. The entire plan had depended on the employment of disparate components not in precise array but in separate waves, like tornado after hurricane, large winds from several directions. The Indians felt those winds. They said so. But when Reno left Custer, he lost the little bit of courage he possessed naturally. Aware of Custer's march on the other side of the river, Reno must have experienced an awful aloneness, magnified by regular quaffs from his liquor container. Of course Reno should have held in the timber, and of course he was a coward for vanishing into the woods before any part of his command and then—having suffered few losses—for rushing out without proper attention to the formation of his battalion and without making any provision for covering its retirement from the field.

Benteen, for his part, was full of prickles and was a mean man when his pride and vanity were tweaked. The idea of being relegated to a reserve role annoyed him—it always had and always would. By his own admission he knew that he was to hurry back to the main trail after his mission to the left. Additionally, he failed to respond promptly to the sound of firing in what he acknowledged was a combat situation, and he played cute with messages that, no matter the ancillary chitchat, ought to have spurred him forward with the mules carrying ammunition.

Facing Captain Benteen at the court of inquiry, Recorder Lee wondered whether Custer could have escaped as Reno had, whether he could have "fled the field with the remnant of his command." Benteen replied, "I think discretion would have been the better part of valor had he done that."[36] Lee posed a similar question to Lieutenant Edgerly, asking whether Custer "could have fled the field with a portion of his command by abandoning the others to their fate." Edgerly answered quite simply: "I believe he fought very desperately."[37]

Indeed, Custer had conducted the campaign by the book, in accordance with the army's nine "principles of war." Once he had elected to go on the offensive (the only real way to win a battle), he developed a simple plan for attacking a clear objective. When that attack failed to achieve the objective, he was obliged to pursue the enemy, using his own wing as the "mass" (or decisive element) in support of Reno's limited assault ("economy of force"). Whether or not one believes that Custer's intelligence before the fact was sufficient, what he knew (or felt) enabled him to achieve complete surprise, as indicated in Sioux and Cheyenne testimony. His deployment of forces ensured a high degree of security (especially for invaluable supplies) if all subordinates performed as expected. Even in unconventional warfare, and even with the disparity in the sizes of the competing forces, he was nearly successful in applying the "principles" that he (the poor student) had learned well enough.[38]

For most people, the easy course would have been to leave the field in the face of overwhelming numbers of the enemy. And yet for Custer, this was a course he could not choose. He was the kind of soldier who despised retreat, who possessed an overweening confidence in his ability as a military leader, and who trusted too much to good fortune. But beyond that, in this instance, he exhibited what General Sheridan rightly called a "super-abundance of courage," and he performed an act so heroic that it truly has few parallels in the annuls of any people's history of war, for good causes or bad.

Of course, this was always a story about more than Custer. It was a story about the Seventh Cavalry, full to the brim with human fallibility, maybe no better than the other regiments active on the western frontier. It was the story of capable officers, those dead like Tom Custer and Yates and Calhoun and those living like Weir and French and Varnum, who opted for the hard duty instead of the soft assignments out of harm's way. It was the story of stalwart scouts, white and Indian. It was the story of the enlisted men, who improvised their own escapes from the Reno battlefield, who held their ground to an astonishing degree with Custer's wing, and who endured a twenty-four-hour siege under nearly constant harassment. And last, but certainly not least, it was the story of the Sioux and Cheyenne warriors who won the battle, not just because some of the soldiers happened to fail but because the Indian fighters were able to use their advantages to the fullest extent of their considerable ability. In their testimony, these Indians confirmed the efficacy of Custer's battle plan, condemned the weakling Reno, and praised the courage of the soldiers during the final phases of the fight.

There must have been a moment when Custer, realizing that Reno had gone and Benteen might not come, touched the bottom of despair. With his brothers, his brother-in-law, his friends, and his command in tow, the rapidly aging "boy general" decided in favor of the men he could not see, took his chances on behalf of the whole regiment, and selected—in full possession of his faculties—the road to living hell. His was a cruel choice for the young men and old who rode with him, but with all of the facts available to them, they might have understood their commander's uncommonly unselfish act. The shame was that President Grant, General Sherman, and General Sheridan—stout fighters in their own right, in their own prime, in their own war—could not begin to comprehend that honorable exit.

"The more I see of movements here the more admiration I have for Custer," Colonel Nelson Miles wrote from the field to his wife several months after the Battle of the Little Bighorn, "and I am satisfied his like will not be found very soon again."[39]

NOTES

CHAPTER 1. A DIRTY LITTLE WAR

1. Josephy, "Indian Policy," 36. Actually, in 1871 Congress passed legislation that ended further treaty-making with the Indians, although existing treaties were still considered binding.

2. Sherman to Libbie Custer, 24 June 1889, Elizabeth Bacon (E. B.) Custer Collection, Little Bighorn Battlefield National Monument (LBBNM). Custer quoted in Henry B. Carrington to Cyrus Townsend Brady, 25 September 1904, published in Brady, *The Sioux Indian Wars*, 387.

3. For a description of the Sioux confederacy and its separate tribes, see Utley, *The Lance and the Shield*, especially 3–4.

4. McDermott, "Custer and the Little Bighorn Story," 96–97; Utley, *Frontier Regulars*, 15, 22.

5. McFeely, *Grant*, 248; Wooster, *The Military and United States Indian Policy*, 14.

6. Wooster, *The Military and United States Indian Policy*, 71–72.

7. Apparently the first use of "Manifest Destiny" was in 1845, by John Louis O'Sullivan, who wrote: "Our manifest destiny is to overspread the continent allotted by Providence for the free development of our yearly multiplying millions." Bartlett, *Familiar Quotations*, 552.

8. The description of the army enlisted man is from the *New York Sun*, quoted in Morris, *Sheridan*, 301; see also Utley, *Frontier Regulars*, 22.

9. The standard biography for Custer remains Jay Monaghan, *Custer: The Life of General George Armstrong Custer* (1959), although a tightly constructed and superbly written work is Robert M. Utley, *Cavalier in Buckskin: George Armstrong Custer and the Western Military Frontier* (1988). Two other Custer biographies are Jeffry D. Wert, *The Controversial Life of George Armstrong Custer* (1996), and Louise

Barnett, *Touched by Fire: The Life, Death, and Mythic Afterlife of George Armstrong Custer* (1996). Unless otherwise indicated, the broad facts pertinent to events in Custer's life are drawn from these volumes.

10. Merington, *The Custer Story*, 95.

11. Sherman to Libbie Custer, 24 June 1889, E. B. Custer Collection, LBBNM. As indicated, Custer's regular army rank was lieutenant colonel, but he is addressed as "general" throughout this book in recognition of his brevet rank of major general (a military courtesy) and in accordance with the usual understanding of his grade.

12. Utley, *Frontier Regulars*, 133.

13. For a full treatment of the Battle of the Washita, see Hoig, *The Battle of the Washita*.

14. Utley, *Frontier Regulars*, 135–36; Josephy, "Indian Policy," 32–33.

15. McFeely, *Grant*, 308–9.

16. Ibid., 311.

17. A sampling of Custer's delinquent behavior and demerits can be found in Connell, *Son of the Morning Star*, 107–8. Besides throwing stones and snowballs, Custer kept cooking utensils in his room, was frequently late, participated in food fights, made a "boisterous noise" in the sink, appeared unmilitary (his hair and beard were too long), and repeatedly swung his arms while marching.

18. McFeely, *Grant*, 316; Morris, *Sheridan*, 346; Utley, *Frontier Regulars*, 196; Flores, "The Great Contraction," 13–18.

19. Quoted in Morris, *Sheridan*, 309.

20. Quoted in Willert, "Does Anomaly Contain Sturgis's Body?" 12.

21. G. A. Custer, *My Life on the Plains*, 22.

22. Nichols, *Reno Court of Inquiry*, 65. The testimony cited herein has been taken from the Nichols volume, which is based on the official transcript of the proceedings as kept by the court stenographer, who himself depended to a large extent on the accounts published in the *Chicago Times*. For a discussion of the versions of the inquiry record, see Liddic, Mercatante, and Bookwalter, "Reno Court of Inquiry."

23. Whittaker, *A Complete Life of General George A. Custer*.

24. Whittaker to the *New York Sun*, 26 February 1879, reprinted in Graham, *The Custer Myth*, 327.

25. A vivid account of Reno's difficulties is contained in Connell, *Son of the Morning Star*, 42–46. For a defense of Reno, see Magnussen, *Peter Thompson's Narrative*, 304–5.

26. Utley, *The Reno Court of Inquiry*, 139.

27. Ibid., 8.

28. Graham, *The Custer Myth*, 308–9, 336–37.

29. Edward S. Godfrey to Robert G. Carter, 14 April 1925, published in ibid., 318–19.

30. Utley, *The Reno Court of Inquiry,* 139.

31. Varnum to Camp, 14 April 1909, Walter Mason Camp Collection, Brigham Young University (BYU). In this letter, Varnum explicitly stated that Wallace "was acting engineering officer and was riding with Custer." The texts of the two memoirs are contained in Carroll, *Custer's Chief of Scouts,* 64–65, 89.

32. Ghent, "Varnum, Reno, and the Little Big Horn." In this article, Ghent makes a good but incomplete case against Wallace.

33. Carroll, *The Benteen-Goldin Letters,* 198, 207, 212, 233.

34. Whittaker to the *New York Sun* in Graham, *The Custer Myth,* 329; and Ghent, "Varnum, Reno, and the Little Big Horn."

35. Camp interview of Frederick Gerard, 1909, published in Hammer, *Custer in '76,* 237–39.

36. Benteen to Robert Price, 6 March 1879, published in Graham, *The Custer Myth,* 325–26.

CHAPTER 2. NATURAL ENEMIES

1. Davis and Davis, *The Reno Court of Inquiry,* 83, 91.

2. Carroll, *The Benteen-Goldin Letters,* 247; Carroll, *Barry Correspondence,* 41.

3. Attorney John Bulkley quoted in Frost, *Custer Legends,* 103.

4. E. S. Godfrey quoted in Dippie, "Custer," 109.

5. Whittaker, *A Complete Life of General George A. Custer,* 632–34.

6. Utley, *The Reno Court of Inquiry,* 139.

7. Carroll, *The Benteen-Goldin Letters,* 196.

8. Connell, *Son of the Morning Star,* 34–39; Hammer, *Men with Custer,* 21–22.

9. Carroll, *The Benteen-Goldin Letters,* 196–97.

10. Connell, *Son of the Morning Star,* 33.

11. Carroll, *Barry Correspondence,* 34, 46. Custer did pay Benteen one dollar in interest.

12. Carroll, *The Benteen-Goldin Letters,* 209, 219.

13. Godfrey, "Some Reminiscences," 159.

14. Carroll, *The Benteen-Goldin Letters,* 252, 259.

15. G. A. Custer, *My Life on the Plains,* 183.

16. *Cavalry Tactics,* 457. As a "general rule," the manual prescribed sorting horses by color.

17. Carroll, *The Benteen-Goldin Letters,* 264.

18. General Orders, 22 November 1868, E. B. Custer Collection, LBBNM.

19. Godfrey, "Some Reminiscences," 168–77.

20. Ibid.

21. Ibid.; Utley, *Life in Custer's Cavalry,* 224.

22. Carroll, *The Benteen-Goldin Letters,* 252.

23. Godfrey, "Some Reminiscences," 174.

24. Hoig, *Battle of the Washita*, 133.

25. Godfrey, "Some Reminiscences," 174.

26. Ryan to W. A. Falconer, 15 April 1922, E. B. Custer Collection, LBBNM.

27. Carroll, *The Benteen-Goldin Letters*, 252.

28. Published in *New York Times*, 14 February 1869, and reprinted in Graham, *The Custer Myth*, 212–13.

29. Carroll, *The Benteen-Goldin Letters*, 238, 280–81.

30. Carroll, *Barry Correspondence*, 42.

31. G. A. Custer, *My Life on the Plains*, 261, 266–67.

32. Ibid., 267.

33. Ibid., 271.

34. Carroll, *The Benteen-Goldin Letters*, 216–17.

35. Benteen to the *Army and Navy Journal*, 6 January 1877, published in vol. 14, no. 24 (20 January 1877); Carroll, *Barry Correspondence*, 36.

36. Carroll, *The Benteen-Goldin Letters*, 206, 294.

37. E. B. Custer, *Boots and Saddles*, 114, 125, 257; Merington, *The Custer Story*, 304.

38. Merington, *The Custer Story*, 262.

39. Carroll, *Barry Correspondence*, 46.

40. Carroll, *The Benteen-Goldin Letters*, 267–70.

41. Ibid.

42. Camp interview of Thompson, 1911, published in Hammer, *Custer in '76*, 247.

43. Carroll, *The Benteen-Goldin Letters*, 200–204, 213–14, 230–31, 234, 270, 275.

44. Ibid., 229.

45. Carroll, *Barry Correspondence*, 30; Carroll, *The Benteen-Goldin Letters*, 258, 262.

46. Carroll, *Barry Correspondence*, 35, 40, 48; Carroll, *The Benteen-Goldin Letters*, 199, 295.

CHAPTER 3. AS FAMILIES GO

1. Carroll, *The Benteen-Goldin Letters*, 272.

2. Ibid., 221.

3. Merington, *The Custer Story*, 193.

4. Ibid.

5. Monaghan, *Custer*, 61.

6. Fougera, *With Custer's Cavalry*, 162, 179.

7. Utley, *Cavalier in Buckskin*, 130; Wert, *Controversial Life*, 311; Fougera, *With Custer's Cavalry*, 67–68.

8. E. B. Custer, *Boots and Saddles*, 143, 181.

9. Wert, *Controversial Life*, 34, 287–88. Also see G. A. Custer, *My Life on the Plains*, 253, and Bighead, "Custer's Last Battle," 364, 376–77. No one has made a persuasive case that Custer had illicit affairs in the West or elsewhere. Indeed, even Benteen (the sole source for many of the stories) dealt only in rumors, which ought to have been corroborated somewhere in the correspondence or memoirs of so-called enemies. Even in Cheyenne histories, the story of Custer's alleged liaison with Monahsetah is written off as a "tale." The myth that Custer was a "well-known womanizer" ought to have been debunked by now, but it persists.

10. E. B. Custer, *Boots and Saddles*, 275–76; Merington, *The Custer Story*, 303–4.

11. The locations and assignments of Seventh Cavalry officers at the time of the expedition can be found in Hammer, *Men with Custer*.

12. Utley, *Cavalier in Buckskin*, 151–53; McFeely, *Grant*, 428–36.

13. Terry to Custer, 16 March 1876, E. B. Custer Collection, LBBNM.

14. E. B. Custer, *Boots and Saddles*, 193.

15. Merington, *The Custer Story*, 236–37.

16. Whittaker, *A Complete Life of General George A. Custer*, 596; Fougera, *With Custer's Cavalry*, 273; Merington, *The Custer Story*, 236.

17. Fougera, *With Custer's Cavalry*, 76, 273.

18. Utley, *Life in Custer's Cavalry*, 275–76. "Troop" and "company" are equivalent terms used interchangeably in this book, even though the army did not officially adopt "troop" for the cavalry company until 1883. Soldiers used "troop" long before it was accepted in the military manuals, so that like the coloring of horses, the practice predated the policy by many years. In addition, my employment of both "troop" and "company" avoids a certain monotony of expression. See Utley, *Frontier Regulars*, 36 n.

19. Connell, *Son of the Morning Star*, 289.

20. McCulloch, "Canadian Who Died at Custer's Last Stand."

21. Utley, *Life in Custer's Cavalry*, 280.

22. Utley, *Cavalier in Buckskin*, 108; Camp interview of Mathey, 1910, Camp Collection, BYU; Utley, *Life in Custer's Cavalry*, 91, 196.

23. Carroll, *Custer's Chief of Scouts*, 24.

24. Merington, *The Custer Story*, 236; Utley, *Life in Custer's Cavalry*, 264–65.

25. Fougera, *With Custer's Cavalry*, 256; Ryan to Libbie, 17 March 1908, E. B. Custer Collection, LBBNM. Ryan said that the only sword carried beyond the Powder River Base Camp belonged to Lieutenant Mathey and that it was rolled up in a bundle of blankets on a pack mule. However, Lieutenant DeRudio claimed that he was the only officer who took a saber on the expedition. See Camp interview of DeRudio, 1910, published in Hammer, *Custer in '76*, 87. Perhaps other officers also ignored orders to leave their sabers behind.

26. Carroll, *The Benteen-Goldin Letters*, 199.

27. Fougera, *With Custer's Cavalry*, 254.

28. Meyer, "Tracking a Custer Indian Fighter."

29. Ibid.; Graham, *The Custer Myth*, 341–42.

30. Utley, *Life in Custer's Cavalry*, 158, 260–61.

31. Merington, *The Custer Story*, 275.

32. Fougera, *With Custer's Cavalry*, 74–75. Also see Willert, "The Wedding Ring of Lieutenant Donald McIntosh," 2–11.

33. Merington, *The Custer Story*, 309.

34. Fougera, *With Custer's Cavalry*, 70.

35. Carroll, *Custer's Chief of Scouts*, 22–23.

36. Whittaker, *A Complete Life of General George A. Custer*, 606.

37. Utley, *The Reno Court of Inquiry*, 248.

38. Cecil, "Lt. Crittenden," 30–36.

39. Marquis, "Pioneer Woman." The recollections are those of Edith Manley, the daughter of Second Lieutenant J. A. Manley of the Twentieth Infantry.

40. Sturgis to Custer, 16 July 1875, E. B. Custer Collection, LBBNM; Fougera, *With Custer's Cavalry*, 233–34.

41. Sturgis to *Army and Navy Journal* 13, no. 50 (14 July 1876): 806.

42. Stewart, *Custer's Luck*, 137–38; Heski, "The Trail to Heart River," 22–30; Koury, *Diaries of the Little Big Horn*, 20.

43. Hunt and Hunt, *I Fought with Custer*, 50.

44. Barnett, *Touched by Fire*, 318.

45. Woodruff to Camp, 15 February 1910, Camp Collection, BYU.

46. Hammer, *Custer in '76*, 83.

47. Carroll, *Barry Correspondence*, 50–51.

48. Merington, *The Custer Story*, 262; Utley, *Cavalier in Buckskin*, 46.

49. Josephy, "Indian Policy," 38; Morris, *Sheridan*, 355.

50. Morris, *Sheridan*, 356–57.

51. Marquis, "Pioneer Woman."

52. Merington, *The Custer Story*, 310.

CHAPTER 4. MEN AND BOYS

1. Nevin, *The Soldiers*, 78; Nichols, *Reno Court of Inquiry*, 358. In the latter reference, Sergeant Edward Davern indicated that the term "striker" for body servant was still in use in 1876.

2. Hunt and Hunt, *I Fought with Custer*, 57. Information on the relationship between Burkman and Custer (based on talks between Burkman and I. D. "Bud" O'Donnell) can be found in Wagner, *Old Neutriment*.

3. *Army and Navy Journal* 14, no. 3 (26 August 1876): 47; Utley, *Frontier Regulars*, 23, 84–85. 91; Nevin, *The Soldiers*, 68–69.

4. Nevin, *The Soldiers*, 72.

5. Hammer, *Men with Custer*, 209. The previous occupations of the enlisted men were also derived from this book.

6. Waldo, "Pioneer Cavalryman Saved"; Kelly, "Death of Early-Day Indian Fighter." Both articles are from the Custer Scrapbooks, the Billings Public Library.

7. Heski, "The Trail to Heart River," 22–30. See especially page 27 for the illustration done by Thomas Marquis based on Edward Godfrey's notes. For Terry's diary comments on Custer's overeagerness, see Koury, *Diaries of the Little Big Horn*, 4.

8. Sergeant Ryan and Private Peter Thompson quoted in Heski, "The Trail to Heart River," 28.

9. Wagner, *Old Neutriment*. 123.

10. Kellogg, "Diary, 1876," 213–22; Heski, "'Digging' and 'Picking' to the Powder River"; Stewart, *Custer's Luck*, 220–22.

11. Cooke, *Cavalry Tactics*, 39. Although this definition was not picked up in the *Cavalry Tactics* of 1874, the term was clearly still in use in 1876. For example, see Benteen's assertion that when Custer returned to Fort Lincoln in the spring of 1876, he changed the organization of the regiment from four battalions to two wings, the right commanded by Reno and the left by Benteen. Carroll, *The Benteen-Goldin Letters*, 281–82.

12. There can be little doubt that Tom Custer was serving as his brothers aide-de-camp. Sergeant Richard Hanley of Company C said that during the Reno scout, Lieutenant Harrington commanded that troop. Camp interview of Hanley, 1910, published in Hammer, *Custer in '76*, 128. Also see Nichols, *Reno Court of Inquiry*, 132.

13. Camp interviews with Edgerly, undated, and McGuire, undated, published in Hammer, *Custer in '76*, 53, 123.

14. Utley, *Cavalier in Buckskin*, 170.

15. Stewart, *Custer's Luck*, 228–29.

16. Goldin, "On the Little Big Horn," 101.

17. Utley, *Cavalier in Buckskin*, 173.

18. Camp interview with Wilber, undated, reprinted in Hammer, *Custer in '76*, 149.

19. Field Order, 14 June 1876, E. B. Custer Collection, LBBNM.

20. Utley, *Frontier Regulars*, 88.

21. Sturgis to Custer, 16 July 1875, E. B. Custer Collection, LBBNM.

22. C. H. Axtell to Libbie, 13 July 1914, E. B. Custer Collection, LBBNM.

23. Merington, *The Custer Story*, 262–63, 267; Waldo, "Pioneer Cavalryman Saved."

24. *Cavalry Tactics*, 457–78. The purchase, training, and treatment of horses is prescribed in excruciating detail. One of the "rules" stated: "After a horse has been assigned, his rider will not exchange him, nor allow him to be used by any other person, without the permission of the captain."

25. Overfield, *The Little Big Horn*, 23–24.

26. Frost, *Custer Legends*, 192–93, 200–201. For a lengthy and rather pointless discussion on the question of Custer's disobedience of orders, see Brady, *The Sioux Indian Wars*, 359–97. The affidavit of Mary Adams (Custer's servant) has been modified in format here only to emphasize the words of the speakers.

27. Stewart, *Custer's Luck*, 241.

28. Overfield, *The Little Big Horn*, 28, 37–38, 83.

29. Stewart, *Custer's Luck*, 242.

30. Hammer, *Custer in '76*, 53.

31. Godfrey, "Custer's Last Battle," 272. This well-known account of the Little Bighorn fight first appeared in *Century Magazine* (January 1892) and was modified to some extent by Godfrey over the years. The version reprinted in Hutton, *The Custer Reader*, is the most complete—see pages 230–31 for Hutton's brief explanation of the changes. The cost of the straw hats is from Reno's testimony in Nichols, *Reno Court of Inquiry*, 573.

32. In assessing the relative fighting strength of the companies, the actual numbers of enlisted men detailed to the pack train on the day of the Battle of the Little Bighorn are included. In this and all other places where numbers of soldiers are discussed, the totals derive from my arithmetic, based on the biographies contained in Hammer, *Men with Custer*.

33. Camp interview with George W. Glenn, 1914, published in Hammer, *Custer in '76*, 135. For an example of men who traded places, see Hammer, *Men with Custer*, 286, where Private Charles Schmidt (L Troop) supposedly obtained the horse of Private Michael Reagan (K Troop).

34. Varnum to his parents, 4 July 1876, and Ryan narrative as reported in the *Montana Tribune*, 1923, both reprinted in Graham, *The Custer Myth*, 240, 342.

35. Hammer, *Men with Custer*, 244, 145, 131–32.

36. Godfrey, "Custer's Last Battle," 273. As must have been the case with many other officers and men, Captain French made out his will before beginning the last campaign. He gave the will to young Lieutenant Jack Sturgis, whom French apparently admired very much, hoping that he himself "might fall and he [Sturgis] be spared." See Willert, "Does Anomaly Contain Sturgis's Body?" 15.

37. From *The Arikara Narrative*, reprinted in Graham, *The Custer Myth*, 30; Wagner, *Old Neutriment*, 137.

CHAPTER 5. HOW THEY LOOKED

1. Hunt and Hunt, *I Fought with Custer*, 53, 56.

2. Gallenne to Rev. Father Genin, 5 July 1876, published in Daniels and Davis, *That Fatal Day*, 17–18.

3. Brady, *The Sioux Indian Wars*, 223.

4. Varnum interview with Charles Bates, published in Carroll, *Custer's Chief of Scouts*, 24.

5. Hutchins, "The Cavalry Campaign Outfit," 319-35. Also see Hammer, *Custer in '76*, 92, and Carroll, *Custer in Periodicals*, 105.

6. Camp interview of George Glenn, 1914, published in Hammer, *Custer in '76*, 135; William E. Morris, unidentified newspaper clipping, published in Daniels and Davis, *That Fatal Day*, 28.

7. Camp interview with Burkman, 1911, and Thompson, 1909, Camp Collection, BYU. Also see Hutchins, "The Cavalry Campaign Outfit," 330.

8. Ellis, "A Survivor's Story," 7.

9. Kanipe to Camp, 4 August 1908, Camp Collection, BYU; Godfrey and Ryan descriptions in Graham, *The Custer Myth*, 345-47; Hutchins, "The Cavalry Campaign Outfit," 330.

10. Hutchins, "The Cavalry Campaign Outfit," 327-28; Godfrey in Graham, *The Custer Myth*, 345.

11. Godfrey, "Custer's Last Battle," 275; Goldin to E. A. Brininstool, 26 November 1928, Earl Alonzo Brininstool Collection, Brigham Young University (BYU).

12. Camp field notes, reprinted in Hammer, *Custer in '76*, 124; Ellis, "A Survivor's Story," 7; Nichols, *Reno Court of Inquiry*, 512; Godfrey, "Custer's Last Battle," 275.

13. *Cavalry Tactics*, 457, 477.

14. G. A. Custer, *My Life on the Plains*, 72.

15. Excerpts from Godfrey's diary in Koury, *Diaries of the Little Big Horn*, 9-10, and Godfrey, "Custer's Last Battle," 277-78.

16. Merington, *The Custer Story*, 310; Carroll, *The Benteen-Goldin Letters*, 177.

17. Merington, *The Custer Story*, 310.

18. Godfrey, "Custer's Last Battle," 277-78.

19. See Gray, *Custer's Last Campaign*, for a detailed discussion of Boyer's life.

20. Varnum to Camp, 14 April 1909, Camp Collection, BYU; Carroll, *Custer's Chief of Scouts*, 59-60, 80.

21. Wagner, *Old Neutriment*, 134, 141.

22. Camp field notes, published in Hammer, *Custer in '76*, 224 n.

23. Carroll, *The Benteen-Goldin Letters*, 177, 180; Camp interview of Rooney, undated, Camp Collection, BYU; Camp interview of Edward G. Mathey, 1910, published in Hammer, *Custer in '76*, 78-79.

24. Carroll, *The Benteen-Goldin Letters*, 162.

25. Godfrey, "Custer's Last Battle," 275.

26. Mathey in Hammer, *Custer in '76*, 78-79; Kipp to Camp, 1 December 1921, Camp Collection, BYU.

27. Carroll, *The Benteen-Goldin Letters*, 163-64, 177-79.

28. Godfrey, "Custer's Last Battle," 278; Camp interview of Herendeen, undated, Camp Collection, BYU.

29. Utley, *Cavalier in Buckskin*, 177–79.

30. Camp interviews of Gerard, 1909, published in Hammer, *Custer in '76*, 230; Carroll, *Custer's Chief of Scouts*, 85–86.

31. Carroll, *The Benteen-Goldin Letters*, 179.

32. Mathey in Hammer, *Custer in '76*, 78.

33. Godfrey, "Custer's Last Battle," 279.

34. Camp interview of DeRudio, 1910, published in Hammer, *Custer in '76*, 83; interview of White Man Runs Him, 1919, in Graham, *The Custer Myth*, 21; Carroll, *The Benteen-Goldin Letters*, 165.

35. Carroll, *The Benteen-Goldin Letters*, 165; Godfrey, "Custer's Last Battle," 279.

36. Annie Yates quoted in Wert, *Controversial Life*, 293.

37. E. B. Custer, *Boots and Saddles*, 270–71, 275.

38. Godfrey, "Custer's Last Battle," 279; C. A. Woodruff to Brady, 3 May 1904, reprinted in Brady, *The Sioux Indian Wars*, 381.

39. Carroll, *The Benteen-Goldin Letters*, 179; Godfrey, "Custer's Last Battle," 279.

40. Carroll, *Custer's Chief of Scouts*, 60–61, 86–87.

41. Carroll, *The Benteen-Goldin Letters*, 180; DeRudio in Hammer, *Custer in '76*, 83.

42. Gerard testimony in Nichols, *Reno Court of Inquiry*, 85.

43. McGuire interview in Hammer, *Custer in '76*, 124; Private Patrick Corcoran to Camp, 4 April 1910, Camp Collection, BYU.

44. Barnard, *Custer's First Sergeant*, 174; Goldin article in Carroll, *Custer in Periodicals*, 106.

45. Varnum to Camp, 14 April 1909, published in Hammer, *Custer in '76*, 60 n; Carroll, *Custer's Chief of Scouts*, 62–63, 87–88.

46. Varnum to Camp, 14 April 1909, published in Hammer, *Custer in '76*, 60 n; Carroll, *Custer's Chief of Scouts*, 62–63, 87–88; Red Star narrative in Graham, *The Custer Myth*, 31–33.

47. Varnum to Camp, 14 April 1909, published in Hammer, *Custer in '76*, 60–61 n; Carroll, *Custer's Chief of Scouts*, 62–63, 87–88.

48. Varnum to Camp, 14 April 1909, published in Hammer, *Custer in '76*, 60–61 n; Carroll, *Custer's Chief of Scouts*, 62–63, 87–88.

49. Red Star in Graham, *The Custer Myth*, 32–33.

50. Carroll, *The Benteen-Goldin Letters*, 180.

51. Varnum letter in Hammer, *Custer in '76*, 61 n; Gerard testimony in Nichols, *Reno Court of Inquiry*, 108.

52. Camp interview of Private James Rooney (F Troop), undated, Camp Collection, BYU.

53. Ryan narrative in Graham, *The Custer Myth*, 241; Goldin quoted in Hammer, *Men with Custer*, 228; Godfrey to Libbie, 6 July 1922, E. B. Custer Collection, LBBNM.

54. Gray, *Custer's Last Campaign*, 237, 241.

55. Monaghan, *Custer*, 70–71.

56. Camp interview of Varnum, undated, Camp Collection, BYU.

57. Carroll, *Custer's Chief of Scouts*, 64, 88.

58. Nichols, *Reno Court of Inquiry*, 134.

59. Ibid., 132.

60. Carroll, *The Benteen-Goldin Letters*, 181.

61. DeRudio in Hammer, *Custer in '76*, 84.

62. Camp interview of Hare, 1910, in ibid., 64.

63. Red Star in Graham, *The Custer Myth*, 33.

64. Camp interview of Varnum, undated, Camp Collection, BYU; Camp interview of Hairy Moccasin, 1911, published in Hammer, *Custer in '76*, 176.

65. Kanipe, "Account of the Little Big Horn Fight," 279.

66. Red Star in Graham, *The Custer Myth*, 33.

67. Roe, "The Custer Massacre," 2.

68. Koury, *Diaries of the Little Big Horn*, 10.

69. Hammer, *Custer in '76*, 84.

70. Donoughue to *Bismarck Daily Tribune*, 17 January 1888, reprinted in Daniels and Davis, *That Fatal Day*, 21.

71. Godfrey diary in Koury, *Diaries of the Little Big Horn*, 10; Carroll, *The Benteen-Goldin Letters*, 181.

72. Newell narrative published in O'Neil, *Sagas of the Greasy Grass*, 26–27.

73. Ryan narrative in Graham, *The Custer Myth*, 241.

74. Hammer, *Custer in '76*, 231.

75. Ibid., 221; Varnum to Camp, 5 May 1909, Camp Collection, BYU.

76. G. A. Custer, *My Life on the Plains*, 327, 363–75.

CHAPTER 6. WHAT THEY SAW

1. Carroll, *The Benteen-Goldin Letters*, 154, 167, 182.

2. Nichols, *Reno Court of Inquiry*, 439.

3. The impetus for my thinking in terms of officer seniority as the basis for wing and battalion responsibilities was Clark, "Seventh U.S. Cavalry Command and Control System, 25 June 1876."

4. Utley, *Cavalier in Buckskin*, 31.

5. Hammer, *Custer in '76*, 63.

6. Nichols, *Reno Court of Inquiry*, 585.

7. Brady, *The Sioux Indian Wars*, 232.

8. Ibid. Brady obtained this information from unspecified "official" sources, but even without identification, many officers in the Seventh would not have wanted Reno to command any part of the regiment.

9. Again, the location and duties of enlisted men relative to the pack train are derived from Hammer, *Men with Custer*.

10. Nichols, *Reno Court of Inquiry*, 528.

11. Stanislas Roy to Camp, 17 March 1909, Camp Collection, BYU; James Court to the author, 6 May 1997. Court, who conducts regular tours through the Bighorn country, said: "There are numerous shallow depressions between the Divide marker and Reno (Ash) Creek, any of which could hide the whole force."

12. E. B. Custer, *Boots and Saddles*, 116.

13. Hunt and Hunt, *I Fought with Custer*, 76.

14. Nichols, *Reno Court of Inquiry*, 560.

15. Overfield, *The Little Big Horn*, 43.

16. Nichols, *Reno Court of Inquiry*, 439, 464.

17. Cooke, *Cavalry Tactics*, 42.

18. Carroll, *Barry Correspondence*, 33.

19. Nichols, *Reno Court of Inquiry*, 457.

20. Carroll, *Barry Correspondence*, 33.

21. Nichols, *Reno Court of Inquiry*, 326.

22. Ryan to Camp, 17 December 1908, Camp Collection, BYU.

23. Hammer, *Custer in '76*, 231. In these 1909 interviews with Camp, Fred Gerard said that soon after passing the Divide, Kellogg asked to borrow spurs because he wanted to keep up with the scouts, even though Gerard suggested he drop back to the main column. Kellogg "replied that he was expecting interesting developments" and wanted to "report everything he could see out ahead." Although Custer had been cautioned not to take newspaper correspondents on the expedition, Terry must have been aware of Kellogg's presence, and in the overall scheme of things, having the media in attendance served the army's and the government's interests, if all went well. A reporter or two accompanied most large army operations, and General Crook took numerous correspondents on his expeditions.

24. Nichols, *Reno Court of Inquiry*, 528.

25. Mathey in Hammer, *Custer in '76*, 78.

26. Nichols, *Reno Court of Inquiry*, 512.

27. Camp interviews of Curley, 1908 and 1909, published in Hammer, *Custer in '76*, 156, 161. For another view on the location of the Lone Tepee, see Meketa and Bookwalter, *The Search for the Lone Tepee*, which concludes that the site was three and a half miles from the river, as opposed to my estimate (and that of Gray, *Custer's Last Campaign*) of four-plus miles.

28. From the June 1916 *Teepee Book*, reprinted in Graham, *The Custer Myth*, 24–25.

29. Ibid., 34.

30. Utley, *Cavalier in Buckskin*, 178–79; Utley, *The Lance and the Shield*, 139–42.

31. The Cheyenne American Horse told George B. Grinnell that two bodies from the Crook fight were left in lodges on Reno Creek. He noted that "the troops discovered these lodges and charged them" and that the Indian scouts saw this. Quoted in Hardorff, *Cheyenne Memories*, 24 n, 28, 152–53. Also see Feather Earring

statement in Graham, *The Custer Myth*, 98, and Camp interview of He Dog, 1910, published in Hammer, *Custer in '76*, 205. The usual mourning period was apparently four days; see Hardorff, *Lakota Recollections*, 100 n.

32. Kanipe answers to Camp questions, undated, Camp Collection, BYU. In one of his replies, Kanipe said that the only place horses of Custer's right wing were watered was "some distance above the burning tepee where we crossed Benteen's [Reno] Creek the last time, which put us on the side with the burning tepee." In this and other Kanipe testimony, there is a strong suggestion that Custer followed Reno for some distance before the right wing crossed to the north side of the creek.

33. Nichols, *Reno Court of Inquiry*, 403; Carroll, *The Benteen-Goldin Letters*, 182.

34. Carroll, *The Benteen-Goldin Letters*, 168, 183.

35. Camp interview of Roe, 1910, published in Hammer, *Custer in '76*, 249.

36. Kanipe story published in *Greensboro (N.C.) Daily Record* (27 April 1924) and reprinted in Graham, *The Custer Myth*, 248–49.

37. Kennedy statement given to Olin Wheeler in about 1900, published in Liddic and Harbaugh, *Camp on Custer*, 156.

38. Donoughue's narrative in Daniels and Davis, *That Fatal Day*, 21. In Hammer, *Men with Custer*, Donoughue is listed as a member of Company K (with Benteen), but from his detailed story touching on seemingly inconsequential incidents, it is obvious that he was serving in some capacity with Reno's battalion.

39. Gallenne account in Daniels and Davis, *That Fatal Day*, 17.

40. Graham, *The Custer Myth*, 289.

41. Hare interview in Hammer, *Custer in '76*, 64–65.

42. Young Hawk narrative in Graham, *The Custer Myth*, 34; Herendeen in Nichols, *Reno Court of Inquiry*, 262.

43. Newell narrative in O'Neil, *Sagas of the Greasy Grass*, 27.

44. Kanipe to Camp, 20 July 1908, Camp Collection, BYU; Magnussen, *Peter Thompson's Narrative*, 119.

45. Donoughue's narrative is in Daniels and Davis, *That Fatal Day*, 21.

46. G. A. Custer, *My Life on the Plains*, 249.

47. George Herendeen said that he and Boyer compared notes on Indians seen out in front as they were crossing the Divide. According to the timing, these sightings appeared to have been different from those Indians observed by Varnum and others from the Crow's Nest. See Camp interview of Herendeen, undated, published in Hammer, *Custer in '76*, 222.

48. Brininstool, *Troopers with Custer*, 129.

49. Herendeen statement published in the *New York Herald* (7 July 1876) and reprinted in Graham, *The Custer Myth*, 258.

50. Nichols, *Reno Court of Inquiry*, 311–12.

51. Gerard statement in *The Arikara Narrative*, reprinted in Graham, *The Custer Myth*, 251. Also see Charles Woodruff letter, 3 May 1904, and the Sioux Rain-in-the-Face's tale (originally published in *Outdoor Life* in 1903) of how Sitting Bull had the

"squaws" erect "empty death lodges" along the bend of the river to fool the soldiers, making them believe that the Indians "were but a handful." Both in Brady, *The Sioux Indian Wars*, 286, 383.

52. Reno to Thomas Rosser, 30 July 1876, published in the *New York Herald* (8 August 1876) and reprinted in Graham, *The Custer Myth*, 226.

CHAPTER 7. A FATAL SEPARATION

1. Nichols, *Reno Court of Inquiry*, 84–85.

2. Herendeen to *New York Herald*, 4 January 1878, reprinted in Graham, *The Custer Myth*, 263.

3. Nichols, *Reno Court of Inquiry*, 276.

4. Ibid., 112.

5. Magnussen, *Peter Thompson's Narrative*, 109.

6. Nichols, *Reno Court of Inquiry*, 560–61.

7. Arikara accounts in Graham, *The Custer Myth*, 31.

8. Camp interview of Hare, 1910, and Hare material mixed in with the 1911 interview of Herendeen, Camp Collection, BYU. In the 1910 interview, Hare said that the knoll was two hundred yards from the Lone Tepee, that from this high ground he saw forty or fifty Indians on a rise between that point and the river, that they were the same ones Sergeant Kanipe would later see, and that he (Hare) would see them again.

9. Nichols, *Reno Court of Inquiry*, 276.

10. Ibid., 139–40; Carroll, *Custer's Chief of Scouts*, 64.

11. Carroll, *Custer's Chief of Scouts*, 89.

12. Varnum to Camp, 14 April and 5 May 1909, Camp Collection, BYU.

13. Camp interview with Gerard, undated, Camp Collection, BYU. See also Camp interview of Strike Two, 1912, published in Hammer, *Custer in '76*, 183, and the Red Bear narrative in Graham, *The Custer Myth*, 39–40, for more on the episode with the Arikaras at the Lone Tepee. Camp interview of One Feather, 1911, in Liddic and Harbaugh, *Camp on Custer*, 128.

14. Nichols, *Reno Court of Inquiry*, 332, 360.

15. Ibid., 188, 199.

16. Kanipe account to Camp, 1908, published in Hammer, *Custer in '76*, 92–93; Kanipe to Camp, 20 July 1908, Camp Collection, BYU.

17. Nichols, *Reno Court of Inquiry*, 86, 251.

18. Hammer, *Custer in '76*, 65.

19. Hunt and Hunt, *I Fought with Custer*, 165. This manuscript was apparently published in *Americana Magazine* in March-April 1912. See the Fred Dustin bibliography in Graham, *The Custer Myth*, 390, including Dustin's conclusion that this was a "compilation by another hand" because it incorporated material from

Reno's official report (hardly surprising) and because it contained unspecified "palpable errors." Perhaps one of the errors that Dustin thought he detected was Reno's admission that he had spoken with Custer, an occurrence indicated in the testimony of Kanipe, Gerard, and Herendeen.

20. Carroll, *Custer's Chief of Scouts*, 64–65, 89; Varnum to Camp, 14 April 1909, Camp Collection, BYU.

21. Gray, *Custer's Last Campaign*, 278–79; Camp interview with Hairy Moccasin, 1911, published in Hammer, *Custer in '76*, 177, 222.

22. Nichols, *Reno Court of Inquiry*, 312.

23. Morris to Brady, 21 September 1904, published in Brady, *The Sioux Indian Wars*, 402.

24. Kanipe account in Graham, *The Custer Myth*, 249, and in Hammer, *Custer in '76*, 92–93. See Gray, *Custer's Last Campaign*, 271, for emphasis on two Sans Arc young men who provided warning to the main village.

25. Nichols, *Reno Court of Inquiry*, 561; Overfield, *The Little Big Horn*, 44.

26. Martin account in Graham, *The Custer Myth*, 289.

27. Reno to Rosser in ibid., 226.

28. Reno statement in *New York Herald*, 8 August 1876, in Graham, *The Custer Myth*, 228; Nichols, *Reno Court of Inquiry*, 584.

29. Nichols, *Reno Court of Inquiry*, 141.

30. Ibid., 251, 276; Graham, *The Custer Myth*, 31, which indicates that twenty-two Arikara scouts crossed the river and nine did not.

31. Nichols, *Reno Court of Inquiry*, 90, 380; Hammer, *Custer in '76*, 106, 145, 148.

32. *Cavalry Tactics*, 476–78.

33. Hammer, *Custer in '76*, 84.

34. Herendeen statement in Graham, *The Custer Myth*, 258; Nichols, *Reno Court of Inquiry*, 87, 251; Hammer, *Custer in '76*, 106, 231.

35. Nichols, *Reno Court of Inquiry*, 87, 251, 578, 588–89.

36. Ibid., 87; Hammer, *Custer in '76*, 231–32.

37. Nichols, *Reno Court of Inquiry*, 561.

38. Ibid., 358, 380.

39. Ibid., 105; Hammer, *Custer in '76*, 232.

40. Nichols, *Reno Court of Inquiry*, 561.

41. Ibid., 141; Carroll, *Custer's Chief of Scouts*, 65, 89.

42. Nichols, *Reno Court of Inquiry*, 561; Overfield, *The Little Big Horn*, 44.

43. Nichols, *Reno Court of Inquiry*, 585.

44. Hammer, *Custer in '76*, 92–93.

45. Kanipe to Camp, undated, Camp Collection, BYU.

46. Russell White Bear interview of Curley in Graham, *The Custer Myth*, 19.

47. Camp interview of Soldier, undated, published in Hammer, *Custer in '76*, 188.

48. Ibid., 191.

49. Sklenar: "Private Theodore W. Goldin," 9–17, and "Theodore W. Goldin," 106–23. Goldin claimed to carry a last message from Custer to Reno. He may have done so, but if he did, the message was never delivered. For information on another claimant (Sergeant Thomas Harrison), see Private Henry Jones to Camp, 30 November 1911, Camp Collection, BYU.

CHAPTER 8. A TERRIBLE FRIGHT

1. The Indian village was obviously not configured in some precise geometric shape. Respects Nothing thought that the site occupied one square mile of land, and Flying Hawk recalled that the camp was about a mile and a half long and approximately a mile wide. See Hardorff, *Lakota Recollections*, 26, 50. Other Indians guessed two or three miles long, with assorted estimates on the width. See Graham, *The Custer Myth*, 69, 79. However, since Indians did not think in terms of acres and miles, such measurements do not have a great deal of meaning. My calculation of lodges loosely situated and forming a village less than two miles in length and about a mile across (from just north of the Garryowen Loop to a bit north of the Miniconjou Ford, and from the river westward beyond the end of the Loop, so that soldiers on the left of Reno's skirmish line could see some part of it), is descriptive of a large village comfortably formed along the Little Bighorn.

2. Utley, *The Lance and the Shield*, 148; Hugh L. Scott interview, 1919, in Hardorff, *Lakota Recollections*, 74.

3. Col. W. H. Wood report, 27 February 1877, reprinted in Graham, *The Custer Myth*, 57–62.

4. Frank B. Zahn interview, 1931, reprinted in Hardorff, *Lakota Recollections*, 92–93.

5. Eli Ricker interview, 1906, in ibid., 26.

6. Narrative published in Graham, *The Custer Myth*, 84.

7. Ricker interview, 1907, in Hardorff, *Lakota Recollections*, 63–64.

8. Camp interview, 1907, in Hammer, *Custer in '76*, 209.

9. Scott interview, 1919, reprinted in Graham, *The Custer Myth*, 97.

10. Walter S. Campbell (a.k.a. Stanley Vestal, used hereafter) interview, 1930, in Hardorff, *Lakota Recollections*, 109–10.

11. Vestal interview, 1932, in Hardorff, *Lakota Recollections*, 109 n. It would be useful if there were some interviews of Sans Arc Lakotas, but I have seen none.

12. Report in the *Pioneer Press*, 18 July 1886, reprinted in Graham, *The Custer Myth*, 88.

13. Ibid., 75, 102, 104 (reprints of various accounts); Hammer, *Custer in '76*, 201; Bighead, "Custer's Last Battle," 366.

14. Ryan to Camp, 29 November 1908 and 21 March 1909, Camp Collection, BYU.

15. Nichols, *Reno Court of Inquiry*, 239.

16. Ibid., 313.

17. Taylor to Camp, 12 December 1909, published in Hammer, *Custer in '76*, 150–51.

18. Nichols, *Reno Court of Inquiry*, 329.

19. Ibid., 240, 376.

20. Camp interviews with O'Neill, Roy, and Petring, all undated, published in Hammer, *Custer in '76*, 106, 112, 133.

21. Daniels and Davis, *That Fatal Day*, 21.

22. O'Neil, *Sagas of the Greasy Grass*, 28.

23. Apparently the Indians held various kinds of dances and celebrations throughout the village during the evening of 24 June. The Cheyenne Wooden Leg remembered them as a "social affair for young people." See Hardorff, *Lakota Recollections*, 100 n.

24. John G. Neihardt interview of Eagle Elk, 1944, in ibid., 109.

25. Red Horse in Graham, *The Custer Myth*, 57; Bighead, "Custer's Last Battle," 366.

26. White Bull, "The Battle of the Little Bighorn," 337–38; *Pioneer Press* story in Graham, *The Custer Myth*, 90. The credit or blame for individual casualties is almost impossible to fix, but the Arikara and other Indian scouts were farther forward and better positioned to do damage to the village. Wild shots from the guns of the cavalrymen may have struck the camp, but the troopers were probably occupied with the force of warriors, primarily toward the foothills. It is generally believed that fewer than a dozen Indian noncombatants were killed, nearly all during the initial phase of the assault. See Hardorff, *Lakota Recollections*, 94 n.

27. Scott interview of Red Feather, 1919, published in Hardorff, *Lakota Recollections*, 83.

28. Respects Nothing in ibid., 26. Although I recognize that "Custer" was a generic expression often used by the Indians to describe the army force, the warning did in fact relate to all components of the Seventh seen by the Sans Arcs and to the dust first detected on the east side of the river. When the last of the Sans Arcs departed the bluffs, they could not have known in which direction Custer (then near the Flat) would move. The soldiers' dust was simply behind them.

29. Hammer, *Custer in '76*, 65, 180–84.

30. Ibid. Also Young Hawk, Red Bear, and Little Sioux in Graham, *The Custer Myth*, 34, 40, 42.

31. Nichols, *Reno Court of Inquiry*, 561; Reno to Rosser in Graham, *The Custer Myth*, 226.

32. Morris in Brady, *The Sioux Indian Wars*, 402.

33. Roy to Camp, 22 December 1909, Camp Collection, BYU.

34. Nichols, *Reno Court of Inquiry*, 328.

35. French to Mrs. Cooke in Graham, *The Custer Myth*, 341.

36. John Ryan, Daniel Newell, and William Slaper in Hammer, *Men with Custer*, 239, 325, 352; Rutten in Hammer, *Custer in '76*, 118. Private Smith's body was never discovered unless it was one of the scorched and unrecognizable heads found in the village after the battle; Turley's remains were later found in the woods.

37. Carroll, *Custer's Chief of Scouts*, 65, 90; Nichols, *Reno Court of Inquiry*, 157, 174, 177.

38. Camp interview of Herendeen, 1911, published in Hammer, *Custer in '76*, 222 n; Herendeen account in Graham, *The Custer Myth*, 263.

39. According to Private Gallenne of Company M, he was holding "six frightened horses" when he got into the timber. Since no other account mentions more than four animals per horse-holder, Gallenne may simply have been mistaken, or French may have made a deliberate decision to modify the norm in order to retain additional M Troop men on the line. See Daniels and Davis, *That Fatal Day*, 17.

40. DeRudio and O'Neill in Hammer, *Custer in '76*, 85, 106.

41. An excellent article on the problems involved in adjusting the sights of the Springfield carbines is Wilke, "A Sight Picture."

42. Nichols, *Reno Court of Inquiry*, 301, 306.

43. Ibid., 222, 252, 314, 316; Hammer, *Custer in '76*, 112; Ryan in Graham, *The Custer Myth*, 242.

44. Hammer, *Custer in '76*, 84, 106, 112, 143, 222, 232; Nichols, *Reno Court of Inquiry*, 216, 562.

45. Nichols, *Reno Court of Inquiry*, 141–42, 216, 562.

46. Hammer, *Custer in '76*, 107; Brininstool, *Troopers with Custer*, 131.

47. Nichols, *Reno Court of Inquiry*, 23, 216.

48. Hammer, *Custer in '76*, 232.

49. O'Neil, *Garry Owen Tid-Bits 6*, 26–27; Nichols, *Reno Court of Inquiry*, 521.

50. Alleged Reno statement to the Reverend Dr. Arthur Edwards, published in *Northwestern Christian Advocate*, 7 September 1904, reprinted in Graham, *The Custer Myth*, 340.

51. Nichols, *Reno Court of Inquiry*, 230. Varnum thought they were alternate files. See Hammer, *Custer in '76*, 61. Paradoxically, Moylan told the court of inquiry that "the firing on the part of the majority of our men was very well regulated," although new men may have discharged their weapons in a wild and random manner. See Nichols, *Reno Court of Inquiry*, 223. Corporal Roy of Moylan's company thought he had fired about twenty rounds, whereas Sergeant Culbertson of the same unit testified that he expended exactly twenty-one rounds. On the other hand, the new recruit Edward Pigford said that he fired only four or five shots, even though his Company M remained on the line longer than the others. It is unlikely that any soldier on the field of battle came close to using up his fifty bullets, since virtually all the men were almost always on the move during periods of engagement ranging from five to maybe twenty minutes. For a variety of

testimony on this subject, see Hammer, *Custer in '76*, 112, 143; Nichols, *Reno Court of Inquiry*, 23, 288, 345, 354.

52. Hammer, *Custer in '76*, 85; Nichols, *Reno Court of Inquiry*, 314, 326.
53. Hammer, *Custer in '76*, 85; Nichols, *Reno Court of Inquiry*, 314, 326.
54. Hammer, *Custer in '76*, 101–2; Nichols, *Reno Court of Inquiry*, 337–38.
55. Camp interview of Heyn, undated, Camp Collection, BYU.
56. Nichols, *Reno Court of Inquiry*, 9–10, 147, 223–24, 287, 293–94, 318.
57. Ibid., 142.
58. Hammer, *Custer in '76*, 107.
59. Nichols, *Reno Court of Inquiry*, 142; Carroll, *Custer's Chief of Scouts*, 66, 90.
60. Nichols, *Reno Court of Inquiry*, 217.
61. Hammer, *Custer in '76*, 232.
62. Ibid., 143; Barnard, *Custer's First Sergeant*, 180.
63. Nichols, *Reno Court of Inquiry*, 224, 246.

CHAPTER 9. HURRY UP AND WAIT

1. Camp interview of Kanipe, 1908, published in Hammer, *Custer in '76*, 97.
2. Ibid., 94.
3. Kanipe to Camp, 7 July 1908 and undated, Camp Collection, BYU.
4. Camp interview of Martin, 1908, published in Hammer, *Custer in '76*, 100.
5. Ibid., 103; Graham, *The Custer Myth*, 289–90.
6. Nichols, *Reno Court of Inquiry*, 388–89, 394.
7. Camp interview of Curley, 1908, published in Hammer, *Custer in '76*, 156.
8. Scott interview reprinted in Graham, *The Custer Myth*, 13.
9. Colonel Tim McCoy interview, 1919, in ibid., 23.
10. Ibid., 24–25 (from June 1916 *Teepee Book*).
11. Magnussen, *Peter Thompson's Narrative*, 121.
12. Nichols, *Reno Court of Inquiry*, 397.
13. See Martin in Graham, *The Custer Myth*, 290.
14. Ibid.
15. Kanipe in ibid., 249.
16. Hammer, *Custer in '76*, 92–95.
17. Ibid.
18. Ibid.
19. No surviving soldiers or scouts testified that Custer sent Benteen a message at any point between the Lone Tepee and the Flat, although Custer might have been expected to do so, if only because the Lone Tepee gambit had failed. From the evidence, the only person who might have carried such a message was the Arikara Stabbed, who supposedly told fellow scout Soldier that he had been out delivering a message to units over to the east, which could have meant Benteen,

the pack train, or even Reno. However, in a separate account, Soldier said that Stabbed had been "detailed to follow up a trail off toward the left and had not gone with the rest of the scouts." In either case, Soldier's stories raise the intriguing but unsupported possibility that Stabbed had been sent to Benteen. See Camp interview of Soldier, undated, in Hammer, *Custer in '76*, 188, and *The Arikara Narrative* account in Graham, *The Custer Myth*, 38.

20. Martin in Hammer, *Custer in '76*, 100.

21. For a copy of the Godfrey map, see Graham, *The Custer Myth*, 126.

22. Nichols, *Reno Court of Inquiry*, 157-58, 174; Carroll, *Custer's Chief of Scouts*, 90.

23. Nichols, *Reno Court of Inquiry*, 101-2.

24. For biographical sketches, see Hammer, *Men with Custer*.

25. Magnussen, *Peter Thompson's Narrative*, 117-22. Although Thompson's story provides some insight into events during the march along the bluffs, some of his recollections are clearly out of sequence, and the end of his narrative is too fabulous to be swallowed as fact.

26. Thompson to Camp, 1909, and McGuire to Camp, 5 February 1909, Camp Collection, BYU.

27. Hammer, *Custer in '76*, 188; Graham, *The Custer Myth*, 38.

28. Scott and Russell White Bear accounts in Graham, *The Custer Myth*, 17-19.

29. Hammer, *Custer in '76*, 156-57.

30. Ibid., 177. Implicit in this 1911 Camp interview of Hairy Moccasin is a distinction between "Custer Ridge" (Sharpshooter Ridge) and Weir Point.

31. From Kanipe's testimony, we know that Company C was on the left of the troops (see Kanipe to Camp, 7 July 1908, Camp Collection, BYU) and that the Gray Horse Troop was near the center of the formation (see Martin in Hammer, *Custer in '76*, 100). Interestingly, the first Maguire battlefield map (reproduced in Graham, *The Custer Myth*, 132) displays Custer's "order of battle" as F, E, L, C, and I in line at about where Sharpshooter Ridge would be located. The source of Maguire's alignment is not known.

32. Hammer, *Custer in '76*, 100, 103.

33. Nichols, *Reno Court of Inquiry*, 398.

34. Ibid., 157. Russell White Bear interview in Graham, *The Custer Myth*, 19.

35. Nichols, *Reno Court of Inquiry*, 343.

36. Hammer, *Custer in '76*, 100; Martin in Graham, *The Custer Myth*, 290.

37. Nichols, *Reno Court of Inquiry*, 390.

38. Photo of the Cooke message in Graham, *The Custer Myth*, 299. The original of the message is housed at the U.S. Military Academy at West Point, New York.

39. Hammer, *Custer in '76*, 103; Nichols, *Reno Court of Inquiry*, 395.

40. Hammer, *Custer in '76*, 101, 104.

41. Ibid., 104.

42. Graham, *The Custer Myth*, 290.

43. Camp interview of Little Sioux, undated, published in Hammer, *Custer in '76*, 181.

44. Soldier in ibid., 189.

45. Curley and Goes Ahead in ibid., 157, 175.

CHAPTER 10. UNREADY RESERVES

1. Nichols, *Reno Court of Inquiry*, 431.

2. Benteen to his wife, 2 July 1876, published in Carroll, *The Benteen-Goldin Letters*, 154.

3. Ibid., 157.

4. Benteen to his wife, 10 July 1876, published in Carroll, *Camp Talk*, 29.

5. Nichols, *Reno Court of Inquiry*, 404.

6. Godfrey, "Custer's Last Battle," 285.

7. Nichols, *Reno Court of Inquiry*, 439; Edgerly to Graham, 5 December 1923, in Graham, *The Custer Myth*, 216.

8. Gibson to Yates, E. B. Custer Collection, LBBNM. For a discussion of Benteen's movements, see Gray, *Custer's Last Campaign*, 258–65. Gray first used "No Name Creek" to designate the valley followed by Benteen back to the main trail. He also placed "the Morass" much closer to the Lone Tepee than, for example, did Kuhlman, *Legend into History*, 86–88. I have adopted Gray's name for the dry stream, and I believe he was correct about the Morass, just as I have used his excellent time-motion study for the entire Little Bighorn operation as a framework for my own analysis, with modifications.

9. Camp interview of Gibson, 1910, published in Hammer, *Custer in '76*, 80.

10. Carroll, *The Benteen-Goldin Letters*, 168, 183.

11. Nichols, *Reno Court of Inquiry*, 433; Carroll, *The Benteen-Goldin Letters*, 287. At the court of inquiry, Benteen correctly concluded that Custer and Reno could have reached the Lone Tepee in under two hours. See Nichols, *Reno Court of Inquiry*, 422.

12. Nichols, *Reno Court of Inquiry*, 433; Camp interview of Gibson, 1910, Camp Collection, BYU.

13. Nichols, *Reno Court of Inquiry*, 430; Carroll, *The Benteen-Goldin Letters*, 184.

14. Graham, *The Custer Myth*, 227.

15. Nichols, *Reno Court of Inquiry*, 431.

16. Carroll, *The Benteen-Goldin Letters*, 169.

17. Nichols, *Reno Court of Inquiry*, 480; Camp interview of Godfrey, undated, published in Hammer, *Custer in '76*, 75.

18. Private Windolph in Hunt and Hunt, *I Fought with Custer*, 81. Private William Morris quoted Private Jan Moller of Benteen's H Troop as saying that the battalion had "walked all the way, and that they heard the heavy firing while

they were watering their horses." See Morris letter in Brady, *The Sioux Indian Wars*, 404.

19. Nichols, *Reno Court of Inquiry*, 513.

20. Camp interview of McDougall, undated, published in Hammer, *Custer in '76*, 69; Edgerly quoted in Gray, *Custer's Last Campaign*, 264.

21. Kanipe to Camp, 9 October 1910, quoted in Hammer, *Custer in '76*, 93 n.

22. Carroll, *The Benteen-Goldin Letters*, 169, 184.

23. Hammer, *Custer in '76*, 93 n.

24. Nichols, *Reno Court of Inquiry*, 480; Godfrey, "Custer's Last Battle," 289.

25. Godfrey interview in Hammer, *Custer in '76*, 75.

26. Nichols, *Reno Court of Inquiry*, 404, 427, 463.

27. Kanipe to Camp, 14 April 1910, Camp Collection, BYU.

28. Nichols, *Reno Court of Inquiry*, 531, 513.

29. J. E. Kanipe, "Tarheel Survivor of Custer's Last Stand," 30.

30. Nichols, *Reno Court of Inquiry*, 504, 529.

31. Kennedy quoted in Liddic and Harbaugh, *Camp on Custer*, 156.

32. McGuire to Camp, 4 December 1908, Camp Collection, BYU. McGuire's statement makes it clear that this event occurred before the mules became mired at the Morass and before Kanipe arrived with his message. Such timing comports with the notion that Custer had paused long enough at the Lone Tepee for the advance elements to be reconstructed and for word to be sent back to the rear components—that is, during the 2:00–2:15 period.

33. Nichols, *Reno Court of Inquiry*, 465, 503.

34. Martin statements in Graham, *The Custer Myth*, 291, and Nichols, *Reno Court of Inquiry*, 390–91.

35. Nichols, *Reno Court of Inquiry*, 404, 407, 432.

36. Carroll, *The Benteen-Goldin Letters*, 180.

37. Nichols, *Reno Court of Inquiry*, 405.

38. Ibid., 404, 432.

39. Edgerly in Hammer, *Custer in '76*, 54–55.

40. Quoted in Overfield, *The Little Big Horn*, 41.

41. Nichols, *Reno Court of Inquiry*, 433.

42. Graham, *The Custer Myth*, 291.

43. Nichols, *Reno Court of Inquiry*, 391–92.

44. Hammer, *Custer in '76*, 54; Edgerly in Graham, *The Custer Myth*, 221.

45. A comparison of Nichols, *Reno Court of Inquiry*, and the *Chicago Times* versions of Martin's testimony indicates no essential differences. One must conclude that Martin deliberately misstated the facts for unknown reasons, possibly having to do with misplaced loyalty, ambitions for a military career, or an inability to carry out preinquiry tutoring. As a *Times* reporter observed, Reno's counsel became frustrated with Martin's inability to fix times, and even the compassionate recorder, Lieutenant Jesse Lee, announced to the court that the only

reason he had called Martin was to confirm that Custer's order to Benteen had been delivered. Indeed, it must have been a very embarrassing moment for all when the recorder apologized for Martin's ineptitude. See Utley, *The Reno Court of Inquiry*, 317.

46. Nichols, *Reno Court of Inquiry*, 440, 442; Godfrey, "Custer's Last Battle," 289.

47. Camp interview of Gibson, 1910, published in Hammer, *Custer in '76*, 80.

48. Godfrey, "Custer's Last Battle," 289–90; Hammer, *Custer in '76*, 75–76.

49. Nichols, *Reno Court of Inquiry*, 405, 433.

50. Hammer, *Custer in '76*, 80, 76.

51. Graham, *The Custer Myth*, 25.

52. Nichols, *Reno Court of Inquiry*, 529.

53. Ibid., 430–431.

54. Carroll, *The Benteen-Goldin Letters*, 246.

55. Carroll, *Barry Correspondence*, 48.

56. Carroll, *The Benteen-Goldin Letters*, 152–53.

57. Camp interview of D. F. Barry (during which Benteen's letters received by Barry were discussed), undated, Camp Collection, BYU.

CHAPTER 11. CHARGE TO THE REAR

1. Nichols, *Reno Court of Inquiry*, 124. Gerard testified that the "first man" shot was "leading horses," but it is not possible to locate this event in time.

2. For various descriptions of the timber area, see ibid., 223–24, 287, 293–94, 318, 555–57.

3. Camp interview of Hare, 1910, Camp Collection, BYU; Hammer, *Custer in '76*, 86, 223, 233; Nichols, *Reno Court of Inquiry*, 156, 231, 298; Utley, *The Reno Court of Inquiry*, 7–8, in which a report of 13 January 1879 quoted DeRudio as saying that Reno's position was "impregnable, and nothing but fear could have prompted his retreat."

4. Nichols, *Reno Court of Inquiry*, 415.

5. Ibid., 104. For a summary of Forsyth's Beecher Island fight, see Utley, *Frontier Regulars*, 147–48.

6. Her narrative is in Graham, *The Custer Myth*, 84.

7. George Bird Grinnell interview of Brave Wolf, 1895, and Soldier Wolf, 1898, both published in Hardorff, *Cheyenne Memories*, 35, 42.

8. Ricker interview in Hardorff, *Lakota Recollections*, 65.

9. Private Newell in O'Neil, *Sagas of the Greasy Grass*, 28.

10. Nichols, *Reno Court of Inquiry*, 142.

11. Carroll, *Custer's Chief of Scouts*, 66, 90; Nichols, *Reno Court of Inquiry*, 88, 127. Gerard stated that twice during the expedition Reynolds had "presentiments" of his death and that Gerard suggested that he see General Terry and get permission

to remain behind. Reynolds did as Gerard proposed, "and General Terry shamed him out of it."

12. Nichols, *Reno Court of Inquiry,* 254.

13. Ibid., 255, 267, 564.

14. Ibid., 563–65, 587.

15. Ibid., 217.

16. Moylan to Fred Calhoun, 6 July 1876, published in *Little Big Horn Associates Newsletter* 25 (February 1996): 9.

17. Camp interview of Heyn, undated, Camp Collection, BYU.

18. Hammer, *Custer in '76,* 107; Brininstool, *Troopers with Custer,* 131.

19. Nichols, *Reno Court of Inquiry,* 255, 284.

20. Ryan account in Graham, *The Custer Myth,* 242.

21. French to Mrs. Cooke in Graham, *The Custer Myth,* 341.

22. Nichols, *Reno Court of Inquiry,* 23, 27–28, 53.

23. Ibid., 256, 286.

24. Ibid., 88, 120.

25. Ibid., 143, 278–79.

26. Ibid., 347; Hammer, *Custer in '76,* 85.

27. Hammer, *Custer in '76,* 112.

28. Private Goldin to Brady, 11 August 1904, published in Brady, *The Sioux Indian Wars,* 272.

29. Hammer, *Custer in '76,* 107.

30. Ibid.

31. Nichols, *Reno Court of Inquiry,* 336; Hammer, *Custer in '76,* 66. Hare told the court of inquiry that Clear was his orderly, although the private is listed in some places as an orderly with Dr. DeWolf. See Nichols, *Reno Court of Inquiry,* 278, 335, and Hammer, *Men with Custer,* 60.

32. Nichols, *Reno Court of Inquiry,* 190, 196; Terry, "A Brave Doctor"; Camp interview of D. F. Barry, Camp Collection, BYU.

33. Nichols, *Reno Court of Inquiry,* 185, 565.

34. O'Neill in Hammer, *Custer in '76,* 107; Herendeen account in Graham, *The Custer Myth,* 264.

35. Hammer, *Custer in '76,* 61; Carroll, *Custer's Chief of Scouts,* 67, 91; Nichols, *Reno Court of Inquiry,* 143, 171.

36. Nichols, *Reno Court of Inquiry,* 191, 206, 281.

37. Hammer, *Custer in '76,* 66; O'Neill, *Sagas of the Greasy Grass,* 29; French to Mrs. Cooke in Graham, *The Custer Myth,* 341–42.

38. Hammer, *Custer in '76,* 118–19.

39. Ibid.; Carroll, *Custer's Chief of Scouts,* 66.

40. Hammer, *Custer in '76,* 85, 112, 223; Nichols, *Reno Court of Inquiry,* 89.

41. Hammer, *Custer in '76,* 119.

42. Ibid., 223–24; Hardorff, *Lakota Recollections*, 101–2. One purpose of the mutilations was to send the victim into the next world in a condition that would prevent him from enjoying the earthly pleasures dearest to him.

43. Hammer, *Custer in '76*, 119; Morris to Camp, 24 December 1909, Camp Collection, BYU; Carroll, *The Benteen-Goldin Letters*, 158.

44. Hammer, *Custer in '76*, 119.

45. Ibid., 133–34.

46. Nichols, *Reno Court of Inquiry*, 350; Brininstool, *Troopers with Custer*, 52; Newell in O'Neil, *Sagas of the Greasy Grass*, 29.

47. Nichols, *Reno Court of Inquiry*, 564, 566.

48. Ibid., 217–18.

49. Ryan to Camp, 11 January 1910, Camp Collection, BYU; Hammer, *Custer in '76*, 119.

50. Carroll, *Custer's Chief of Scouts*, 67, 91.

51. Ibid.; Hammer, *Custer in '76*, 61.

52. Nichols, *Reno Court of Inquiry*, 231.

53. Red Horse accounts in Graham, *The Custer Myth*, 56–62.

54. Hammer, *Custer in '76*, 224–25; Nichols, *Reno Court of Inquiry*, 259.

55. For a representative sample of the variations on their story, see DeRudio to the *New York Herald*, 30 July 1876, and Gerard's story from *The Arikara Narrative*, both reprinted in Graham, *The Custer Myth*, 251, 253–56; Hammer, *Custer in '76*, 86 (DeRudio) and 233–36 (Gerard); Brininstool, *Troopers with Custer*, 133–50 (O'Neill).

56. Hammer, *Custer in '76*, 134.

57. Ibid., 224; Graham, *The Custer Myth*, 264; Nichols, *Reno Court of Inquiry*, 257.

58. Nichols, *Reno Court of Inquiry*, 98–99, 316–18; O'Neill in Hammer, *Custer in '76*, 108.

59. Nichols, *Reno Court of Inquiry*, 551–52, 499.

60. Taylor to Godfrey, 20 February 1910, published in Graham, *The Custer Myth*, 343–44.

61. Godfrey memorandum for Brady, published in Brady, *The Sioux Indian Wars*, 374.

CHAPTER 12. CALLING FOR COURAGE

1. In the competition for bragging rights, the three Crows who departed clearly resented Curley's assertion that he was present until near the end of the fight, possibly because he was too young to be claiming so much for himself. For examples of their conflicting testimony, see their accounts in Graham, *The Custer Myth*, 21–25, and Camp interviews in Hammer, *Custer in '76*, 174–79.

2. The latest to make a major attempt at resurrecting Curley's reputation was Gray, *Custer's Last Campaign*.

3. Camp interview, 1910, published in Hammer, *Custer in '76*, 166.

4. Ibid.

5. Ibid.

6. Meringtom, *The Custer Story*, 303; E. B. Custer, *Boots and Saddles*, 69; Whittaker, *A Complete Life of General George A. Custer*, 151.

7. For comments on the value of the pack train, see Corporal John Hammon's statement to Charles E. Deland, 28 February 1898, Fred Dustin Collection, Little Bighorn Battlefield National Monument (LBBNM).

8. Russell White Bear interviews in Graham, *The Custer Myth*, 18–19.

9. Ibid.; Camp interview, 1913, in Hammer, *Custer in '76*, 172.

10. Her narrative is in Graham, *The Custer Myth*, 86.

11. Grinnell interview of White Shield, 1908, in Hardorff, *Cheyenne Memories*, 52.

12. For Soldier Wolf's comments on noncombatants crossing to the east, see ibid., 43; for families going to Chasing Creek, see Ricker interview of Respects Nothing, 1906, in Hardorff, *Lakota Recollections*, 26.

13. Zahn interview of Moving Robe Woman, 1931, in Hardorff, *Lakota Recollections*, 93.

14. Grinnell interview of Little Hawk, 1908, in Hardorff, *Cheyenne Memories*, 62.

15. Marquis interview of Wooden Leg in Graham, *The Custer Myth*, 105.

16. Weston (based on Camp questions) interview of Two Eagles, 1908, in Hardorff, *Lakota Recollections*, 146.

17. Grinnell interview of Tall Bull (1898) and White Shield (1908) in Hardorff, *Cheyenne Memories*, 47, 52.

18. Weston (based on Camp questions), 1909, in Hardorff, *Lakota Recollections*, 155–56.

19. Hardorff, *Cheyenne Memories*, 43.

20. For mention of the proposition that some small number of soldiers from E Troop waded into the water, see Fox, *Archaeology, History, and Custer's Last Battle*, 313.

21. The "anthill" description was used by John Two Moon (Grinnell, 1908) as well as by Two Moon himself (Dixon, 1909) in Hardorff, *Cheyenne Memories*, 66, 131.

22. Statement made to Lieutenant Charles Roe of the Second Cavalry in 1882; see Roe, "The Custer Massacre," 3.

23. Hardorff, *Cheyenne Memories*, 43.

24. Brust, "Lt. Oscar Long's Early Map," 8.

25. Holly, "Indian Accounts," 67.

26. A number of Indian witnesses said that soldiers dismounted. For examples, see Hardorff, *Lakota Recollections*, 155; Hardorff, *Cheyenne Memories*, 52, 62; Graham, *The Custer Myth*, 89.

27. Scott interview of Red Feather published in Hardorff, *Lakota Recollections,* 85.

28. Dixon, *The Vanishing Race,* 174.

29. Hamlin Garland's interview of Two Moon, 1898, published in Hardorff, *Cheyenne Memories,* 102.

30. *Pioneer Press* account in Graham, *The Custer Myth,* 92.

31. Scott interview of Feather Earring in ibid., 97–98; Ricker interview of Nicholas Ruleau (repeating Red Hawk's testimony), 1906, in Hardorff, *Lakota Recollections,* 42.

32. For examples of Curley's using "Custer" when he obviously meant components of the command, see Hammer, *Custer in '76,* 157–58, 162.

33. Newspaper account of 15 July 1876 reprinted in Graham, *The Custer Myth,* 11.

34. Trinque, "Elusive Ridge," 3–8.

35. Ibid.

36. Interview of Ruleau in Hardorff, *Lakota Recollections,* 43.

37. Fox, *Archaeology, History, and Custer's Last Battle,* 316–17.

38. Camp's paraphrase of Curley's meaning, in Hammer, *Custer in '76,* 158.

39. Among the burial parties, Lieutenant Godfrey's Company K was assigned the center of the battlefield, moving south to north. He said that his men buried fifteen to twenty men in one place, by implication the first group of bodies he encountered, and he noted that they found "a good many" cartridge shells where the troopers appeared to have made a stand. See Nichols, *Reno Court of Inquiry,* 495. Sergeant Kanipe is the primary source of the information that Finley and Finckle were found on the western portion of Calhoun Ridge. See Hammer, *Custer in '76,* 95 n.

40. Camp paraphrase of Curley, published in Hammer, *Custer in '76,* 158. This 1908 interview was conducted on the battlefield, and Camp's notation indicates that the termination of Yates's withdrawal was at the Finley marker.

41. Liddic and Harbaugh, *Camp on Custer,* 123.

42. Weston (questions from Camp), 1909, in Hardorff, *Lakota Recollections,* 166.

43. Grinnell interviews in ibid., 43, 47.

44. Many Sioux and Cheyenne survivors indicated that this was the case. In addition, Benteen asserted that in his explorations of the battlefield, he crossed and recrossed the river many times; he added that he thought one could do so "almost anywhere." See Nichols, *Reno Court of Inquiry,* 418.

45. Curley's July 1876 account in Graham, *The Custer Myth,* 11.

46. Hammer, *Custer in '76,* 163.

47. Ibid., 158, 167. From Curley's description, it is clear that he saw less than a full company depart for Finley, but he must have only assumed their annihilation because of their vulnerable position. When Curley departed, Custer and Tom had just left the vicinity, and it is unreasonable to conclude that the C Troop platoon could have been eliminated that quickly.

48. Russell White Bear interview in Graham, *The Custer Myth*, 18.

49. Hammer, *Custer in '76*, 164, 169. For an excellent analysis of Curley's escape, see Gray, *Custer's Last Campaign*, 373–82.

50. Hammer, *Custer in '76*, 159.

51. Nichols, *Reno Court of Inquiry*, 69.

52. Dixon interview of Two Moon, 1909, in Hardorff, *Cheyenne Memories*, 130–31.

53. Camp interview of He Dog, 1910, in Hammer, *Custer in '76*, 207.

54. G. A. Custer, *My Life on the Plains*, 89.

55. For information on Indian weapons, see Fox, *Archaeology, History, and Custer's Last Battle*, 77–79.

56. See ibid., 175–82, for an analysis positing that Custer was looking for a ford as an offensive maneuver to threaten the noncombatants.

57. Vestal interview of White Bull, 1930, in Hardorff, *Lakota Recollections*, 112.

58. Camp interviews of He Dog and Tall Bull, 1910, published in Hammer, *Custer in '76*, 207, 213.

59. Scott interview of He Dog, 1919, in Hardorff, *Lakota Recollections*, 76.

60. Ricker interview in ibid., 33.

61. Taylor to Camp, 19 November 1909, Camp Collection, BYU.

62. According to various sources, Foley's body was the first found by the burial parties. It was located on the elevation north of Medicine Tail Coulee and several hundred yards from the river. See Roy to Camp, March 1909, 12 March 1909, and undated interview, Camp Collection, BYU; Roy and DeRudio in Hammer, *Custer in '76*, 86, 116.

63. At the court of inquiry and elsewhere, surviving officers commented on the position of some fraction of Company L in nearly skirmish order. For example, see Moylan and Edgerly in Nichols, *Reno Court of Inquiry*, 236, 453.

64. Weston (based on Camp questions) interview, 1909, published in Hardorff, *Lakota Recollections*, 168.

65. For example, see ibid., 138, 184.

66. Marquis interview in Graham, *The Custer Myth*, 105.

67. Bighead, "Custer's Last Battle," 370.

68. DeRudio in Hammer, *Custer in '76*, 87. The exact number of E Troop found dead in a ravine is not known; twenty-eight was most frequently mentioned by survivors.

69. Nichols, *Reno Court of Inquiry*, 304, 67.

70. Various sources in Hardorff, *Lakota Recollections*, 170 n, 86.

71. Compare the arguments in Fox, *Archaeology, History, and Custer's Last Battle*, with those of Michno, *The Mystery of E Troop*. I am inclined to accept the latter thesis for the simple reason that the E Troop soldiers did not have the time or the opportunity to proceed on foot as a coherent unit down from Cemetery Ridge, across Cemetery Ravine, over the next hump, and into Deep Ravine, where

warriors had been concealed before launching attacks and to which they probably withdrew.

72. Dixon, *The Vanishing Race*, 176.

73. Utley, *Custer and the Great Controversy*, 88.

74. Garland interview in Hardorff, *Cheyenne Memories*, 103.

75. Brust, "Lt. Oscar Long's Early Map," 7.

76. McDougall to Godfrey, 18 May 1909, reprinted in Graham, *The Custer Myth*, 377.

77. Ryan to Camp, 17 December 1908, Camp Collection, BYU.

78. McDougall said that half of E Troop was found in a ravine and half outside, and he observed that most of the men were lying on their faces and had been shot generally "in the side." See Graham, *The Custer Myth*, 377, and Nichols, *Reno Court of Inquiry*, 535. Private Frank Berwald of Company E (with the pack train) told Walter Camp that he saw First Sergeant Frederick Hohmeyer and three privates (Richard Farrell, William Huber, and Albert Meyer, all of E) together in a gully, again suggesting some measure of unit cohesion. See undated interview, Camp Collection, BYU.

79. Bighead, "Custer's Last Battle," 368–69.

80. Marquis interview of Wooden Leg in Graham, *The Custer Myth*, 105.

81. Ibid., 106; Dixon interview of Two Moon, 1909, published in Hardorff, *Cheyenne Memories*, 131–32.

82. Camp interview of Little Wolf, 1918, in Hardorff, *Cheyenne Memories*, 90.

83. Dixon interview of Two Moon in ibid., 131.

84. Like Foley, Sergeant Butler has been viewed as a last messenger from Custer, but given Custer's knowledge of warriors in his rear, that seems most improbable. In his famous account of the battle, Godfrey concluded that Butler had fought bravely until the end because "near and under him were found many empty cartridge shells." Godfrey, "Custer's Last Battle," 305.

85. The "suicide boys" were Cheyenne and Lakota young men who had vowed to die in battle. See Don Rickey Jr., interview, 1956, published in Hardorff, *Cheyenne Memories*, 168 and 168 n; John Stands in Timber's narrative is also found in an undated newspaper article among miscellaneous clippings at the Billings Public Library. Apparently, a warrior would whip another man's pony on occasion in order to promote participation in, and to instill enthusiasm for, an approaching battle.

86. Hardorff, *Lakota Recollections*, 113 n; Lee to Camp, 24 May 1910, Camp Collection, BYU.

87. Vestal interviews in Hardorff, *Lakota Recollections*, 108–26.

88. Ibid., especially 124–26 for White Bull's description and map of coups.

89. Ibid.

90. Ibid., 60 (Ricker interview, 1907)

91. Ibid., 157 (Weston/Camp interview, 1909)

92. Ibid., 167.

93. For officers' comments on the Keogh sector, see Nichols, *Reno Court of Inquiry:* Lieutenant Maguire (some sort of skirmish line), 17; Wallace (men killed running in file), 67; Edgerly (an irregular line, some retreating faster than others), 453.

94. See Edgerly's description of bodies at the Keogh sector in Hammer, *Custer in '76,* 58. Corporal Wylie told Camp that Trumpeter Patton lay across Keogh's chest—see interview published in ibid., 130.

CHAPTER 13. WITHIN HEARING, BEYOND REACH

1. Nichols, *Reno Court of Inquiry,* 191.

2. Ibid., 565, 206.

3. Ibid., 410.

4. Ibid., 443.

5. The variations in Martin's memory are reflected in separate Camp interviews, 1908 and 1910, published in Hammer, *Custer in '76,* 101, 105.

6. Carroll, *The Benteen-Goldin Letters,* 185; Reno report in Nichols, *Reno Court of Inquiry,* 642.

7. Nichols, *Reno Court of Inquiry,* 54, 218, 370, 443. I have used "the Reno Enclave" to designate the ground that Reno's forces defended for nearly two full days.

8. Carroll, *The Benteen-Goldin Letters,* 243.

9. Nichols, *Reno Court of Inquiry,* 482, 243, 246–47.

10. Ibid., 281.

11. Ibid., 371. In this portion of his testimony, Culbertson said that the men did in fact fill canteens in the river during the trip. Under any other circumstances, getting water was certainly a sensible thing to do, even if only a dozen canteens were filled.

12. Godfrey, "Custer's Last Battle," 290–91.

13. Nichols, *Reno Court of Inquiry,* 160, 57.

14. Ibid., 352.

15. Ibid., 373.

16. Ibid., 444; Edgerly in Graham, *The Custer Myth,* 220.

17. Nichols, *Reno Court of Inquiry,* 408.

18. Ibid., 581.

19. Camp interview of Fox, published in Liddic and Harbaugh, *Camp on Custer,* 94–95. As a member of Weir's Company D, Fox could have been situated to hear such a conversation, which is reformatted here to emphasize the participants' statements.

20. Nichols, *Reno Court of Inquiry,* 444.

21. Edgerly to Graham, 5 December 1923, published in Graham, *The Custer Myth,* 217; Carroll, *The Benteen-Goldin Letters,* 199.

22. Nichols, *Reno Court of Inquiry,* 582.

23. Ibid., 290; Hammer, *Custer in '76,* 66.

24. Godfrey, "Custer's Last Battle," 292; Nichols, *Reno Court of Inquiry,* 483.

25. Nichols, *Reno Court of Inquiry,* 467.

26. Ibid., 529. Private Jacob Adams, who was with the pack train, said that when they reached Reno Hill, they "could hear sharp firing on the right, presumably from Custer's command." See Ellis, "A Survivor's Story."

27. Camp interview of McDougall, undated, published in Hammer, *Custer in '76,* 70.

28. Camp interview of Harrison, 1911, Walter Mason Camp Collection, Denver Public Library.

29. Nichols, *Reno Court of Inquiry,* 444; Hammer, *Custer in '76,* 56; 1881 account in Graham, *The Custer Myth,* 220.

30. Camp interview of Wylie, 1910, published in Hammer, *Custer in '76,* 129.

31. Nichols, *Reno Court of Inquiry,* 444; Hammer, *Custer in '76,* 56.

32. Hammer, *Custer in '76,* 129–30.

33. Nichols, *Reno Court of Inquiry,* 445.

34. Ibid., 291.

35. Kanipe, Martin, Thompson, and Watson all knew which way Custer had gone. Perhaps the last man to arrive from the Custer front was Private Gustave Korn of Keogh's I Troop; Korn's horse had run away with him while Custer was in the vicinity of Medicine Tail Coulee. There is evidence that Korn did return to the Reno Enclave, that he would not speak of his experience to fellow soldiers, and that he was later interrogated on the subject at Fort Lincoln. See Henry Jones to Camp, 17 May and 2 June, 1911, Michael C. Caddle to Camp, 2 October and 8 November 1909, and Camp interview of James Rooney, undated, all in Camp Collection, BYU.

36. Various interviews published in Hammer, *Custer in '76,* 56, 66, 76; Carroll, *The Benteen-Goldin Letters,* 215. For Edgerly's depiction of the disposition of forces, see Nichols, *Reno Court of Inquiry,* 445–46.

37. Nichols, *Reno Court of Inquiry,* 428.

38. Ibid., 409.

39. Ibid., 180.

40. Ibid., 372.

41. Ibid., 38, 59; Carroll, *The Benteen-Goldin Letters,* 208–9. By Lieutenant Wallace's count, Company A had five wounded, M had two, and G had none. Also, he noted that G had only eleven killed during the valley fight. If true, and if eight or nine soldiers from Company G were with Herendeen in the timber, a full twenty or so troopers should have been available once the unit reached Reno Hill. This was just another example of the little lies that apparently served no fathomable purpose.

42. Nichols, *Reno Court of Inquiry*, 161.

43. Carroll, *Custer's Chief of Scouts*, 92.

44. Camp interview of Pigford, undated, published in Hammer, *Custer in '76*, 143.

45. Ibid., 76 (undated Camp interview).

46. Ibid., 67 (1910 Camp interview).

47. Nichols, *Reno Court of Inquiry*, 567.

48. Ibid.; Camp notes quoting Hare in Hammer, *Custer in '76*, 67 n.

49. Hammer, *Custer in '76*, 76.

50. Nichols, *Reno Court of Inquiry*, 445–46.

51. Ibid.; Hammer, *Custer in '76*, 56–57, 130. See also Camp interviews of Thomas Harrison in Camp Collection, Denver Public Library, and published in Hammer, *Men with Custer*, 59.

52. Nichols, *Reno Court of Inquiry*, 445–46; Camp interviews of Thomas Harrison in Camp Collection, Denver Public Library, and published in Hammer, *Men with Custer*, 59.

53. Nichols, *Reno Court of Inquiry*, 446, 485.

54. Ibid., 568.

55. Godfrey, "Custer's Last Battle," 295–96.

56. Nichols, *Reno Court of Inquiry*, 357; remarks made by Godfrey at Annual Dinner of Order of Indian Wars (25 January 1930) and included in Godfrey, "Custer's Last Battle," 307–8; Koury, *Diaries of the Little Big Horn*, 12.

57. Nichols, *Reno Court of Inquiry*, 491.

58. Sklenar, "Captain Benteen's Ugly Little Secret Exposed," 8–14.

59. Nichols, *Reno Court of Inquiry*, 470, 505, 509, 575.

60. Hammer, *Custer in '76*, 144; Camp interview of James Boyle, undated, Camp Collection, BYU.

61. Hammer: *Custer in '76*, 114, and *Men with Custer*, 215.

62. Hammer, *Custer in '76*, 130.

63. Camp interview of McGonigle, 1908, published in Hammer: *Custer in '76*, 152, and *Men with Custer*, 247.

64. Nichols, *Reno Court of Inquiry*, 245.

65. Camp interviews of Hanley, 1910, and McGuire, undated, in Hammer, *Custer in '76*, 127, 125. Kanipe confirmed McGuire's participation; see his answers to Camp questionnaire, undated, Camp Collection, BYU.

66. Carroll: *The Benteen-Goldin Letters*, 210, and *Camp Talk*, 32.

67. Nichols, *Reno Court of Inquiry*, 493.

68. Ibid., 491–92. See also Camp interviews of Charles Windolph and James Boyle, undated, Camp Collection, BYU.

69. Ibid., 449–50.

70. Ibid., 500, 644–45; Edgerly letter in Graham, *The Custer Myth*, 317.

71. Nichols, *Reno Court of Inquiry*, 492.

72. Wagner, *Old Neutriment*, 164.

73. Goldin letter, published in the *Janesville Daily Gazette*, 8 July 1886; Goldin to Brininstool, 13 August 1924 and 28 February 1928, Brininstool Collection, BYU.

74. Liddic and Harbaugh, *Camp on Custer*, 161.

75. Carroll, *The Benteen-Goldin Letters*, 149, 206.

76. Carroll, *Custer's Chief of Scouts*, 94; Hammer, *Custer in '76*, 63.

77. Godfrey, "Custer's Last Battle," 307, 309.

CHAPTER 14. HONOR BOUND

1. In one example of Weir's erratic behavior in the weeks following the battle, he reportedly partied hard into the wee hours, became unsocial, fell or jumped into a stream, refused help in getting out, then rode in totally disheveled attire at the head of the column into Fort Lincoln the next morning. See Connell, *Son of the Morning Star*, 284.

2. Hardorff, *Cheyenne Memories*, 63.

3. Hardorff, *Lakota Recollections*, 149.

4. The various postmortems are unclear as to the precise location of Lieutenant Smith's body, except that it was on or near Last Stand Hill, but Lieutenant Maguire's final battlefield map places it to the northwest, about where the first-aid station should have been situated. For a copy of the map, see Nichols, *Reno Court of Inquiry*, 636.

5. Hardorff, *Lakota Recollections*, 159.

6. Hammer, *Custer in '76*, 87. DeRudio told Camp, "These horses were all sorrels from Company C."

7. G. A. Custer, *My Life on the Plains*, 95.

8. Runs-the-Enemy in Dixon, *The Vanishing Race*, 175.

9. Lone Bear in Hardorff, *Lakota Recollections*, 160; White Shield in *Cheyenne Memories*, 56.

10. For a wide range of sightings, see various Indian witnesses in Hardorff, *Lakota Recollections*, 32, 77, 88, 159; Hardorff, *Cheyenne Memories*, 67, 103, 111, 150; Wooden Leg in Graham, *The Custer Myth*, 105; He Dog and Flying By in Hammer, *Custer in '76*, 207, 210; Bighead, "Custer's Last Battle," 371.

11. For some detail on the location of bodies, see Michno, *The Mystery of E Troop*, 138, 163-64, 215, and Fox, *Archaeology, History, and Custer's Last Battle*, 180, 219. Also, Lieutenant Mathey claimed he buried Kellogg's body between Custer's position and the river; see Hammer, *Custer in '76*, 79.

12. Hammer, *Custer in '76*, 87.

13. Hardorff, *Cheyenne Memories*, 104; Hardorff, *Lakota Recollections*, 59-60, 96, 121-22 (White Bull's list of twenty-seven), 161. See also Hammer, *Custer in '76*, 267 (White Bull's list of twenty-six).

14. Godfrey, "Custer's Last Battle," 307, 309.

15. Connell, *Son of the Morning Star*, 78.

16. Hammon statement to DeLand, Dustin Collection, LBBNM.

17. Nichols, *Reno Court of Inquiry*, 549; Hammer, *Custer in '76*, 95 n.

18. Godfrey, "Custer's Last Battle," 310; Hammon statement to DeLand, Dustin Collection, LBBNM.

19. Comment in Hardorff, *Lakota Recollections*, 121–22 n; and hearsay information in Hardorff, *Cheyenne Memories*, 141.

20. See Kanipe and O'Neill in Hammer, *Custer in '76*, 95–96, 110; Hammon statement, Dustin Collection, LBBNM. Since O'Neill and Hammon actually participated in burying Custer, their information carries more weight.

21. Ryan to Camp, 17 December 1908, Camp Collection, BYU.

22. E. B. Custer, *Boots and Saddles*, 55–57, 133.

23. Wooden Leg in Graham, *The Custer Myth*, 105; Bighead, "Custer's Last Battle," 370.

24. Edgerly, Hare, Godfrey, and DeRudio in Hammer, *Custer in '76*, 58, 68, 77, 87; Edgerly in Graham, *The Custer Myth*, 220; Godfrey, "Custer's Last Battle," 310.

25. Glenn in Hammer, *Custer in '76*, 136.

26. O'Neill in ibid., 110.

27. Herendeen in ibid., 226 n.

28. Hedren, "Holy Ground," 204 n.

29. Overfield, *The Little Big Horn*, 37.

30. Quoted in Morris, *Sheridan*, 363.

31. Quoted in Whittaker, *A Complete Life of General George A. Custer*, 579.

32. E. B. Custer, *Boots and Saddles*, 221–22.

33. Nichols, *Reno Court of Inquiry*, 624.

34. Lee to Libbie, 27 June 1897, reprinted in O'Neil, *Garry Owen Tid-Bits 6*, 36–37.

35. Merington, *The Custer Story*, 304.

36. Nichols, *Reno Court of Inquiry*, 438.

37. Ibid., 454.

38. Hattaway and Jones, *How the North Won*, 711–13.

39. Quoted in Hutton, *Phil Sheridan and His Army*, 320.

Selected Bibliography

UNPUBLISHED SOURCES

Brininstool, Earl Alonzo. Collection. Harold B. Lee Library, Brigham Young University, Provo, Utah.

Camp, Walter Mason. Collection. Denver Public Library, Denver, Colorado.

———. Harold B. Lee Library, Brigham Young University, Provo, Utah.

———. Lily Library, Indiana University, Bloomington, Indiana.

Clark, Dennis, Lt. Col. "Seventh U.S. Cavalry Command and Control System, 25 June 1876." Seventh Annual Symposium, Custer Battlefield Historical and Museum Association, Inc., Hardin, Montana. 25 June 1993.

Court, James. Letter to author, 6 May 1997.

Custer, Elizabeth Bacon. Collection. Little Bighorn Battlefield National Monument, Crow Agency, Montana.

Custer Scrapbooks. Billings Public Library, Billings, Montana.

Dustin, Fred. Collection. Little Bighorn Battlefield National Monument, Crow Agency, Montana.

Holly, Jim. "Indian Accounts Paint Last Stand Picture." Seventh Annual Symposium, Custer Battlefield Historical and Museum Association, Inc., Hardin, Montana. 25 June 1993.

NEWSPAPERS AND JOURNALS

Army and Navy Journal
Janesville (Wisc.) Daily Gazette
Little Big Horn Associates Newletter
Research Review: The Journal of the Little Big Horn Associates

BOOKS AND ARTICLES

Ambrose, Stephen A. *Upton and the Army.* Baton Rouge: Louisiana State University Press, 1964.

Barnard, Sandy. *Custer's First Sergeant John Ryan.* Terre Haute, Ind.: AST Press, 1996.

Barnett, Louise. *Touched by Fire: The Life, Death, and Mythic Afterlife of George Armstrong Custer.* New York: Henry Holt and Company, 1996.

Bartlett, John, comp. *Familiar Quotations.* 1855. Reprint, edited by Emily Morison Beck, Boston: Little, Brown, 1980.

Bighead, Kate, as told to Thomas B. Marquis. "She Watched Custer's Last Battle." In *The Custer Reader,* edited by Paul Andrew Hutton. Lincoln: University of Nebraska Press, 1992.

Brady, Cyrus Townsend. *The Sioux Indian Wars: From the Powder River to the Little Big Horn.* New York: Indian Head Books, 1992.

Brininstool, E. A. *Troopers with Custer: Historic Incidents of the Battle of the Little Big Horn.* 1952. Reprint, with an introduction by Brian C. Pohanka, Mechanicsburg, Pa.: Stackpole Books, 1994.

Brust, James. "Lt. Oscar Long's Early Map Details Terrain, Battle Positions." *Greasy Grass* 11 (May 1995): 5–13.

Carroll, John M., ed. *The Benteen-Goldin Letters on Custer and His Last Battle.* New York: Liveright, 1974. Reprint, Lincoln: University of Nebraska Press, 1991.

———. *Camp Talk: The Very Private Letters of Frederick W. Benteen of the 7th U.S. Cavalry to His Wife, 1871 to 1888.* Mattituk, N.Y.: J. M. Carroll, n.d.

———. *Custer in Periodicals: A Bibliographic Checklist.* N.p.: Old Army Press, n.d.

———. *Custer's Chief of Scouts: The Reminiscences of Charles A. Varnum.* Lincoln: University of Nebraska Press, 1987.

———. *The D. F. Barry Correspondence at the Custer Battlefield (The Juciest Ones Being from Capt. Benteen).* N.p., n.d.

Cavalry Tactics: United States Army. New York: D. Appleton, 1874.

Cecil, Jerry. "Lt. Crittenden: Striving for the Soldier's Life." *Greasy Grass* 11 (May 1995): 30–36.

Connell, Evan S. *Son of the Morning Star.* New York: Promontory Press, 1984.

Cooke, Philip St. George. *Cavalry Tactics: or, Regulations for the Instruction, Formation, and Movements of the Cavalry of the Army and Volunteers of the United States.* Vol. 1. Philadelphia: J. B. Lippincott, 1862.

Curtis, William E. "Custer's Scouts." *Inter-Ocean* (Chicago), 14 July 1876. Reprinted in *Big Horn–Yellowstone Journal of 1876* 2, no. 1 (winter 1993): 17–21.

Custer, Elizabeth B. *Boots and Saddles: or, Life in Dakota with General Custer.* 1885. Reprint, with an introduction by Jane R. Stewart, Norman: University of Oklahoma Press, 1961.

Custer, George Armstrong. *My Life on the Plains; or, Personal Experiences with Indians.* 1874. Reprint, with an introduction by Edgar I. Stewart, Norman: University of Oklahoma Press, 1962.

Daniels, Karen L., and E. Elden Davis, eds. *That Fatal Day: Eight More with Custer.* Howell, Mich.: Powder River Press, 1992.

Davis, Karen L., and E. Elden Davis, eds. *The Reno Court of Inquiry: The Pioneer Press, St. Paul and Minneapolis, 1878–1879.* Howell, Mich.: Powder River Press, 1993.

Dippie, Brian W. "Custer: The Indian Fighter." In *The Custer Reader,* edited by Paul Andrew Hutton. Lincoln: University of Nebraska Press, 1992.

Dixon, Joseph K. *The Vanishing Race: The Last Great Indian Council.* New York: Bonanza Books, 1913.

Dustin, Fred. *The Custer Tragedy: Events Leading Up to and Following the Little Big Horn Campaign of 1876.* El Segundo, Calif.: Upton, 1987.

Ellis, Horace. "A Survivor's Story of the Custer Massacre." *Big Horn–Yellowstone Journal of 1876* 2, no. 2 (spring 1993): 5–11.

Flores, Dan. "The Great Contraction: Bison and Indians in Northern Plains Environmental History." In *Legacy: New Perspectives on the Battle of the Little Bighorn,* edited by Charles E. Rankin. Helena: Montana Historical Society Press, 1996.

Fougera, Katherine Gibson. *With Custer's Cavalry.* Caldwell, Idaho: Caxton Printers, 1940. Reprint, Lincoln: University of Nebraska Press, 1986.

Fox, Richard Allan, Jr. *Archaeology, History, and Custer's Last Battle: The Little Big Horn Reexamined.* Norman: University of Oklahoma Press, 1993.

Frost, Lawrence A. *Custer Legends.* Bowling Green, Ohio: Bowling Green University Press, 1981.

Ghent, W. J. "Varnum, Reno, and the Little Big Horn." *Winners of the West* 13 (30 April 1936).

Godfrey, Edward S. "Custer's Last Battle." In *The Custer Reader,* edited by Paul Andrew Hutton. Lincoln: University of Nebraska Press, 1992.

————. "Some Reminiscences, Including the Washita Battle, November 27, 1868." In *The Custer Reader,* edited by Paul Andrew Hutton. Lincoln: University of Nebraska Press, 1992.

Goldin, Theodore W. "On the Little Big Horn with General Custer." *Army Magazine,* June and July 1894. In *Custer in Periodicals: A Bibliographic Checklist,* edited by John M. Carroll. N.p.: Old Army Press, n.d.

Graham, W. A. *The Custer Myth: A Source Book of Custeriana.* Harrisburg, Pa.: Stackpole Books, 1953. Reprint, Lincoln: University of Nebraska Press, 1986.

Gray, John S. *Custer's Last Campaign: Mitch Boyer and the Little Bighorn Reconstructed.* Lincoln: University of Nebraska Press, 1991.

Greene, Jerome. *Evidence and the Custer Enigma: A Reconstruction of Indian-Military History.* Silverthorne, Colo.: Vistabooks, 1995.

Grill, "Mon Tana Lou." "Little Knife, Uncapapa Sioux Who Fought Custer, Had His Own Version of Little Big Horn Battle." *Billings Gazette,* June 1926.

Hammer, Kenneth, ed. *Custer in '76*. Provo: Brigham Young University Press, 1976. Reprint, Norman: University of Oklahoma Press, 1990.

———. *Men with Custer: Biographies of the Seventh Cavalry*. Hardin, Mont.: Custer Battlefield Historical and Museum Association, 1995.

Hardorff, Richard G., comp. and ed. *Cheyenne Memories of the Custer Fight: A Source Book*. Spokane, Wash.: Arthur H. Clark, 1995.

———. *Lakota Recollections of the Custer Fight: New Sources of Indian-Military History*. Spokane, Wash.: Arthur H. Clark, 1991.

Hattaway, Herman, and Archer Jones. *How the North Won: A Military History of the Civil War*. Urbana: University of Illinois Press, 1983.

Hedren, Paul L. "Holy Ground: The United States Army Embraces Custer's Battlefield." In *Legacy: New Perspectives on the Battle of the Little Bighorn*, edited by Charles E. Rankin. Helena: Montana Historical Society Press, 1996.

Heski, Thomas M. "'Digging' and 'Picking' to the Powder River." *Research Review: The Journal of the Little Big Horn Associates* 11, no. 1 (winter 1997): 11–17.

———. "The Trail to Heart River." *Research Review: The Journal of the Little Big Horn Associates* 9, no. 2 (June 1995): 22–31.

Hoig, Stan. *The Battle of the Washita: The Sheridan-Custer Indian Campaign of 1867–69*. Lincoln: University of Nebraska Press, 1979.

Hunt, Frazier, and Robert Hunt. *I Fought with Custer: The Story of Sergeant Windolph*. New York: Scribner's, 1947.

Hutchins, James S. "The Cavalry Campaign Outfit at the Little Big Horn." In *The Custer Reader*, edited by Paul Andrew Hutton. Lincoln: University of Nebraska Press, 1992.

Hutton, Paul Andrew. *Phil Sheridan and His Army*. Lincoln: University of Nebraska Press, 1985.

———, ed. *The Custer Reader*. Lincoln: University of Nebraska Press, 1992.

Jones, Archer. *Civil War Command and Strategy: The Process of Victory and Defeat*. New York: Macmillan Free Press, 1992.

Josephy, Alvin M., Jr. "Indian Policy and the Battle of the Little Bighorn." In *Legacy: New Perspectives on the Battle of the Little Bighorn*, edited by Charles E. Rankin. Helena: Montana Historical Society Press, 1996.

Kanipe, Daniel A. "Account of the Little Big Horn Fight." *Montana Historical Society Contributions* 4 (1903).

Kanipe, J. E. "Tarheel Survivor of Custer's Last Stand: The North Carolina Cavalryman Describes the American Thermopylae." Edited by Bill Boyes. *Research Review: The Journal of the Little Big Horn Associates* 7, no. 2 (June 1993): 22–31.

Kellogg, Mark. "Diary, 1876." *Montana Historical Society Contributions* 9 (1923).

Kelly, Tom. "Death of Early-Day Indian Fighter Recalls Events Prior to Custer Battle." Newspaper clipping, 25 November 1951. In Custer Scrapbooks, Billings Public Library.

Kidd, J. H. *A Cavalryman with Custer: Custer's Michigan Cavalry Brigade in the Civil War.* 1908. Reprint, with an introduction by Robert M. Utley, New York: Bantam Books, 1991.

Koury, Capt. Michael J. *Diaries of the Little Big Horn.* Bellevue, Nebr.: Old Army Press, n.d.

Kuhlman, Charles. *Legend into History.* 1951. *Did Custer Disobey Orders at the Battle of the Little Big Horn?* 1957. Reprint, combined edition, with an introduction by Brian C. Pohanka, Mechanicsburg, Pa.: Stackpole Books, 1994.

Liddic, Bruce R., and Paul Harbaugh, ed. *Camp on Custer: Transcribing the Custer Myth.* Spokane, Wash.: Arthur H. Clark, 1995.

Liddic, Bruce R., Frank Mercatante, and Tom Bookwalter. "Reno Court of Inquiry." *Research Review: The Journal of the Little Big Horn Associates* 11, no. 1 (winter 1997): 18–23.

Magnussen, Daniel O., ed. *Peter Thompson's Narrative of the Little Bighorn Campaign, 1876.* Glendale, Calif.: Arthur H. Clark, 1974.

Marquis, Thomas B. "Pioneer Woman Saw Custer and Soldiers Depart." Newspaper clipping, n.p., n.d. In Custer Scrapbooks, Billings Public Library.

McCulloch, W. J. "Canadian Who Died at Custer's Last Stand." *Hamilton Spectator,* n.d. In Custer Scrapbooks, Billings Public Library.

McDermott, John D. "Custer and the Little Bighorn Story: What It All Means." In *Legacy: New Perspectives on the Battle of the Little Bighorn,* edited by Charles E. Rankin. Helena: Montana Historical Society Press, 1996.

McFeely, William. *Grant: A Biography.* New York: W. W. Norton, 1981.

McIntosh, Donald. "Letter to his wife, Molly, June 22, 1876." *Little Big Horn Associates Newsletter* 24, no. 4 (May 1995): 7.

Meketa, Ray, and Thomas E. Bookwalter. *The Search for the Lone Tepee.* N.p.: Little Horn Press, 1983.

Merington, Marguerite, ed. *The Custer Story: The Life and Intimate Letters of General George A. Custer and His Wife Elizabeth.* New York: Devlin-Adair, 1950.

Meyer, Eugene L. "Tracking a Custer Indian Fighter." *Washington Post,* 27 March 1980.

Michno, Gregory. *The Mystery of E Troop: Custer's Gray Horse Company at the Little Big Horn.* Missoula, Mont.: Mountain Press, 1994.

Miles, Nelson A. *Personal Recollections and Observations.* Chicago and New York: Werner, 1896. Reprint, with an introduction by Robert M. Utley, New York: Da Capo Press, 1969.

Millis, Walter. *Arms and Men.* New York: Putnam's Sons, 1956.

Monaghan, Jay. *Custer: The Life of General George Armstrong Custer.* New York: Little Brown, 1959. Reprint, Lincoln: University of Nebraska Press, 1971.

Morris, Roy, Jr. *Sheridan: The Life and Wars of General Philip Sheridan.* New York: Crown, 1992.

Nevin, David. *The Soldiers.* Alexandria, Va.: Time-Life Books, 1973.

Nichols, Ronald H., comp. and ed. *Reno Court of Inquiry.* Hardin, Mont.: Custer Battlefield Historical and Museum Association, 1992.

O'Neil, Tom, comp. *Garry Owen Tid-Bits 6.* Brooklyn, N.Y.: Arrow and Trooper, 1992.

———. *Garry Owen Tid-Bits 9.* Brooklyn, N.Y.: Arrow and Trooper, 1993.

———. *Garry Owen Tid Bits 10.* Brooklyn, N.Y.: Arrow and Trooper, 1994.

———. *Sagas of the Greasy Grass.* Brooklyn, N.Y.: Arrow and Trooper, 1992.

Overfield, Loyd J., II, comp. *The Little Big Horn, 1876: The Official Communications, Documents, and Reports.* Lincoln: University of Nebraska Press, 1971.

Rankin, Charles E., ed. *Legacy: New Perspectives on the Battle of the Little Bighorn.* Helena: Montana Historical Society Press, 1996.

"The Reno Court of Inquiry." *Pioneer Press* (St. Paul and Minneapolis), 1878–79. Reprinted as Karen L. Davis and E. Elden Davis, eds., *The Reno Court of Inquiry: The Pioneer Press, St. Paul and Minneapolis, 1878–1879.* Howell, Mich.: Powder River Press, 1993.

Roe, Charles F. "The Custer Massacre." *Army and Navy Journal,* 25 March 1882. Reprinted in *Big Horn–Yellowstone Journal of 1876* 2, no. 3 (summer 1993): 2–4.

Sklenar, Larry. "Captain Benteen's Ugly Little Secret Exposed." *Research Review: The Journal of the Little Big Horn Associates* 12, no. 2 (summer 1998): 8–14.

———. "Private Theodore W. Goldin: Too Soon Discredited?" *Research Review: The Journal of the Little Big Horn Associates* 9, no. 1 (January 1995): 9–17.

———. "Theodore W. Goldin: Little Big Horn Survivor and Winner of the Medal of Honor." *Wisconsin Magazine of History* 80, no. 6 (1996–97): 106–23.

Stewart, Edgar I. *Custer's Luck.* Norman: University of Oklahoma Press, 1955.

Terry, M. E. "A Brave Doctor." *St. Paul (Minn.) Pioneer Press,* 3 May 1878. Reprinted in *Big Horn–Yellowstone Journal of 1876* 2, no. 4 (autumn 1993): 2–5.

Trinque, Bruce A. "Elusive Ridge." *Research Review: The Journal of the Little Big Horn Associates* 9, no. 1 (January 1995): 2–8.

Utley, Robert M. *Cavalier in Buckskin: George Armstrong Custer and the Western Military Frontier.* Norman: University of Oklahoma Press, 1988.

———. *Custer and the Great Controversy: The Origin and Development of a Legend.* Pasadena, Calif.: Westernlore Press, 1960.

———. *Frontier Regulars: The United States Army and the Indian, 1866–1891.* 1973, Reprint, Lincoln: University of Nebraska Press, 1984.

———. *The Lance and the Shield: The Life and Times of Sitting Bull.* New York: Henry Holt, 1993.

———, ed. *Life in Custer's Cavalry: Diaries and Letters of Albert and Jennie Barnitz, 1867–1868.* New Haven: Yale University Press, 1977.

———, comp. *The Reno Court of Inquiry: The Chicago Times Account.* N.p.: Old Army Press, 1972.

Wagner, Glendolin Damon. *Old Neutriment.* Boston: R. Hill, 1934. Reprint, with an introduction by Brian W. Dippie, Lincoln: University of Nebraska Press, 1989.

Waldo, Edna Lamoore. "Pioneer Cavalryman Saved from Fate of Custer's Soldiers in June 1876 by Horse He Didn't Have." Newspaper clipping. In Custer Scrapbooks, Billings Public Library.

Wert, Jeffry D. *The Controversial Life of George Armstrong Custer*. New York: Simon and Schuster, 1996.

White Bull, Chief Joseph, as told to Stanley Vestal. "The Battle of the Little Bighorn." In *The Custer Reader*, edited by Paul Andrew Hutton. Lincoln: University of Nebraska Press, 1992.

Whittaker, Frederick. *A Complete Life of General George A. Custer: Through the Civil War*. Vol. 1. New York: Sheldon, 1876. Reprint, with an introduction by Gregory J. Urwin, Lincoln: University of Nebraska Press, 1993.

———. *A Complete Life of General George A. Custer: From Appomattox to the Little Big Horn*. Vol. 2. New York: Sheldon, 1876. Reprint, with an introduction by Robert M. Utley, Lincoln, University of Nebraska Press, 1993.

Wilke, Lynn H. "A Sight Picture: Paint and Feathers." *Little Big Horn Associates Newsletter* 28, no. 5 (July 1994): 4–6.

Willert, James. "Does Anomaly Contain Sturgis's Body?" *Research Review: The Journal of the Little Big Horn Associates* 11, no. 2 (summer 1997): 2–16.

———. "The Wedding Ring of Lieutenant Donald McIntosh." *Research Review: The Journal of the Little Big Horn Associates* 10, no. 2 (June 1996): 2–11.

Wooster, Robert. *The Military and United States Indian Policy, 1865–1903*. New Haven: Yale University Press, 1988. Reprint, Lincoln: University of Nebraska Press, 1995.

INDEX